"*In Search of the Lost Feminine* beautifully illustrates the shift from prehistoric partnership societies to the warlike dominator era we are struggling to leave behind. Through legend, folklore, and vivid pictures contrasting the worldview of the Minoans and the later Greeks, Craig Barnes brings to life what was—and can be again."

—*Riane Eisler, author of* The Chalice and the Blade,
Sacred Pleasure, *and* The Power of Partnership

"An intellectual feast by a detective of unusual powers who has locked onto a mystery of world-historic proportions, and, by golly, I think he has solved it. Along the way he offers one breathtaking revelation after another. The result is a major reinterpretation of Western culture."

—*Walter Wink, award-winning author and
professor of biblical interpretation at
Auburn Theological Seminary*

"Combining the rare alchemy of a literary scholar, legal practitioner, and explorer extraordinaire, Craig Barnes dares to rewrite the history of Western civilization and vividly resurrects the woman as our vessel of rebirth. A must-read for anyone who worries that we have lost our way."

—*Gail Sheehy, author of* Passages *and*
Sex and the Seasoned Woman

In Search
of the
LOST
FEMININE

Decoding the Myths That Radically Reshaped Civilization

In Search of the LOST FEMININE

Decoding the Myths That Radically Reshaped Civilization

Craig S. Barnes

FULCRUM PUBLISHING

GOLDEN, COLORADO

Library of Congress Cataloging-in-Publication Data
Barnes, Craig S.
  In search of the lost feminine : decoding the myths that radically reshaped civilization / by Craig S. Barnes.
    p. cm.
  Includes bibliographical references and index.
  ISBN 1-55591-489-6 (pbk.)
  1. Sex role—History. 2. Patriarchy—History. 3. Minoans. 4. Mythology, Greek. I. Title.
  HQ1075.B356 2005
  305.309182'1—dc22

2005032942

ISBN-13: 978-1-55591-489-9
ISBN-10: 1-55591-489-6

Printed in Canada by Friesens Corporation
0 9 8 7 6 5 4 3 2 1

Editorial: Haley Groce, Faith Marcovecchio
Cover and interior design: Ann W. Douden
Line drawings: Ann W. Douden
Maps copyright © Full View Mapping, LLC
Author photo: Sally Hayden von Conta

Fulcrum Publishing
16100 Table Mountain Parkway, Suite 300
Golden, Colorado 80403
(800) 992-2908 • (303) 277-1623
www.fulcrumbooks.com

To goddesses and peacemakers,
old and new,
conservationists, and singers of stories,
and especially to
Will, Lisa, Tom, and Molly,
who fill me with hope.

In real life,
illusions can only transform our life
for a moment,
but in the domain of thoughts and the intellect,
misconceptions may be accepted as truth
for thousands of years,
and make a laughingstock of whole nations,
mute the noble wishes of mankind,
make slaves from people and lie to them.
These misconceptions are the enemies
with which the wisest men in the history
of mankind try to struggle.
The force of the truth is great,
but its victory is difficult.
However, once you receive this victory,
it can never be taken from you.

— Arthur Schopenhauer

CONTENTS

Acknowledgments   *xiii*

Introduction

    Rewriting the Story of Western Civilization   1

I

Minoan Artifacts Challenge the Inevitability of Patriarchy   9

    The Mystery of Minoan Civilization   13

    An Expectation of Rebirth or Immortality   23

    Time as a Circle Rather Than a Line   33

    The Troubling Question of War   44

    Crete and the Issue of Female Sexuality   52

    The Ecstatic and the Divine as Inseparable   60

    Five Values Dramatically at Odds with Patriarchy   64

II

The Collapse of the Minoan World   67

    The Invasions of 1600 BCE: A War Culture Emerges   68

    The Theran Explosion: The Loss of Faith in Mother Earth   71

    The Growth of Trade: The Diminishment of Daughters   79

    The Great Civil War over Marriage: The End of Women-Centered Culture
        in the Eastern Mediterranean   82

III

A Warrior Civilization Emerges   91

Four Hundred Years of Chaos Sets the Stage   91

Values Shaped by Storytellers   96

An Exaggerated Feminine Is Made Monstrous   102

Mother Earth Is Overthrown   108

Jason Resists the Many Shapes of Seductive Women   113

Odysseus Rejects Calypso   124

Homer Poses the Choice between Love and Property   136

Clytemnestra Is Sacrificed on the Altar of Marriage   145

Marriage Destroys the Mother-Daughter Bond   151

Daughters Die for Civic Good   157

A Multitude of Myths to Tame, Punish, and Disparage Women   161

Oedipus, the Lost Son   169

A Glorious Monument Enshrining the Subordination of Women   175

Biblical Patriarchs Match the Greek Story   187

IV

Objections to the Warrior Civilization   195

Jesus Carries Forward the Eleusinian Symbolism of Grain and Wine   197

Jesus Takes On the Threat of Military Destruction   203

Ancient Beliefs Spring Up among the Celts   209

A Short-Lived Islamic Challenge   211

The Metaphor of the Holy Grail   214

Devil Talk and Witch Burnings   220

Closing the Book on the Patriarchy   226

V

History as a Choice of Stories   231

Women Coming Home to Dignity   233

The Declining Utility of War   238

Another Story All Along   241

Appendix

Success and Failure in Women's Wages
and Employment in America   247

Endnotes   *249*

Bibliography   *265*

Index   *271*

About the Author   *286*

Acknowledgments

My appreciation for the muted tragedy in women's history was profoundly affected by seven years of litigation in a wage case on behalf of nurses employed by the City of Denver. The judge in that court would not allow an examination of the historical roots of gender discrimination. Many years after the case, in personal pursuit of some explanation for patriarchy's assumptions, I was led back through the history that I had hoped to present in court—back through witch trials, medieval history, through Rome to Greece, and eventually back to the Minoans of ancient Crete. Not until reaching 1500 BCE did an adequate explanation begin to illuminate the actions of the Denver court in 1976. This volume is therefore written in part as an effort to demonstrate more fully than could be presented in any court the antecedents of our current patriarchal condition. As it turned out, such gathering of evidence was not only unheard of in our courts but, at that time, was not available *anywhere*. To finally assemble the story is one of the reasons for this book.

Riane Eisler's groundbreaking analysis of the origins of patriarchy in *The Chalice and the Blade* changed my view of history. Without this combination of story, archaeology, and fresh insight, it is doubtful that my work would have been conceived or written. I am also indebted to Walter Wink, who has woven together history, sociology, and theological insight in many works, especially in *Engaging the Powers*. Both Eisler and Wink have read portions of this text, and I am deeply grateful for their support. Robert Graves's *The Greek Myths* opened my eyes to the probable political instructions in those old stories. Morgan Farley has been an inspiration and a careful consultant. Peter Struck, Ruth Bamberger, Jack Pike, and Hal Bolton also have read portions of this text and improved it, though its continuing failures are none of their own. Finally, I am indebted to Bob Baron, Sam Scinta, and Haley Groce of Fulcrum Publishing for their unflagging support, which has sustained me through many a revision.

Additional grateful thanks go to Elizabeth Sackler for her encouragement throughout the project and especially for her introduction to the curatorial staff of the Goulandris Museum of Cycladic Art in Athens, who spent extremely valuable time familiarizing me with their splendid collection. I am also indebted to Harry and Emelia Rathbun for weeks of conversation about the teachings of Jesus.

Beyond all these I am indebted to my wife, Mikaela, who has endured years of repeated conversations about the probable and improbable meanings of pots and jars, butterflies and bees. Without her constant encouragement, history would have had to stay the way it was.

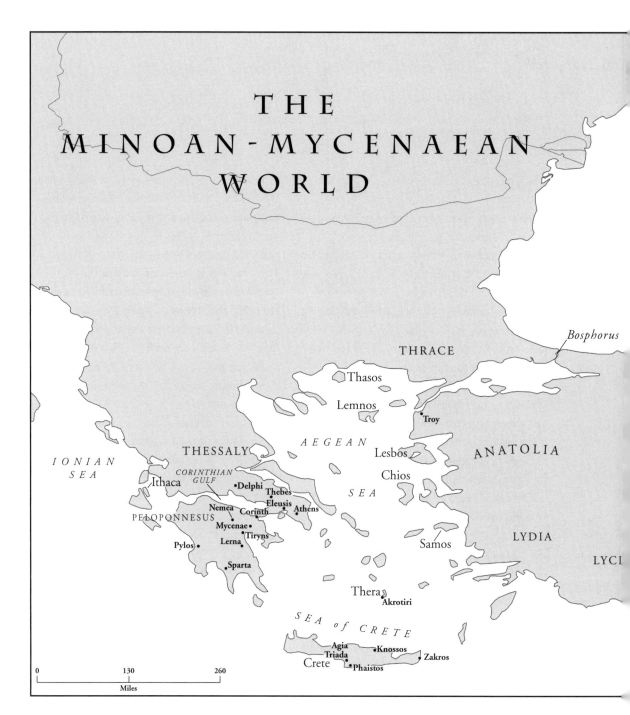

THE MINOAN-MYCENAEAN WORLD

THRACE

Bosphorus

Thasos

Lemnos

Troy

AEGEAN

THESSALY

Lesbos

ANATOLIA

IONIAN SEA

CORINTHIAN GULF

Ithaca

Delphi

Thebes
Eleusis

Chios

SEA

Nemea
Corinth
Athens

PELOPONNESUS

Mycenae
Lerna
Tiryns

Samos

LYDIA

Pylos

LYCI

Sparta

Thera

Akrotiri

SEA of CRETE

Agia
Triada
Knossos

Crete

Zakros

Phaistos

0   130   260

Miles

N

BLACK SEA

COLCHIS

AMAZON COUNTRY

ARMENIA

MEDITERRANEAN
SEA

Full View Mapping, LLC

Introduction
Rewriting the Story of Western Civilization

For thirty-five hundred years the story of Western civilization has been told with a political slant that worked for the cause of the victors of the great Trojan War of 1220 BCE. For all this time we in the West have been told that the suppression of women, the heroics of war, and the neglect of female ecstasy are natural and inevitable, the givens of history. We have viewed our condition through the lens of those norms that served one victorious culture but destroyed another, and we have been encouraged to believe that the older culture never even existed. For all this time we have shortchanged human nature, exalted our weakness, and disparaged our deepest instincts toward peacemaking and reconciliation, toward nurturing and the cycles of the seasons. We have been on a course that has resented the instinct toward moderation and maturation, has suppressed the "civil" in "civilization," and has elevated the mighty or the brutal as if it were some inexorable, bestial instinct that could not be resisted. For all this time we have therefore, tragically, at the cost of untold millions of lives and millennia of unbearable pain, denied an inward knowing of decency and compassion and persecuted an inner divine, as if these human characteristics were *un*natural, as if these decencies were *not* included in the genetic code, and as if militarism, monarchy, misogyny, and hierarchy *were* included within the genetic code. Through all this denial, however, again and

again throughout this same long evolution of time, like a root fire or a flame that would not die, there was an inward knowing—a gnosis, an inimitable hope, an inner feminine—that repeatedly flared up to illuminate and shine light into that patriarchal world. Each time it did so, the flame revealed aspects of human nature that the heroic patriarchal story did not reveal. Unbeknownst to those who repeatedly raised this fire of inner being, two millennia before on the islands of the eastern Aegean, Minoan civilization had also glorified these alternate values. In the centuries since 1500 BCE, Minoan insights kept popping up in other situations and other cultures and in so doing made clear that the earlier Minoan experience had not been an anomaly, was not an aberration or a mystery of the deep past so much as an early and vivid example of some innate quality of the human that does not ever go away.

I am a former lawyer who spent many years of his life nose-to-nose with other lawyers in the intense heat of the courtroom. I am therefore by nature an advocate, having at one time quit the law to seek a PhD in politics and then, because of the urgency of the real world, in turn left academia (without the PhD) to return to the passionate involvement of the streets. Out of all this comes the desire to describe the larger picture of how Western civilization got to the place where it is. Chiming in with Homer and Hesiod and the author of Genesis to say, oh yes, let the Muse sing once more indeed, but this time with a truer, clearer, more historically accurate voice.

In a quick overview my tale begins with the undeniable but almost forever buried archaeology of Minoan civilization and the modern discovery of how a remarkable people portrayed women, ecstasy, sexuality, time, and war. Then it moves to four dominant causes that brought off the great cultural collapse after 1500 BCE, when all this was systematically destroyed. Three causes were in some way accidents of history, geology, and trade. But the fourth cause of the great collapse was not an accident. An invention of stories, myths, and folktales seeking to rationalize and justify the suppression of the Minoan culture was the most important. Of all the causes for our rationalization of patriarchy and its demonic children, this was the one—this mythological justification, this romanticization in story and verse—that was the most egregious and did the most to solidify our continued denial of what civilization could become. I will therefore look to these myths to see what they accomplished on behalf of the patriarchy and how stories once considered inscrutable suddenly become scrutable when the need for sons became clear, or the need for heroes, or the need to corral women into a marriage to protect a man's estate. Finally, there has been resistance that flared to the surface in the Mysteries at Eleusis only to be suppressed again, arose anew in the teaching of the seer Jesus, but was stamped out once more. This resistance burned along the ground through the teachings of the Gnostics, then flared up in Ireland among the mystics of the Middle Ages. Each time it was tramped down like a weed blaze, suppressed with wet blankets of patriarchal

norms again and again until modern times when, in an explosion of archaeological discovery, we have uncovered once again the ruins of ancient Minoan civilization. These ruins are so distinct, so unlike our own expectations of power and dominion, and so unlike our drivers of empire and self-indulgence that they inevitably raise the question: "How could this be?" How could some civilization so unlike our own have survived for so long, and is there any remnant that remains today?

Stories and pictures organize a culture's attention and the use of its treasure. Stories and pictures are therefore apt to be more the driver for oppression—of anybody—than the evil nature of any human, male or female. It is the storied ground, for example, that precedes and nourishes the actions of a Vladimir Ilyich Lenin or a Martin Luther King Jr. For good or evil, each lived with one eye forever on a perceived story of history. The purpose here will therefore be to demonstrate how the patriarchal story at first came to infiltrate the mythology of the Western world and how, also, those papyrus-bound tales have never been far from the flame of dissent, a flame fanned by those who beheld in their own imaginations a vastly different social alternative and who have never quite gone away.

I have waded into territory where scholarship cannot be sure, have forged ahead in the manner more of the trial lawyer or perhaps even the poet. I admit to great fear where my own scholarship falls short, but cannot yet deny the need to tell the story that has appeared out of my own experience negotiating in wars of ethnic cleansing, trying lawsuits for women's wages, and experiencing the brutalities of empire or the wonder of sexuality and family love.

This does not serve to keep me within the narrower confines of reductionist research, but rather to turn my attention, much as did the originators of the patriarchal story, to the tale of how we got here, how we got to where civilization hangs in the balance today, and, like these first storytellers, to the task of reframing the story for my own times.

When I was in the fifth grade I attended a small three-room country school on the prairies of eastern Colorado. My five classmates and I were taught the lessons of the dragon's teeth of Jason and the season-changing disobedience of the goddess Persephone. We were led into the mysteries of a culture that had been reinforced in schools since the seventh century BCE—that is, without interruption for twenty-eight hundred years. By the time I was in high school, as fate and the consequence of war would have it, I actually lived in Athens, Greece. The city was marvelous, as yet unrecovered from World War II, gentle by the sea, unclut-tered. It was a time for falling in love. Not only with my local high-school goddess but also with the gleaming Parthenon in the moonlight, the long clean beaches of Sunion and Marathon, the mystery of Delphi, and the mixture of elegance and detail in the marble preserved from ancient times. Underneath these wonders lay the spectacular Greek explosion of culture and knowledge that had birthed modern civilization. At the Parthenon I learned that some scholars attributed Greek rationalism to the god Apollo and some compared the Greek miracle to the rules for life set down by Jehovah, rules which rose above the whims or passions of any human. Whether one was attracted to the rationalism of Apollo or the justice of Jehovah, this objectivism had, in its time, wrought a mind change that unleashed a powerful new force in

Western history. Men began to break things down into their parts—to analyze behaviors, attribute some to one god, some to another—and as they did this they were creating a new understanding of detail. At the same time it seems to have become more difficult to maintain any concept of the whole.

The result, my teachers said, of the new rationality was an explosion of discovery and a culture that would become the foundation of Western progress. Within five hundred years the Greeks had reached stunning new heights in literature, drama, architecture, medicine, biology, anatomy, and philosophy. These achievements were of such magnificence that ever since they have been hailed as "the Greek miracle." Not until the Renaissance of the late Middle Ages would such an explosion of creativity and rationality occur again in the West.

What my teachers did not say, however, was that the price paid for these achievements was the destruction, wherever possible, of a different way of seeing the world that had prevailed before Greek civilization rose to dominate the region. Vibrant cultures that had been alive on the islands of the eastern Aegean and probably also on the Greek mainland as well as in Anatolia and the Levant were destroyed because their lingering values threatened the new order. Widely diverse peoples—with whom the Greeks were in obvious proximity and in constant commercial exchange—had apparently maintained a more communal relation to the land and its riches and had viewed women, ecstasy, and time as more benign than did those who controlled the new civilization. These islanders also viewed war as less useful. Altogether, their world view contained within it a serious threat to Zeus's new Olympian order, and as a result the

Greeks, wherever they could, extinguished it.

We have not known until recently about this collision of civilizations because the islanders did not leave a written history. We are left with only artifacts, ruins of walls, and pictures on seals, figurines, and pots. To try to interpret what was honored or highly valued, taking our clues only from physical objects, is extraordinarily difficult. Some scholars argue that it is impossibly subjective. And, these scholars add, if we cannot tell what earlier civilizations valued, we cannot honestly say that they disagreed with the predominant Greek civilization or that the Greeks intentionally destroyed them. The gist of this approach, which has dominated scholarship for the last fifty years, is that because pots are difficult or because walls don't speak, they are close to inscrutable.

But frescoes on walls are not meaningless. In many cases more can be drawn from pictures than from words. A rich texture of preliterate culture is not only possible to discern from the archaeology, it is richly rewarding. If one were to track *only* the changes in the pictures, the graphics, and the images, one would see a dramatic difference in the objects and subjects portrayed from one civilization to the next, from Minoans to Greeks. These pictorial differences *alone* suggest that between 1500 BCE and 800 BCE, culture in Greece and its surrounds was undergoing a monumental change, one from which we have not yet fully recovered.

The story begins in the eastern Aegean Sea. The time is before the modern era. Literature was first introduced into Western culture about 750 BCE. There was some Greek writing before this time, but it was mostly of shipping records and commercial transactions. The earlier civilizations on the islands of the Aegean—Crete, Thera, Lemnos, Chios, and Cyprus—are therefore not known to us through their literature or their own stories. It is for this reason that these cultures are called "prehistory." They flourished, literally, before the first histories were written. One might expect that they were also primitive. That was in some ways clearly true. But it was certainly not uniformly true. What is more likely true is that many of these cultures did not conform to the values that eventually became mainstream in the West. They were nonconforming and therefore not only considered prehistoric but also were considered for most of the last three thousand years as less artistic, less refined. Robert Graves once wrote of the "savage bee goddess." Archaeological finds of the last one hundred years show, however, that while this savagery may have been true in part, it was also certainly untrue in other and equally important parts.

Western history has until now been told largely as the story of civilizations descending from Sumeria and Babylon, Egypt and Greece, and, finally, Rome. Within these confines our first great literature arose either in the biblical stories around 1000 BCE or in the Greek mythology that began to be written about 750 BCE. There were, of course, extensive Sumerian, Babylonian, and Egyptian myths that had accumulated in the two millennia before the rise of Greece, but these Middle Eastern sources have remained outside the bedrock of Western lore, beyond the immediate study of most Western schoolchildren, and of less significance to the shape of modern values. By contrast, twenty-eight hundred years after the Greek tales were written, American schoolchildren were still reading translations of *The Iliad* and *The Odyssey,* just as did children in fifth-century classical Athens. Of course the biblical stories are bedrock in the West as well, and so there are really two major sources of modern European, and hence American, mythology. Stories from these two sources have been continuously retold over this entire period. It is for that reason that I will concentrate here on these stories, taking them down to their patriarchal roots.

After the decline of Minoan culture, about 1200 BCE, a so-called Dark Age settled onto the eastern Aegean and Greece. During the course of the next four hundred years, the Greeks in a newly emerging civilization unleashed a storied assault upon their predecessors. The stories drew contrasts between Greeks who followed Zeus and those who did not pay primary allegiance to the sky god, the former attacking the latter with vehemence and color, with pictures and images of demons and monsters. The encoded attack was in stories that we today call myths, perhaps because we do not understand them. To the contrary, however, it is probable that at the time, those who listened to these tales understood them very well. These myths were their cultural history, the means of identification of an emerging people. By these stories they distinguished themselves from the old and in so doing laid the foundations of much of what was to come in the next three thousand years. In the manner of a trial lawyer poring over corporate documents within which lie secret clues to his case, I will therefore examine these myths for encoded messages. They are messages that laid the foundations of Western civilization.

This approach and this project comes from the fact that many years ago, as a young trial lawyer, I pursued a wage case on behalf of Denver's nurses. After five years in preparation, a three-week trial, hundreds of exhibits, multiple notebooks of statistical analysis,

and days of expert testimony, the trial judge ruled from the bench without taking the matter under ten minutes' advisement. After weeks of testimony and years of preparation by myself and others, without taking time to collect his thoughts or to write them down, he hastily ruled against a whole class of plaintiff nurses, 95 percent of whom were women. As a result, graduate nurses in Denver continued to be paid less than tree trimmers.[1] Without knowing the history of suppression, this judge had accepted the public persuasion of the ancient Greeks, both in his conclusion about the roles of women and in ruling that they had caused their misfortune themselves. The long history upon which I embark in this volume is therefore not merely an academic exercise. This is not an angels-on-the-head-of-a-pin problem. This is a current problem with deep roots embedded in the stories we tell our children, with consequences that show up in a million paychecks and a million absent benefit packages, or worse, in physical and emotional abuse.

In the 1980s, some years after finishing the nurses case, I was engaged in what is called Track II diplomacy, or, that is, nongovernmental negotiations concerning nuclear issues in Moscow, and in the 1990s was involved as a mediator-negotiator between the sides engaged in horrific ethnic cleansing in the Caucasus of the former Soviet Union. Even later, spanning a period of some years, I negotiated under contract for the U.S. government in Central Asia. These negotiations were on the periphery of the area where Sam Huntingdon of Harvard has predicted the West will experience an upcoming war of civilizations. If there is such a war unfolding, my diplomatic conversations were at the beginnings, in stiffly hierarchical Moscow, in Christian Armenia, in Muslim Azerbaijan, in formerly nomadic Kazakhstan and Kryghistan. In some of these disputes, communities of people who often had lived for centuries in peace, had intermarried, shared businesses, and raised their children together were suddenly stirred to passionate violence against one another. From politicians, on television, and in the press, flames of ancient stories were then fanned so that former friends suddenly began to kill one another. These peoples were modern victims of an old technique of political mythmaking—telling stories of origin in order to manipulate modern powers. The vice president of Armenia led me and my colleagues through a story of Armenian history, tracing their myths all the way to the beginning of the Common Era in AD 340. Weeks later, the vice president of Azerbaijan did the same, only Azeris would trace their myths to Persia and ancient Sumeria. Each ethnic group made claims of right to a certain territory based upon their myths, and they were myths in the common sense—only partly history and equally made up to frame a current political agenda. One day I realized that that is precisely what the Greeks had done at the beginning of the first millennium BCE, and that we, too, in the West were living out our own results of some of the same stories.

Some will argue that the Greeks were not at war—in their mythology—against anyone and that their stories were not original to them or specifically designed to overcome the influence of the Minoans. It is true that much of Greek mythology has echoes in tales of the Babylonians, Sumerians, Hebrews, and other cultures of the ancient Near East. Commerce between cultures of the second millennium was widespread. A thriving international exchange in goods, ideas, stories, words, and jewelry dominated the last half of the second millennium, and the ancestors of Homer and Hesiod and Genesis participated in that commerce. Griffins and sphinxes and animals and heroes are repeated in Greek pictography as they also appeared in Babylon or among the Hittites or Assyrians or Egyptians. Greek mythology, therefore, did not arise out of whole cloth. Professor M. L. West of Oxford has presented an elaborate and compelling case that Greek poets looked eastward for the derivation of many of their stories.[2] Thus, we now know that incidents of some stories from Greece have clearly identifiable elements of similar stories from *The Epic of Gilgamesh* or other early myths, and it may well have been that an equivalent political struggle occasioned similar myths in those Eastern realms in the centuries before the rise of Greek civilization. Having said that, however, it is also clear that none of these earlier stories from Sumeria or Babylon or from among Assyrians or Egyptians contain a figure quite like Jason, or Heracles, or Oedipus, Penelope, or Clytemnestra. There is no Medea or Scylla, no Charybdis or Electra.[3] In their particulars, these Greek stories are distinct; they were fashioned from what must have been common elements—common, that is, to them and to their Eastern cultural relatives—but out of these elements they shaped particular and focused stories relevant to their own situation during that period from the fall of Mycenae in about 1200 BCE to the rise of Western literature in about 750 BCE. Therefore, while it may be said that Odysseus was, for example, "on a long journey home" and that "the journey home" is central to some other myth of the Near East such as *The Epic of Gilgamesh*, it is not true that the hero of that epic had to pass by one after another *female* danger or abided in a culture of *female* disparagement. It is equally not the case that *The Epic of*

Gilgamesh or any other of the Near Eastern epics is fought over a marriage, as the Trojan War was fought, or that any of these Eastern stories celebrates the sacrifice of daughters (like Iphigenia, Polyxena, or Otionia) or concentrates on the dangers of the lost son (as in Oedipus). M. L. West has, it is true, pointed out that many of the earliest Sumerian writings contain advice from a father to a son, but this is patently not the same message as that which lies embedded within the father-son stories of Jason, Oedipus, or Telemachus, all of which we will visit here and all of which portray sons seeking to confirm their patriarchal rights. It is not therefore a safe conclusion that, because of Eastern influence (and certain Eastern elements mixed with the Greek myths), the Greek myths were copies from some earlier age created to solve some problem of Babylon or the Near East. It is far more plausible that these stories constitute a Greek response to problems presented by women-centered cultures that surrounded them. Thus, in these pages I will depart from a probable scholarly consensus that the Greeks were not original in their stories and will argue that in most ways relevant to establish their patriarchy they *were* original and responding to their particular conditions. I will do so based on the weaving of materials from the stories, or myths, and also on pots and in celebrations for men or women, on public monuments enshrined in marble, and on the political and historical chaos of the times.

In the last one hundred years we have unearthed a great deal of new information. Now for the first time we can see what Plato and Aristotle could not see because they did not know, even in classical times, what Aegean civilization had been like before the myths. The evidence had been buried, literally, and remained buried until the late nineteenth and early twentieth centuries of the modern era. As a result we can now see that whereas before the myths women had been portrayed benignly, after the myths they were portrayed as dangerous. Whereas before the myths battles had not been glorified, after the myths battles and heroes came to center stage. Whereas before the myths nature was represented hopefully and expectantly through flowers and bees and snakes and monkeys, after the myths nature was given the shape of angry, erratic, and vengeful gods represented by thunderbolts and earthquakes, while symbolic snakes were turned vengeful and demonic. These changes were ushered in by a massive storytelling campaign that provided the intellectual and psychological climate for a patriarchal property system. Within that system, as a result, women and their sexuality had to be suppressed, the view of nature and war had to be changed, and man's relation to time had to be reoriented.

Robert Graves cast early light on this first war of civilizations and later so did Elise Boulding, Marija Gimbutas, and Riane Eisler, all of whom wrote in the twentieth century. Each did a remarkable job uncovering the existence of cultures before the Greeks that did not share Greek values and that were eliminated by them. There was, among these scholars, including Joseph Campbell, a tradition that warlike nomads had swept down from the steppes of Asia bringing patriarchy and oppression and that the origins of misogyny were from these nomads. A furious intellectual debate then raged through the 1990s over the issue of who these nomads were, why they had not left more evidence, what language they spoke, where their pots and houses were. In the end, many modern scholars, including many women, turned to critique Campbell and Gimbutas and the so-called nomad theory.[4] In addition, when the evidence was insufficient to establish these nomadic invasions in a certain time and place or to establish whether they were outsiders or insiders, the critics began to disparage not only the Campbell-Gimbutas theory of invasions but also the whole of the "goddess movement." Critics disparaged the idea that there ever had been a universal Mother Earth goddess or that there ever had been a peaceful society or that there ever had been anything like nomadic invasions that caused a change to patriarchy. They argued, with substantial justification, that there had never been proof of matriarchy or a universal goddess in western European history.[5] With less justification, however, they went beyond these reasonable questions about nomads and a universal Mother Earth goddess to dispute whether women had ever been more prominent in Western culture and whether some pre-Greek societies were *women-centered*, or egalitarian, or peaceful. As a result, scholarship has since settled back into a comfort zone with its time-honored patriarchal conclusions.

The consequences of the old mythology have been continuous and in some cases disastrous. The myths of Demeter and Persephone and Adam and Eve, together with all their brethren, have unfortunately laid a foundation for oppression and subordination, ridicule and killing, and physical and psychological abuse that has affected the lives and the survival of millions ever since. Recent generations have happily opened up the possibility of a mind change, a possible revolution of consciousness, perhaps the first such change since the rise of Greek and Middle Eastern civi-

lization. That shift in consciousness, however, is not yet complete, and some issues such as the utility of war are on the cusp. Millions continue to think that war works. Others have shown political success and possibility for change on a grand scale without war. That issue is hotter today than ever. The foundations of that debate, too, were laid twenty-eight hundred years ago.

Of a part with these two great debates is the current effort of many to regain a connection with the earth and its natural processes, to overcome an alienation that was also born in that time long ago when the snake was banished and the fertility of the soil was subordinated to the majesty of property won by conquest and power. This debate, too, is at the center of modern politics, the sides divided by the competing beliefs that we are placed on this earth, like Zeus and Jehovah, to subdue and regulate its riches or the belief that we are sprung from the earth, are totally dependent upon it, and could never subdue it at all. In this debate, for some, God is external, forced there by the incomprehensibility of time and infinity, and for others God is within, inimitable, indescribable, and therefore not possible or necessary to name.

Will the butterfly of a postpatriarchal mind emerge from the chrysalis? Will a new, less-heroic consciousness recapture and restore any of that package of perceptions of those who preceded the heroes? The complete answer to that question does not lie in these pages. But these pages will explain in some detail the story of how we got to where we are now. The story retold in this way will give us a platform from which, should we choose, we might make a new beginning.

I
Minoan Artifacts Challenge the Inevitability of Patriarchy

Both Greek mythology and early biblical writings refer to a distant past, a human history in a certain place that they do not any longer know well, as if they had heard thereof but never seen it or quite believed it. It was a place, they each said, in a different time, in a world before their time. This older time was not just the time of a different mind or a time of a different religion, but, more than this, was a time of human civilization in a certain different location. That location—the ground, its nature—was this time's chief characteristic rather than its ideology, its wars, or its kings. In this place, peace was the order of the day, nature gave freely of her fruits, and men and women partook of them without strife.

The earliest Greek writers said that when men and women had lived in this place it had been wonderful, and they called it the Golden Age. In the beginning, they said, before all the anger and chaos of Greek times, there had been peace and harmony among peoples, and death had been no more troublesome than sleep. Greek storytellers said that this was an age of joy in which no one had had to work too hard, the women were beautiful, and there were lovely goddesses to watch over men. They said that the children came, the fish were plentiful, and the seasons turned.

Similarly, over on the other side of the Aegean Sea, on the coast of the Levant, the Hebrews recalled those distant times as if one were in the Garden of Eden, and they too had a recollection that was more gentle and abundant. In the Garden, they said, there was no consciousness of nakedness, and before writing, before awareness of our differences, life had been eternal and sweet. All this lay in their memory and their stories only, because it was before any books.

When writing did come to Greece in about the eighth century BCE, Hesiod, the first of his fellows (of whom we know) to explain the origins of his people, looked back and gave labels to those different times that lay in their past. The Golden Age was the first, he said, of five ages and was followed by the Silver, which was not quite so good, and then the Bronze, a great deal worse. Next came an age of heroes and then his own time, the worst, when gods were angry and men were degenerate, cruel, and unjust.

Perhaps the earlier images were fantasy and Hesiod and the biblical writers were making this all up. Or maybe they simply indulged wishful thinking born of the human need to project an ideal past. Or maybe, on the other hand, this mythology of the Golden Age was rooted in cultural memories that had been passed along over the centuries and that recalled actual times when life had been more settled, more benign, the fields more fruitful. I believe that the record will show that the latter is plausible and that the echoes of an earlier civilization persisted in mythology long after those earlier civilizations had been destroyed. The case can be made, not for paradise, but for the fact that war is not eternal or ever present, that the suppression of women and its accompanying misogyny are not ever present, and that the disconnection from the earth and the urge to dominate nature are not as universal as we have thus far believed.

The example that makes all this plausible is the Minoan civilization, which lasted from 2500 BCE to 1500 BCE. Minoans lived in Crete and the Cycladic islands of the eastern Mediterranean. They did not write stories but produced remarkable palaces, indoor plumbing, colorful paintings, and graceful pottery. Their civilization was funded by an elaborate and far-flung sea trade. Thus, they were neither isolated nor limited in their contacts and were not poor by the standards of the times but rather, to the contrary, were quite wealthy. Neither was their civilization short lived; Minoan culture endured much longer than many of the warring empires that were to follow. The Mycenaeans, the Hittites, or the Assyrians, for example, all came and went within less than five hundred years, but the Minoans lasted for at least one thousand.

Minoan achievements were not modest, and yet the extraordinary fact is that until one hundred and fifty years ago, historians from Herodotus to Thucydides to Gibbon knew almost nothing of them. Until the twentieth century, storytellers, historians, and philosophers did not have any evidence of some bright past that lay in time beyond Greece or the Hebrew tradition, and so most scholars were apt to say, and still do say, that Hesiod's description of the Golden Age reflects a general yearning of humans for some idealized past or is some unrealistic projection, an idea of paradise. Greek myths contained some scattered evidence of the Minoans, but most of this was a coded rejection and provided no clue to the abundance, riches, or beauty of their lives. Today, the common view is still that Minoan civilization had been substantially and permanently erased in 1500 BCE.

As it turns out, however, a memory of Crete and the Minoans, an echo, was unintentionally being carried forward by the very myths that were intended to dispose of them. Today, as a result, we can rediscover Minoan culture partly through recently discovered archaeology and partly by studying the details of ancient myths, which when pieced together provide a mosaic of values that Greeks and early Hebrews intended to reject. That rejection, first written down twenty-eight hundred years ago, has without question influenced Western civilization ever since. In order to understand modern values or to appreciate the bedrock of American culture, it is therefore not sufficient to refer only to the Enlightenment or to the Middle Ages or even to ancient Rome or to all that the Romans inherited from Greece. As a result of what has been learned during the course of the last one hundred years, we can now say that our Western story begins earlier than we thought. It begins with those who came and went in the millennium *before* the Greeks.

At the very beginning of this story, in 2500 BCE, Crete and Thera (two islands about seventy miles apart in the eastern Mediterranean) were centers of modest means. The famous civilizations of the times were still in Babylon and down in Egypt. The lands we today call Turkey and Palestine were occupied by mostly village cultures, or perhaps even nomads, and seem to have been substantially patriarchal. These mainland cultures were ruled by kings, and they were also cultures that worshipped all manner of gods and goddesses. During the period from 4000 to 3000 BCE, tales glorifying female gods were gradually being replaced by tales of male gods who were taking over. The rise and fall of gods on the Asian/Egyptian mainland has been widely documented and can be traced elsewhere.[1] Suffice it to say that war and patriarchy had gradually become embedded in the mainland of Asia Minor and down into Egypt by the beginning of the second millennium.

At around the same time, about 2100 BCE, there was widespread destruction all across Greece and on the mainland of what we today call Turkey. We assume that wars were the means of destruction. Most scholars have also assumed that there was movement of populations from one area to the next and that whole peoples were changing locations, so that new

languages were percolating into Anatolia (today's Turkey) and also into the Argolid (today's southern Greece). New pottery types were spreading, and some archaeologists have tried to trace movements of so-called "Indo-Europeans" down out of Asia into the Near East and Greece. There is, however, widespread disagreement about the sources of these Indo-Europeans or even whether they migrated or where they migrated to. For our purposes it is enough to know that it is widely assumed that whoever they were, these people moving about the eastern Mediterranean in 2100 BCE are commonly believed to have been patriarchal and warlike.

In the midst of this broad picture of movement and destruction, Minoan civilization stands apart. Not only were Minoans occupants of islands in the physical sense, they also occupied islands of a culture that was neither patriarchal nor warlike. That is, at a time when Greek culture was extremely primitive and undeveloped and when trade among Greek villages was minor or nonexistent, there were grand palaces emerging on Crete and the Cretans were developing vast trade throughout the Mediterranean world. Minoans traded with Anatolia, down to Palestine and Egypt, and as far west as Sicily. They traded exquisite pottery that shows up in the graves of the Mycenaean kingdom over on the Greek mainland. By this time it is about 1700 BCE. Over in Anatolia there is widespread destruction and warfare. Babylon is soon to be ravaged by Hittites. The Hittites are establishing power, which they will hold for four hundred years before they too sink into the sands of oblivion. In about 1625 BCE the Egyptians will be ravaged by a people they call the Hyksos and a large part of their territories will be taken over by these apparently foreign invaders.

It is in this context that we look to the island civilization of the Minoans, surrounded on all sides by aggressive kingdoms. The purpose of this book is to show how, in a curious and backhanded way, the suppression of those Minoans seems to have become a permanent theme, a subtext, in the thinking of the European world.

The Mystery of Minoan Civilization

The graphic art of Minoan civilization surprises us with rare and unexpected beauty. It includes flowers, vines, and trees as well as swallows kissing, women dancing, and dolphins leaping. It includes nature scenes that today we only put in children's storybooks, but in 1500 BCE these colorful scenes were ubiquitous in palaces and in smaller dwellings, on pots, on tiny seal rings. The creatures in the paintings were

Fig. 1. Blue bird fresco from the palace at Knossos, Crete, dating from between 1600 and 1400 BCE. Herakleion Museum, Crete. See also gallery following page 78. PERMISSION OF THE GREEK MINISTRY OF CULTURE

probably symbols. There were many griffins (a creature with a bird's head, a lion's body, and a snake's tail—some combination doubtless intended to convey a message). In Greek mythology, griffins were ferocious and would eat men alive, but in the Minoan paintings, they are sitting calmly by the throne in the great room of the palace at Knossos or pulling chariots on the side of the famous sarcophagus of Hagia Triada, and they don't look ferocious at all.

In addition to griffins there are hundreds of paintings from Minoan civilization of birds, snakes, and octopuses. Some say the sky, the ground, and the sea—where these creatures lived—are aspects of the Triple Goddess, but others doubt that such a Triple Goddess ever existed and claim that it is a figment of legend and imagination. The Triple Goddess is a little like the Holy Grail. Either you see her or you don't. For those who see her, there are flowers in combinations

Fig. 2. Kissing swallows on a portion of the Spring Fresco. Akrotiri, c. 1500 BCE. National Archaeological Museum of Athens. See also gallery following page 78. PERMISSION OF THE GREEK MINISTRY OF CULTURE

of three in the wall frescoes of Thera; there are three levels of altars surrounded by worshiping women in the frescoes of Knossos on Crete; there are three seasons of the moon—waxing, full, and waning—both carved into seal rings and painted on the walls in Crete and Thera; and there are three stages of womanhood—the maid, the mother, and the crone—painted into the frescoes from Thera. Still, the patriarchal mind is difficult to persuade, and it is reasonable to call for a more sophisticated form of analysis, some form of triangulation, something that goes beyond "this means that." It is a fair request. The analysis must go beyond "this is a beautiful woman and therefore she is a goddess," because if "woman means goddess," then any fresco could mean anything.[1] Some correlations between symbols, some relation between the elegant woman and her context or other symbols found together with her, must be attempted.

Fig 3. The Spring Fresco, with shapes of women (or stones) arising out of the ground, arms and heads of lilies, which are themselves often in clusters of three in bud, full bloom, or dying. Akrotiri, Thera, about 1500 BCE. National Archaeological Museum of Athens. See also gallery following page 78. PERMISSION OF THE GREEK MINISTRY OF CULTURE

There is an astonishing number of colorful wall frescoes that have recently been uncovered on the island of Santorini (once known as Thera). In some rooms women's shapes have been painted as if the female form is arising directly out of the earth. These are in some ways the equivalent to other clay figurines found in Crete that feature women rising out of not the earth but the trunks of trees. Or there are clay figurines of women who have heads of birds or bees, as if women were somehow of a kind with the earth, the trees, and things that fly. Minoans spent time on graceful lines, bright color, and contrast. Walking through museums in modern times, one suddenly sees a bright blue bird among olive branches, or over there a blue dolphin leaping above the waves, or over here a red and brown partridge in tall yellow grasses. If we were expecting them to be primitive, the visual impact is wholly surprising. If we had Cretan writing or Cretan Kant or Hegel or Plato, we would still encourage a person to see the magnificent frescoes and their flowers, just to get the feel of a culture that is more vivid than words can describe.[2] The Greeks told tales of this very same civilization as if it were ruled by an evil King Minos, a king who demanded tribute in the form of

Fig. 4. A gold ring showing women dancing with arms raised in exaltation, snakes and chrysalises, flowers, and a small figure floating in from the distance. An evident portrayal of female ecstasy. Herakleion Museum, Crete. PERMISSION OF THE GREEK MINISTRY OF CULTURE

the sons and daughters of Athens and who fed Grecian youngsters to the voracious half-man, half-beast—the evil Minotaur in the labyrinth. The Greeks also say that Minos's wife had been so carried away with passion that she mated with a great bull and that is how the Minotaur was conceived. Theseus, one of the first heroes of Athens, was the one who put an end to all this barbarism, and thereafter came the beginning of civilization as we know it. But the wall paintings and pots and figurines that have been uncovered in the last one hundred and fifty years do not show the barbarity that the Greeks described. There are some wild contradictions here that the literature has not yet resolved.

There was some early Cretan writing that no one has yet been able to translate; we will not find the truth by reading, not yet. Unlike Egypt of about the same time, there are no lists on Minoan walls of rulers or names of battles that great kings had won. There are no frescoes or friezes that show conquests, no lists of queens or matriarchs. They left us no names for *any* person or any god who lived in this colorful setting. They were more interested, it seems, in nature and the seasons, the moon and the dolphins, than they were in individuals or individual gods. We do not have even any invoices or records of court administration such as those that existed at the same time in Egypt or Babylon. Instead we have only griffins, figurines with snakes wrapped around women's shoulders, figurines with women's bodies and birds' heads, or figurines of women with hands that look like bees' feet (fig. 4).

Often, on small golden seal rings, women can be seen dancing under the moon. On a famous black vase, men are singing as they come in from the fields (fig. 5). Here or there a fresco seems to portray an important event: a celebration of the fleet coming home, with a woman in the center of the reviewing stand; women gathering saffron, perhaps before a ceremony; bull leapers in community games; or a burial.[3] The feel of the whole is expectant, the way spring feels after a long winter.

All four major palaces in Crete seem to have included sanctuaries with sacred axes, sacred horns, and pouring jugs for wine or oil or perfumes. Two of them also had little stairways leading down to enclosed spaces where there may have been water for bathing. Perhaps these little basins were for purification. Sir Arthur Evans, the first excavator of the ruins of Knossos on the island of Crete, called them "lustral basins." Water anywhere is a source of life, and at the palace at Zakros there was water right in the compound, bubbling up from an underground spring. Not one of these palaces—not Knossos, Zakros, Mallia, or Phaistos—was surrounded by fortifications. All four were built in open areas between mountains that were much higher, and none of them had high enclosures or watchtowers or moats or slits in the walls. It seems clear that while the people of Crete and Thera spent a great deal of time painting monkeys and partridges, they did not spend so much time, or any at all, preparing for any sort of siege.

Fig. 5. Harvester's vase portrays men in song, smiling, with rakes on their shoulders. Herakleion Museum, Crete. PERMISSION OF THE GREEK MINISTRY OF CULTURE

At Knossos, the largest palace, drinking water was piped in from miles away. If there had been a risk of siege, they would have had to find the water inside or take the palace to where the water was. By contrast, in the mighty fortress of Mycenae, built around 1300 BCE on the mainland of Greece, an extended bulge in the walls was added to encircle a stairway to a deep spring, certainly to resist the threat of siege. This feature never appears at any palace on Crete. What is remarkable, therefore, is not that the Cretans were interested in nature, birds, and octopuses, but that this interest is not balanced with any sort of evident interest in siege and war.

Crete and Thera did engage in far-flung trade, the same as we do, and were confronted with obvious dangers, the same as we are, but neither in their art nor in their palace construction did they preoccupy themselves with enemies. They had widespread influence throughout the Mediterranean, yet their trade goods and religious objects showed an expectation of a benign future. Their original pottery designs and copies of such designs are found in the mountains of ancient Greece and the ruins of cities from Asia Minor to Italy.[4] They did not, however, create images on this pottery of an angry god, of a god at the top of some pantheon, or of a hierarchy of gods. There are images on seal rings of men and women in prayer, but these scenes seem at least as ecstatic as fearful. It is not clear whether these prayers are, as has so often been supposed, prayers to supplicate or placate angry divinities or, equally plausible, of excited communion with a beneficent nature. It is also commonly supposed that their sacrifices were intended to propitiate or to quiet the anger of the gods. There *is* evidence that Minoans went to the mountains to pray, to throw their arms upwards in exaltation, to dance, to swirl and swing under the moon, but there is *no* evidence that they went there to *placate*. For one reason or another there is little in any of the scenes that they painted on the walls or carved in their rings that shows either them in fear or their gods in anger.

Fig. 6. Partridge fresco, a frieze in a caravan serai near Knossos, Crete. The subject matter is sharply in contrast to friezes in Greek culture, which is to follow. Herakleion Museum, Crete. See also gallery following page 78. PERMISSION OF THE GREEK MINISTRY OF CULTURE

Fig. 7. A seal that appears to show dancing satyrs, bees, and animals surrounding a woman under a new moon. Herakleion Museum, Crete. PERMISSION OF THE GREEK MINISTRY OF CULTURE

Fig. 8. One example of scores of Minoan figurines of women not shaped to a likeness, seeming to indicate the feminine in general more than any individual in particular.

Something about the feminine was uniformly honored in Minoan culture. They made hundreds of little figurines of women. We do not know why these were significant to them. The figurines have been found on altars, in graves, and even discarded. Perhaps they thought of women as lessening the pain of death, as if women might lessen death's impact or the feminine or regenerative power might even help to overcome death's duration. These figurines are not carved to a likeness and clearly represent the feminine more than any individual woman. There are men in their frescoes and on the seal rings, sometimes as clay figures dancing, but the largest number of all figures and images, by a vast majority, are women (fig. 8). The feminine is not always shown as divine, but it is in all cases honored. In the Minoan materials there is no picture of a woman being dragged by the hair, speared, or attacked by a man. Most often women are in the center; sometimes men are bringing them fish or oils or gifts. There is no certain link between their central position, which is commonly shown, and matriarchy, which is not definitively shown. Maybe women had political control, maybe they did not. Often they are dancing and undulating as if building to some sensual or sexual communion (figs. 4 and 7). In no case are they being chased about by men in the heat of passion, as will be common later on in the Dionysian orgies of Greece. Here, by contrast, there is a quiet dignity among these women. Very often they are dressed splendidly with many-layered, embroidered dresses, flowers in their hair, lovely necklaces around their necks. Minoan women are famous for the fact that often, but not always, their gowns are open in front, breasts exposed without a hint of self-doubt or fear (fig. 9).

Fig. 9. A common Minoan depiction: a seal showing three bare-breasted women performing a ceremony before trees and an altar.

There are, of course, many ways in which the civilization of the Minoans was primitive; it was a time before great roads, before literature, before money, before iron and steel, before dramatic arts and the emerging science and mathematics of the Greek miracle one thousand years later. It is perhaps not wise to create an image of paradise out of our own hunger or hope for a better world. All agree that modern observers ought to be careful about projecting their own values backwards.

These artifacts and pictures, however, are not projection. These are simply the evidence of what was there. There is no speculation that women are the repeated and central subject of this art. These objects are what Minoans spent their time looking at or putting on altars or into graves. The focus in their material is not individual, personal, self-aggrandizing, or combative. This is not because one wishes that there may have been paradise in human history, but because no pot bears an artist's name, no seal ring shows two men fighting. Later on, in classical Greece, pots were often signed, the gods painted thereon were often identified in writing, and warfare was the constant theme.

In Crete and Thera these preoccupations are completely absent, not because we wish they were absent, but because they are absent.

From about 2000 BCE to 1500 BCE these two islands, Thera and Crete, were centers of influence, power, and commerce. In a way, they were at the fountainhead of Western history. Then they were mysteriously erased from our records. In the course of three hundred years after 1500 BCE, Minoan influence dramatically disappeared. So complete was the destruction of their memory, so comprehensive the rejection of their values, that the knowledge of their sophistication was buried from their time until this and has only been unearthed for less than one hundred and fifty years, some of it for even less than thirty years. The evidence available today was therefore not available for more than thirty-four hundred years and was not a part of the early histories of Herodotus, Thucydides, or even Plato, who did not know what is known today.[5] This generation is therefore privileged to be among the first, after thirty-five hundred years, that can begin to speculate about a culture that seems to have been profoundly different from our own, not only physically, but emotionally and psychologically.

An Expectation of Rebirth or Immortality

It is not easy to assign meanings to artifacts. "This means that" is too easy and not subject to corroboration. But when a method is applied to certain Minoan artifacts that have multiple characteristics, there is a possibility to find some single meaning that arises from the combinations. One cannot just say, "a monkey means joy" and leave it at that. However, one can ask—if a figurine combines say, a snake, a woman, and a tree—what is it about these three elements that conveys a coherent message? That simple question takes an observer beyond a "this means that" calculation. Meanings for some of these pictures, rings, vases, pots, and walls may then be plausibly assigned and, when often repeated, may even leap out.

The first proposition of this analysis is that art was, in those times, labor intensive and probably not wasted on subjects without social significance. When some artist took time to carefully design and paint blue birds on a graceful pot, the intention is likely to have been for more than decoration alone. Or, if the focus were beauty itself, then the elegant pot depicts the value in beauty. It is probable, too, that larger questions were on Minoan minds, much the same as they are on that of any human. Everyone has to deal with death somehow. Everyone has to deal with space and time, disappearance, rebirth, sadness, and loss. Men and women of ancient Crete would no doubt have stood at the sea's edge and wondered where the sun goes, how it dies and is reborn. They would certainly have hurt when a child died and rejoiced in the flowers of spring. A culture sophisticated enough to build

boats and sail with the stars across the Mediterranean, complex enough to build multitiered palaces, to hammer gold and carve onyx; a culture that irrigated wheat and exported olive oil, that piped drinking water and had indoor plumbing, would most surely have had a view of life and death that was reflected in their art. In the search for meaning in their artifacts, these subjects are as likely to be there as any other.

Fig. 10. Monkeys were widely represented in Minoan art leaping through trees, gathering eggs, and scampering, as these are, through a field of white crocuses. Thera Museum, Santorini. PERMISSION OF THE GREEK MINISTRY OF CULTURE

Most of the pots of ancient Crete and Thera have only one image, such as a flaming sun, an octopus (fig. 11), or a spiral; or, they may have fish or wheat or birds. Most of the figurines, similarly, also have one image, a woman or a man (although there appear to be many more women figurines than men), and often they are dancing or singing. When there is only one image, it is entirely speculative to imagine what that image may have meant. The image may have meant nothing more than a woman dancing or an octopus, just what it appears to be. It goes too far, for example, to say that a picture of a woman means "goddess." On the other hand, there are quite a large number of Minoan images or figures that are not of just one life-form but that combine life-forms. These are the ones that by their very nature suggest an abstraction. A woman growing out of a tree is not just a woman; she is an idea. These combination images, therefore, are a promising place to start.

There are women rising out of the ground in the frescoes at Thera (fig. 3), there are clay figurines of women with bird heads, and there is a seal ring that portrays a beehive on top of a human female's body. Underneath the beehive is a body with breasts and bird's wings.[1] Such combinations never, of course, occur in nature. There are Minoan vases, or pitchers, that have breasts and wheat sheaves painted on the sides and have birds' beaks in the place of the spout.

The images are again combined, and it cannot be because they occur that way in nature, so they must be put together in these combinations to communicate some thought. The mystery is to figure out *what* thought. It may be impossible to say what a single snake meant when it appeared by itself, but it may not be quite so impossible when the snake occurred in combination with other features, such as the woman and the tree.

Fig. 11. A typical example of Minoan pottery with one image. The octopus is a common subject; this pot is from the museum in Herakleion, Crete. PERMISSION OF THE GREEK MINISTRY OF CULTURE

In an oft-repeated clay form, a woman is seen arising out of a tree base or, that is, is associated with a tree. Often, in the little carved seals that were used to impress images in clay, a woman seems to have a bee head or bee hands. She is part woman, part bee. In one very common and widespread figurine—with many variations—she has a woman's body with a bird's head and bird's wings (fig. 13). In another case the base is solid, quite like a tree. These little bird-woman-tree combinations can be seen today in Crete but also were found in prehistoric Mycenae, Thebes, Thera, and Athens. They were small, portable, and often gaily painted, and were found in graves and in storerooms; they were everywhere. What could be the meaning of the combination of the bird, the woman, and the tree?

Fig. 13. Drawing of Minoan seal ring with combination bird-woman figure.

Fig. 12. Drawing of a Minoan seal showing a figure with a woman's body, a bird's wings and tail, and a beehive for a head. This is a clear example of an intentional combination of images to create some abstract meaning.

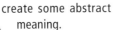

The resolution of this mystery may, in turn, open a door to understanding Greek myths that followed several hundred years later. As curious as it seems, the little figures from Crete may therefore provide a key to understanding certain of the most important stories that lie at the foundation of Western civilization. The chapter on Odysseus will make this more clear. In Thera there is a splendid little nippled ewer with a beaklike spout (fig. 14). An ewer is a pottery vessel, like a pitcher, that is already potentially a symbol because it holds some liquid. Then to this vessel of enrichment are added the beak of a bird, the nipples of a human female, and, on a similar pot (not the one in figure 14) is painted a picture of wheat. The wheat is not just sprouting or in early season; it is full-grained, as it appears just before the harvest. The question, again, is why were these features combined?

Fig. 14. An elegant nippled ewer excavated from the ruins of Akrotiri at Thera. The vessel combines symbols of a bird and a woman. Thera Museum, Santorini. See also gallery following page 78.

Such combinations are common in Minoan pottery, and in all cases, these associations are harmonious, tending to increase the meaning of the piece. They are additive and, one would have to believe, consistent, so that there would be nothing about the bird that cancels the meaning of the woman or nothing about the bee that is inconsistent, but rather, something about them all that is the same or, at minimum, adds to create a single message.

What is it then that is the same about a bird, a bee, and a woman? They are not all sweet, because the bird is not. They do not all fly, because the woman does not. They do not all nurture, because the bee does not. What if we then add to this mix the tree? What is similar to the woman and the tree, or, because the women arising out of trees often have either bird heads or doves in their crowns, what is similar about birds, trees, and women? Trees and birds go together, but women do not nest in trees, except by the wildest stretch of imagination. There must be some other connection. Women are often portrayed with snakes, too, and sometimes in the same figures in which they arise out of tree bases, or, that is, there will be snakes in the crown rather than birds. Is there, conceivably, any characteristic of birds, women, and snakes that links them? What about birds, women, and wheat, as on the ewer from Thera? If we find it, can we unlock the code of ancient Minoan values?

First of all, there is nothing to link birds, women, and bees or wheat in their physical characteristics. Birds and women are totally different creatures. There is nothing in their habitats that is the same. Snakes and women do not live in trees, and birds, most bees, and most women do not live in the ground. Conceivably, they are brought together because they are so different, that is, to represent the universe of possibilities. But then why not a woman with an octopus, also a common symbol, which is about as different from a woman in physical shape as you can get? Octopuses occur over and over on Cretan pots and jars, but the octopus and the woman never come together on the same pot or even on the same seal.[2] Nor does the woman appear on the side of a pot with the bull, except in bull leaping, which is obviously a commemoration of another sort. If Cretans had seen themselves as the later generations of Greeks saw them and had thought of mating women with bulls, maybe then they would have appeared together in some sort of fertility combination, but they do not. They do not come together sexually, not even as opposites, perhaps representing the masculine and the feminine. It cannot be argued that these multiple creatures define the known universe or, that is, gain their importance from their difference, which could be far greater if different well-known subjects were combined. They do not all bring new life, they are not all metaphors of fertility, they do not all die at the same time, and they do not die in the same way.

Nor do they define the universe of daily life. The pots do not combine bulls on one side and chickens on the other, or goats, sheep, fish, pigs, deer, or eagles. These normal creatures show up sometimes, but not in those seals or on those pots or wall paintings that combine images into one figure. They do not show up as evident representations of some unified concept.

The images that show up most often in combination are birds, bees, snakes, women, trees, and wheat. They are not physically, emotionally, habitually, or sexually alike, nor do they reproduce in the same way or on the same schedule. But they do share two features. First, they are all alive. Second, they all have a way in which they either bring about or signal rebirth or the return. Birds go away in the winter and return in spring, as do bees, as do snakes, as do the leaves on trees, and as does the wheat. That leaves only women, who do not go away in winter. But women's fertility goes away every month and returns every month, and their children are the mark of human return, endlessly, over time. Women are the human vessels of return, which is the equivalent of what the wheat, trees, snakes, or swallows do in spring. They are the agents of human continuation, or, that is, if there is anything close to spring in the human experience, it is women who are our agents of the endless return.

Fig. 15. Clay figurine of a woman with doves in her crown. She is rising out of a form most scholars identify as a tree, and therefore combines in herself these three images. Herakleion Museum, Crete.

Fig. 16. A clay woman figurine with snakes in her crown, combining the meaning of snakes, the crown, and the woman. Herakleion Museum, Crete.

Either these careful combinations and their elegant forms were intentional or they were accidental, and to suggest that work of such sophistication and grace in so many repetitions was accidental seems to violate the care and attention that each pot or each figure exhibits. In some ways, therefore, these images are as clear as if written on a papyrus sheet. They combine the human female with those particular creatures or life-forms that share one feature: that each return after some period of absence. Here, one must be careful. This is not, apparently, woman in her image as mother alone, because she is in company with—combined with—creatures that do not mother. This is not fertility alone, or nature, or awe, or womanhood, by itself. When the images are combined they are not completely consistent with these traditional

explanations. Combined, they signal more than some physical fact, more than fertility, more than motherhood; they signal something more conceptual.

Many vases portray the sun, but none are linked to the image of a woman. Many images portray the moon as well, but relatively few are connected directly to symbols of women. There is more here therefore than just the celebration of fertility, because the moon would be tantamount to a signal of woman's monthly fertility. There are birds, snakes, and women who grow out of trees or out of the ground and who sometimes have heads like bees, but they are not shown pregnant or with sows—a common fertility symbol. We must go back to the more abstract idea, not just of fertility, but of the return, the constant continuation. Now, therefore, while it is also true that the sun and moon are honored as well, repeatedly, on pot after pot, here there is a difference. The sun, portrayed often and brilliantly, is not portrayed in association with breasts or women's bodies. The sun is on its own. On the other hand, the *combined* symbols combine *life*-forms. If we saw women together with the sun, it might signal cycles. But if the combination is women and all things that live, it must signal not just continuation, not just the cycles of the seasons, but the cycles of *life*. Profoundly, that is another way of saying "rebirth." Rebirth not of a specific sort, because many sorts are combined, but as a concept. And because these forms are ubiquitous, rebirth must be a central feature of their universe.

In this light, a certain extraordinary frieze from a ceremonial room in the palace at Zakros, at the eastern end of the island of Crete, is highly illustrative. It was once a continuous frieze, running just below the ceiling around all four walls for a distance of twenty-six meters, and consisted of large continuous spirals linked together. At each center of the spiral there is a molded shape in the form of a woman's breast. It is rendered in high relief, painted in white with a colored rosette at the center, and the spiral wraps around one such high relief to the next all the way around the chamber.[3] What could this mean unless it is another way to suggest some connection between nourishment and human life, not only once, but unendingly? The spirals are continuous, with no endpoint and no beginning. And what does that mean, except that life spirals on, or, simply, that death can be overcome?[4] There is a second wall-paneling in the museum at Herakleion with a pattern of breasts surrounded by spirals. The first of these from Zakros is not, therefore, an accident or an anomaly of only one palace. Some commonly understood symbolism is present here.

Fig. 17. Molded breasts linked by ever continuing spirals that decorated the ceiling around all four walls of a large hall at the palace at Zakros. Herakleion Museum, Crete.

In ancient times portions of sacrificed bulls or goats were placed on the altars high in the mountains or, later on, on altars of Zeus or Poseidon. It is a common phenomenon of nature, even today, that when carcasses fester in the open they are apt to pick up bees. Indeed, bees seem to be hatching from the meat. Some people imagine plausibly that in Cretan times this phenomenon, especially when it occurred upon the altar, was evidence of regeneration caused by the death of the sacrificed bull. New life was hatching out of the sacrifice! The bee embodied a suggestion that from death, life mysteriously reappeared. On one delicate gold Cretan pendant—a gem almost certainly to be worn by a woman—two bees hold a balled treasure, probably a honeycomb, in their feet between them. The pendant is graceful and radiant. The wings are diaphanous, the eyes

expectant. These golden bees and the golden treasure they hold all point to the natural world rather than any commercial or man-made world. Seen altogether, in the Minoan civilization the crocuses point the same way; swallows kissing and graves that open to the eastern sun all point this way. Combined, these images convey the concept of unlimited, dependable returns of spring. They do not point upward to Zeus or outward to Jehovah or to an end or a single beginning, but, to the contrary, are suggestive of repeated new beginnings inherent within the principle of life itself.

Fig. 18. A golden pendant on which two bees hold some sacred object between them in a posture of reverence. Herakleion Museum, Crete.

PERMISSION OF THE GREEK MINISTRY OF CULTURE

Fig. 19. A thousand years after the decline of Minoan civilization, women, wheat, and pomegranates were still portrayed together as in this third-century carving of the goddess Demeter. Corinth Museum.

Woman is not separated from, so much as embedded within, this naturally regenerating order. The message is therefore not the value of women by themselves. It is rather more the value of regeneration. That was the transcendent principle of which women were a representative part. The abundant and repeated message of Minoan civilization was that the natural order tends to regenerate life from death. The closest thing to that that we can see in our human society, their artifacts say, is female.

It may seem curious at first, but women in later mythology are also associated with death. There are also hundreds of figurines of women found in ancient grave sites before the Greek mythology. There is, later, the Greek goddess Hera, known to preside over both life and death,[5] and the goddess Persephone, the goddess of the underworld, who is in constant association with her mother, the goddess Demeter, the goddess of growth. A marble carving in Corinth shows Demeter holding both a wheat sheaf and pomegranates—three symbols on one monument: life, death, and new life. These carvings were actually produced much later, in Corinth (fig. 19), but they are all carryover symbols from an earlier, probably Cretan, age.

Even by the later time of this carving in Corinth, the Greek goddess Demeter was said to control the seasons and embodied the qualities of woman and the seasonal cycles, in combination. That concept therefore cannot be said to have ended with Thera and Crete in 1500 BCE. Demeter's prominence began shortly after the Cretan and Theran decline. If Demeter was therefore associated with both life and death, and if the figurines of women found in Thera and Crete that preceded them are also associated with both life and death, it is a small leap to think that Demeter and Hera received these well-documented characteristics from their ancestors at Crete and Thera. But while in later classical times the ability to influence the return was confined to only the goddesses, in earlier times, in the Cretan figurines who do not name any goddess, the return seems to have been associated with all women. If this is true, it was a magnificent statement. Without separating out some supernatural figure, they seem to have been in awe of the continuation of life itself and of all women, who were the vessel of permanence for humans.

Life and death in continuous cycles, or spirals from breast to breast, are the signal of life's continuation, which is simply another way of saying endless rebirth. Endless rebirth is a way of thinking about immortality. That is what is there, again and again, in bold signals in clay models, on friezes, and on pots. Through their very beings, their bodies, their milk, and their children, women of Thera and Crete were offering endless spirals, an endless continuation of fertility and rebirth, and, therefore, something like immortality—the idea that life could go on forever.

Time as a Circle Rather Than a Line

Our culture thinks of time as linear. Most cultures do. In fact, today one has to look far and wide through anthropology texts to find news of people who do not see time as a line. For example, there is one modern study of Trobriand Islanders who have no past tense or future tense in their language. Everything is now. According to Dorothy Lee, who studied these people some thirty years ago, it has controlled the way they see life, death, and conflict. They don't fight among themselves all that much. They don't fear death. That is quite interesting, but is it important? It might be. Once we know that such an attitude is possible, that there can be people like this, then we have to ask whether the Minoan culture was more like us or more like the Trobrianders. It might be one way to explain why they had so little to do with war. If time is a circle, those who die are apt to come back. War would then be less effective than we imagine it. Is that a sound possibility for Minoans?

Within the last few years, archaeologists have uncovered a small ancient city on the island that is today called Santorini. In prehistoric times the island was called Thera, and the ruins of the small town are now called Akrotiri. The Akrotiri remains are very old, dating back to about 1500 BCE. The culture here is closely related to that of Crete, and its art and pottery are similarly focused on natural themes. Here, modern archaeologists have discovered not only pottery and utensils but also rooms in which the walls are decorated by substantially intact frescoes bright with red, yellow, orange, brown, blue, and green paintings. In one of these rooms, three sides are covered by painted scenes that are now called the Spring Fresco (fig. 3). Here the excavators have uncovered an astonishing array of painted lilies—some just budding; some in full, orange flower; and some bending to time, dying. Above the lilies are swallows poised in midflight, beaks just barely kissing. Directly above these swallows are full moons, and overall there is a feeling of expectation created by the fullness of the color and combinations of symbols. There are also, and centrally, several mysterious shapes arising out of the ground. These shapes look like no tree or plant known to man, and yet they are sprouting lilies. The shapes might be stones embedded in the earth. But several of them look uncannily like the bodies of women. If they were stones, they seem unnatural, because they appear to be in motion, swaying or perhaps even dancing. If they were women, they are again not quite natural, because in each place where there should be hands or heads there are clusters of lilies. The lilies are not rigid, as in some Egyptian painting, or for purely symbolic purposes but are natural and realistically colored. Except it is not realistic for blooms to arise from either stones or the arms of dancing women. Once again we seem to have symbols in combination. Some of the lilies are only budding, tight and closed. Some are in full bloom, bright and beautiful. And others are bent over, wilted and dying. The shapes of the stones (or women) from which these flowers grow are similar to shapes of women dancing on seal rings found in Crete. But in this case, instead of bees' hands or bees' heads there are lilies where the heads and hands should be. Moons and mating birds hovering above and behind the curious shapes suggest cycles.[1] The budding, blooming, and dying flowers also suggest cycles. Taken altogether, these frescoes and the Cretan seal rings reinforce our earlier conclusion that Minoans saw a connection between cycles and women. The women seem so connected to the ground they are arising out of that they are practically indistinguishable from it, or at least inseparable.

The Spring Fresco was painted at a time of high Minoan civilization, before the collapse and subsequent Dark Age.[2] Therefore, after the Dark Age, when the Greeks no longer put the figurines of women in graves, it would signal more than a change in burial practices. Taking female figurines out of the graves would very likely also mean a change in the cyclic expectation in which women had played an indispensable role. Now women and the future were to be separated. The post–Dark Age stories, which we today call myths, must have been intended to give some explanation of how women were taken out of the center, where they had been in Minoan times.

It is in one of these stories that Heracles went to the underworld and stole the apple of immortality. In telling this story, the bards announced the end of the belief in endless, recurring cycles. Heracles was something like a founding hero for the Greeks. He was at the head of the line. Modern readers will remember that he was given twelve tasks, or labors, that he had to accomplish. Each of these was filled with symbolic meaning. One such adventure was to capture the Cretan bull. That seems a fairly evident symbolic attempt to overcome Cretan influence. Heracles was of a new ethnic stock, probably part of a new inward migration,

and new language group (Greek); thus, capturing the Cretan bull would have signaled a break with the Minoan past. In the same spirit Heracles was to attack the many-headed Hydra of Lerna and the lion of Nemea; these also happen to be two place-names on the mainland of Greece. We will return to these stories later in the text, but first, it is of significance here that the last of his labors was to steal the apple of immortality from the underworld. By making this a part of the story, the Greeks seemed to be announcing that immortality was in their hands from that time forward. This would be a direct rejection of the Minoan meanings that we have construed earlier. Whereas the combinations of symbols on Minoan pots and walls signified that women were the key to immortality, Heracles stole the symbol, suggesting that the Minoans were no longer to be believed. It must be understood that the Heracles stories were, for the Greeks, stories of origin. They were canonical records of ancestry by which the Greeks explained how they had come to control the mainland and how they had subdued that country for all time. In general the Heracles stories therefore record a great conquest, and in particular they record this change of views about immortality. The Greeks announced to the world that they had literally stolen the concept.

Time itself—the envelope concept, the abstraction of time—would then go from cyclical to linear. Rather than using the sun and the moon or wheat, the woman, and trees as a model of the operation of the cosmos, rather than using symbols of growth recurring in continuous predictable cycles, it now appeared that, thanks to Heracles' theft of immortality (the apple), the rule of cycles would no longer apply to humans. Life itself would no longer be cyclical.

Fig. 20. Heracles in the underworld stealing the golden apples from the tree guarded by a snake, an evident claim by the Greeks that they had ended the Minoan claim to produce immortality through the vessel of a woman. COPYRIGHT © THE TRUSTEES OF THE BRITISH MUSEUM

Today in the West we do not imagine time as circular. There would be no idea of "progress" in a circle, and we value progress very highly. We base our lives, our economy, and our politics upon the idea of progress and therefore upon precisely the opposite idea: that time is a line. We would have to make a special effort to even imagine what circular thinking would be like.

Dorothy Lee, the anthropologist of whom we have spoken earlier, observed that an island people of modern times in the Solomon Sea, the Trobrianders, live only in present time and have no past or future tense in their language. She makes clear that in a cyclical mind the nature of expectancy, motivation, and satisfaction is different from that in the linear mind of the modern commercial world. Every Trobriander activity is spoken of as "now." The long linear progress of history is spoken of nowhere.

Linear thinking leads naturally to the idea of progress, but circular thinking does not. It thus makes a huge difference which model one adopts. The nature of expectancy, motivation, and satisfaction are all affected. There may be no *becoming* in circular thinking, or at least no future not measured in repetitions—season after season, winter after winter, inexorable, inevitable, dependable. If all is "now," comparisons are less likely. In our culture a linear sentence usually leads to some sort of conclusion, a kind of emotional climax. There is movement and then the drama of the ending, where the meaning lies. For us progression along the line is omnipresent and inescapable and determines our sense of accomplishment, our reality, and our sanity.

Dorothy Lee observes that what makes us sane would, however, be insane for the Trobrianders:

Past, present, and future are presented linguistically as the same, are present in his existence, and sameness with what we call the past and with myth, represents value to the Trobriander. Where we see a developmental line, the Trobriander sees a point, at most swelling in value. Where we find pleasure and satisfaction in moving away from the point, in change as variety or progress, the Trobriander finds it in the repetition of the known, in maintaining the point; that is, in what we call monotony. Esthetic validity, dignity, and value come to him not through arrangement into a climactic line, but rather in the undisturbed incorporation of the events within their original, nonlineal order.[3]

Inhabitants of ancient Crete may have held a view closer to that of Trobrianders than to the time clocks of modern industry. Sameness is of value to the Trobriander, while change is not: "To him value lies … in the incorporation of all time within the same point," Lee says. There is a placidity in this focus. Trobrianders show little annoyance when they are interrupted. The interrupted moment is not an occasion of loss, according to Lee, but simply a new occasion. Hierarchy, comparison, and dominance are reduced in importance. A cyclic or static view of time therefore also softens one's view of causality. Events and experiences merge, losing definition and separateness. Interestingly, this lack of emphasis on separation and hierarchy is also evident in Minoan art.

Other studies show that there once existed and there are still small pockets on earth of a so-called "preconquest" consciousness in which knowledge is rooted in feeling, a kind of liminal awareness. Such cultures display a conviction shaped by a sensuality that does not promote abstract thinking but rather what feels good.[4] There is a kind of benign honesty and openness among such peoples, an "integrative empathy and rapport" with the world around them. There is more feeling than analysis, and unfortunately, rationality brought by modern culture may even kill the feeling. The description of this preconquest thinking calls to mind the evident optimistic expectation, or good feeling without rational explanation, that so many observers have noted in the art of ancient Crete and Thera.

The breakthrough of Greek rationalism would have brought an end to any of this preconquest thinking in Crete, as it later brought an end to the emotional anchor of most of modern civilization. Rationalism arrived, and sensuality as a mode of being came to be identified with sex, sin, and dissolution. We cannot tell with certainty if sensuality was the core of the Cretan system or if circular time was their model, but the frescoes and artifacts are more apt to point that way rather than toward a strict kind of Greek rationalism. Later, the storytellers came along and put faces on players in the transition, told how Apollo the sun god slew the Python at Delphi. The Python was a great snake identified by most scholars as an emblem of an earlier earth religion—certainly not with rationality—and most likely the Python was an extension of the earth cults on Crete. So Apollo came along and slew the symbol of the preconquest mind and put in its place the mind of reason. After that the West never produced a culture of lively art filled with partridges and monkeys, dolphins and flowers, and women growing out of the ground.

Three Minoan-age tombs found at Koumasa on Crete suggest the plausibility of circularity not only for the heavenly bodies but also for human life, or, that is, for human rebirth. These tombs were round and had a small opening facing east to the morning sun.[5] At a certain time of year, the sun would have predictably penetrated the opening and life seems to have been expected to reemerge. Some scholars see here an evident anticipation of rebirth: time goes around, life goes around, and death is not an ending but a stage in a continuation.[6] People come back, like the birds do or the wheat does.

The famous Hagia Triada sarcophagus[7] is another pointer to a circular expectation. It was found in southern Crete, and Hagia Triada is the name of the site from whence it came. It has been marvelously preserved, with colorful pictures on all four sides. On one side the pictures show elegant women presiding over a funeral ceremony; another side shows women presiding over a sacrifice; and on another women ride in chariots pulled by griffins; all this bounded on every side by spirals. On the side showing the funeral ceremony, the cuckoo of spring (or of death), which some say is a raven, sits on a double-edged axe. Growing next to the bird and the axe is an olive tree, holy with its mythical dew-catching leaves, and beside

that is a basket of fruit. The sarcophagus is itself of course only necessary because of death, but it is ringed with images that suggest an indissoluble connection between death and return.[8] All these images begin to pile up and point toward the same cultural optimism about the cycles.

Fig. 21. Women presiding over a funeral ceremony, which takes place beside two double-edged axes, one with a bird perched on top. Portion of the depiction on the famous Agia Triada sarcophagus. Herakleion Museum, Crete.

Another small piece of evidence on the question of immortality is a famous black stone vase in the museum at Herakleion[9] (fig. 5). Men are bringing in the tools from the fields, their heads lifted to the skies, their voices lifted in song. Maybe it is the joy of this year's harvest, or maybe it is the joy of the eternal harvest, as if these men knew the secret of eternal grain. Crete is not a paradise in which death does not occur. It has more the look of a place in which death is not final. The wheat stalk must wither and the seed be buried before it will return. When it is properly buried, it will indeed return. Death in that case is not a horror or tragedy; it is rather a link, and not only a link but is seminal. Without it, life does not go on. Death *causes* life.[10]

If that were the belief of ancient Cretans, then the more dramatic the death, the more likely the rebirth. Or perhaps a significant death would be necessary to assure a significant rebirth—that is, the rebirth of a whole community. If someone wanted to speed the rebirth of a friend, maybe it would be enough to sacrifice a bird or shape a little figurine of a woman. On the other hand, if the chief priestess wanted to bring back the whole city, maybe it was time for a bull. Legend has it that the chosen bull was often white and the finest one available. The sacrifice might of course have been, as so many have supposed, to propitiate the vengeance of nature or to ward off destruction by storms and angry fate. But the sacrifice could just as well have been intended to speed the cycle of rebirth. The Cretans may quite reasonably have had the thought that neither life nor death by itself was whole but that together they might form a completion. Great symbols shaped like bulls' horns arrayed the walls of the Cretan palace at Knossos,

an evident reminder of the interconnection of both fertility and death.

Nanno Marinatos, a modern scholar and foremost interpreter of the frescoes of Akrotiri on the island of modern-day Santorini, believes some frescoes there depict an initiation of young women by an encounter with death: "The novice has to die symbolically in order to be born again in a new life and assume a new identity," Marinatos says.[11] If she is right, the women of Thera were tapping into truths that other cultures of ancient times were also exploring. The Tao Te Ching said:

> Between their births and their deaths,
> three out of ten are attached to life,
> three out of ten are attached to death,
> three out of ten are just idly passing through,
> Only one knows how to die and stay dead
> and still go on living.[12]

Later, in modern times, the same sentiment can be found among our most honored poets. "Die and become/ Til thou has learned this/ Thou art a dull guest/ On this dark planet," says Johann Wolfgang von Goethe in *Selige Sehnsucht*. T. S. Eliot expressed the thought exquisitely in the *Four Quartets*:

> Every phrase and every sentence is an end and
> a beginning,
> Every poem an epitaph. And any action
> Is a step to the block, to the fire, down the sea's
> throat,
> Or to an illegible stone: and that is where we
> start.
> We die with the dying:

See they depart, and we go with them.
We are born with the dead:
See, they return, and bring us with them.[13]

Christianity, too, offers a saying known as the Great Paradox: that one must lose his life in order to save it.[14] Were these also the sentiments of the Minoans? Is this what they, too, were saying? We cannot know, because no "sayings" were preserved. But we can see that the messages inherent within their paintings, carved on their seals, painted on their pots, and incorporated into their figurines are consistent with the idea that life and death are inseparably bound.

If Cretan initiation of young women as depicted on the walls of Akrotiri is any guide, and if Marinatos is correct that initiation was a rite of passage recognizing the procreative power of death, then Cretan religion was not primitive. Perhaps the point should be made with more emphasis. The procreative power of death is a profound realization. It is so elusive that most of Western society is today sheltered from it. It is said, however, by those who have grasped this truth that its recognition is freeing, liberating, and divinely inspired. Unlike moderns, Minoans seem to have had no fear of death. The Hagia Triada sarcophagus is covered with images of wide-eyed, not at all sad, expectant women and with spirals not gray but of bright reds and yellows.

Westerners usually imagine that Cretans made animal sacrifices to avoid some impending calamity. We tend to see sacrifice as the Greeks saw it: to ward off disaster or divine wrath. It is equally plausible, however, and perhaps more likely in a world in which everything that goes around comes around, that Cretan sacrifices were not to ward off evil so much as to consecrate, or even to speed, new life. From the example of the seed, death would be seen as a step toward inevitable regeneration, as part of a cycle, as a turning point rather than a cliff. Hesiod, writing seven hundred years after the fall of Minoan civilization, looked back on these times as the Golden Age. People, he admitted, "lived with happy hearts. … Death came to them as sleep."[15] The scholar Robert Graves reached a similar conclusion: "Death to them was no more terrible than sleep."[16] Some commentators think this is also why Minoans were peaceful.[17] If war killed women, it would interrupt the cycle of life by cutting off the direct source of renewal. That would not be desirable if life's continuation was the preeminent value. Further, if death causes rebirth, nothing much will be gained by killing all the men. Seeds, properly buried, will sprout again. Kill them all and they will only come back.

It is consistent that Minoan art lacks images of specific deities. A woman in the center of a large fresco at Akrotiri, for example, is located above and is larger than other women; she is dressed more elegantly and served by fantastic creatures—a monkey and a griffin.[18] Many people say that she must be a goddess. But who can be sure? If we look at the Sistine Chapel in Rome, we can tell who in the image is God. There is no doubt. This is true over and over in Christian imagery. In Greece, there were Athena, Artemis, and Apollo, and they were repeated so often with accoutrements that positively identify each of them that there can be no doubt who was who. The woman with the helmet and the Gorgon aegis is always Athena. The woman with the bow is Artemis. But in Crete there is no such repetition and no such certainty. There is not a name or a common figure or a repeated figure anywhere. Not on the walls, not on the rings, not on the pots. The Cretans did not spend time and effort either building up a goddess or god or glorifying their names.

Which leads back to the concept of time as a circle, not a line. There has to be a beginning and an end to a line. A line itself cannot, by definition, explain what is either before its beginning or after its end. This is important if we are talking about the envelope of time, which is supposed to encompass everything that ever was. Linear time simply cannot do that. Humans who imagine time as a line—like the Greeks and most everyone since then—are left therefore with an unknown Other. The child asks the question, What came before the beginning? This is not a problem with circular time because everything goes in a circle and every thing joins to every other thing. In circular time there is no outside Other to explain, no void, no before or after.

Which means that when the Greeks took time linear, when Heracles stole immortality, they were confronted with a void outside and beyond the ends of their line. This presented a series of unanswerable questions: What *caused* the beginning? Or, What ending causes no further sequence of events? What ending is *not* a cause? It is a very difficult conundrum for rational thinkers. The questions create, inexorably, a need for an external Other, for some Jehovah or Allah or God of the Universe, for some name for the great void that is off beyond both ends of the line. This in turn makes death a problem: with no return in store, death is more like stepping off a cliff. Something has to catch us from the fall. An external God? A heaven and a Hades would help. If a human is like a plant, we sprout back up (circular), but if a human is not like a

plant, we have to go somewhere (linear).

If time is a circle, as the Cretans suggest with their unending spirals, then today is tomorrow's yesterday and also tomorrow's tomorrow; and then everything that is, is past, present, and future all at once; and everything that is, is here all the time. The concept cannot really be expressed by the mechanism of a linear sentence. But readers, on the other hand, will all most certainly have had some experience, some sense of unification with their environment or their friends that was limitless and timeless. That is the experience of circular, boundless, nondirectional time. When we have these experiences we can appreciate what it means to say there is *no* Great Other. The absence of a single famous goddess whose name was known to all of Crete then makes sense. Those who experienced that sense of unification, that boundless identification with the cycles of life and death, would not have needed an Other. They would not have needed some figure to fill the void at the end of the line of time; they would not have needed an equivalent of Athena or Artemis or Jehovah. It is probable that there was no representation of gods and goddesses in Minoan art because there was no inexplicable external void and there was no end.

Tablets recovered in Knossos and in Pylos from the late Bronze Age (after the peak of Minoan civilization) begin to describe the mother goddess as "Potnia" or "The Lady," without another specific name.[19] "The Lady" is not yet divided into parts. "The Lady" as an appellation does not imply "power over" so much as "presence with." It might be another name for what we today call the divine feminine. Four hundred years later, in the eighth century, The Lady will take on the form of Potnia Hera, or Potnia Athena, but in the earliest tablets she is not differentiated and is not glorified as even the "great" lady.

Maybe the Cretans had a central goddess and maybe they didn't, but there is no treatment of the subject at all like that of their Greek descendants or even as was common at the equivalent time in Egypt or Sumeria. Minoans did have pictures of unnamed, exalted women and a small number of exalted males, all who were clearly respected or venerated, but saying that these people worshipped "the goddess" or even "a" goddess is not much safer than saying that they worshipped a god.[20] Pictures of well-dressed women and men may or may not make them divine. As for potential "gods," or male divinities, there are so few pictures or seals that present candidates for that honor that they are even less plausible than goddesses.

Later, Greek myths tell us that one of the names for the earth goddess that came from Crete was Semele.[21] The word sounds like the Russian word for "earth," *zemleye*. Maybe they are connected.[22] If so, then to this day the goddess Semele had a name that meant, simply, "earth." If she was also from Crete, as the myths uniformly say, then there might have been a Cretan earth goddess. Such a conclusion is consistent with common sense. They are two similar words, and Russia is not so far from where all this happened that it might not have picked up the word *zemleye* from

Fig. 22. A typical example of one of a great many Minoan pots decorated with a spiral and, in this case, one that encircles a bulge on the vessel that suggests a woman's breast.

Semele in some three thousand years of travels.[23] In the best case the name of the woman points toward the fertile earth. But the key notion is that the woman is only the pointer. The earth is the real thing. The earth is what is divine.

If, in looking back from modern times, one attempts to penetrate the mysteries of the "earth religions" or the cultures in which the earth and all its creatures might be seen as one, that search leads not so much toward the exaltation of women as separate from or superior to men or even to each other. Rather, the symbolism suggests women sharing the name and space of the fertile earth; the earth as *zemleye* and the woman as Semele, her closest human equivalent. The Spring Fresco from Thera then makes more sense. Those strange shapes rising out of the ground, growing lilies in the places where heads and hands should be, may indeed be women.

The mythmakers who came after this time said that Zeus ravished Semele and got her pregnant. Then Semele wanted to look Zeus in the eye, to know the shape of her lover. It may simply have been a tale, spun with tongue in cheek, to reverse the old game. When women were at the center of cultural life they always knew who their children were, though the fathers did not. In the new Olympian order this story may be saying, with some arrogance, Now the woman wants to know who the father is. We will not tell you. Metaphorically, and perhaps more importantly, Earth wanted to see what the Sky God looked like.

But these later storytellers said that it is not smart for a woman to look upon the god who loves her. When her request to see him was granted, Zeus turned into a mighty thunderbolt and Semele was burned up. The Greeks might as well have said, Don't try to understand the external God; if you do, it will kill you. This story may have been intended to erase the residual attraction of an earlier Minoan earth goddess (Semele from Crete), or it may have been directed toward the believers in the earth religions as a caution against trying to understand the sky god, or the external deity: the sky god punishes any attempt to limit him by understanding. If this was the message, it would have been similar to the message given to Eve, who tried to eat from the tree of knowledge of good and evil. In the Levant when these biblical passages were written, women who might have been associated with Sophia and wisdom were being told that they were supposed to submit and not attempt to understand.

The profound effect of these later Greek stories was to explain that the power of fertility had been separated from the earth and exported heavenward, where it could never be directly known. This is an important divorce, this separation of fertility from the natural order achieved by banishing fertility to heaven with some external god who cannot be seen. The centuries between 1500 BCE and 800 BCE might therefore be called the time of the Great Divide, marking the time before and after which humans shifted the power of regeneration to an external god. This divide signals the time when humans sent regeneration to the heavenly authorities, divorced it from women and from the natural cycles, separated life from death, and put rebirth into the hands of an unreliable and erratic force. They called this force God or Zeus or Jehovah.

In Minoan art there are not many men in comparison to the number of women. Occasionally there are men, but on the whole the seals and walls are far more apt to show women. We do not know why this is. It may have been that men were less important. It may have been that they were so important that they were not to be shown in graven images. Still, it is surprising that we do not see even one male who is clearly a king or a priest. We do not see any women who are certainly priestesses, either, but there are many women who are portrayed larger, elevated above others in the picture, or to whom gifts are being brought (See, for example, figs. 4 and 9). These women could have been honored mothers, priestesses, or goddesses. From the vantage of our own time (after the Great Divide), most scholars call these honored figures goddesses.

To call them goddesses, however, is risky, because in the Christian tradition there is the constant repetition of a single honored woman, the Virgin Mary, and her picture is always exalted. And even though her pictures live on and on for two thousand years, the Christian canon states very definitely that she is not a goddess, that she is mortal. To say there-fore that these women in Minoan art are goddesses is to think Western, modern, and dual. It is to see things as either mortal or godlike. It is to participate in the very distinction that the Olympians delivered to the West—lock, stock, and barrel—after the Great Divide: there are gods up there and not down here, and gods are not like people. Profoundly, Minoan art does not express this same distinction. They saw women rising out of and as part of the earth or min-gled with birds or as friendly with snakes, in all likeli-hood because they had a more unified view of the universe than everybody who came after them or cer-tainly more so than moderns do. Nature and repro-duction, the cycles, the moon and the sun, and fishing and hunting all get more attention than newborns or crones, who get no attention at all. Life at the extremes, at either end, did not seem to confront or trouble anyone—perhaps because in a spiral world there are no extremes.

The Troubling Question of War

The strangest thing by far about the artifacts and ruins of ancient Crete and Thera is not what is there but what is *not* there. On all the materials that archaeologists have carefully cleaned—all the pots and seal rings and sarcophagi—there are no pictures of men at war. Hundreds of seal rings are each quite individual and full of splendid detail. Sometimes they have men standing in a row; sometimes they have women dancing; sometimes there are stags leaping or even a woman or a man carrying a stag. Sometimes athletes are leaping over bulls or fishing, or there is a horse standing alone in a boat. The owner of that seal may have imported the first horse to Crete or exported the first one; or maybe he was impressed with the idea of a big horse in a small boat, which must have been a bit of a shock, in 1700 BCE, for both the boat and the horse. Daily life is carved in minute detail on these tiny seals. Monkeys, birds, swans, altars, and sacred trees appear again and again. But what is not seen again and again is men at war. On hundreds of Minoan seal rings there seems to be only one—or maybe not even one—picture of men fighting, and there are no scenes at all of men engaged in organized combat.[1] Nor are there any such scenes on the walls. There are no frescoes of great kings leading fine armies or of charioteers dashing into combat. By contrast, later on in classical Greece there are literally hundreds and maybe thousands of scenes of Heracles and Zeus in combat with the Centaurs or with the Giants, or Achilles in combat with the Amazons or with the Trojans, or Theseus battling the Amazons, or Athena in combat with the Giants, or Poseidon in combat with Athena. Battle is the coin of the Greek realm. The same can be said for Egyptian artifacts of the period, which also show kings and their conquests.

Fig. 23. Cretan seal showing a bull leaper, who could be either male or female. Herakleion Museum, Crete.

Fig. 24. Seal impression of a horse in a boat. The date of this seal, perhaps as early as 1700 BCE, may make this one of the first horses that the Cretans had encountered.

War is everywhere on Greek pots, on metopes, in friezes, on money, on cups—everywhere an artist had a chance to draw. But in Crete there is no such preoccupation. On a wall painting from Thera, there is a scene of a naval fleet with men tumbling over the boat into the sea, probably drowning (fig. 25 has a portion of this fresco.) These men may be in battle—some distinguished scholars say that they certainly were—but there is no actual fighting taking place, and these sailors may as well be in a shipwreck. There is no enemy in this painting. On all the Greek pots and carvings there is an enemy: a Centaur, an Amazon, a Giant, Medusa, somebody. Always the point of the Greek scene is to show some obvious evil that a good young man would surely want to kill. But in the naval wreck on the walls of Thera, there is no enemy at all, no one to identify as evil, and no contest. In this single, famous naval fresco, there are also five men with shields lined up on land, and there are armed warriors occasionally on other frescoes. Crete had swords and shields and, at least once, they lined them all up, five in a row. There was apparently a sort of minimal attention to war, an acknowledgement of its existence, or it might equally be true that a few police were needed and that these five men with weapons do not signal war so much as domestic crowd control.

Fig. 25. Naval fleet fresco from Akrotiri, Thera, dating from about 1500 BCE. This is some sort of procession with honored persons, but it is not a battle scene. Another portion of this fresco depicts men falling off a boat, probably drowning. They may be battle casualties or storm casualties, but there is no enemy in the picture to show that it is some battle. See also gallery following page 78. PERMISSION OF THE GREEK MINISTRY OF CULTURE

Fig. 26. Looking eastward from the site of the palace at Phaistos. Similar broad, gentle plains stretch in each direction from the palace, which was not, therefore, in a fortified position. This setting is typical of all four of the great palace sites on the island of Crete.

But Crete did not—and on this no scholar would disagree—glorify war. Crete did not make a culture of war. Its cities and palaces were not fortified. Not one of its most important and wealthy palaces had a single cyclopean wall of those gigantic stones that later characterized Mycenae and Tiryns or even Athens. Crete did not leave to posterity pictures of heroes spearing other heroes or women. Some say we have just not found the evidence and that there has always been war. Those of this opinion point to the occasional bronze swords, double-edged axes, and figure-eight shields. But the argument for war, if it is

based upon the evidence, is slippery. It is true that there are a few swords and some ceremonial shields in the museum at Herakleion, and there is the painting in Thera of sailors drowning. But the weight of the evidence points the other way. There is extensive, repeated, and indisputable evidence in the artifacts that Cretans engaged in fishing, hunting, and dancing and that they celebrated the octopus, the bird, the snake, the bee, and the dolphin. All these pictures and artifacts must be weighed on one side of the ledger, suggesting that war was simply not what these people were thinking about. To the point, on the other side, that this must have been a war culture—as it is imagined there must have been a preoccupation with war in all ancient cultures—are the three sailors drowning and five warriors with shields standing at the ready in the painting from Thera. Even as these soldiers stand quietly, however, they are surrounded by dozens, perhaps hundreds, of others in the same fresco who are walking, standing, talking, and definitely not fighting. The soldiers (police) are there, but the scene is not a battle scene. Nor is there any battle scene anywhere else to be found in all the thousands of Minoan representations.

The overwhelming preponderance of the evidence is that war was not in any sense the central preoccupation of these people. There aren't any pictures of powerful or leadership-type males. There are no lists (as noted earlier) of rulers in Crete, no lists of heroes in battle, no lists of queens who bow to kings, no lists of individuals of any kind. There are cups with boxers and wrestlers on them but no lists of winners in boxing, running contests, or bull leaping. No lists of gods and goddesses, no names of gods on the pots, no temples to gods like Ares or to killer heroes like Heracles.[2] If the evidence is important, then the *weight* of the evidence is also important, and the weight is that individual male emblems of superiority and conquest were not featured in Crete. More than this, they are entirely absent. No propagandist for war was making his living in Crete.

Westerners live in a culture in which technology, and especially war technology, is reinforced by economics and religion. To suggest an ancient culture that did not glorify war may be irreligious or heretical. Some people argue therefore not from the evidence but from principle, which is safer when arguing religion. There must have been war in Crete, it might be said, because war is natural to humans. There was war in Babylon and in Sumeria as early as 3000 BCE, so naturally there would have been war on the islands of Crete and Thera by 1500 BCE. Human beings are violent, the argument goes, and the Cretans were human, so they must also have been violent.

But war may not be natural at all. Men certainly do get angry and strike out—an occurrence that is unhappy, quite natural, and repeated. Such flare-ups are usually of short duration. Few men, on the other hand, like to march all in the same direction and sleep in the mud and take orders for years at a time, which is most *unnatural* and requires training. It is a most unusual and most unnatural man who wants to spear babies and an even more unusual man who will do what he is told to do by some other man, all day long, day after day. Eat now; sleep then; throw your spears into the crowd—it is all unpleasant duty. It took years for the Persians to march on Athens in the fifth century BCE, and all that time they had to keep all their men walking in the same direction like cattle, fully fed and with their spears sharpened. A war is not an outburst; it is a grand organizational campaign.[3] A campaign, everyone marching in the same direction all at once, is not genetically determined for any creature on earth—except possibly for ants and once in a while for ducks or cows—but certainly not for humans. Before the Trojan War, Agamemnon had to spend months rallying the Hellenes to his cause. Then he had to get a fair wind for his ships, and to do that he had to cut his daughter's throat. This can't be an instinctive thing. Some Persian did not simply get angry one night and strike out at a Greek because the genes in a man or the nature of man made him do it.

Weapons, ox carts, and ships have to be made, sandals and food need to be regularly resupplied, and soldiers have to be rallied and kept in good spirits. Man's relatively lazy nature and inbred genes are simply insufficient for this gargantuan task. War is not irrational human violence but rather is dramatically and precisely the opposite. It is the result of a whole culture carefully, rationally, and systematically massing its monies, its young men, its horses, its metals, and its psychic enthusiasm all into the pursuit of some story. Without the story, they won't do all the rest.

More than this, the evidence is overwhelming that men have to be trained, desensitized, and given a rationale for killing. They shrink from it naturally. In World War II of the modern era, 75 to 80 percent of riflemen did not fire their weapons at an exposed enemy, even to save their own lives and the lives of their friends. This was such a problem and so undeniably the natural reaction to combat that the U.S. military was forced to undertake a radical change in training and conditioning. By the time of the Vietnam War in the 1960s, and entirely because of such training and desensitization, the nonfiring rate had been reduced to only 5 percent.[4] Men could be trained to kill, but more importantly, they *had to* be trained to kill. Without such training, even with massive propaganda and encouragement, they are apt to shoot into the air.

Precisely because killing is not natural, the only way such effort is conceivable is when the civilian population together with the soldiers who come from that population give consent, and for this there is usually some grand purpose, some larger than life, or larger than death, cause. That thing that is bigger than any one of us is what gives war a chance. It is the war story that makes the sacrifice worth it. President George W. Bush, finding his war in Iraq increasingly unpopular, would, if he could, rally his country to the export of freedom and democracy. Winston Churchill sought to rally the English to their finest hour "if the British Empire and all its dominions should last 1,000 years." Pericles' funeral oration summoned Athens to believe in that city's unique contribution to civilization. Even before him, Heraclitus, his Greek ancestor, pronounced the new age of war for the Hellenes: "War is the father of all and king of all." Such a saying, such a philosophy, is one of the discoveries of the by-then exploding Greek civilization. They thought they were onto something new that had made them great for all time.

Nothing of the kind was to be found anywhere in the culture of their Minoan ancestors.

Early in Greek history, after the Minoans and before Pericles and even before Heraclitus, the storytellers were those who served the purpose of anchoring Greek culture in heroism, and it was heroism through which a man might become immortal. Heroism and immortality soften the impact of the massive amount of death that war breeds. The story told to the people therefore had to create an objective of such importance that men were willing to march in the same direction, year after year, from Persia to Athens or back the other way. On the other side there had to be a story Athenians thought they were living that made them willing to pay their share of the defense at Marathon or a story to give them courage to face the Persians in the great and decisive naval battle at Salamis. Therefore, in addition to the warrior's training, to make an army there had to be a story. Story was necessary to make an unnatural act seem natural.

A pot in the British Museum features Heracles killing a Centaur, and another in the same place shows Achilles killing an Amazon queen (fig. 27). In museums all over Europe there are Greek pots with similar scenes. On the metopes of the Parthenon, carved just before the outbreak of the final war with Sparta, there were four different wars held up to the citizens of Athens to remind them of their glorious war history. At Olympia there are carvings on the frieze of Zeus's wars. At Corinth there are great white marble carvings of more wars with Heracles subduing the Amazons. In the Getty Museum in Santa Monica, more pots with more Greek wars. In the Los Angeles County Museum of Art, more pots with more Greek wars.

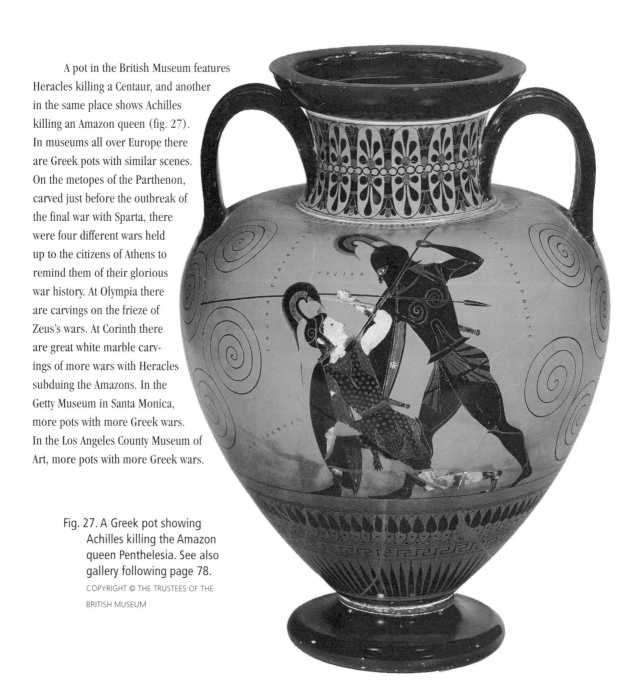

Fig. 27. A Greek pot showing Achilles killing the Amazon queen Penthelesia. See also gallery following page 78.

The ground for all this, the soil without which war does not grow, is the war culture. That is what the pots and friezes and metopes are all for; it is what they reflect. It takes a war culture to support the massive cost and pain of war. This is therefore the extraordi-nary significance of the Minoans. Surprisingly, during the early Bronze Age, Minoans are testament to the fact that *not everyone* shared the war culture. Further, the war historian John Keegan confirms that there had been a thousand years with no evidence of war in

Fig. 28. One of a multitude of later Greek/Roman carvings of war, this one shows Heracles subduing an Amazon warrior. Corinth Museum.

Crete, tracing back to at least 2500 BCE. There had been fourteen hundred years of little or no war just across the Mediterranean in Egypt, Keegan says. Simply, these two regions did not share the war culture that was at that same time sweeping through much of Mesopotamia and Hellas. Not one pot from Thera or Crete shows one man doing the work of a "hero." There are museums full of pots with dolphins leaping, swallows flying, and myrtle bending in the wind. There are no rows of pots depicting Achilles spearing the queen or Heracles trouncing the Centaurs; there are no pots or artwork of any equivalent.

Of course the Minoans must have been violent and peevish and selfish and shortsighted and all the other unpleasant things that human beings are. But peevishness does not provide the system, the rationale, or the organization for war. Some modern scholars have objected, asserting that to say that there was no war culture in Crete is to say that Crete was paradise. Rosemary Radford Reuther, a distinguished ecofeminist, argues against projecting paradise onto Crete.[5] Hers is a gentle form of ridicule of those who might overstate the case for "the goddess" or for the "matriarchy" or for a culture of benignant goodness. Any place without war would be too good to be true. The larger point is right, of course. One cannot be talking about a Cretan paradise as if one were thinking that once there was a historical Garden of Eden or that once there was a loving island where all women lived like Homer's Calypso, indulging in free love and gentle flowers and attending only to life, children, the seasons, and dancing under the moon. During these same years there was abundant war at places all around the region. There is no evidence that the people of Crete treated each other with more skill or handled the crises of life and death without fear or sadness. That would indeed be paradise.

Granting this narrow point, the larger truth is still that it takes a massing of resources, a societal commitment, a focusing of attention, and a gathering of psychic energy to bring together the thousand ships that were said to sail against Troy or to bring together the thousands of soldiers who were said to defend Athens against the Persians. It takes an ideology or a story, and there is simply no evidence for this story in Crete or on the island of Thera. Some ships and some soldiers, yes; a culture of ships and soldiers, no. Rather, the record is of a thousand years of some other focus, not only ignoring war but perhaps inextricably bound to this inattention. They must have had some other focus on the meaning of death, the meaning of sexuality, and the tight bond between humans and the natural order. It understates the point therefore to say that the Minoans were like us in other ways and simply did not wage war. The difference between us is probably far greater than that. The difference extends to the whole Western cultural norm. It extends to our view of time and how we push women out toward fairy tales of trivial beauty instead of linking them into the natural order. It might even extend to our view of ecstasy and the place that we give to sexuality.

Crete and the Issue of Female Sexuality

In biblical literature there are repeated exhortations against the whore of Babylon and other whores who will ruin the lives of the early Israelites. These references and numerous others have led some to conclude that there was an ancient practice in Canaan and along the coast where the Philistines lived, a kind of ritual sexuality.[1] Men went to the temple to make love to the priestess. Now it is called prostitution. When this practice was sanctioned by the religion of Ishtar–Astarte, it might have been seen as one step toward heaven, and Samson apparently thought so too. The Bible takes pains to signify that such a temple is not sanctioned by the patriarchy of Jehovah and tries to keep Samson out of there. But where were these temples, and what did they look like?

For millennia we have not known. Now perhaps we can speculate. At Zakros, on the east end of the island of Crete, archaeologists in the last forty years have excavated an ancient Minoan palace with a courtyard, a lustral basin, a shrine with multiple sacred objects, and access from there to a set of individual rooms. Libation jars of the most elegant crushed crystal, marble, and steatite were found in the shrine room. Sacred double-edged axes were found engraved with lilies and plant leaves. Excavators found a seal ring showing a woman kneeling with a butterfly hovering behind her. Disintegrated boxes lay among the remains of embossed spirals, as well as jugs shaped like bulls heads, called *rhyta*, elegant and smooth and polished in black and gold. The sacred room was next to the lustral chamber, which was probably used for bathing or purifying. The entry to the sacred room was closed and singular. Only one way existed to get to this place. The organization of the rooms suggests that a celebrant went past the purifying lustral chamber, washed with sacred oil from a beautiful marble amphora with lovely, elegant curved handles, and came back up the stairs to the little sacred room where someone met him and some type of ceremony took place. There was not space for more than a few people, so it must have been quite intimate in there. Also in that chamber the excavators found more sacred jars for sacred oil and more libations, and next to that chamber were the sacred axes, more oil, another little carved butterfly, and animal heads in clay to use for pouring all these wonderful oils.

All these things were in one of those temples or one of those sacred areas that existed at the time that the Israelites were settling in Canaan and struggling to get rid of the Philistines and the whore of Babylon. The Israelites repeatedly claimed that the Philistines came from Crete. The prophet Amos said of the Lord, "Have not I brought up Israel out of the land of Egypt, and the Philistines from Caphtor [Kaphtor] and the Syrians from Kir?"[2] (In the Bible, Crete is called Kaphtor.)[3] Jeremiah says, "Behold, the waters rise up out of the North and shall be an overflowing flood and shall inundate the land . . . because of the day that cometh to spoil all the Philistines . . . for the Lord wishes the extermination of the Philistines, the remnant of the country of Kaphtor [Crete]."[4] To this day, Philistine as a term of opprobrium is associated with lewd, drunken, or lascivious conduct. The Bible therefore traces such conduct, which is to be resisted, back to Crete. The easternmost seaport of Crete, the one closest to Palestine (where the Israelites were), is the place we have been describing, called Zakros. This city featured a palace or a temple with a sacred site filled with symbols that might tell us what the Israelites were talking about.

There were lilies and spirals and bulls and butterflies and axes and oils, and all of them could mean just about anything. Or they could be put to the test we used before. If one thing, a lily, say, might mean sexuality, then, if we find lilies there, the suggestion that this palace was one of those temples of sexuality is a possibility. And of course there is a large literature saying that was exactly the meaning of the lily.

Fig. 29. An ivory butterfly from Zakros with an evident message of metamorphosis. Herakleion Museum, Crete. PERMISSION OF THE GREEK MINISTRY OF CULTURE

Still, one lily by itself is a thin basis for argument. But if a lily, dancing, washing with sacred oils, bare-breasted women, and dark chambers are found together, sexuality is a more likely meaning; it is at least suggested by the combination. And if the axe is everywhere a symbol of consecration, as it surely is because it is present again and again at Cretan altars, and if the axe bears engravings upon it of the lily, and if the lily is associated with sexuality, then sexuality is not profane but rather of the sacred.

This is a long way to go to prove that at one time on the island of Crete, sex might have been sacred. There is no sacred text here to prove the case, just Israelites protesting loose sex in the temples. And this is just one sacred site, and there is a long distance between biblical stories and Cretan culture. So no one knows for sure.

Lilies are, however, not entirely without reputation. According to Barbara Walker, throughout the ancient world they were associated with sexuality. She traces the idea back in history and notes numerous instances in which the symbolism of the stem (male) of the lily within the enclosing outer flower (female) is said to represent the physical act of love. There are a great many pictures of lilies on Crete and Thera. There were lilies on the walls of Knossos and on the walls of a little town called Amnisos and of course on the axe at Zakros, and they are all over the walls in the town archaeologists are digging up at Thera. So lilies are a constant of Minoan culture, and maybe they are associated with sexuality and maybe they are not. But if someone claims that they are, there is, according to Walker, at least considerable historic evidence to support the claim.

The bull is not entirely without reputation

either. It is associated with male virility, for reasons that may be obvious. The butterfly is also not without association; it is associated with the chrysalis and rebirth, which in human terms comes through as sexuality and virility, which is a parallel message to that of the bull and the lily. In the sacred chamber in Zakros—the place that the Israelites thought the Philistines came from—there is a figure of a woman kneeling with a butterfly behind her. There was another exquisite, small marble butterfly in the storeroom next to the sacred shrine, which is next to the lustral basin. And all these are next to the Ceremonial Hall, where there are separate doors to enter small individual spaces and another door to go out.[5]

Outside, beyond the Ceremonial Hall, is a grand courtyard. This is where the archaeologist who dug up the ruins of Zakros thinks the people probably gathered under the light of oil lamps to dance and sing and practice their religious rites.[6] No one knows what these rites were.

Unless, of course, the Israelites were right. Maybe the Philistines from Crete were sexual and ecstatic. Maybe the celebrant danced in the courtyard, then went in to purify in the lustral basin, then went to the small sacred shrine to be washed in oil and anointed, and then was led by a priestess to one of the small rooms in the Ceremonial Hall, where they then made love. It would be folly to say that this was definitely so. It would be folly to say that it was definitely not so. But if one of the great mysteries is, Well, what were these temples like, these temples that the Israelites condemned? or What were the centers of sin like, these places where Samson met Delilah?, then the palace at Zakros may provide a clue. And if the students of the goddess cults[7] are right that they were not

sin centers at all but rather central to worship and reverence, then these rites were apt to include not only sensuality but also sacred meaning. There were spirals at Zakros on pots, on the frieze (as we have mentioned earlier), on all kinds of sacred objects in this room. A spiral is an abstraction, a symbol, and next to the axes and the butterflies, these do not indicate some temporary or casual experience like prostitution. The spirals, the butterflies, and the chrysalises all suggest some ritual expectation of life's continuance, and sexuality in that context is not profane.

It is certainly true that any observer can see whatever he or she subjectively intends and that it is risky to go about saying what artifacts mean. But this is the tradition, not just among lawyers, but also among archaeologists. Very famous archaeologists of the last century have said about Zakros or Knossos or Phaistos, for instance, that certain rooms were "king's" rooms or "queen's" rooms. Sometimes they say that very large buildings are "palaces." But the truth is that everyone is making this kind of thing up simply because these building complexes were large and fine. On none of these great "palaces" is there a marker from 1500 BCE written by the people who lived there saying that these rooms had to do with royalty, kings, or queens, or even with men or women. Some rooms are larger or more dramatic than other rooms, and so Western people, who for two thousand years have lived in a patriarchal system, say, Well, these were royals and the largest room was for the king and the next largest was for the queen. Archaeologists of great renown write this way, and the explanatory signs on the walls of these excavations, which are read by thousands of tourists every year, all use the word *king* or *queen*, as if they knew. But there is no original writing to support these claims and no indication of gender for one room or another. Nothing like, say, mirrors and perfumes in one room and swords and shields in another. Nothing like pictures of men or women. It does not say "This is a man's room" or "This is a woman's room," and there is no reason to think that this was the case other than that it would be so if it were medieval Europe. This is therefore nothing more than extrapolation from modern experience backwards: because this would be the king's place in medieval Europe, it would have been the king's place in ancient Crete. But archaeologists are just guessing.

The same thing is true for almost everything one says about Cretan religion. It is quite common to read books that say there was a Cretan deity of animals and another of trees and another of snakes and another of the sea and that sometimes these overlapped and sometimes they did not and that in most cases they were women goddesses and in some cases men and on and on. As if we knew. Wherever there is a woman standing on an obvious altar, the inclination of modern writers is to say, Well, she's up there, so she must be a goddess. Or because a woman is holding on to and praying to a tree, some say, Well, the tree must be a god incarnate. This is very speculative. We have no idea if these trees were thought to actually embody a god. It is quite enough to simply say that the woman is honoring the tree. Some people honor trees even today. One woman in the American Northwest climbed up into a tree and lived in it for two years to protect it from destruction, simply because, as she explained, it was a magnificent form of ancient life. She did not say that the tree was a god incarnate so much as that she had reverence for it as a tree. Still, it is the custom among modern archaeologists and students of the ancient world to say that when a woman is worshipping a tree, it must be because the tree is a god. As if it makes more sense to worship a tree that is really a man than a tree that is just a tree.

One writer says of the famous snake goddesses of Knossos that one statuette "shows how a priestess dressed for a religious ceremony to transform herself into a deity."[8] This is quite wonderful but has to be entirely conjecture. If there were a series of symbols showing ecstasy and opium or women on the way to becoming goddesses, say, in stages or partially heaven-bound or some such thing, it might make sense. But for us to imagine that a woman holding snakes and looking quite transfixed is on her way to "transforming herself into a deity" is an example of a very energetic modern imagination.

We cannot of course say that the large and especially fine rooms such as we find at Zakros and Knossos are not royal rooms, and we cannot say that there were not kings and queens or very important people. There probably were such important people, because there are always differences and inequalities in any human society. The point is not that there were no kings and queens so much as to notice that some very famous archaeologists look at the size of the rooms and their high ceilings or a large chair, and with nothing more than this to go on, say "throne" and "royalty." When they do that they are merely projecting modern values backward. This is not a crime. We probably all do it. Archaeologists are apt to read descriptions by the Egyptians of a "leader" from Crete and translate "prince," as if a leader would naturally be a prince. But if we can do it for kings and queens and snake goddesses, we can also do it for objects that indicate a high degree of sexuality. When we see a

Fig. 30. An elegantly dressed woman with her bodice open gathering saffron beside a river under a gaily bedecked starry sky. This idyllic, sensuous scene lives on the walls of Akrotiri, Thera, from about 1500 BCE. Thera Museum, Santorini. See also gallery following page 78. PERMISSION OF THE GREEK MINISTRY OF CULTURE

butterfly, a chrysalis, a lily, oil, and lustral basins for washing; and seal rings honoring dance; and women with open bodices swaying under the trees, it is certainly not any greater extrapolation to say that something sexual was going on there. We commonly and perhaps mistakenly say that something royal was going on there. The method of reasoning is the same if we say something sexual was going on here, and the conclusion has considerably more evidence to support it. The large complexes or sacred centers of Minoan life of the same and earlier periods may have been trade centers or royal residences or little villages of activity. Whatever they were, they had not only large courts for bull games and sacrifices, but they also had inner chambers for small and intimate meetings, arrayed with bottles of perfume and oil and walls covered with lilies, mating swallows, swinging monkeys, and dolphins leaping. We cannot tell if Zakros was one of those sacred places that included lovemaking, not for sure. But we can fairly suspect.

There is one more intriguing clue. Some years after the Zakros civilization was lost, the dolphin came to be associated by the Greeks with Aphrodite, goddess of sexuality.[9] Some scholars have also seen a semantic connection between the Greek word *delphis*, meaning "dolphin," and *delphys*, meaning "womb."[10] Which raises the question whether earlier Minoan images of leaping dolphins—before the words—

might have implied sexuality. The dolphin, usually bright eyed and leaping, is repeatedly portrayed on wall frescoes at Knossos and on pots and jars from Thera. Popular modern culture holds that the dolphin is the only other creature in nature that engages in sex for the fun of it. Was the dolphin in Minoan art therefore a suggestion of sexuality? It is a question that cannot be answered for certain, but it is another piece of evidence that points toward the possible use of some of these rooms and ceremonial jars as aids to sexuality. In a larger aspect, again, the meaning is greater than pleasure or fun. There is a terracotta figure from

Fig. 31. Dolphins are ubiquitous on Minoan pots and frescoes. Some have associated the etymology of the word *dolphin* with "womb," or, that is, have attributed a symbolic meaning to them, associating them with the promise of regeneration. These are from the palace at Knossos. Herakleion Museum, Crete. See also gallery following page 78.

Fig. 32. This woman from a fresco found in the palace at Knossos, Crete, has carefully coiffured hair, a fine gown, lipstick, and evident beauty that is celebrated and in no sense depreciated or diminished. Unlike later Greek paintings, her beauty is not being attacked. Herakleion Museum, Crete. See also gallery following page 78.

sixth-century Greece in which Aphrodite is holding a casket and standing on the back of a dolphin.[11] If the casket represents death and the dolphin represents the womb or new life, then the goddess is the feminine that connects the two. She is standing on one while holding the other, and the whole picture is in motion—that is, a complete metaphor for death cycling round to life. It is in this sense again that sexuality has its greater significance.

If there *was* anything sexual going on in these places, the Israelites did not approve of it, as they told Samson when he went to see Delilah: Samson, that's a nice place, but it's not your place. If Delilah would have had a child, nobody would have known if it was Samson's or someone else's. And if it was someone else's, it would not qualify to carry on the legitimate male line. The male line is enshrined in what are called "the begats" in the Bible. These begats make up a rather large proportion of Genesis: so much, in fact, as to leave open the suspicion that a primary purpose of that story was to establish a male chain of title. It is not possible to establish a patriliny through women like Delilah, which is why, even though she may be beautiful, her place is not the place of the fathers and her temple was not their temple.

Whether at any one of the four great sites of ancient Crete (Zakros, Knossos, Phaistos, or Mallia)

or in the small intimate rooms covered with lilies in Thera, the Israelites make it very clear that there was ritual sexuality somewhere beyond and before Canaan and that it is to be overcome not just as a threat to the property system but as a threat to their religious institutions. (Which of course are often interwoven.) The later Greek myths make it clear that they too strongly feared sexual women. Possibly this was because if sexuality were to be honored, glorified, and made a part of religious worship of seasons and nature, it may have been very difficult to get people to change or to give it up. If sexuality were, further, made a part of the explanation of life and death, and if that greater understanding were united with a powerful and wondrous physical experience, who would want to give it up? A thousand years later Aphrodite, the goddess of love, was still painted and sculpted with the dolphin and the dove. She was sometimes called Aphrodite *pandemos*, "of the people," her sexuality labeled as a kind that ties all the population into a common bond of nature, a kind of loving in which everyone can share. Aphrodite *pandemos* "involved the ritual of temple 'prostitution,' a service offered freely on behalf of the goddess, for which there were always long queues," which suggests that even in later years the idea of ritual sexuality persisted.[12]

The Ecstatic and the Divine as Inseparable

In modern times there is often an equivalence between sexuality and ecstasy, as if to know one were to know the other. Certainly sexuality can lead to ecstasy. But it is a great mistake to equate the two as if ecstasy were only available through sex. The ecstatic experience is an out-of-body experience, other-worldly, and literally indescribable. It is so uncontrolled, so boundaryless, that it represents a threat to all that has boundaries. There are many examples, old and new: men and women who dance together; circles of them who sway in the sun in a Native American pueblo; women who sway under the moon on the golden seal rings found at Knossos; people who sing sacred music together in modern times and in old; people who climb to mountaintops to pray and lose themselves in the grandeur and expanse of creation; people who swim with dolphins; people who wander among the flowers, picking them for their hair; and people who leap through the air on the backs of bulls. All experience ecstasy. Ecstasy spans time and space and culture. People who love one another and make love experience ecstasy. To hold the baby that comes from that loving brings an ecstasy that cannot be described. The mystical experience of deep meditation or prayer, the experience of being alone in the One, is ecstatic.

These are experiences that are often life changing. One or two can be important enough to organize and permeate the rest of one's days. And yet when we come to describe our ecstatic experience to others, words often fail. Words are little frames of definition

that tend to contain the meaning of a thing or bring the sense down or hem it in. The ecstatic experience isn't like that. We are apt to come closer to the ecstatic with something other than words—with music or getting lost in unexpected laughter or even with our art, painting, or sculpture. Sometimes these activities are more effective than words, and they serve as portals to ecstatic communion. However it comes, ecstatic communion is some of the rarest and most joyful of human experience.

Moderns are more apt to distrust ecstasy or to be uncomfortable with its lack of definition. There are so many ways it can go wrong. A lack of boundaries is dangerous to social order, dissolves discipline, and unwinds the clock. None of these dangers is trivial. One is not wrong to be cautious. Lives may be destroyed, children may be born, careers changed, all because of a single ecstatic experience when boundaries were neglected. When, therefore, moderns look at the dolphins leaping on the walls of ancient Knossos or the bull leapers or the small Cretan pots shaped like opium pods, we are apt to think simply of big fish, sport, and drugs. We are apt to trivialize it, to protect against it. Ecstasy is rare and can change a life; thus, it may be dangerous.

In his famous nineteenth-century poem, the German poet Goethe has his hero, Dr. Faust, fall in love with the goddess Helen. She is more beautiful than all creation, and he would give his soul to hold her. Dr. Faust has only this one thing, this love of his goddess, that he desires in life more than any other. In

Fig. 33. Minoan pots shaped in the form of opium pods. PERMISSION OF GOULANDRIS MUSEUM, ATHENS

desperation he makes a pact with Satan. The devil agrees and will give him what he desires. In return he must never utter the words "Abide with me." He must never seek to hold the ecstasy permanently to himself. Dr. Faust willingly and happily agrees. Satan leads the would-be lover to the underworld, and seeing glorious Helen at last, the doctor is enraptured. Helen is kind to him and lovely. He approaches her and seeks to take her into his arms. The moment has come. He wraps himself around her and then suddenly and inexplicably she explodes in fire and destruction. Helen vanishes, and Dr. Faust is badly wounded and

very nearly dies. He sought the ecstatic experience and it nearly killed him. The poem was Goethe's warning to modern man: beware the dangers of love. Beware the excesses of the otherworldly communion. Beware the ecstatic goddess and all she stands for.

This warning is prefigured by the Greeks. They warned of ecstatic women who romped in the hills. They warned of Dionysian orgies. They warned of Calypso's love. They warned of Medea's enchantments. (We will examine these stories below.) They warned of wine not mixed with water. They warned of hubris. They warned of Aphrodite's "possession." They warned not without reason. All these can take a man to delusion and destruction.

And all these storied rebuttals point to the probable fact that someone before them was more comfortable with ecstasy than either we, or Goethe, or the Greeks were. The signs of it are everywhere in Crete and Thera. It is seen among the women gathering flowers, in the uplifted eyes, and in the eyes of the famous snake goddesses staring off into another dimension. It is seen among clay figures of men and women dancing together in circles, in the fact that they are naked (fig. 35). It is seen among the women dancing under the new moon, arms lifted into the air, calling in tiny spirits (fig. 4), or among women with opium pods in their crowns, arms lifted in expectation (fig. 36). It is seen among the men coming in from the harvest with rakes on their shoulders and their heads lifted in song (fig. 5). It is seen among the young men and women flying through the air over the horns of magnificent bulls, defying death (fig. 34).

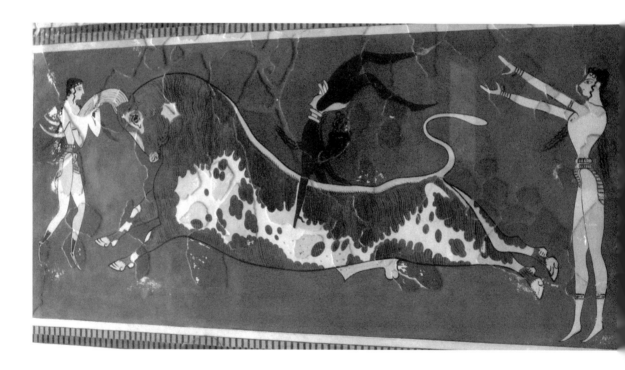

Fig. 34. Men and women both participated in bull leaping, depicted in this fresco from the palace at Knossos, Crete. The male is red and is vaulting off the bull's back while a female dancer engages the animal's horns and prepares to follow. Clearly, the exhilaration of such an experience would have produced a kind of ecstasy. Herakleion Museum, Crete. See also gallery following page 78.

Fig. 36 (below). Clay figurine of woman, arms raised in exaltation, opium pods in her crown, an evident celebration of ecstatic experience. Herakleion Museum, Crete. PERMISSION OF THE GREEK MINISTRY OF CULTURE

Fig. 35 (above). Clay figurines of naked males and females dancing, perhaps dating from about 1800 BCE. Herakleion Museum, Crete.

In our modern culture we limit the ecstatic experience, or try to, to controlled circumstances or to a controlled few who are specially prepared. We cannot tell for certain from artifacts alone whether the Minoans limited this experience as we do or whether they were more comfortable with it. But, as with sexuality, it appears that they were far more comfortable than we are. The wall paintings and figurines neither demean nor glorify ecstasy or even place it at the center of their culture. But neither is it marginalized. It is here and it is there, on this ring and that pot, on this wall of lilies and in the form of that leaping dolphin. It has its place throughout.

Five Values Dramatically at Odds with Patriarchy

It is clear by now that for at least a thousand years before 1500 BCE, there flourished on the island of Crete and among its neighbors a culture apparently quite unlike our own. The greater significance is that it was not simply more primitive, as one might expect, but in some ways more delicate, more hopeful. Frescoes from the time are alight with orange and yellow lilies, ivies, and poppies; there are reds and ochers in the fertile soil, bright-eyed dolphins leaping from the sea, blue monkeys swinging from the trees, swallows lightly kissing, and clear-eyed boys honoring attractive women. The evidence points to profoundly different core values from those of Homer and Genesis—that is, different from those built into the foundations of Western civilization. A very brief summary will serve to highlight the enormity of the difference between their archaeology and what will one day be ours.

Characteristic in the abundant evidence from Crete and Thera (and in some cases from early Mycenae) are these five themes:

1) Honor given to life-forms that die or disappear and are reborn: the tree, the bee, the snake; an implication of life as sufficient to perpetuate itself indefinitely. Therefore, death is not anywhere portrayed as evil but rather as a link between cycles and therefore a *cause* of life, which goes on continuously and (before individualism) is a way of imagining human immortality.

2) Time seen as circular: in cycles, seasons, revolving indefinitely, forever. This creates a greater sense of presence in the moment, because every moment is both past and future. Progress, which is a function of linear time, is not a fixation.

3) The feminine principle is honored at the center of cultural life. Images of women substantially outnumber men and are central to iconography, painting, ceremony, and public life; women are dressed elegantly and are honored on reviewing stands and mountaintops while men bring them gifts, and never once are men seen harming them.

4) Sexuality (including women) is celebrated in symbol, in dance, and in bare-breasted statuettes and is encoded in the symbols of lilies, dolphins, fish, and snakes.

5) Ecstasy, joy, and grace are celebrated in paintings, carvings, and figurines of bull leapers, of women dancing on the mountain, of dolphins leaping above the waves, of swallows kissing in midair, of gentle, obeisant griffins, and in some pottery vessels as elegant as any ever produced.

On the other hand, absent and *not* celebrated in Minoan archaeology are other themes that one might ordinarily expect were we to suppose this to be simply a primitive culture of our dark past:

1) Minoans do not often portray most of the ordinary creatures of the earth, such as spiders, ants, cows, mice, chickens, sheep, or goats. They do not put these symbols in the

center of their sacred scenes or in multiple sacred repetitions. A few such representations do exist, but on balance they rather substantially ignore those things that do not go away in winter or that would not symbolize rebirth in the spring. The exception of course is the bull, which seems to have been of great importance not because it was ordinary so much as for the contrary reason that it was the grandest of all domesticated creatures and its death therefore the most significant. The death of the bull is likely to have been the precursor to new life, and even the bull would then be related to the idea of rebirth.

2) Minoans do not present, glorify, or make an example of men presiding over or subduing women.

3) Minoans do not glorify men at war, men fighting, gods at war, or gods fighting.

4) Minoans do not put in the center of their pictures, seals, pots, walls, or figurines any spears, swords, or graphic scenes of violence between humans. Public places do not dignify conquest. Public places, such as we know them, appear to have been large courtyards for dancing, bull games, or crowded ceremonies of women, perhaps even for ritual sexuality.

5) Entirely absent is any sign of glory for kings or hierarchy. If there is a hierarchy that might be said to be indicated by those pictures of women elevated on high chairs or on mountaintops, the symbol in the exalted position is either a woman of beauty or a woman experiencing ecstasy or—in one case—a man with arms uplifted in reverence. At the top of this hierarchy, if it is hierarchy at all, is either the female principle, the principle of beauty, or the principle of reverence, all of which contrast mightily with the Western hierarchies that were to follow.

6) Minoans do not celebrate brutality to women, not once, not in thousands and thousands of representations.

In the last one hundred years, therefore, an archaeology previously unknown to Western men and women has presented to us the evidence of a civilization unlike any that have come since and that was in some ways substantially more benign. If this conclusion confounds our idea of progress, it may be because we, as creatures of linear time, are unable to step into the mind of revolving seasons without losing hold of our own certainties. It disturbs our world view and what we consider to be grounded or predictable. To admit a civilization more benign than our own confronts our self image, and such a conclusion would be difficult, in part because without our identity as people of progress, our own very sanity would be threatened. These are not therefore conclusions that Westerners can easily come to. And yet the archaeology is there now—at last, after thirty-five hundred years—for all to see. It is not anyone's fault that we did not know all this before. It would only be our fault if we were to ignore it now.

How extensive was the Minoan paradigm? Was it limited to the islands? Or was it suffused throughout the Mediterranean world? There are indications of temple sexuality through ancient Canaan and at places with names strange to us today—ancient Lydia, Lycia, Samos, Lemnos, Samothrace, and Phrygia—as well as among the prehistoric fertility goddesses of mainland Greece. There is a substantial literature on the goddess cultures, or so-called matriarchal cultures, that maintains that such views were widely held.[1] Unfortunately, to be able to confirm the agreement of these peoples with Minoan peoples on Crete and Thera requires a research beyond the scope of this book. What is of paramount importance, however, is that it was the influence of the Minoans and not necessarily that of Lydia, Lycia, et cetera, that lay in the immediate past of those Greek storytellers who were to give birth to Western literature and mythology. As we shall soon see, Heracles in Argos, Cadmus in Thebes, and Jason in Thessaly were set in the fourteenth century immediately following the decline of Crete, and these heroes came with conquest and patriarchy on their minds. Heracles killed the Hydra, captured the Cretan bull, et cetera; Cadmus killed a dragon; Jason voyaged past a vast array of loose women. All these dragons, women, and demons were said to have been resident in their places long before the heroes came. Our earliest mythological stories therefore are stories of overcoming, *and what is being overcome is very often coincidentally similar to the values displayed on Cretan and Cycladic pots, vases, wall paintings, and rings—that is, to the very values listed in paragraphs one through five, above*. There is even some similarity among the biblical tales and the older symbols of the snake and the apple, so it is

likely that biblical tales were also of cultural displacement, especially of cultures in which women had been more prominent.

Scholars have long despaired to know who the Amazon women were or who the Centaurs were or what purpose they and other demons like Scylla and Charybdis served in our mythology. Greek storytellers set these creatures up in evil opposition to their own culture, which was that of the invading Hellenes. Today, these mythological figures and a multitude of others are thought by many to present an insoluble mystery. But if we examine these creatures as symbols of peoples who already lived on the mainland and on the surrounding islands, then Amazons, Centaurs, Scylla and Charybdis, et cetera are very likely explicable. We shall see in the following text that the evidence is abundant that these figures seem to represent the values of the single most influential culture that immediately preceded the Greeks, the Minoans. Seeing that, we approach a revolutionary new understanding of how our patriarchal property system was at first idealized and then justified. At the same time we might come to see how a different culture that honored women, sexuality, and ecstasy, that had no reverence for war, and that had a circular view of time was systematically suppressed. The suppression, however awful, seems to have been neither easy nor ever quite permanent. The flame of these ancient nonpatriarchal beliefs has been fueled by some unquenchable heat that has emerged over and over throughout these last thirty-five hundred years.

II

The Collapse of the Minoan World

At least four causes brought Minoan civilization to an end: invasions, expanding cultures of trade and war that increased the need for sons, the great volcanic explosion that crippled Crete and destroyed the island of Thera, and the development of a sharply misogynist mythology. There is more going on, therefore, than merely the invasion of patriarchs or the evil that lurks in the hearts of men. Modern scholars have been right to be skeptical about that simple solution or the casting of blame in such a simplistic way. On the other hand the suppression of Minoan values was also far less than natural or preordained and was not somehow a given of human nature or of rising commercialism. Misogynist mythology was not dictated by any of the other so-called natural causes. It was not required by invasions, trade, or the devastating volcano. Misogyny was gratuitous and certainly politically motivated and, in the end, long lasting and brutal in its effects.

The Invasions of 1600 BCE: A War Culture Emerges

In the nineteenth century of our Common Era there was a theory that the earlier cultures of the ancient world (including the Minoan world) had been matriarchies. In the 1970s and 1980s it was common to embellish these theories with the hypothesis that there had been at one time a single earth mother or a single goddess religion widely spread across the Near East, including Crete. The matriarchies and the goddess religions were thought by many (led most prominently by Joseph Campbell) to have been thereafter deposed as a result of incoming invasions of Indo-Europeans who had been warlike and patriarchal. The theory was that these invaders were nomadic and accustomed to killing and that they brought with them horses and war chariots. Somewhere along the way they had developed a fabulously powerful composite bow constructed of both wood and bone that could be accurate at two hundred meters. Because they were accustomed to herding sheep and goats, they were good at riding skillfully among their sedentary village adversaries, cutting off stragglers and outsiders, turning them from the herd, and mowing them down.

John Keegan, a war historian, describes the onset and spread of these wars as epoch making:

> About 1700 BCE a Semitic people, known to us as the Hyskos [*sic*], began to infiltrate Egypt through the Nile delta and soon set up a capital of their own at Memphis. A little later, Mesopotamia … was overrun by people from the northern mountains between modern Iraq and Iran; they appear to have made themselves overlords of the ancient inter-riverine kingdom by 1525 BC. Shortly afterward Aryan charioteers from the steppe lands of eastern Iran, speaking an Indo-European language, entered the Indus valley and utterly destroyed its civilization. … the adoption of the war chariot and the imposition of the power of war charioteers throughout the centres of Eurasian civilization in the space of some 300 years is one of the most extraordinary episodes in world history.[1]

While a great many causes therefore undoubtedly contributed to the decline of women's influence and the conversion to patriarchy, it is difficult to imagine a more effective first cause than impalement, dismemberment, death by drowning, rape, slavery, and the utter destruction of whole villages. This would be enough, in most cases, to force a change of religion for anyone who survived. Compared to the incentive caused by left-brained thinking or the gradually decreasing economic power of women, brutality works immediately. There is no evidence of an invasion of the islands of Crete and Thera, and so it is unlikely that these two oases were the immediate victims of this forced change in thinking. It is, however, highly likely that if there were any surviving cultures on the mainland of Asia Minor or Greece that held to the Minoan values, that these would have been swept before this assault. Therefore, in those outlying areas where the earth religions were practiced, this brutality was a likely first cause that contributed to bringing about an immediate rejection of women's leadership, open female sexuality, faith in rebirth, and matrilineal descent. To this extent, the theories of Joseph Campbell and his followers seem to have been correct.

Invaders seemed to come from different directions—sometimes from the north, sometimes from the south. From the south, out of Egypt came a band who scourged the old symbols and laid waste wherever they went.[2] The process is recounted in Exodus:

> Then Moses stood in the gate of the camp, and said, Who is on the Lord's side? Let him come unto me. And all the sons of Levi gathered themselves together unto him. And he said unto them, Thus saith the Lord God of Israel, Put every man his sword by his side, and go in and out from gate to gate throughout the camp, and slay every man his brother, and every man his companion, and every man his neighbor.

> And the children of Levi did according to the word of Moses: and there fell of the people that day about three thousand men. …[3]

Because brothers were killing brothers, the biblical fight could not have been simply about ethnic origins or even about who was the son of whom; they were sons of the same father. Rather, this biblical passage reflects a horrifying religious contest, a war among their own peoples brought on by the claims of one to act in favor of "the Lord" and others who must have claimed they were acting in favor of a more archaic set of gods or even goddesses. Scholars now also place the arrival of an invading people—bringing war chariots—into Greece at about 1600 BCE.[4] These

invaders spoke an Indo-European language that evolved into Greek, which gradually became the new common speech on the mainland. The transition in Greece therefore presaged and was probably similar to the later conversion described so vividly in Exodus. The second millennium seems to have been a period of religious and territorial turmoil in both the biblical lands and across the Aegean in Greece.

In both cases the invasions of outsiders ushered in a collision between male gods and those preexisting earth goddesses who were everywhere to be found. All the famous Olympian goddesses—Athena, Hera, Demeter, Artemis, Hestia, and even Aphrodite—seem to have had independent existences on the mainland of Greece prior to the arrival of the Indo-Europeans. There are no names for them before the Greeks, and therefore they may have been like those Minoan figures, with different reverential images in different villages. Sometimes they served as symbols of renewal and hope, sometimes they were associated with the hearth, sometimes with childbirth, sometimes with a river or a stream, sometimes with sexuality, or sometimes with grain or the hunt. All were divine feminine representations combining the wonder of life and death but without titles or with mostly local titles.

Now all these Greek villages that held such wonder for the feminine or for life's regeneration, by whatever name, were forcefully converted one by one during a period of one thousand years. Many of their divinities were given Olympian names. Some carried on images of the past and merged old and new. Athena, whose earliest worship was probably a fertility cult in the mountains of Arcadia, never ceased wearing snakes around her waist, reminders of her ancient earth origins. Demeter was always remembered to have come from Crete, perhaps the last prosperous center of the earth religions. Aphrodite was said to come from Cyprus, was always an outsider, and was never considered to be trustworthy. The new invaders were clearly troubled by sexuality in women. Hera, Zeus's wife, never fully accepted her demotion from the position as reigning deity of Mycenae and perhaps Sparta. The Olympians converted her into a goddess of marriage, but there was nothing about the model wife that was happy. It is not as if the Greeks thought of marriage as a love match. Marriage, to Hera, was an institution of suppression, and it is quite likely that this is how women during this one-thousand-year conversion experienced it. Greek wives, having once not been wives at all and not corralled and controlled in marriage, but freer and at the center of religious or cult worship, would have fully understood why Hera was angry, scheming, and jealous. In sum, all the local goddesses of the old earth religions were tamed after the invasions of 1600 BCE, and for the next thousand years the tales about their taming became the stuff of the myths that tried to imprint a stamp of inevitability.

These invasions, therefore, accompanied by brutality and the forced subordination of earlier goddess figures (representations of the divine feminine), were among the first pressures that would eventually destroy the Minoan legacy. Beginning in about 1700 BCE, the mainland of Greece and the coastal areas of the Aegean began to be devastated and the goddesses were brought under the control of male gods. In these places war replaced fertility as the acknowledged source of prosperity. But this was not the whole story, was not a complete explanation for the decline of Minoan values.

Fig. 37. This portion of a larger wall painting from Akrotiri, Thera, shows women in the central boxes of a reviewing stand observing the arrival of a naval fleet. Unlike any pictography of the later Greek period, here women in a civil ceremony occupy the most prominent positions. The painting is clear evidence that women were not only honored but also held public authority. See also gallery following page 78. PERMISSION OF THE GREEK MINISTRY OF CULTURE

The Theran Explosion: The Loss of Faith in Mother Earth

Over the last fifty years scholars have debated the precise date of the volcanic explosion on the island of Santorini (Thera), but the most recent evidence puts it at just the time when the influence of Crete and other Minoan cultures was dramatically replaced by that of the Mycenaeans—that is, by Greek-speakers. That would make it probable that the explosion itself and its aftermath opened the doors for foreign invasion, or at least the rise of foreign powers, to offset Minoan influence. The picture of how it all happened is traced through archaeology.

Fira, a small town on today's island of Santorini, sits on a cliff one thousand feet above the blue Aegean. From here on a summer's day, in every direction one sees the sea glistening silver and blue gray in the passing sun, mottled occasionally by a few clouds. In a small, well-ordered museum in this modest town sits a little pitcher that was dug out of the volcanic ash that covered the island in a giant blanket thirty-five hundred years ago. The pitcher has a long elegant beak; the shaping of the neck is graceful and bends down to a rounded jug that is clay colored but blended with hazy pink, like sunset clouds moving over the sea. On the breast of the pitcher are two nipples, discreet and

tasteful (fig. 14). In the same museum case is a smaller pot around which dolphins are leaping, and beside it is yet another with swallows in flight, swooping and diving (fig. 38). The proportions of all these vessels are exquisite. The drawing is delicate and lively. The flight of the birds is exactly as the swallows leap and fly along the chalk cliffs of Santorini today. The dolphins seem to be laughing. Nearby in the museum is a tiny wall painting of a red dragonfly and light green myrtle branches caught in warm sunlight.

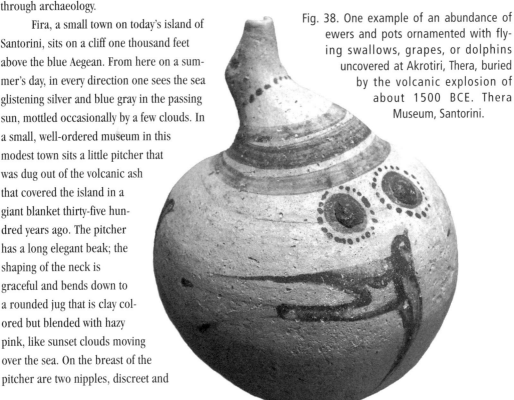

Fig. 38. One example of an abundance of ewers and pots ornamented with flying swallows, grapes, or dolphins uncovered at Akrotiri, Thera, buried by the volcanic explosion of about 1500 BCE. Thera Museum, Santorini.

Another pot has a sheaf of wheat, another a bunch of grapes, and another a splay of olive leaves. An art scholar writes of these presentations with awe and says that it is impossible to view the Bronze Age Minoan material without sensing joy.[1] Some have written that these may have been the finest pots ever produced in Europe.

These vessels were all buried—along with wall frescoes of elegant bare-breasted women, with houses and a whole village—as a result of a horrific volcanic explosion that occurred about 1500 BCE or possibly as late as 1470 BCE. The eruption at Thera was cataclysmic and probably more awful than any in the history of humankind. More than any theory of patriarchy, more than any explanation of invading nomads, more than any Indo-European change in customs, the ash that buried the pots and the villages of Thera probably produced the psychology, the state of mind, that buried Minoan civilization.

The island of Thera had been a little less than ten miles long and ten miles wide and in the center rose to a height of at least one thousand feet, while some have posited it was as high as more than three thousand feet.[2] The central part of this nine square miles of rock and stone was suddenly and horrifically lifted into the air and dropped into the sea, leaving an area submerged that had once been about one hundred square miles of land, some of it certainly inhabited.

The ash layer that covered the houses in the remaining part of the island (the little Bronze Age town of Akrotiri) was more than ninety feet thick. The dust and ash from the immediate explosion shot up and away and drifted over all but the southern part of Crete and blew on the winds as far as Cyprus, Egypt, and Anatolia. It deposited ten feet of ash in the sea twenty miles away and sent a tidal wave, variously estimated from fifty feet to three hundred feet high, rushing toward Crete. The speed of this giant wave is reckoned to have exceeded one hundred and fifty miles per hour. In twenty to thirty minutes it would have reached all the way from Thera to the shores of defenseless Crete.

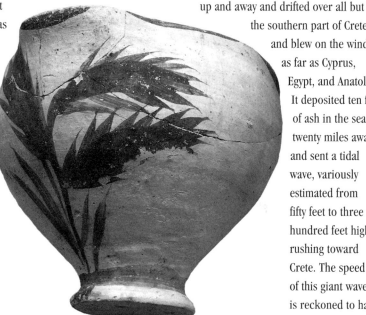

Fig. 39. A wheat or barley design on a vessel uncovered at Akrotiri, Thera. One of the earliest bits of evidence that celebrations of wheat, which later occurred at Eleusis and in the ceremony of the Last Supper, derived from a long history of honoring grain. Thera Museum, Santorini.

The seaside palaces at Zakros and Mallia would have had no other warning than to see the flames on the horizon and to hear the awful roar of the earth literally arching her back and retching up her innards. In 1816 an explosion of the same or lesser size in Indonesia created a year without summer, thus spreading famine in Russia and the United States. It is certain that the combination of sun-darkening, earthquake, and tidal wave would have ripped asunder the very tissue of Minoan community.[3] It is in that sense that the psyche of these communities would have been changed.

When the sea rushed in to swallow up the island of Thera, when a tidal wave rushed across the coasts of Crete and Naxos and most surely as far as the Greek mainland and Asia Minor, when the soils of neighboring countries were covered with ash and the seasons delayed, suddenly the cosmology of the people who made the exquisite little pots must have had to change. Not only was Thera no longer a whole island, it had substantially vanished. Not only was Cretan agriculture under a coating of ash, the skies were darkened, the sun cooled. This Theran explosion, which today we know to have been four times the power of Krakatoa in Indonesia (some recent scholars say as much as nine times that power), had to have shaken the very foundations of faith of the people of the Aegean. It would have delayed the dependable cycles of planting and fishing, deadened temporarily the fruitfulness of both land and sea, and cast a lingering cloud over their skies and their hearts. It would have upset any idea that the world was benign, that the gods were benign, or that life and death were predictable. All this happened, according to the most recent estimates, in about 1500 BCE. It is inevitable,

in hindsight, that the explosion led to a crisis of faith, to an inability of the nature religions to explain the vicious, brutal, and unearned destruction that rose up out of the earth itself.

It is unlikely that after the explosion on Thera the people of the region could picture their earth, its seasons, or its benignant nature as dependable or predictable. Less and less after Thera did they picture women as central to survival or Mother Earth as the source of all life. Mother Earth had exploded in their faces, quite literally, and they would have been wary of her now, more apt to try to propitiate Zeus the Thunderer, Poseidon the Earthshaker, or Hades, lord of the Underworld. All three of these had shown up in the explosion, and from this time on their names begin to appear in primitive writing. All three are appropriate to describe the unexpected forces that seemed to have descended upon the earth in one horrendous moment.

The Thera explosion immediately precedes the decline of Minoan civilization and was certainly among its main causes. Some say that the earthquakes weakened the palaces and that the warlike Mycenaeans came and settled in. Some say the Mycenaeans conquered the Minoans. But there is no evidence of a fight or a war, so people may say there was a fight because it is hard to imagine such a change without a fight. On the other hand it is at least as likely that the Mycenaeans were friendly to the Minoans and came in to bolster a devastated country. There is a great deal of similarity between Minoan art and Mycenaean art during the early period before the explosion, and they may have been allied in spirit. Whether the Mycenaeans came peacefully or as hostiles seems to depend on the eye of the observer now, thirty-five hundred years later.

Other than Plato's reference to the lost Atlantis one thousand years later, there is not a collection of myths relating to this explosion. There is no doubt that it occurred. But there seem to have been few people left afterward to describe it. Or maybe the ones who had suffered the losses were taken over, became slaves, or emigrated, becoming refugees in a generally hostile world where they did not have the status of storytellers. Or maybe the trauma was like a great accident, which often leaves people speechless and unwilling to talk about the event itself. Catastrophes are not easily relived. Psychologists today report that people who live through horrific natural disasters do not sit around the fire and happily reminisce. Men who come back from war seldom reminisce about life in the trenches. Or maybe those who experienced it directly, on Thera and Crete, were themselves buried or swept out to sea, leaving others at a distance to remember only the thunder and the earthquake and the roar of the sea.

Until the beginning of the twentieth century, Western scientists and historians knew almost nothing about what lay under the ash left behind by the Theran explosion and therefore almost nothing about ancient Minoan civilization. There was no Acropolis to look upon and remember, no Roman Coliseum as a reminder, no man-made landmark to spur the inquiry. Not one monument was left above the surface of the earth.

The Greeks told tales of vicious and evil King Minos, but no one really had any idea about his world or the civilization of these wonderful palaces at Zakros and Knossos or the pottery or the wall paintings contained within. Many of the most exquisite wall paintings on Santorini, further, have only been

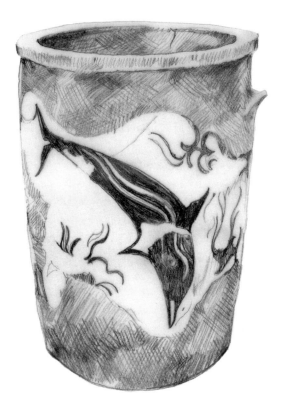

Fig. 40. A lovely dolphin vase from under the ash at Akrotiri. Thera Museum, Santorini.

unearthed in the last thirty years: the elegant women of Thera, the lilies, the swallows kissing, the full moons, and the monkeys swinging were simply not known for all these thousands of years. They were buried and out of sight while much of the story of Western history was being imagined without the information that these artifacts contained. They were not known to great historians of the modern era, such as Edward Gibbon or Alexander Pope. They were not known to Dante or Augustine or Virgil or Pausanias. They were not known to the great historian of Athens, Thucydides, or the first historian of the West,

Herodotus.[4] They were not even known to Homer and Hesiod, those first poets who wrote down the stories after the Dark Age in the eighth century BCE. The theory and explanation of Western cosmology, the religions of Judaism and Christianity, and the formulation of patriarchy all took place when the only information about Crete and Thera came from the stories told and passed on by the Greeks for some seven hundred years after the explosion. These stories seem to have had no contribution from the Cretans themselves or from the Therans. It is as if the explosion of 1500 BCE had literally blown them off the map.

In a sense the explosion of 1500 BCE marks a boundary between (Western) history and prehistory. The story of Western civilization as we have always known it seems to begin with Mycenae, the next great civilization to rise after that of the Minoans. Mycenaeans had settled into the Greek mainland from about 1900 BCE but only gradually gained influence on the Peloponnesus, so that they were only slowly rising to full power by about the time of the Theran explosion. By 1500 BCE they were thriving, probably as a kingdom controlling trade routes through the Greek mainland. Their artisans had extensive contacts with the Cretans, modeling their frescoes and pottery on Minoan styles. In the early centuries Mycenae had been a minor civilization compared to the far-flung trade of Crete and Thera, but after the explosion it rose to great significance, perhaps in the vacuum created by the Minoan silence.

It is from Mycenae that the first threads of our Western mythological history become specific. The heart, the center of power, was a citadel atop a small hill overlooking a broad and fertile agricultural plain on the mainland of Greece in a region called Argos.

Today, still, it appears as a site of great cyclopean walls dominating the surrounding plains, and in those days it controlled a narrow pass that lay nearby on the land route to Corinth, Thebes, and Athens. By 1300 BCE Mycenaeans had extended their empire to all these cities. They dominated the Peloponnesus and controlled Sparta, Argos, Tiryns, Lerna, and Nemea— all those place-names familiar to persons who track the exploits of Heracles. In Mycenae before Heracles they had honored Hera, a goddess of life and death, of fertility and the seasons. Hera's time would have been at the beginning of the Mycenaean era, perhaps even before the decline of Crete and before the great explosion on Thera.[5] Then it seems that at some point, probably after the explosion, Mycenaeans added the worship of Zeus, Athena, and the remaining Olympians. The explosion probably discredited Hera as much as it did the Cretans. These were not good times for the earth and therefore also not for the earth goddess, and after the explosion the Mycenaeans became definitely warlike.

According to the myths the goddess Hera was forced to become the unhappy wife of Zeus. Her "marriage" may signify the conquest of villages by people who were converted at the point of a spear to believe in Zeus the Thunderer and Poseidon the Earth-shaker. As they lost these battles one by one, these people may also have lost faith in the ability of Hera, the benignant mother of seasons, to protect them. A force greater than the change in the seasons had taken over their lives, and this was the force of violent, erratic nature represented by the Theran explosion. From that event primitive Indo-European invaders seemed to have derived Zeus, Poseidon, and Hades. In the ensuing cynicism and chaos also came Heracles,

Fig. 41. This ewer has a bird's beak, a necklace, and a spiral, which seems to be interchangeable with the nipples in its message of continuity of life. Thera Museum, Santorini.

the warrior hero, the conqueror of old symbols. The storytellers would spin the whole cataclysmic change to say that Zeus had been sleeping with or ravishing many women and that his son Heracles was clearing the way of all the old evils. All of which was probably allegory to explain Mycenaeans or Dorians conquering and subduing villages one after the other through the course of the second millennium. The significance to history is that these would have been villages that had previously been more dependent upon women, either as priestesses, queens, or even as goddesses. Later on, the storytellers would also describe Hades' abduction of Persephone (herself a representative of the old religion of the earth mother) as a marriage. The allegorical "marriage" of Mycenae's Hera to Zeus, king of the invaders, is also likely to have been forced, representing the takeover of Mother Earth's Mycenae by warriors such as Heracles.

It has always seemed a bit inscrutable that Zeus, the king of the gods, would have had such an angry wife as a goddess of marriage. But it is not inscrutable if the myths are seen as propaganda for a massive political and cultural change that had been ushered in by the combination of growing sea trade, its accompanying increase in wealth, the spreading systems of war, and the growing need for sons. (More on this below.) It is less inscrutable if the earth religions are seen as destabilized following the Theran explosion. It is not inscrutable at all if Hera is seen as a representative of those old earth religions that were being displaced, being forced into the patriarchal fold, and being symbolically integrated more or less against the combined wills of a huge population of women who must have resisted or found Hera's subordination a symbol for their own.

Hera, who had been all-powerful as a fertility and seasons goddess in Mycenae, never shows up in any Greek mythology to support Zeus. She is, further, forever pestering Zeus's illegitimate son, Heracles. He is "illegitimate" because he was born of a mortal, in other words, Greek, woman, and therefore not from Hera—that is, not from the older religion. Hera, in anger, sends snakes to kill Heracles on the day he is born. Because she was the original reigning goddess in the region, her act of sending snakes is probably telling us that her followers resisted the takeover by the Indo-Europeans or patriarchs. Very likely her townspeople did not like being forcefully converted to Zeus's worship and her resistance is symbolic of theirs. Two towns near to Mycenae, where Hera had been supreme, were Lerna and Nemea, and two of Heracles' great "labors" took place in those towns. It is likely that those "labors" that are set in these towns are allegory for their conquest and that Heracles stood, in the popular mind, for the invading forces that suppressed them. Heracles and the invaders were almost certainly deposing earth goddesses and subjecting people to a new patriarchal religion. In one story Heracles wrestled with Antaeus, a Giant and a direct descendant of Mother Earth. This Giant could only be defeated if his feet could be lifted off the ground. To break the old earth worship, therefore, Heracles had to break the physical connection of Antaeus to the raw ground. The symbolism was remarkably explicit. Heracles, son of the sky god, fought Antaeus, a descendant of Mother Earth, by lifting him up in the air and breaking his connection to his divine mother. This was the only way Antaeus (and all others of similar belief) could be beaten.

Hera had originally been a figure associated with snakes, much the way the snake goddesses of Crete seem to have been. It was Hera who sent the many-headed Hydra in Lerna to defy Heracles and Hera who was forever bedeviling the many women—some say they were moon goddesses—with whom Zeus was constantly forcing "sexual" unions, which was more likely an apologist's way of describing forced political unions. Hera remained a danger. She represented the old order that, on Thera at least, had blown up in their faces. She had at one time been responsible for the regular seasons and had suddenly gone very unreliable. Her followers apparently did not abandon her entirely, so that Zeus's warriors had to keep her in the pantheon on Olympus just to keep her people in line. But after the Thera explosion, the earth goddess was in steady decline.

Fig. 42. Heracles lifting Antaeus. At the end of the Bronze Age, farmers, worshipers of Mother Earth and her sons, could only be overcome if they were literally separated from contact with the earth.

Fig. 1. Blue bird fresco from the palace at Knossos, Crete. See page 13.

Fig. 2. Kissing swallows on a portion of the Spring Fresco. See pages 14–15.

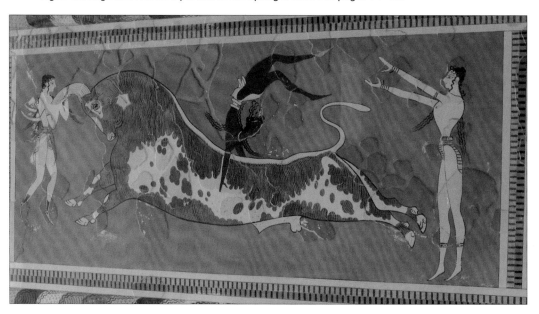

Fig. 34. Men and women both participated in bull leaping, depicted in this fresco from the palace at Knossos, Crete. See page 62.

Fig. 3. The Spring Fresco is part of the ruins of Akrotiri on the island of Thera.
See pages 14–15, 33.

Fig. 31. Dolphins on a fresco at the palace at Knossos, Crete. See page 57.

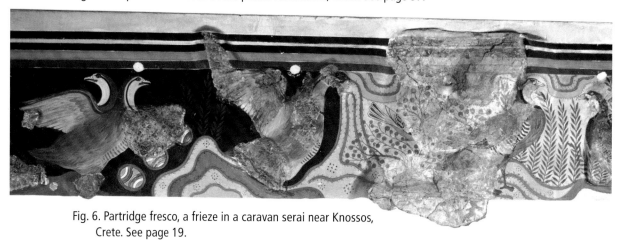

Fig. 6. Partridge fresco, a frieze in a caravan serai near Knossos,
Crete. See page 19.

Fig. 14. An elegant nippled ewer excavated from the ruins of Akrotiri on Thera. See page 26.

Fig. 27. A Greek pot shows Achilles killing the Amazon queen Penthelesia. See page 49.

Fig. 30. An idyllic, sensuous scene found on the walls of Akrotiri, Thera. See page 56.

Fig. 32. A woman from a fresco found in the palace at Knossos, Crete.
See page 58.

Fig. 37. Women watching from the central boxes of a reviewing stand as a naval fleet arrives. See page 70.

Fig. 25. Naval fleet fresco from Akrotiri, Thera. See page 45.

The Growth of Trade: The Diminishment of Daughters

The civil wars and the explosion were not by themselves the whole cause of women's suppression. Neither is the coming of nomads and invaders a complete explanation. Wars did not simply spring from the evil minds of aggressive men. Conflict arose more fundamentally from the need to control new riches. Wars during these years were most often fought to plunder wealth or grain or women, all forms of property. Warriors came home loaded with loot or slaves; these were a soldier's payment. Therefore, they needed to be able to store the material and—as their booty grew—they needed to be able to continue to hold it longer than their own lives, to be able to give it to a next generation who could protect it. As they became increasingly wealthier, accumulating more than they could immediately consume, they would also have needed counting cycles that lasted longer than the monthly cycles of the moon or annual cycles of the sun. They would have become property holders for terms of years and thieves of the now-massive accumulations of others, thus in many ways outlasting the seasons. They would have begun to value symbols of conquest as opposed to symbols of fertility, because conquest, or so it seemed, produced security for an even longer term. They would have needed symbolic heroes of pillage and rape, such as Heracles, in increasingly greater degree than symbolic nourishment of the crops, such as Demeter, the goddess of grains, represented. They would have begun to find gods of war, such as Ares, or turned earlier fertility goddesses, such as Athena, into half one thing, half another; in Athena's case, it was half warlike, half wise.

In the late phases of the Bronze Age, near the decline of Crete, there was trade in gold, ivory, ebony, lapis lazuli, and amber all across the eastern Mediterranean into Anatolia and as far as Mesopotamia. Egyptians sent gold, alabaster, amethyst, ivory, ostrich eggs, scarab seals, stone and faience vases, and ornaments to Greece. Mycenaeans sent pottery to Troy, Egypt, and Sardinia. Silver and copper went from Cyprus to Crete, Pylos, and Argos. Olive oil went from Knossos to Mycenae and probably to Egypt.[1] This trade required long sea voyages that were more easily undertaken by men who, not ever being pregnant, would not have to cope with big bellies while rowing the long oars or hoisting sails and who did not have to nurse and care for babies while fighting off pirates. Men could leave home for long periods, while women would have extended times when being at home was far safer. The Hittites invaded down from Anatolia to Babylon, sweeping up riches as they went. The Mycenaeans fought against Thebes; the Sea Peoples conquered much of Egypt. As, in the second millennium BCE, this trade spread out across the Mediterranean and as wars to steal the very rich results of this trade also spread in its wake, sons became more central to both offense and defense. In this way, gradually over time, protection of the long-term seemed to depend more upon sons than upon daughters. An underlying cause of patriarchy was therefore probably more than just brutal invaders who mastered the art of war on land. Joined to those invasions was also the changing economics of the sea. Nomads needed sons to conduct war on horseback or in chariots. Marauding sea peoples needed sons to man the oars. On a farm women were at least as useful, if not more useful, than men. But in the late Bronze Age, more and more wealth was coming from trade and conquest rather than fields of grain or woven rugs or daughters.

If men themselves could not live forever, their influence could live on through the wealth and property that they left behind. This would be in marked contrast to measuring security by when a village had enough daughters to beget children for another generation. Now the need became to insure that the property would be left only to one's own sons and not to the sons of some other man. It is therefore a great mistake to think of Homer's *Odyssey* as being about a loving marriage or about Odysseus, the hero, coming home to his beloved wife, Penelope. In the very first chapter of that great book, Telemachus, the son of Odysseus, says, when asked by Athena whether he is the son of the hero of the Trojan War:

> My mother says indeed I am his. I for my
>   part
> do not know. Nobody really knows his own
>   father.[2]

Within the first 215 lines of *The Odyssey,* Telemachus thus states the great problem that patriarchy was intended to solve. A son of a queen or a temple priestess might have many possible fathers. "My mother says that I am his" is the signature statement of a matrilineal culture, and this is the social condition with which Homer copes throughout. Penelope, the queen of the island of Ithaca, is a woman of the old order, and Homer is showing us Ithaca's transition. Telemachus's anguish is that he wants to be the son who knows who his father is. It is the father, the pirate, the raider, who brings home the new wealth. It is no longer enough for only the mother to know. And so, while "my mother says that I am" is the signature statement of the matrilineal society, it is the fundamental problem for the patriarchy. Homer gets to it within the first 215 lines and takes the rest of the book to work it out.

In *The Odyssey* when Athena thereafter arrives at Ithaca to check the situation, she is admitted to the courtyard where the suitors are gathering to feast at Penelope's, and therefore Telemachus's, expense:

> There she found the haughty suitors. They at the moment in front of the doors were amusing their spirits with draughts games, sitting about on skins of cattle whom [*sic*] they had slaughtered themselves, and about them, of their heralds and hardworking henchmen, some at the mixing bowls were combining wine and water, while others again with porous sponges were wiping the tables and setting them out, and others cutting meat in quantities.[3]

Throughout this tale Telemachus does not worry that Penelope is lonely or that she is without protection or that, after twenty years of waiting for her husband, she is wasting her life. He worries only that already they are "cutting meat in quantities," and it is literally driving him to distraction. Underneath all its adventures therefore—and the point of its moral lesson—*The Odyssey* is about ending this abuse, not just for this hero and his son but as a moral lesson for all

Greeks. If Penelope remarried, Telemachus would lose his claim to her property because, presumably, before patriarchy it would go with Penelope to the new husband and their children. Nor does Telemachus express concern about his father, Odysseus, as a human being. He is concerned, he tells us again and again, that all his goats and sheep and pigs are being eaten by men who want to marry his mother and take the rest. His concern is the race against time, the hurry to get his father home before his mother remarries. This race provides the drama for the whole book. This is therefore a story about a rightful claimant getting home in time to save his property for his son, and this property, we learn immediately, is that which is accumulated from raids and piracy all across the Aegean. Odysseus no sooner gets home and protects his property by killing off all the suitors then he turns around and leaves Penelope once again. *The Odyssey* is about protecting a marriage, but it is not about married love. That kind of special affection between a man and a woman, the affection of the heart, he left behind earlier on his journey—a matter important enough for a much more detailed discussion later on in this text. "By my love have I made him my husband," said glorious Calypso, who had already loved him for seven years. "That's what you think," said the Olympian gods—the gods of the new culture of the invaders—who sent him back to Penelope.

These traders and raiders, so often at sea or at war, would have to know absolutely, without doubt, who their sons were and who their sons were not. This could only be accomplished if monogamous marriage for women became sacred and enforced by both religion and law. The laws all around the Mediterranean world would come soon enough in Leviticus and Deuteronomy and from Solon and Psistratus. But first the morality upon which the laws were based had to be articulated and assimilated. This was the role of the early stories of Jason, Odysseus, Agamemnon (also treated at length below), and for that matter, of Adam and Eve. A woman had to be married or else the patriarchy could not work, and the patriarchy had to work because everyone's growing wealth had raised the new requirement that there be sons left behind to protect it.

The Great Civil War over Marriage: The End of Women-Centered Culture in the Eastern Mediterranean

Invasions, trade, and the Theran explosion all therefore combined to usher in the increased need for sons and a new culture that recognized the evil and erratic nature of Mother Earth. These were preconditions to the great cultural shift that brought about the end of Minoan influence and values. From changes in the role of Hera, described above, it can already be seen that gods and goddesses were being shaped anew to adjust to these changing conditions, to the incoming peoples, and to the arrival of great new wealth. It was the storytellers who would rationalize these changes, give them sacred import, and make conversion compelling. In addition, epic stories were then created, memorized, and told and retold to describe the agonies of the wanderer Jason in search of his patrimony and of his troubles with his wife, or the hero Odysseus and his journey to regain his wife, or the warrior Heracles and his battles with Zeus's wife and his own wives. These grand tales emerged in the four hundred years after the decline of Mycenae but attempted to depict times before that decline. They were grand tales of origin and claims by chieftains to parts of Greece or to some of the islands. The greatest of these epic tales were those told by, or attributed to, the blind poet Homer. In turn the greatest of Homer's tales was his recounting of a great civil war between those Greeks who lived on the mainland of Greece and those who, sharing a similar religion but not yet sharing the same social custom with regard to marriage, lived in Asia Minor in the city of Troy.

Just as the war between the north and south of the United States determined the fate of slavery, the Trojan War determined for all time—or at least until modern times—the status of marriage in patriarchal society. After that great conflict—which allegedly lasted ten years—Western history gradually turned away from the values of defeated Troy. These were values that had no doubt lingered from earlier civilizations like that of the Minoans. Troy seemed to have been allied in spirit and perhaps even in practice with the Cretans. They were renowned for treating women more openly than did the Greeks, and nearby Phrygia was renowned even after the war for what patriarchs called its "orgiastic" cult.[1] Symbols from Cretan cults such as the double-edged axe and the so-called "horns of consecration" have been related by scholars to traditions of ancient Anatolia, cheek by jowl with Troy.[2] The war was therefore important for more reasons than just the fact that the Greeks won and the Asians lost. Of even greater significance to history has been the mythical status of that war, wrapped in glory and self-congratulation, lodged forever in the Western mind by the poet Homer. His portrayal gave history a vivid picture of how the new patriarchal culture finally stamped out the last of those remaining cities that placed a high value on women and ecstasy and a lower value on marriage.[3]

The war is usually reckoned about 1225 BCE—that is, about three hundred years after the Thera explosion. In the wake of this war, a Dark Age descended over Crete and the Greek mainland, over the villages that had centered their attention on the

moon and regeneration and the naturalness of death. After this time villages were turned (allegorically by the power of Heracles' sword), to concentrate on the Thunderer, the Earthshaker, and the awfulness of Hades. It was after this war that the die was cast, after which the old influences of Crete and Thera would gradually fade away.

The Trojan War was not about religion or goods or territory. By this time, three hundred years after the explosion on Thera, people on both sides shared a belief in the Olympian gods. When the war was over, further, the Mycenaeans did not seize Troy as a part of their empire. They simply destroyed the city and went home. It was not about copper or shipping or ivory. Troy had none of these. It was not about revenge, for there was no history of war or conquest between the Hellenes and the Trojans. It was not about controlling Black Sea trade or defeating the Persians. The winners did not stay in Troy to control the entry through the isthmus into the Black Sea, and they did not create new relations with the empires eastward into Anatolia. This was a war, rather (as the protagonists claimed in their own words), to defend a marriage. It makes perfect sense in the thirteenth century BCE, when marriage was being solidified as a foundation of mainland Greek patriarchy. By this time it had become abundantly clear that marriage was the institution without which a patrilineal property system simply could not be maintained. Therefore, controlling Helen was important for more reasons than that she was beautiful or that Menelaos, her husband, was brokenhearted. Her decision to move around from man to man would destabilize the whole of the patriarchal property system.

We have the story from the perspective of the Greeks (the winners) and not from the Trojans, and the most we know of it is from the ruins of the city and Greek mythology. The most detail comes from Homer, but there were other versions and other storytellers, and from them all came a lore that was eventually known by every Greek. The story provided the first great heroics upon which the Greek character was said to be founded. Three thousand two hundred years later, the names of its characters are still familiar to Western readers, and its stories are still taught in our schools.[4] We know of Achilles, the warrior; and Helen, "the most beautiful woman in the world"; and Agamemnon, the leader of the Greeks; and Clytemnestra, his wayward wife. We know of Odysseus, the crafty one, meaning that he did not always tell the truth; and we know of his loyal wife, Penelope, who waited twenty years for her husband to come home. From Homer's specific recounting we know of the habits and details of the Bronze Age, of the styles of war, traditions of hospitality, the hearth, and sacrifices to the gods.[5] *The Iliad* is one of the foundation documents of Western civilization. It provides a clue to the politics and issues that divided the eastern Mediterranean only three hundred years after the decline of the Minoan world.

The conflict begins when Paris, a young prince of Troy, runs off with Sparta's beautiful queen Helen. No one in Troy seems to have been too upset that Paris brought home a new bride or that Helen had freely chosen for herself with whom she would live. Troy therefore in all probability was more like Crete in its pairing customs than, say, patriarchal Mycenae or the homes of the contemporaneous patriarchal biblical kings. In this sense it is plausible that Troy was a predecessor in the line of those loose traditions that

the biblical texts later condemned. Sparta, too, may have had residual connections to the older traditions that offered more freedom to women or that treated women with the respect and dignity shown on the walls of Crete and Thera. Sparta was one of a few well-known places where the goddess Hera had been worshipped before the coming of Zeus, Heracles, and their lot. Hera, by all mythical accounts, and as we have seen, was not comfortable in Zeus's bed. She had been converted to the role of a married woman, but in her earlier incarnations there is archaeological evidence that she had been a goddess of the earth religions, of the seasons, and of life and death.[6] If she had been dominant in Sparta before the coming of the Greeks, she might have shared the view that women could have several sexual partners. Even in Homer's times Sparta was a likely place for Paris's seduction of Helen because women in that city were apt to have more than one mate, sometimes even several. That was common knowledge in the lore of Homer's times. Virginity, chastity, and fidelity were never rated as highly in Sparta—even hundreds of years after the Trojan War—as they always were in Athens.[7]

Helen and Paris assumed a freedom that Menelaos, the king of Sparta, however, did not grant. By this time, under Zeus's patriarchal rules, monogamy in marriage had become very important for women. In addition, everyone said that Helen was ravishingly beautiful and that Menelaos wanted her back perhaps for that reason too. Some scholars think that Helen was also, as a priestess of the moon goddess, Menelaos's connection to the divine. As such, she was the basis of his claim to the throne. Many scholars, such as Robert Graves, who have written about the so-called earth religions and the freedom of

female sexual conduct in those times have assumed that union with a priestess or union with a queen was the way in which a man established his claim to property. Therefore, if Menelaos lost Helen, he would probably also have lost his estate and his position as king. He may have wanted her back not only because she was beautiful but also because without her he would have lost all status.

The abduction of Helen by the prince of Troy—or, in her mind, simply her choice of a new lover—created therefore an archetypal conflict, a classical confrontation of civilizations or, more precisely, of property systems. Patriarchs who were taking control of Greece were imposing the institution of marriage in order to control from whom women might have children, thus limiting who might make a claim upon a man's growing wealth. The goddess Aphrodite, who came from Cyprus and was not a dependable supporter of Zeus, had in this case upset a man's claim to a kingdom. That Aphrodite was regularly and constantly a problem for the patriarchs indicates that at the beginning the new order was having trouble dealing with open female sexuality and therefore having trouble in establishing the male line.

To help solidify their positions, patriarchs now contrived to invoke the blessings of the gods. To get something right with the gods would be to gain alignment with the natural order of the universe and, they hoped, guarantee their patrilineal claims for all time. They were not far from wrong. The myths thus begin the story of the Trojan War with a contest between three goddesses vying for approval. Before the war there had probably been a hundred different goddesses for a hundred different islands of culture throughout the Minoan and Mycenaean worlds. These goddesses would all have been in contest for the loyalties of various villages. The Trojan War therefore begins with three goddesses quarrelling.

The storytellers say that a lesser goddess named "Strife" decides to cause a little trouble. She throws a golden apple down among three of the most prominent goddesses: Aphrodite, Athena, and Hera. Upon the apple is written the provocation "For the fairest." This sets off a beauty contest that is not good for public order. Consternation results, and there is trouble brewing on Olympus. Zeus thereupon presents the golden apple to the young mortal Paris, the prince of Troy, and says to him, "Since you are as handsome as you are wise in the ways of the heart, … [I] command you to judge which of the goddesses is the fairest." Paris is reluctant. It is a vainglorious man who will judge among the gods, and the act is most likely to be fraught with serious consequences. He is right about that. Hera, to win her case as the fairest, offers to make Paris the richest man alive. "Oh," Paris says, "I will not be bribed!" Next, Athena offers to make Paris victorious, handsome, and wise. He says, "Well, that is very nice, but I am a humble herdsman, not a soldier." Then Aphrodite sidles up to Paris without any clothes on and says to him, "You must be the handsomest man in Phrygia. … Why don't you move to the city and lead a civilized life? What have you to lose by marrying someone like Helen of Sparta, who is as beautiful as I am and no less passionate? … You can have her if you like."

"How is that possible, if she is already married?"

"Heavens! How innocent you are! Have you never heard that it is my divine duty to arrange affairs of this sort? I suggest that you tour Greece with my son Eros as your guide."[8]

The rest, as they say, is history. Paris straightaway gives the golden apple to Aphrodite, and the goddess keeps her word and gives to him the beautiful Helen. The lady had a husband, but she and her lover consider this a small matter, and together they elope. They sail away to live with Paris's parents, brothers, and sisters in Troy. That is all as it might have been in late–Bronze Age cultures in which women were sexually free, or, that is, as we imagine cultures scattered through Anatolia and around the Mediterranean before patriarchy. Paris and Helen would have been acting according to the norm before the rise of great wealth had begun to create such a premium for sons.

Menelaos, the betrayed husband, sends out a call to his brother, Agamemnon, in nearby Mycenae to help fetch the untamed wife, a woman who does not yet know the rules of patriarchy. The brothers then enlist all their neighbors to join the chase, and they form a sort of twelfth-century-BCE posse. Then the Trojans, who lived across the Aegean Sea in Phrygia, enlisted their neighbors, too, and the dispute ultimately developed into an Aegean civil war.[9] The list of chieftains on each side is so long and so accurate that is has been said that Homer's descriptions of the territories from which they each came were used by later generations to conclude territorial disputes.[10] We can therefore say with some authority that the Greeks considered this accounting not only myth, but also history. Phrygia, the region in which Troy was located, was (as we have already noted) well known for its orgiastic pursuit of the cult of the Great Mother[11] and therefore probably also relationships between women and more than one man. There is further evidence that matrilineal institutions had prevailed in the region before the coming of the Hellenes, and in one set of stories the city of Troy was originally first colonized by Cretans.[12] The issue in the civil war was very likely therefore not only about the retrieval of Helen; it was probably also about whether the Greek patriarchs would enforce the rules of marriage against a group of eastern cities that had rallied together to defend old sexual and religious freedoms.[13] The time period is right for cultural and religious transition: the earth mother had been discredited by the explosion at Thera, and the social mores of the old earth religions were under great pressure to yield to religions honoring the male line.

According to the winners—who wrote the story—the gods took sides, and those defended by the married goddess Hera and the virgin goddess Athena defeated the side of the sensual and beautiful Aphrodite. From the perspective of a cultural war, this is at least a caution about female sexuality, the hypnotism of which may cast a trance over any man just as it did the Prince of Troy. Paris was an apt example. He was captivated by Aphrodite, and, thus blinded, he upset two kingdoms and chaos broke loose all across the eastern Mediterranean. Aphrodite was apparently the *principle* of sexual irresponsibility, while Helen was the practice of it here on earth. The fighting would go on for ten years. In the course of that time, Aphrodite is wounded on the battlefield. Paris pays with his life for violating the rules of monogamy. The religious and cultural message is that sensuality must be resisted if Zeus's order and peace are to be maintained. The Trojan War is therefore a story at two levels involving both principles as exemplified by gods and practice as lived by mortals. The Olympians battle for patriarchal principle, while the people's struggle demonstrates how that principle can be vindicated by heroic men.

The story of the three goddesses and Paris with his apple sends a clear signal of another kind. According to storytellers, in the ancient tradition, a woman would offer to a man an apple as an invitation for a sexual rendezvous. When the priestess of the Triple Goddess offered the apple, the tryst came with the promise of immortality.[14] The association between the apple and immortality was therefore a profoundly important one in religious terms. The patriarchs played off this story but added a twist. The Trojan War begins when they reverse the roles and have a man offer the three goddesses an apple for which they must compete. The Olympians thus put a man in charge of the sexual offer and additionally break apart the aspects of divinity. Instead of one Triple Goddess with three aspects there are now three goddesses, each with a separate aspect. In the patriarchal story Paris is to decide which of the three is more beautiful, and that turns the goddesses into competitors set against each other. This competition is further evidence of the chaos of the times, as divinity had become the subject of a tug-of-war instead of a unifying principle. There is a parallel reversal of symbols in Genesis. Rather than Eve as a representative of the eternal life force or as extending the apple as an offer of life to her worshipper, she is castigated and made ashamed of her gift.

In yet another Greek version of the apple story, in his Eleventh Labor Heracles steals the golden apples that had been Mother Earth's wedding gift to Hera. The goddess had planted these golden apples in her own divine garden, where they were guarded by a dragon. In the story Heracles kills the serpent/dragon and steals the apples, taking them to the new patriarch in Mycenae. Heracles, a son of Zeus, thereby cut short, or terminated, the gift of golden fruit of immortality, which was the most cherished inheritance from Mother Earth. All of this added significance to the story of Paris and the three goddesses. We may not be familiar with these associations today, but it is quite obvious that listeners of Homer and the bards of the eighth century BCE were familiar with them. It is also quite apparent that the stories were intended to tell them who was who and who would win out in the great political struggles of the times.

On one side in the Trojan War were the tamed goddesses, Hera and Athena, both of whom were by then under the control of Zeus. On the other side was Aphrodite, who more than any other was the symbol of the old promise of immortality achieved in part through sexuality and in part through union with the most ecstatic and holy. Throughout the myths Aphrodite is characteristically very difficult for Zeus or anyone to control. There is still an awe toward her in Homer's language when he describes her being wounded by a mortal on the field of Ilium:

> Through her bright veil the daring weapon
> drove;
> The ambrosial veil, which all the Graces wove;
> Her snowy hand the razing steel profan'd,
> And the transparent skin with crimson stain'd.
> From the clear vein a stream immortal flow'd,
> Such stream as issues from a wounded god;
> Pure emanation! Uncorrupted flood![15]

This is perhaps the first war of civilizations that ever there was. At the end of the contest, marriage wins and love loses. Sexuality loses; Aphrodite's side loses; and interestingly, Achilles, the hero of the Trojan War, also loses, but in an unexpected way. He is killed

in battle by an errant spear that strikes him directly at the weak point in his heel where his mother had held onto him when she dipped him into a potion to make him invulnerable. It is just at that point—the point of the mother's grip—where he was speared. Oh, noble Greeks, beware the grip of the mother! That is the meaning of the Achilles' heel.

Achilles' death is also used by the Olympians to usher in a new understanding of death, one which may have been spreading since the mindless, unearned devastation of the volcanic explosion on Thera. Death is now portrayed as a long, dark existence in Hades, where human shades wander endlessly. It is no longer purposeful as the agent of new life or with the promise of rebirth but rather has become tragedy without meaning. A hero is one who dies too soon. The word *hero* was derived from *Hera*, who was formerly the goddess of revolving seasons, but now *hero* would come to signify the young man who died too early or whose seasons had been cut short.[16] Before, according to the world view of the earth religions and probably of the Minoans, death had been linked with the promise of rebirth. Now, in the new religion, death had become a dark abyss.

In Homer's *Odyssey* the main character, Odysseus, at one point goes down into the underworld and meets the dead Achilles. Odysseus tries to persuade the fallen hero not to be sad. Achilles, he says, you are king of the dead. "Now in this place you have great authority over the dead. Do not grieve, even in death, Achilles." The dead hero answers:

> O shining Odysseus, never try to console me for
> dying.

I would rather follow the plow as thrall to
    another
man, one with no land allotted to him and not
    much to live on,
than be a king over all the perished dead.[17]

By the time of Homer's recounting of the Trojan War, the goddess Hera, who once might have offered a positive view of death, has been substantially robbed of that message. Earlier, she reigned supreme over life and death, surrounded by griffins, lions, trees, and birds. Her worship involved the certainty of the cycles. She was a goddess who aided in the coming and the parting. She offered both loss and gain or, that is, balance. In Homer's hands, however, she becomes the angry, bestial wife, the trickster woman. The goddess who in former times stood at the heart of the mystery of death and was often described in Greek lore as the "tamer" or the one who brings death, is now herself tamed as a wife, and death is made meaningless.[18]

One after another the markers of the old religion are being altered or radically modified. In Minoan religion women are central, glorious, decorated, openly alluring, and the object of devotion. In Homer's work, women are pawns. The first chapter of *The Iliad* begins with Agamemnon—who is married—refusing to give up rights to a captured slave girl. The girl's father has come to his camp to plead for his daughter's return. Agamemnon rejects the old man; he will have his woman. This selfishness reflects badly upon the leader of the armies that have come to defend marriage. The god Apollo therefore enters the scene and speaks for Mount Olympus. He urges Agamemnon to let the girl go back to her

father. Agamemnon agrees, but only if handsome Achilles will give him the slave girl whom *he* has won. Achilles responds more or less, "Are you kidding?" and in a rage announces that he will leave the war. Less than six hundred years after Crete and Akrotiri, women have been changed from central religious figures to chattel, and wars are to turn upon the trading of them.

Some have argued that the Trojan War was not about marriage at all. Troy, they argue, was the strongest fortress in the northern Aegean: it had a dominant position at the intersection of ancient trade routes by land and sea, and it was the master of accumulated treasure. The seizure of Helen was therefore a mere pretext, an excuse, for the sack of one more city in a series of sackings.[19] Other towns, not only Troy, were also attacked at about this time, including towns on the islands of Lemnos, Lesbos, Pedassos, and Lyrnessos, in all of which women and cattle were seized.[20] The hypothesis is that these attacks must have been for loot, because there was loot. But a war fought to secure the patriarchy secures *all* property, generally, rather than just the property that pirates could pick up on a few raids. The import of a battle to secure patriarchy is far, far greater. It is unlikely that Homer would write 450 pages of lyrical, metered poetry about an act of piracy.

To trivialize the Trojan War as merely one among a long history of raids and coastal piracies, one must overcome three arguments. The first is that the combatants themselves said that the conflict was to enforce a marriage. Any argument to the contrary must assert that the participants were engaging in a sort of diplomacy, a façade of lies to cover a greater secret. But pirate raiding is not a greater secret. One might reason that because in the twenty-first century we are accustomed to war for oil, they in those days might have been accustomed to war for gold and women. The weakness in this approach is that it applies modern values to an ancient situation. Because we would not fight a war over marriage, therefore we argue that they did not. They were most likely concerned with the same things we are. This is clearly ridiculous.

The second, and substantial, impediment to the argument that this war was just one in a long series of piracies is that the protagonists did not do what pirates do. They did not move up and down the coast. They did not do what Achilles and Odysseus both did before and after the Trojan War; they did not raid, sack, and move on, sometimes winning, sometimes losing, but always moving on. Agamemnon and his armies stayed on the attack against one city (Troy) for ten whole years. This is a very long raid. If they had only wanted loot, there were far easier places to get it. Piracy works because it is quicker and cheaper than trade. A ten-year war is neither quicker nor cheaper. Even the Persians in their wars against the Greeks in the fifth century did not stay on the march for ten years. No one who wanted to seize a warehouse of grain or a treasure of gold would spend more grain and more gold to get all this than he might gain.

And third, it does not accord with the looting theory that both sides assembled masses of allies, mighty forces of neighbors. The Trojans enlisted on their side the Amazons and Aphrodite. Listen to Homer describing the armies of Agamemnon, on the other side, assembling on the shores of Greece. The language is in the classic lyrical translation of Alexander Pope:

Thus o'er the field the moving host appears,
With nodding plumes and groves of waving
   spears.
The gathering murmur spreads, their trampling
   feet
Beat the loose sands, and thicken to the fleet.
With long-resounding cries they urge the train
To fit the ships, and launch into the main.

This does not sound like a pirates' raid. Next Agamemnon's hordes are urged on by the super-righteous queen of the gods:

Shall Troy, shall Priam, and the adulterous
   spouse
In peace enjoy the fruits of broken vows?
[…]
Shall beauteous Helen still remain unfreed,
Still unrevenged a thousand heroes bleed?
Haste generous Ithacus! Prevent the shame
[…]
Your own resistless eloquence employ
And to th' immortals trust the fall of Troy.[21]

It is hard to imagine a mere pirates' raid thus blessed by the immortal gods or as one in which the gods find justification in enforcing a marriage. Then Homer begins a section of *The Iliad* famously called the catalogue of ships. Some say that it was written separately; some say Homer gave it to us. But no matter who wrote it, the catalogue gives no support to the claim that the Trojan War was a mere coastal pillage.

According to the catalogue, leaders from the plains of Boetia send fifty ships, each with 120 warriors. But these warriors do not come from only

Thebes or from one Boetian town; they are from *all* the various towns of Boetia, as if *all* were involved, as if this were a contest like the First World War of modern times in which men rose up out of the fields and plains of America to do their part. That is what Homer says happened for Agamemnon. The Phocians send forty ships, led by the great warrior Ajax and other stalwarts of the country too numerous to name. Euboea sends forty more ships. Athens sends fifty more. The Argives send eighty ships. Sixty more come from Sparta, ninety from Pylos. On and on the counting goes, until on the other side, across the Aegean in Troy, men look out from their walls and see a mighty hoard assembling. Not to be outdone, the call goes out from Troy to all her foreign allies:

> In just array let every leader call
> The foreign troops: this day demands them
> all."[22]

The roll call of Trojan allies begins with a son of Aphrodite, who takes a leading role. The goddess, his mother, started the war by telling Paris that he could run away with Helen. Now her son leads the lists and then Homer describes the others; the call to warriors, kings, and fighting men goes on for pages.

This was not some coastal raid amid a long century of coastal raids. This was not a piracy to collect a few women. This was not about loot. Homer presents this saga, page after page, as a great turning in the history of the Greeks. Because of that turning, we know that it was also a great turning in the history of the West. This was the war upon which, from their own words, the institution of marriage depended and this, perhaps more than any other, is the foundation myth of Western patriarchal history. It was among the very first to be written down and is among the few with the most lasting effect. It would not be important or disturbing that it was about marriage were it not that at that time, in the eighth century BCE, the institution of marriage was an institution of forced religious conversion and brutal suppression. As we have seen, marriage at its beginnings was an institution for the protection of patriarchal property rights and not for the souls of either men or women. The Trojan War was fought to solidify the former, and Homer's *Iliad* glorified the fact that at last the case was settled.

III

A Warrior Civilization Emerges

Four Hundred Years of Chaos Sets the Stage

In the year 1200 BCE, only a quarter century after the Trojan War, chaos began to descend upon the eastern Aegean world. Great palaces were burned to the ground on the mainland of Greece in Mycenae, Tiryns, and Lerna; on the islands in Samos; and on the coast of Asia Minor in Biblos and Ugarit. Both sides of the Aegean were in flames. It was about the same time that a tide of nomads migrated up from Egypt into the territory of Canaan and the Philistines. They pillaged and burned cities along the way. Down came Jericho and, one after the next, cities such as Ai, Libnah, Lachish, Eglon Hebron, and Debir, a waterfall of names that roll off the pages of history into an ocean of oblivion. From Pylos, on the west coast of the Adriatic, all across the Aegean world to Anatolia, the destruction

came. The destroyers came on horseback and by boat. They came with composite bows and were known by many descriptions. They were led by kings and built temples to thunder gods or nameless gods or gods blended together into combinations. Wherever they went they compared women to horses, to property, and to slaves. In a thousand years there had never been so many cities burned one after the next. The great warriors of Mycenae, who had only just gotten back from the magnificent Trojan War, landed at home, and in a historical minute their empire collapsed around them. Their military might had once stretched from Argos to Thebes to Athens on the mainland of what we now call Greece, across to the island of Crete, and then on across to the coasts of the eastern Mediterranean to Troy, in what is today Turkey, and to Biblos, in what might today be Palestine. Then the whole Mycenaean empire just sank out of sight like a small craft that took on too much water and slowly sank into the waves. Within the same few years another empire, the Hittites, also collapsed and sank under the sands of Anatolia, not to be rediscovered for three thousand years.

There had been wars before. But this was more than war. This was widespread collapse. The end of one time and the beginning of another. A silence settled over the Aegean world.

Some say the coastal destruction had come from Sea Peoples laying waste to all in their path. Some say that in Greece it was the Dorians, invaders from the north, or nomads from Central Asia, or Armenia, or the steppes of Russia. Some say that it was none of these, that it was a drought caused by hot winds and thus a crop failure so bad that people in Greece just picked up and moved out—but only after they had risen up in hordes and burned the palaces of their leaders, stealing all the grain. Still others imagine that the descendants of Agamemnon, Achilles, and Odysseus turned on one another—as indeed the legends say—and laid to waste their own empire.

Whether it was one of these disasters or all of them put together, in about 1200 BCE the eastern Mediterranean plunged into a Dark Age that lasted four hundred years.[1] When it emerged the culture had become more brutal. Now, the stories they told glorified a pantheon of erratic and vengeful gods, and people were led to fear both the divine and death. These grim tales were thereafter told and retold in schools, in theater, in literature, and in politics; were painted on vases; were carved on friezes in limestone and in marble; and were engraved indelibly into the Western mind. Since then, not only in Greece but also in Asia Minor, father gods have held sway over the seas and skies, over the weather and our futures; man has answered the riddle of life with the reply that he is the solution, he himself, and that his cleverness will make him more successful than his honesty and his property, more important than his women.

By 800 BCE women had become the target of widespread vilification. The Greek poet Hesiod wrote at about this time that Pandora, the first woman, was the source of all men's suffering, was "the ruin of mankind." There was little in the evidential world to explain this harshness. Women, objectively speaking, were, and are, subject to most of the same infirmities as men, but not all of them and certainly not more than men. Women are or may be wonderful, brilliant, and beautiful, and they have a miraculous capacity to create life. Women are or may be—and no doubt were at that time—for the most part more tender, and at least as good—if not decidedly better—at human relations than men. Given the evidence of the last ten thousand years, they are less apt to organize armies of destruction and at least as given to healing, dancing, and singing as are men. Why, therefore, would Hesiod, one of the very first poets in our history and in the history of literature, claim with utmost seriousness that women were the ruin of mankind? To say that women are more dangerous than men may be true in some limited respects but certainly not in most respects that would have been important in the agrarian and shipping economy of the eighth century BCE. Women did not go on pirate raids or lead armies trampling through the grain or have the authority to make or break contracts. They did not plunder economies or sink ships. They did not carry off boy babies or leave a legacy of vivid pictures on walls or pottery showing women killing men they did not like. For the most part they spun, worked in the fields, bore children, cooked, and generally led lives synchronized to the months and seasons. Why, then, call them "ruinous"?

At about this same time, another far more famous poet, Homer, began to describe history's earliest women as supernatural figures and gave them names such as Calypso, Circe, and Scylla. Homer said that they were all very dangerous. Calypso lived only for passion, and passion could paralyze a man. Circe was an enchantress who turned men into pigs. Scylla, once a rare beauty, ate men for lunch. After Hesiod and Homer, the stories multiplied. Some said that the descendants of Pandora were Harpies who would steal a man's food, or that they were Furies, whose ecstatic orgies would lead women to run raving through the woods eating raw deer and, if a poor man happened by, they would eat him too. In many ways the stories of women were caricatures of seductive or fatal characteristics of mortal women who seem to manipulate men and thus destroy them.

For at least one thousand years before Homer, the people of the Aegean had been apt to make little figurines that showed women merged into birds, with arms uplifted, as if women could fly. These little figurines were spread all across the eastern Mediterranean throughout the Mycenaean world, buried in graves and on altars. Maybe the figurines were symbolic of priestesses or maybe they were symbolic of all women. Homer addressed these figurines too. Or at least he made a caricature of a beast that looked suspiciously like these figurines. He called them Sirens—half woman, half bird—and he said that they were known for an irresistible seduction. In making a caricature of the bird/woman figurines, he was in all likelihood making a statement about the widespread culture from which those figurines had come. He said that a Siren held out the possibility that, through her embrace, a man could achieve knowledge. Such a delusion, Homer said, would certainly kill a man. When these little figurines were first put on altars or laid in graves, in the millennia before Homer, they had a benign connotation. The discussion of Minoan figurines, earlier, revealed a great many combinations of figurines of this type. Before the Dark Age these figurines are full of hope and joy. After the Dark Age they were transmogrified into Sirens and became sinister in the extreme.

This was a watershed, this four hundred years of the Dark Age after the Trojan War, and what emerged was new in other ways. Now wars, in general, were glorified; immortality, the idea of it, was redefined; prophecy was controlled; and wine was diluted, its ecstasy feared. The consequence of this new mythology was to bring heroes to the front and send decent women to the back rooms of the households, where they were not to be seen and not to have commerce with men who were strangers. The law of Athens allowed that a widow might be transferred to her husband's brother, to a friend, or to allies in war, as if she were property. At this same time women's sexuality was charged with dark foreboding and women were subjected to the twin requirements that they be either virgin or married, the *sine qua non* requirement of any patriarchal order. Now, too, time went linear, and the value of the individual rose above the value of the community.

All this has been bedrock in the West ever

since. From this foundation a civilization emerged in Greece that has rightfully been the wonder of the Western world, producing democracy, science, theater, medicine, and biology and in a hundred ways laying the ground work for modern civilization. In the Middle East a religion arose that honored justice, the weak, and the law and required respect for one God.

But at no time did the new Greek miracle or the new Judaic religion recover the qualities of respect for women and beauty and the cycles of life, which had been the characteristics of the civilizations they replaced. At no time in the last twenty-eight hundred years have women been accorded the dignity and respect that they enjoyed in the island civilizations before 1200 BCE. At no time has the world revisited the culture without war that had been characteristic of the Minoan civilization for the preceding one thousand years. Ever since Homer the world has glorified heroes of battle and mothers who gave up their daughters to the good of the state or even, if need be, sacrificing them, literally, on the altars of power. Ever since Genesis women seeking connection to the divine have been directed to seek salvation through their husbands and male intermediaries. Ever since the Sirens and the apple of Eden, men have been directed to seek knowledge in some way other than through the feminine.

We will return to these stories of Sirens and the apple in more detail, but it is well to note that it was at this point, when chaos set in upon the Western world after 1200 BCE, that the storytellers worked with these symbols. These times saw the destruction of cities on the Greek mainland and the coasts of Asia and the collapse of the Mycenaean and Hittite empires. In this context of general collapse, the symbolism of Sirens

and the apple of Eden likely runs deeper than just a warning about embracing women—that is, is more than a warning against sexuality. The Sirens, after all, had bird bodies, which hold no sexual allure. The warning is rather against the larger concept, the very concept of the feminine, and it was this larger concept that was not to be embraced, upon pain of death.

Out of the chaos of these times therefore would come a conscious and intentional separation from some part of nature, not just a woman's nature, but of nature itself, a part that we today might call the divine feminine or the power of natural regeneration. The rupture of culture from that natural connection would, as it turned out, be more or less permanent. In the early 1800s of the modern era, the German poet Johann Wolfgang Goethe would occupy the whole of his *Faust* with man's search for the equivalent of Helen of Troy. When Dr. Faust sought to claim the goddess-like woman for his own, she exploded in his arms. The goddess was not the answer for Dr. Faust, but someone else was: a simple country girl, Margarete. Dr. Faust had impregnated the young girl, and in due course she died an awful death. But in her simplicity and forgiveness and capacity for love, Goethe revealed the true agency of transformation. Satan instructs Faust, as Western history has done all men, that the doctor must never seek *permanent* connection to the feminine. He must not even utter the words "Stay with me." But in a sort of nineteenth-century rebellion, Goethe, in the last words of the poem, rejects the Faustian bargain and grants to his hero reunion at last with Margarete, whom he now calls the Eternal Feminine.[2] *Das Ewigweibliche Zieht uns hinan*. "The eternal feminine pulls us on."

Three thousand two hundred year after the

general collapse of 1200 BCE, Goethe was still trying to overcome the trivialization of feminine beauty passed on through the figure of Helen. He was trying to recapture the larger concept of the eternal feminine, which seems to have been first discarded in the chaotic ages at the beginnings of the patriarchy. The patriarchs had accomplished this feat through their stories. First they sang these stories and then they wrote them on papyrus and engraved them in stone.

Goddess-like Helen had not originated with Goethe. But after nearly three millennia, the German poet was still trying to understand what these stories were truly meant to convey. He did not live in a time of complete cultural and religious freedom, and therefore he made his attempt indirectly, through a very long poem. Because we are no longer constrained by the same social fetters, we might now attempt an analysis that is more direct.

Values Shaped by Storytellers

A class of storytellers came to prominence during the period after the Trojan War, and these were the people who created the template of values for Western history. Their influence has been enduring. They were the ones who attempted to find meaning in the social chaos of the times and to establish new values that would replace the Minoan values. These storytellers therefore must be attended, described, and given credit or blame for laying the groundwork of patriarchal history. There had never before that time been a Western literature; there had only been records of sales transactions and payments, but in 1200 BCE even such commercial records disappeared. The Dark Age was dark in part because after 1200 BCE no one in Greece could write anymore. In the absence of writing, the storytellers took over.

Again, the time is during those four centuries following the Trojan War. Trade between cities dwindled to a trickle. Few and far between were those travelers who came with news of happenings on the other side of the dark and stormy waters. Sea captains with tales and knowledge of events in Egypt, Crete, or Cyprus would have unloaded their hides, pots, or ivory at the port of Tiryns or Pireaeus or Iolcus and waited for returning vases, pots, or olive oil to accumulate to ferry back, maybe to Troy or to Samos or Ugarit. During these years there were very few of these traders, and we are forced to imagine them because the archaeological evidence of such trade is almost non-existent. The most adventurous of the few, if we imagine further, would have had stories of the Black Sea

and the great wilds beyond, of the steppes of Asia. "There is a golden fleece," some such sea captain might have said, "greater and more golden than any fleece owned by any king in all of Greece. It is owned by the king of Colchis."

A golden fleece was no miracle, in fact, because it was the custom in some parts of the world to filter sediment out of river water by staking a sheep's fleece onto the sandy bottom and allowing it to catch tiny particles. If a person put such a fleece into the right stream, it might even catch up a little gold. When that happened it would be a likely subject for storytelling. "What is more," a wandering sea captain might spin into his tale, "there was a Greek who went all the way to Colchis and brought just such a fleece back to Thessaly."

Now, in those days, when people did not read or write, they would have used graphic symbols to identify certain familiar people or places or even attitudes. Phrases like the "wine-dark sea" and the "rosy-fingered dawn" or objects like the lotus or the lily or the apple would be used as shorthand for people, places, or even weather conditions. The apple was a favorite. It showed up in the stories everywhere, as did the pomegranate. Moderns might think that these fruits appeared in stories as accidents, without intention or connotation. Far more likely is that they all had associations from folktales and traditions. The Bible story of the fig tree, for example, is still understood by millions to connote something about sexuality. Homer says, in the same vein, Watch out for the lotus and the lily, and there is a fig tree beside the sucking monster, Charybdis. The repeated implication is that something sexual is going on when these images are mentioned. The pomegranate, with a hundred luscious seeds, is said to implicate fertility, which must have been very important in cultures dependent upon reproduction. And then there was the spiral, a symbol with such a connotation of eternal existence that today books are written just to document all the cultures that gave the spiral such meaning.[1]

A golden fleece seems to have been associated with kings and probably also with the patriarchal right to be a king. Such symbols therefore had political meanings. Jason's pursuit of the fleece later became a mainstay of Greek mythology. One might imagine a wandering sea captain who began the spread of these stories when he landed at some seaport such as Corinth and reported, "There was a golden fleece that used to belong to Thebes, but it was stolen off to Colchis, and a man named Jason had to slay a dragon to get it back." Which raises the next question: What are dragons? Or, more usefully, What are dragons supposed to mean when the story is clearly political, is clearly about who has the right to rule some certain territory?[2]

Dragons are exaggerated snakes. They evoked a memory of places where snakes were honored or worshipped. Inhabitants of ancient Crete fit that category. Women are represented in Cretan figurines with snakes wrapped around their shoulders and arms. Women were associated with snakes in Colchis too, and in Lydia, Lycia, Phoenicia, and even in Delphi, which was nearby to Thebes, where the story of the golden fleece originated. If snakes were domesticated—and we know from the Egyptians and the

Cretans that snakes were indeed common to many cultures—perhaps they were symbols of a culture that was thought by the storytellers to be altogether dangerous. In that case the most dangerous of all would have been the culture represented by the largest snake of all, the dragon that breathed fire. Some might have said, Oh, no, those people just worship snakes, but the men telling stories for political effect might have been tempted to respond, Well, then, not just snakes but dragons! I am making this up, of course. Except I am not making up the fact that dragons meant *something*. To think that they were just to frighten children or ignorant men does not do the storytellers or the dragons justice.

Dragons' teeth must have conveyed some symbolic meaning too.[3] Sometimes cities controlled by the snake-worshipping women did have armies: Delphi was an example, Thebes was probably another, and perhaps Colchis as well. This would give some substance to the idea that dragons' teeth could be planted and would come up as warriors. There were at least two stories of that happening, once in Thebes and once in Colchis. If the dragons' teeth were the symbols for armies controlled by snake-worshipping women, it might make sense that they were "planted," as the stories said, because planting was the mode by which the women's cultures gained strength. The planting would therefore itself be a symbol pointing to these cultures. When, as the storytellers said, the teeth came up as warriors, these would signify agricultural societies turning militaristic. When, as happened repeatedly in the stories, the warriors who had sprung from the ground were then incited to turn against each other, it may well have signaled civil war. All this would be summarized in a brief sentence from the storytellers:

"And the army which sprang from the dragon's teeth was about to kill Jason but instead the warriors all turned on one another."

While this all may seem surreal to modern audiences, it is highly likely that audiences of the early first millennium BCE knew exactly what the storytellers were talking about. Why else tell the stories? Certainly not to confuse. "A community presents itself … through the myths that it transmits," explains a modern French professor, Luc Brisson. Brisson is explaining why Plato concluded that the ancient myths were intended to convey values and indeed sometimes even to arouse the public and to modify mass behavior.[4] The myths were not, that is, intended to be mysterious at all, but rather, to the contrary, to mold public opinion and certainly to be understood.[5] If Plato was correct, then our job today is to try to understand what all those symbols and images were intended to, and most certainly did, convey. What were the poets trying to tell their listeners, and how did they want them to modify their behavior?

In the Dark Age and before, Athens had made war against Thebes and Thebes had turned on Mycenae and Mycenae had turned back on Thebes and Thebes had turned back on Athens. Once a city raised a great army, the fighting seemed to go round and round in circles. The dragons'-teeth armies may well have symbolized the chaos of war during the four hundred years of the Dark Age. We can conjure up a conversation:

"Up in Colchis, it was a mess," explains an imaginary sea captain.

And so the stories must have grown from simple reports to tales of origin, conquest, and glory, of the way things were before the great destruction of 1200 BCE. Maybe they remembered the glory of Agamemnon and Achilles at Troy, or maybe they even remembered the sweet flowers and gentle women of Crete, before Troy. Some would want to explain the destruction of the glorious, winding labyrinth of Knossos or the bull court at the palace at Mallia, where a man used to be able to sit in a city without walls and gaze out across the dark sea, unafraid. Some, those who had been the farthest east and on their way to Egypt, would have seen the lustral basins at Zakros or the lovely lilies on the walls at Thera, where the women went about with open bodices and dragonfly necklaces and where they danced in the moonlight. Maybe some even told of times before Mycenae when the Cretans traded from Italy to Egypt and women were more open and dangerous in the way they lived.

In the centuries that followed 1200 BCE, the storytelling sea captains gave way to professional bards who roamed the Aegean world. The bards are not imaginary. They most certainly existed.[6] They learned after a time to codify verses and meter them so that they were easier to remember. They developed conventions of verse and speech and were the performers of their time, perhaps even soothsayers, sometimes voices of prophecy, and they were welcomed from village to village. When they spoke of Giants or the shape of these Giants' crescent shields or the lion skin that Heracles wore or the snakes in Medusa's hair, they were speaking in symbols, or codes, probably the same way we today understand the political connotations of "rock-ribbed conservative" or that someone is a "Red." We don't spell it out every time, but we mean much more than rocks and colors. No doubt the ancients spoke in the same way of nectar and dragons and the golden fleece, of Sirens and Cyclopes, Circe and Calypso. Some say that the snake symbolized immortality because it shed its skin and is in a sense constantly reborn. Some say the moon was associated with women and fertility and that therefore wherever we find snakes and women and moons, we are seeing signs of fertility worship. A majority of scholars are apt to say, however, that there are too many meanings to settle on only one. The moon does not mean just one thing, but many things in many different villages or cultures. The unfortunate consequence of this admitted difficulty is to make it easy to discourage finding any meaning at all. For some two thousand years most scholars and historians have therefore looked backwards and doubted that we could know just who the Amazons or the Cyclopes were or if there was a Trojan War at all. And yet we know that the tales are full of signals: uncontrovertibly, a helmet on a goddess always means Athena, and a club and lion skin are symbols for Heracles, et cetera, and that therefore some practical connotation was certain. We must conclude that while all meanings were indeed local, some meanings were more than local and were widely understood.

In the last century Jungian psychologists have admirably excavated important psychological insights from these tales. There can be no doubt that such insight is present in the myths, as it is in all great storytelling. But where one might differ from the Jungians is to doubt that such insight was the primary purpose of such stories. And where I differ, further, from those others who are mystified by mythology in general is that I think the evidence is overwhelming that these tales were told for a definite political and historical purpose. The purpose might vary from tale to tale, from village to village, from century to century,

might be a little different in Thebes than in Argos, a little different in Athens than in Corinth. But more striking than these differences is a continuity that runs through them. The thread that connects them is this: they are all (here I agree with Plato) intended to be educational and for instruction, and secondly, the ultimate purpose of the great majority of the tales was *political or cultural* persuasion. I believe that the psychological insight observed by the Jungians was therefore used for this—to the Greeks'—larger purpose. I come to this conclusion because of the context, the archaeology, and the way that the monuments, artifacts, and stories all weave together to present the increasing importance of sons in the property system.

This chapter is a setup, therefore, to explain why it is so important to examine our ancient myths. When they are put under a microscope, they reveal the origins of patriarchal propaganda. To prove this case we must in turn look at the context, which is good scientific practice. For archaeologists, if a clay figurine is found in a trash pile, it might mean one thing. If it is found in a grave, it might mean another. The same must be applied to myths, and most of the myths we are talking about originated at the dawn of a new pan-Hellenic, or Greek, culture. The men in the tales were uniformly heroes in combat, in conquest, in piracy, or in war. That is, the stories were being circulated after 1200 BCE, at the beginning of a new individualism and a time of political chaos and opposition. Therefore the bards circulated stories that were like newspaper or local history reports and were most certainly not exercises in self-indulgence or misty romance. These reports were likely to have had relevance to this chaotic time and to have been part of the effort to bring an end to instability. They were likely also to have had relevance to the changing economics of imperial trade among those who replaced the Mycenaeans and the Hittites. The tales were probably also topical on religious questions, as much to explain the changing times as to amuse, as much to persuade as to inform. They were to help people get a grip and to decide whose side was winning and whose was losing. In such conditions they would be akin to today's political polemics.

The bards sang at length about death, life, immortality, the content of women's character, the content of civil duty, and the prowess of true manhood. They took sides. Their stories were of opposition: a hero conquering a lesser rival, or Greeks prevailing over foreigners, or marriage prevailing over sexual freedom for women. They praised certain people and disparaged others. They praised Odysseus, the crafty; Achilles, the brave; Theseus, the bold; and Heracles, the all-purpose cleaner of the stables of Greece.

As the centuries unfolded they began to identify and single out the gods. These they pictured often in their own image, sometimes vengeful, sometimes wise, and sometimes erratic, watching over the hunt or the fishery or the river or the olive grove. Athena was the protector of the olive trade and weaving; Poseidon controlled the sea and horses; Artemis ruled the hunt; Zeus held power over the weather, while Demeter controlled the seasons, or sometimes it was Hera and the seasons or maybe it might even have been Persephone. War and piracy were sweeping the land, and there was confusion and overlap, as if to suggest that most of these gods had had incarnations before the wars and some had come from different places, perhaps with similar functions, before they were all brought together in the Greek pantheon. It

is likely that each god or goddess had an origin independent of the other and that when the Greeks consolidated their territorial power, they consolidated the gods in order to consolidate political control. People were not limited to just one god per subject, even for subjects as important as childbirth and death. Hera, in ancient Mycenae, was sometimes associated with death and spring and other times with marriage. Then Artemis came along, and she was sometimes associated with childbirth and other times associated with virginity; it depended upon which village and what time. Hera may have been the dominant divinity in Mycenae before Zeus, who seems to have been imported after the troubles and maybe as a result of the troubles. And so it went. Mostly it seems that all the stories were in some way intended to help people choose sides. Where there had been an Athena on one side, there was often a Poseidon on the other. Where there was Zeus on one side, there were often Titans on the other, or Cronus, or Giants. Or Zeus overpowered someone and banished him (Prometheus, for example); or wedded someone and subordinated her (Hera); or raped someone (Semele) and bred upon her a new god (Dionysus). These were stories of explanation, of rationalization, of the ascendance of some villages and the decline of others. By their nature they seem to be early attempts at persuasion or claims asserted by followers of Zeus or Athena, attempting to establish priority for possession of certain lands. These are the subjects—allegiance, territory, power—of what we today call politics. The myths, that is, were intensely political.

Whenever they could during these early years, any village that was in play for power claimed direct descent from Zeus or Apollo or Poseidon, as if to claim a chain of title as against the dragons, or the dragon women, or the illegitimate children of seductive women. Gradually, the tripartite worship of earth, water, and sky—once dominant on the island of Crete and identified by vivid pictures of the snake, octopus, and bird—was replaced by a cosmology of three angry brothers who raped, oppressed, and incinerated the weak. One of these brothers, Zeus, the all-powerful, could even give birth by himself. This was not so surprising. Over in the Levant they had a new god, Jehovah, who could do that too.

While these stories were being passed about during the Dark Age, a new construction of the world was emerging, perhaps at campfire after campfire, until gradually a new model of reality was shaped. While this new construction certainly borrowed elements of Near Eastern mythology, it was intended to create a new Greek consensus.[7] This consensus praised Athena and Apollo, urged sacrifice to Artemis and Zeus, and gave a place to Ares, the god of war, and to Hephaestos, the smithy who they said had molded the first woman out of clay and tears.

In all these honorings, however, Greek storytellers did not honor the ancient beliefs in civilized, magnificent Crete.[8] This island had long been the glory of the Aegean, and its connections to the Greek mainland were legion. Its religious shrines had been at Delphi; its pots had been bought and sold in Thebes, Pylos, and Athens; and its wall paintings and female votives were copied and buried in graves in Mycenae and Argos. But when the storytellers went about during the Dark Age re-creating the heroic history of their people, they did not favorably describe Knossos, the

palace of flowers and dolphins, or Thera, the island of lilies and swallows, or even the beautiful women who adorned the frescoes in the palaces of Crete. Rather, the opposite was true. When the storytellers came to speak of ancient Crete, they heaped her with scorn and the suggestion of evil.

Greek tales held that Crete had a bad king, Minos, who, among other things, had made war against the Athenians in Syracuse. And Crete was said also to have had a lusty queen, Pasiphaë, who was of such ungodly passion that she made love with a bull and from this bestial union produced the Minotaur. This Minotaur was a brute—half man, half animal— that stalked the labyrinth and ate young men and women and nearly killed Athens's Prince Theseus.[9] For millennia Minos and Pasiphaë have been stand-ins for all that was bad in Crete and all that the Athenians and the Greeks were meant to replace.

But when today's archaeologists look at the on-the-ground reality of Crete, there is no evidence for King Minos's or any king's existence, or for the bestiality, or for the mistreatment of servants, slaves, or women. There is no foundation for the Minos stories other than that the palace at Knossos was elaborate, with winding corridors and dead ends, and was clearly in itself some kind of labyrinth.[10] The palace might have been a place where early Athenians were drawn because of its culture, women, bull games, paintings, or its religion, and it might have been a place from which young people did not return for any of these reasons. The archaeology gives us that much. It does not give us a bull ring with a king in charge or a queen who betrayed him.

An Exaggerated Feminine Is Made Monstrous

Among all the propagandists of the patriarchal order in the early first millennium, there were three who stood out. In order of significance, the first was Homer, whose glorification of war and marriage laid down the basic template. He wrapped it all in elegant storytelling, in some of the most human and winning drama to be found in Western literature, unmatched perhaps until Dante or Shakespeare. His stories were metered and left the reader falling gently forward, slipping into the patriarchal mind as subtly as low clouds drifting in on a warm summer's afternoon. Homer led readers away from lands and times of female enchantment and onto the shores of marriage and mayhem. It is a testament to his artistry that for twenty-eight hundred years the rest of us have taken the transition for granted.

The second great propagandist was the author or redactor of Genesis (whoever that was), who wrapped the sacred fruit in evil and sent the sacred snake into exile and the sacred woman into a subordinate world. She was now beholden not to God, not to the universe, not to nature's rules, but to the rules of her husband. This author so cloaked Eve in guile and independence that female charm and intelligence have been systematically deprecated ever since, her sexuality boxed into rules for this and that, now and then, always at the behest of a man or a male god. He or she or they, whoever wrote Genesis, went on to make it seem acceptable that Lot should try to escape Sodom by offering his daughters to the townsmen for their unbridled pleasure. It is not a promising beginning for early women in the Levant.

The third great publicist for the Western patriarchal paradigm was Hesiod, a shepherd-poet, an everyman who lived near Thebes in eighth-century Greece. He is the one who wrote that the first woman, Pandora, had been "the ruin of mankind." His hometown of Thebes was and still is on the edge of mountains through which winds an ancient trail to legendary Delphi. Thebes lies above a vast, fertile agricultural plain, and during Hesiod's times the city was in more or less constant war with its neighbors across the plains to the north or with Athens to the southeast. For a time the city had been under the control of Mycenae, which is much farther south in the Peloponnesus across the isthmus of Corinth. Thebes therefore had been under the heel of empire, and its people knew chaos. There were also, however, ancient Theban connections to the culture of Crete. Today in the museum in that city, one can still see both those Siren figures that are so common to the Minoan culture and even a seal ring that features bull leaping, a sport in great vogue in earlier times in Crete.[1] Thebes was certainly in contact with Crete during its heyday. By the time of Hesiod, however, it seems to have been consciously severing that connection.

Hesiod is the first writer in the Western tradition to give his countrymen a deep, storied rationale for controlling women. Quite simply, he made them hateful. He took his readers back to the very beginning, as he saw it, of life. At first, he claimed divine inspiration—from the Muses—thereby making his story incontestable:

> We start then, with the Muses, who delight
> With song the mighty mind of father Zeus
> Within Olympus, telling of things that are,
> That will be, and that were, with voices joined
> In harmony.[2]

This is good, richly textured storytelling, both here and in Homer. Eventually we are going to hear a story of Echidna, but first Hesiod sings of the nine muses "whose one thought is singing and whose hearts are free from care." When moderns speak of the earliest storytellers, such as Homer and Hesiod, we are not therefore speaking of clumsy braggarts or superficial ideologues. Hesiod is laying the groundwork here for a persuasion that rings true. Like any modern novelist, he mixes the good with the bad. The Muses touch a man with wisdom, and a wise leader is wise in this:

> When public harm is being done
> To the people, they [the Muses] can set things
>   straight with ease,
> Advising with soft words. And when a lord
> Comes into the assembly, he is wooed
> With honeyed reverence, just like a god,
> And is conspicuous above the crowd,
> Such is the Muses' holy gift to men.[3]

Struck (as he claims) by the wisdom of the Muses, the poet begins his tale with authority. He writes that chaos was first before everything. Then came Mother Earth, who birthed the hills, valleys, sky, ocean, and many lovely goddesses. One of these early goddesses was Rhea. Mother Earth also birthed a son (named Cronos), the Titans, and some Cyclopes. The progeny of Mother Earth were not all good. Among them was Echidna, who was more snake than human. Echidna was definitely female. She did not marry, but she bred repeatedly. This is probably what Greeks thought of Minoan women. Echidna's bestial offspring were the Sphinx, the Nemean Lion, the dragon in Colchis, the Cerebrus, and the Chimera. These creatures variously combined features of the dragon, the lion, the snake, the goat, and the dog; ate raw flesh; and breathed awful fire. Echidna's breeding companion was Typhon, and it was said that he was the wind and horror that comes from volcanoes. It was a potent match. At the beginning the earth was covered with snakes and demons and the sky was filled with howling winds, fire, and chaos.

It is likely that there are political connotations. In Hesiod's imagination there must have been at least a hundred villages that still honored the Minoan practices and resisted the cult of Zeus with its patriarchal norms. Typhon was said to have a hundred dragon hands. This is a likely metaphor for some hundred villages that honored the snake goddess or for women who were not afraid of snakes and who may have resisted Zeus worship. Women as far away as Eve in the Garden of Eden were also handling snakes. The practice was very widespread, indeed. Eve was probably an earth goddess too, before the people of Jehovah got hold of her.

Hesiod's hometown was Thebes. It was a strong political center quite far to the west of the island of Thera, where the volcano had exploded in 1500 BCE. Thebes is not near the coast, so it would not have been hit by any tidal wave caused by that eruption.

After the explosion Greeks more directly in the path were inspired to name the awful gods Zeus the Thunderer and Poseidon the Earthshaker. At the distance of Thebes, however, it is more likely that the name for the horrific event was Typhoon—that is, big wind. The gale quite likely would have carried the dust and ash clouds upland and affected agriculture at Thebes. New scientific evidence about the massive nature of the explosion is only being published in the recent months and years, and it is possible that those who, for all these centuries, overlooked a connection between Hesiod's Typhon and the Theran explosion just didn't know what we know today. Certainly even Hesiod did not know the exact nature of the case, because by his time Thera was seven hundred years under the ash, and there had been no literary writing in the interim. But he might have heard stories of the great disaster. Modern authorities do confirm that Typhon is the source of the word *typhoon* and that Typhon is also associated with volcanoes.[4] This is odd, considering that volcanoes are not common in Greece. If his story was not born from the Theran volcano, what other could it have been? It might have related to Mount Aetna in Italy, but that volcano did not tear apart the center of Minoan culture the way that the explosion on Thera had done. Neither was it so devastating in its effect to wipe out a whole island, as had been the Theran explosion. That horrific event in 1500 BCE is certainly the best candidate, and the psychological effects are likely to have made an indelible impression all over the eastern Mediterranean.

Echidna was a distorted "dragon." Typhon had "dragon" hands. Thebes had been settled for the patriarchs by a man by the name of Cadmus, and the legend was that Cadmus had been forced to slay a "dragon" before he could settle into town and take over. But no one in Hesiod's time ever really *saw* a "dragon," so we have to ask who or what does Cadmus's "dragon" represent? Why is there a "dragon" at the beginning of patriarchal time in Thebes?

From archaeology today we know that Thebans had a strong connection with Crete. In modern Thebes there is a fine little museum that houses, for example, more than forty female figurines with birds' wings and birdlike heads. These came mostly from grave sites, and not one of them is male. These are similar to those in Herakleion's museum in Crete, where there are also a great many such figurines, all of which seem to date from before the decline of Minoan civilization. There are no male figurines with wings in either place. Thebes had traded with Crete and imported seal rings from palaces such as Knossos and pots from Thera—like that beautiful Theran ewer with nipples and bird's beak noted in earlier pages. In the museum in Thebes there are also grave boxes decorated with processions of women dressed like Cretan women, or with bull leapers made famous by Crete, or with horns of consecration, the sacred symbol of Crete. There are ancient pots featuring the double-edged axe and the figure-eight shield, always also at sacred sites in Minoan Crete. There are even spirals on the pots, as in Crete and Thera, and on burial boxes, as on the famous Hagia Triada sarcophagus from Crete. Large stone horns of consecration at Thebes are of a size to complement a palace or shrine, just as they did at Crete. Wall frescoes of bare-breasted women are indistinguishable from those of ancient Crete. Small pottery figurines of women, so common to Mycenae and even more abundant in Crete, are also found here. Painted on a pot are a lion and a sphinx, symbols pointing back at least to ancient Mycenae and Nemea, which overlapped Crete and had strong ties to it. With all these accumulated similarities, it is a fair reckoning that the people who were driven out of Thebes when the first patriarch came had once shared a culture with Minoan Crete. Further, the first wars of Cadmus and his battles against the "dragon" must have been necessary to replace a culture with a great many Minoan features.

This Minoan culture therefore lay in the background of the poet Hesiod when he wrote how the new powers came to control his world. He might have actually used in his daily life vases like these in the Theban museum today, or seen sarcophagi like those with the spirals and the doves, or pots with the axes and symbols from Crete. He would have been in the center of the political and religious turmoil wrought by four centuries of war after the collapse of the Mycenaean empire. Not everyone around him would have been eager to change religions or, that is, to change over to Zeus. So Hesiod waded in and gave his fellow citizens a story that would help to separate the old from the new, the old earth cults from the new Olympians.

According to Hesiod the first dragon lady was Echidna, who was "fierce of heart, nothing like any mortal man, unlike any immortal god, for half of her is a fair-cheeked girl with glancing eyes, but half is a huge and frightening speckled snake; she eats raw flesh in a recess of the holy earth."[5] Typhon, her mate, has a great fight with Zeus, and he is wondrous awful, the largest monster ever made:

> On his shoulders grew
> A hundred snaky heads, strange dragon heads

With black tongues darting out. His eyes flashed fire
> Beneath the brows upon those heads, and fire
> Blazed out from every head when he
> looked round.[6]

From his thighs downward he was nothing but coiled serpents, and his arms—which reached a hundred leagues in either direction when he spread them out—had countless serpents' heads instead of hands. His brutish ass-head touched the stars, his vast wings darkened the sun, fire flashed from his eyes, and flaming rocks hurtled from his mouth.[7]

Hesiod is laying out a world-changing battle in which one of the protagonists has volcanic characteristics. The struggle was literally and figuratively titanic:

> As the lord [Zeus]
> Arose, mighty Olympus shook beneath
> The immortal feet, and Earth [Gaia or Rhea]
> gave out a groan.
> The purple sea was seized by heat from both
> [Zeus and Typhon]
> From thunder and from lightning, and from fire
> The monster bore: the burning hurricane
> And blazing thunderbolt. The whole earth boiled
> And heaven and the sea. The great waves raged
> Along the shore, at the immortal's charge,
> And endless quakes arose. Hades the lord
> Of dead men down below trembled for fear,
> And the Titans, they who live with Kronos, down
> Under Tartarus, shook at the endless din
> And fearful battle.[8]

This is terrific. Hades is trembling, Titans are shaking, and according to some, Zeus was even dismembered by Typhon, and his parts were hidden in a cave.[9] It could have been the end of the Olympian story. "Endless din and fearful battle," warns Hesiod, but finally Zeus threw Typhon to the ground, "lashed him with a whip and mastered him. … [A]nd great Earth groaned."[10] "Great Earth," of course, is Mother Earth, patroness of the old order in which women had been central and the cycles of the seasons paramount. This is how, at last, Mother Earth and her ilk were vanquished. The victor, Hesiod proclaims, is Father Sky. The transition has not been peaceful, consensual, gradual, or even natural. Mother Earth and her progeny have been "mastered" after "endless and fearful battle." Now Hesiod's stories begin to accord with the change in pictures on the pots; here the archaeology and mythology coincide.

At some time after all this, says Hesiod, Cadmus, the human, comes to Thebes. He slays another dragon, probably a descendant of Echidna and Typhon, and—in this version—puts Zeus back together again. Given the abundant evidence that Thebes and Crete had enjoyed plentiful social and artistic connections, it is likely that restoring Zeus meant dismantling the earlier Minoan-influenced culture. This would mean setting aside the pre-Olympian custom of honoring women and the Cretan view of cyclical time and immortality. When Typhon was overcome, therefore, the whole package of the preexisting Minoan culture would have been symbolically rejected. Why else proclaim Cadmus as the first patriarch of Thebes? He was more, that is, than just first father. He was founder of a new Theban order, and as he is said also to have brought the alphabet from Phoenicia, is probably founder of a new Hellenic order. This is the manner in which the early patriarchal stories embellished what they knew of actual history, and these are the encoded roots of Western patriarchal values.

If we need more of a signal that Cadmus brought a war between the old and the new and that the change to patriarchy came through war rather than as a peaceful migration—or as some say, a "natural evolution"—we need only to look at the details of the story. Cadmus was said to have killed the "dragon" that he found in Thebes and crushed its head with a rock, whereupon Athena appeared and told him to sow its teeth in the earth. Cadmus did as bidden and cast the teeth into the ground—that is, into soil that would have been sacred and holy for Minoans or early residents of Thebes. Instead of wheat sprouting, however, armed men sprang up and began to clash their swords and pound their shields. Cadmus was immediately in great danger from an army produced by Mother Earth, formerly queen of divinities. Cadmus heaved a stone into the center of all these earthborn warriors, an act that provoked them to fight among themselves. The symbolism is made clear by the context: in the years preceding this story, Mycenae and Thebes and Athens—all the old communities that had had extensive ties to Crete—had all been fighting among themselves. Cadmus proves that Mother Earth's children will kill each other off by fighting among themselves. Similarly, Athens (also with strong ties to Crete) had been going through a conversion. Athena had ended up in that city as a warrior-goddess, but in earliest times she had actually been a fertility goddess in Arcadia.[11] Similarly, in Mycenae Hera had been goddess of childbirth and seasons. She was subordinated to Zeus, and each of these changes came during the

Dark Age, when there was endless war throughout the Greek mainland. That, then, is the symbolism of the dragon's teeth. In Thebes Mother Earth's warriors had all fought each other until they were exhausted, and the followers of Zeus were the last ones standing. Cadmus the patriarch then took over. He had also brought with him the alphabet, which provided the means to write the story down and seal the victory for all time. Or, at least, seal the victory until the story could be changed, which is the purpose of this book.

It would not take much imagination for the men of Thebes to know that they were not the friends of Hesiod's Echidna or her offspring—the Sphinx, the Hydra, or the Chimera. Such evils that descended from Mother Earth bore female names, many of them had breasts, and they all were rooted in the caves in the once sacred ground. Someone probably knew each village name, now unknown to us, where the changeover to Zeus or his cohorts occurred. Some village or some battle or some change of heart would be signaled by Hesiod's reporting that Hyperion "mastered" the goddess Theia, that the goddess Rhea was "forced" by Cronos, or that the goddess Hera was "married" to Zeus. The verbs that mark the rise of patriarchy are not gentle; the nouns for women are ugly. Hesiod came from the area where Cadmus slew "the dragon," where Oedipus finished off "the Sphinx," just over the hill from where Apollo slew "the Pythia," and just up the road from where the Athenian men annually celebrated the Apaturia, a festival commemorating the brotherhood, the tribe, and marking their places as descendant sons of Zeus.

Zeus had won the war of religious cults in some small part because, in times still very much full of violence and indecision, Hesiod and Homer told the best stories and won the war of words. The battles on the ground had been fought and were over, but the victors needed apologists, someone to explain and give doctrine to the victory, to make it right with the gods and right with universal truth. Then Hesiod, the shepherd, stepped forward and made poetry out of conquest, Homer made heroism out of civil war, and the people of the Western world settled into twenty-eight hundred years of acceptance. In the end it was to be these stories, as much as the swords, that legitimated and insured the continuation of the patriarchy.

Mother Earth Is Overthrown

It was in the years after the Thera explosion that Hera, Athena, Aphrodite, and Artemis were given names. On the seal rings of Crete, there are many images of a prominent woman, perhaps a goddess, lording over deer and lions. Perhaps one of these prominent women may have been an early version of Artemis. There are also the famous snake "goddesses" of Knossos, possible predecessors of Athena, who often shows up years later with a snake wrapped around her waist. Some scholars say Athena had an incarnation as a fertility goddess in Arcadia, which is not distant from Mycenae, before she joined the crowd on Mount Olympus. Maybe Arcadia was a stepping stone from Crete, but by the time we know Athena she had a name, was said to have been born from the head of Zeus, was virgin, and was definitely not in the fertility business. There is also the abundant sexual energy that floods the initiations of young women portrayed in the wall paintings of Thera, or the lilies of Amnisos (on Crete), or the lily room of Thera. All these may be precursors of Aphrodite.

The names first show up on tablets displaying early writing now described as Linear B. These tablets were uncovered at Knossos in the remains that were rebuilt after 1500 BCE, after the Theran explosion. It was almost as if the storytellers first looked around in despair and had a need for some way to address this thing, this demon energy that had overwhelmed them from the sky and the water, that had shaken down untold destruction on the land. How to name this power so great that no human had ever experienced it before? On Crete a wave possibly as high as 325 feet had just hit them from outside, from somewhere incontrovertibly inexplicable and out of the ordinary.

"What was that?" survivors might have asked.

It must have been that in the face of this unknown but undeniable power, some name had to be found. Just as they would eventually describe the force of the unseen hand of passion as the power of the goddess Aphrodite, they would need some name for the unknown force behind the power of lightning and fire, tidal waves and death. It is not hard to imagine that out of the Theran explosion therefore came some explanation: "That was Zeus, Poseidon, and Hades," fixing names to horrors.

So vicious, inexplicable, and unearned had been the explosion that it seemed as though the forces of nature were almost bent on vengeance or an angry whim, acting in a manner similar to those who get angry out of pride, malevolence, or for no reason at all. In fact, unprovoked, the explosion must have seemed purely malevolent. Maybe such malevolence explains why this force at first had to be objectified, and thus, after some centuries every cosmic thing had a name. They called the rosy-fingered dawn Eos and the rising sun Helios and the thunder Zeus. It is a mystery why the god of the sea, Poseidon, was also called the Earthshaker. But maybe again the explanation is that in the beginning of this usage, at the time of the volcanic explosion, they all experienced the earth shake and roar and then the massive wave came right on its heels. It is altogether likely that the horrible shake and the sea were bound together in the popular mind after that first awful eruption of 1500 BCE. Later, over generations, it turned out that the Thunderer kept repeating his threats (thunderstorms), while the Earthshaker (because there were no more great tidal waves) seemed to settle down. When the skies darkened for a midday storm, the people again ask, "What is that?"

"Still Zeus," says the storyteller. "Never far away." Or when wars were won or lost or homes were destroyed by fire, "That's Ares," says the storyteller. Ares was in the crowd with Zeus and was among the most unpopular of all the gods. And so the stories built upon each other.

In Minoan times no separation of the parts is evident, but by 1200 BCE, at the beginning of the Dark Age and thereafter, all the parts have names. Hera has appeared and become dangerous to Heracles; Artemis, the virgin, eventually comes round to challenge Niobe, the fruitful human mother; and when someone says, "I was taken over. I lost myself," the storyteller explains, "It was Aphrodite." Men who feel sexual passion in the morning are simply pursued by Eos. But men possessed or taken over by sexual passion in midday—thrown off their feed—have been nailed by Aphrodite. Jealous women are bad, like Hera, who never adjusted to being subdued by Zeus. Maybe it was because before this, during the Dark Age, she had her own little dominion in Mycenae, and somehow after that got "married." Unions with Zeus never had anything to do with consent. The best women in this new world were strong and virgin, like Athena, herself born from the head of Zeus, forever ready to work for civic good, helpful to heroes in war, and scornful of women who misbehave in ways that

dilute the patriarchal line.

Demeter and Persephone had also become partially Olympianized. Of them all, they seem to have the clearest ties back to Minoan cultural values, but the *Homeric Hymn to Demeter* of the eighth century begins and ends with them both firmly controlled by the will of Zeus. There was no escaping the takeover of all the preexisting deities, and the mother-daughter pair are no exception. All these figures therefore are taking on their essential characteristics in the years before writing was reborn, years in which their only fame came from stories passed from village to village during generations of war and political chaos.

When writing finally reemerged in the eighth century BCE, it was the farmer-poet Hesiod who first put a good face on the new patriarchal lineup. He admitted that civilization in the earliest of times had been golden, wonderful, and luxurious and that death was no more terrible than sleep. People lived with happy hearts, untouched by work or sorrow. There was no fighting. But this was very far back, he said. Hesiod could not know, of course, of the painted walls and elegant pottery of Minoan Crete that were by then at least four hundred years destroyed. Nor could he have known of the lovely women of Thera whose images had lain under one hundred feet of ash for even three hundred years more. Still, there must have been some resonance of these earlier times in legend and story, and Hesiod shared a view with the writers in the biblical tradition who had also described a Garden of Eden. Both Hesiod and the author of Genesis acknowledged that this earlier age contained a place so unlike their own that they described it as paradise. Back before all this fighting, Hesiod said, there was a time when men were happy and at peace, and the earth gave up her fruits unasked. All this ended with the coming of chaos and war and the subsequent obvious need to gain control and reestablish stability. Coincidentally, Zeus's three daughters, according to Hesiod, were Peace, Justice, and Order. Three hundred years later, when commentators in the classical period tried to unravel the meaning of Hesiod's poetry, some of them would argue that names such as Zeus and Hera had been intended as code—some said they were embedded riddles—standing for some larger concept.[1] In light of what is known from archaeology today, it is quite likely that these commentators were right to consider the poems as filled with symbolism. But rather than being code, or riddles, it is more likely that following all those years of unrest and tribulation, Hesiod and his fellow poets desired to put a favorable face on the new order. The stories were probably not so much riddles as they were propaganda.[2]

There is an evident political purpose in Hesiod's story of creation, and it has a decided sexual connotation. Hesiod fantasized that prior to the current gods, people lived in a sort of happy state in which time was not a factor. The landscape was lush and alive. There was plenty of ease for sleeping. The reigning god was Uranus, who seemed uninterested in time, much as the Minoans might have been uninterested in time.[3] Nobody worked very hard. But then Uranus was castrated. The deed was done by young Cronos, his son, with a sharp flint sickle. Thus, the end of that first age came when the father of the gods was rendered impotent, an evident message of both religious and sexual powerlessness. The impotence was imposed upon him by his own son in an age when sons were becoming increasingly important both in the mythology of patriarchy and in the practical business of commerce and war. It cannot therefore be without enormous social and political significance that Cronos, the castrator, vindicates the importance of sons and proves the sexual impotence of his father, who was the reigning god from the previous epoch. As such, Uranus's fortunes had been intimately connected with Rhea, the reigning goddess of the earth. Rhea had been at least as important, if not more so, as Uranus (according to Hesiod and all accounts), though he only played the role of consort and not much more. The event of Uranus's castration therefore signals a change in the nature of both religion and politics and of time and eternity—that is, of man's view of immortality. As a consequence, it also signals the shift in moral authority from women to men.

Cronos carries a name that we have either confused or intentionally associated with linear time. Even the Greeks eventually came to think of Cronos as Father Time, or as Chronos. From that day to this, Father Time still carries his sickle, and every year cartoons reaffirm the image of the old bearded man with sickle in hand. After three thousand years this is still a symbol of what linear times does: it cuts a person down. No one had thought that about circular time.

Hesiod does not say *where* the Golden Age was. He might have been referring to some place like Canaan, which in the mists of history the biblical author described as "a good land, a land of brooks of water, of fountains and depths that spring out of valleys and hills; a land of wheat and barley, and vines and fig trees and pomegranates, a land of oil olive, and honey."[4] The Golden Age could also have been in Crete. In any case the end of that halcyon time was signaled by the fact that Uranus had been castrated. What is plausible from the story, but perhaps impossible to verify, is that linear time itself was the new idea that eroded the old order. In which case there may lie embedded in this oldest of the patriarchal creation myths a validation that earlier civilizations, including Crete, saw time as endless, as a cycle, or as merging present and future. The rational followers of Zeus, Athena, and Apollo began to parse things out and time went linear, and Uranus was done for, done in by Cronos—or maybe Chronos.

Patriarchy was not quickly established, however. Cronos, who rearranged time into a line the way we imagine it today, had also been instructed to be wary of his own sons, one of whom would in turn displace him, even as he had displaced his father. Hesiod is describing the beginning of patriarchy. Gods getting castrated was not a good sign for patriarchs. Sons who might displace their fathers was an unsettling idea too. The age of sons is going to be altogether dangerous. As a result Cronos swallowed his own first two sons as soon as they were born. Cronos's wife, Rhea, was of course immediately angered, and when her third son was born she presented Cronos a stone wrapped in swaddling clothes, which he swallowed. The infant saved by this deception was Zeus, who was taken off to Crete to be raised in secret. Once again there is a connection to Crete, this time apparently to allow later generations to claim that Zeus knew whatever Cretans knew and possessed whatever wisdom Cretans had. When Zeus eventually grew up, he disguised himself and went back to see his father, to whom he administered a powerful emetic. Thus the patriarchy truly gets going when Cronos explodes up from his innards two new male gods, Poseidon and Hades. Their appearance is an uncanny reminder of the great vomiting explosion of Thera.

"Where did Poseidon come from?" someone asks.

"You saw him belching forth from Thera," says the storyteller. "That was the result of the emetic."

"And out came Hades too?"

"Death swept out and took over all of Thera and Crete," says the storyteller, "and that was the end of one time and the beginning of another. That was the end of Cronos's time and the beginning of Zeus's time." I am again, of course, making this up, being a storyteller talking about storytellers. But we actually know more about Crete than the eighth-century storytellers did, so maybe it is reasonable to project where their ideas came from.

It is evident from these stories that at its foundation Western mythology is grappling with two issues: time (or death) and sexuality (the source of life). When Uranus was castrated, ending his ability to carry on the values of the old age, drops of his blood were said to fall to earth and three females sprouted from the blood and soil of the old religion. These were the famous three Furies—vengeful, ferocious, and maneating. Unlike Eve, who passively accepted her relegation to second place in the scheme of things, the Furies of Greece were never passive. A remnant of female power from the previous culture forever hung on in the new age and continued to plague the religionists of Zeus.

As a result the Furies would become symbols in Greek mythology of some danger present from the beginning of their epoch, which they considered to be the beginning of time. The Furies were known as a danger that comes in threes, and if the Triple Goddess was known in her three personas as maid, mother, and crone, all three were offended. Thus, at the

beginning we are given a civil war: on one side are those whom Hesiod considers the new realists and those who understood the awful power of Zeus, Poseidon, and Hades; on the other side are those whom he considers to be bitter losers, the followers of the earth goddess Rhea, whom he calls the Furies.

The gradual takeover of the patriarchy is therefore presented in stages: Cronos takes over from Uranus, time goes linear and produces thunder and lightning (Zeus), the angry sea (Poseidon), and death (Hades), and these three become the great, incontrovertible powers. Three women (the Furies, or the Triple Goddess, or the three aspects of Woman, Lion, and Snake in the Sphinx—there are many threes in the early female images) are replaced by three men.

The women are left furious but powerless. Their value is in the cycles of life, but reality has produced destruction borne in the sky, carried on the sea, and followed by undeniable death.

Since life is no longer circular, war, too, now becomes practical. As the storytellers explain, war can actually cut off a family, end a village permanently, and cause a final end not possible when death was thought to be only a productive stage in a continually repeating cycle. Women may be furious at this change, but they are impotent to resist it. After all, Thera exploded on their watch. Thera birthed the Thunderer, the Earthshaker, and Death. Thera was their home, and she did them in.

In Search of the
LOST FEMININE

112

Jason Resists the Many Shapes of Seductive Women

There is more difference between the values represented on pots in Crete and those in the eighth century BCE than there is difference between those of the eighth century and those of today. We share more values of Hesiod's time than Hesiod shared with the Minoans. The ancient stories therefore represent the very minute detail of a historic and dramatic departure, a turning, and concealed within them is information that shows just how much the tellers knew exactly what they were doing. Take, for example, the famous story of Jason and the Argonauts.

Jason was a man who wore no shoe on his left foot. In the eighth century this was a certain clue that Jason was a fighter. He could get the best traction when he held his shield in his left hand and thrust it forward over his left leg, his shoeless toes gripping the soil. His is one of the foundation stories. He was young, broad-shouldered, and had a look of supreme confidence. He was unmarried, though not because of his uncouth left foot so much as that no queen thereabout northern Greece was looking for a king. In those days (maybe 1400 BCE) some became kings by being sons of kings, but others traced their royal line through their queens, so even more young men became kings by marrying well. Warlords roamed the wilds of Greece hawking a new religion that recognized the brutalities of Zeus, Poseidon, and Hades and diminished the blessings of Mother Earth. Warlords, by definition, needed sons who could also become warlords. Sons were useful to fight and die and gain kingdoms that would be more secure than those that depended upon women.

In the manner of the times, Jason was in need of a queen, a title, a country, and heirs. That much is easy. From there the story presents one of the great mysteries of ancient mythology. What is it about, truly?

As soon as he was born, Jason was cast out into the wilderness. His father was a king who could not protect the boy or raise him as a young prince because he would be killed by his Uncle Pelias, an evil usurper who had seized the throne. It was dangerous in these times to be the son of a king. It was perhaps dangerous to be a son in general. In more recent times there have been cultures that left infant females out in the hills to die. In those times, during the transition away from the dominion of the goddess Rhea and before the warlords of Zeus, it apparently was the custom that sons rather than daughters might be left in the hills. Daughters may still have been more highly valued. Jason was therefore set out on a hill and then saved by shepherds, as was the custom in these early stories of patriarchal ascendance. People who travel and herd sheep are distinguished from farmers in these and in many biblical stories, and there is often a preference for the pastoral heroes. Some say that that is because the biblical ancestors and those who first migrated into Greece were nomads. They were herdsmen who came and unseated the settled farmers and brought with them stories that honored shepherds more than farmers. That might be the meaning of the fight between Cain and Abel. One was a farmer, the other a shepherd, and the shepherd gets the better reputation. If there is a parallel in the Greek stories, it is that Jason (perhaps) and Oedipus (certainly) were saved by shepherds, which tells us immediately that they were protected by that culture that drew its line from nomads, from shepherds and goatherds who did not live at one place on the land. No wonder the Jason story, one of the foundation stories of Greek myth, has to do with a man trying to find a place to settle and establish his claim and that it begins with him abandoned out in the hills.

While still a young man, Jason was educated by a Centaur by the name of Cheiron. Cheiron also taught Asclepius, Achilles, and other famous heroes. Jason's training therefore was at the hands of a beast who was extremely learned and cultured, which is itself a contradiction. Horses are sometimes wise in their way and men in theirs, but seldom do we get the image of a wise horse-man combination. Unless we assume that the listeners to the tales of the eighth century were utterly stupid and gullible, we must assume that they did not expect to send their children to learn from wise men who had the bodies of horses. Anyone who actually raised horses or lived among them would know that no such thing ever actually existed.

Which is of course contrary to the opinions of most interpreters of mythology for most of our history. Most tend to think, as if modern men were smarter than ancient men, that the listeners to these tales were gullible and primitive. But these people could navigate the wide Mediterranean by the stars and make copper into bronze and spin fine pots; they could engineer twelve-foot-thick cyclopean walls by lifting single stones weighing many, many tons to levels of thirty, forty, and even fifty feet; they could calculate the exact day to expect the solstice and the exact midpoint between solstices; they had mastered the alphabet and elaborate writing; and they could write great poems and twenty-five-volume histories. Nevertheless, the usual modern interpretation is that they were superstitious enough to think that a horse-man combination was real.

That is possible, but it is unlikely. Before the alphabet and therefore before these written myths, there was obviously a middle ground of coded phrases or symbols and ideas that could be represented not by letters but by figures of speech or location names or even fruits or animals. Whole thoughts could be expressed in code. A woman with a helmet was a common code for Athena. A man with a trident was code for Poseidon. An apple, with or without Aphrodite present, would be code for sex. A pomegranate would probably symbolize fertility and sometimes death, as if bound together in some earlier understanding. A snake would be code for a primitive people who came before the Greeks, who lived closer to the ground, or for an evil that was sometimes tamed, sometimes not.

In this common use of symbols to stand for concepts or as shorthand for tribes or gods, we have to assume that *Centaur* was the name given to symbolize something, someone, or some time when men and horses were combined in some way. Maybe they were riders or warriors of skill so great that they had earned a reputation for never separating from their horses, even in times of great danger and action.[1] Or one might assume that they were men from the steppes of Central Asia, where they lived with their horses so closely that they seemed like brothers, or that they never camped or slept without their horses by their sides and were known as inseparable.[2] Or, to the people of the eighth century, when a storyteller said, "Centaur," the listeners all might know that he was talking about a small band of, say, one hundred Asians or nomads or invaders or "some horseman not from around here." Or maybe they were herders, outriders who, like American cowboys, never married and always rode, but when they came to town they came with voracious sexual appetites. Such a range of possibilities is at least as rational as the hypothesis that all the villagers (who saw horses every day) sat around the fire and trembled that they might be assaulted or raped or even taught by some horse-man. And such an imagined symbolism gives a good deal more credit to the intelligence of the people of that time than to think that they were all gullible primitives. If the people of the eighth century, that is, were intelligent enough to produce a poet of the power and imagination of Homer, it is highly likely that they were also intelligent enough to understand symbols. Today moderns call certain sports teams of fifty or one hundred warriorlike men "Broncos" or "Mustangs" or "Terrapins," and no one doubts that these are symbols. The Centaurs might have been the first of these wild bands.

Later on in Greek mythology, Centaurs play a huge role and show up on famous carvings on the Parthenon, on the temple of Hephaestos, at Olympia, and on all manner of pots. But as important as Centaurs obviously were, today no one knows either who they were or why it makes sense for one of them to teach the young man with no shoe on his left foot, the boy by the name of Jason. The storytellers had in mind someone or something, but we just don't live close enough to the time to know for certain who or what.

We are told that Jason's Uncle Pelias had stolen Jason's father's kingdom. Pelias of course did not want to give the kingdom back. Finally, after some extensive persuasion, Pelias agrees to return the kingdom to Jason, but only if Jason will first sail off to the farthest reaches of the Black Sea, to Colchis (which is today called Georgia), to fetch home a certain very wonderful golden fleece. This is the foundation of the story that follows. The hero must make a long journey, seize a golden fleece from a dragon or whatever other dangers are there, and bring it back to Thessaly.

Colchis, where the fleece hangs from a tree, is dense with trees and bountiful in summer, a land of fruits and vineyards and broad rivers. Traders in ancient times who wanted to reach the Caspian Sea and the inlands of what is today Central Asia or even China would likely have sailed the Black Sea to Colchis, which affords the best crossover point. From there they would have traveled inland, working their way along the Caucuses above what is today Armenia and Azerbaijan, sailed again across the Caspian, at which point they entered into the real wilderness. So Colchis was a sort of jumping-off point to the wilderness of the north and east (a trading route later followed by Marco Polo), much as in the nineteenth century of our era St. Louis was the jumping-off point for the great plains of America. This is where Jason was sent to find and capture the golden fleece.

It may seem self evident that any adventurer of those days would have wanted to find a ram with a golden fleece and would have traveled half the world to get it. Its value is supposedly clear to any schoolchild, and three millennia of rural children who may also have raised sheep might have been expected to say, Well, yes, a golden fleece would be very wonderful. But most especially rural children and their parents would also know that never in all their lives had

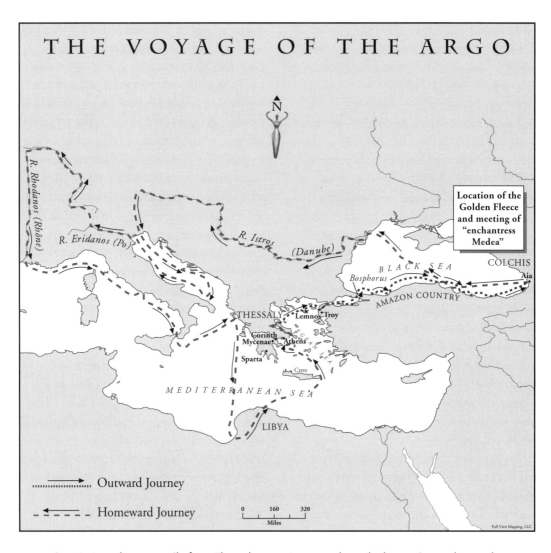

Fig. 43. Jason's route sails from Thessaly, past Lemnos, through the straits, and past the Amazons to Colchis, where he is to claim the golden fleece.

they ever seen any such thing growing on a sheep and that a golden fleece on a live sheep would not only have been special, it would have been fantastic. It would have been out of this world. It would have been magic. But magic symbolizing what, then?

This fleece had been on the back of a fine ram that had thoughtfully flown a previous young hero who was escaping from Thessaly to Colchis. That's what the storytellers said. That had all happened before Jason. So the ram was not only golden but it could fly and it had carried an earlier hero on its back. Then, when it landed in Colchis and delivered that first young man (not Jason) safely to that city, the ram volunteered itself to be sacrificed to Zeus. It gave up its life so that its wonderful fleece could hang from a tree at a shrine to the father god. The story thus gives us a golden fleece on a flying ram with enough religious consciousness to engage in self-sacrifice. This is a very special ram indeed. Jason was supposed to go to Colchis and bring this fleece back to Greece or, that is, back from the edge of civilization to the heart of civilization.

Today we do not know why the golden fleece would be the key to Jason getting his kingdom. We do not know whether it was important because it was from the back of a life-giving ram or conversely because it was life-giving it was—for that reason— golden. Or perhaps it was special because it had been offered in worship of Zeus rather than some other god or goddess. It seems almost disrespectful to argue that a flying, spiritually conscious golden ram had no greater meaning than to entrance schoolchildren and village primitives down to modern times. Thus the very rationale of this famous trip is a mystery, at least on the surface. Except we must continue to remember

that it was somehow the key to Jason becoming king, the key to his patrimony, and, in the event, the foundation of Greek patriarchy.

At the beginning Jason travels on his famous boat, the *Argo*, up through the islands of the Aegean. He takes with him fifty notables from all over Greece. Here there is clear symbolic meaning. All of Greece is represented on the *Argo*. Heracles is there. The two famous brothers from Sparta, the Dioscuri,[3] are there. There is a bee master from Athens, and Atalanta, "the virgin huntress." There is a son of Ares, the god of war; a son of Hermes, the messenger god; and another of Apollo, the god of reason. The boat is full of famous names of ancient Greece, and therefore the voyage of Jason must have some significance for the emerging Greek culture as a whole. This is a foundation story: How did we, the Greeks, get the golden fleece? This is how. What does it mean that we got it? No one ever says. Probably it is assumed in the eighth century that everyone knows. The problem is that twenty-eight hundred years later we don't any longer know.

At their first stop, on the island of Lemnos, the travelers find a colony of women who have either expelled or murdered their husbands (the legends are mixed). These women are living alone in search of some new males to make them pregnant so that there can be a future generation of Lemnians. The Lemnians are like Amazons and need men for only one small purpose. The sailors of the *Argo* oblige and sail on.

It seems demeaning to put a story of sailors and sex at the beginning of a heroic journey that the Greeks will tell of again and again and again for generations. The incident raises questions: What was the significance to their listeners of these sexual exploits, and what was the meaning of women who controlled their own island, their own futures, and who did not need men as husbands? Why, even more mysterious, does Jason oblige these women who do not believe in the patrilineal line? He is on a trip the very purpose of which is to regain his patrimony, his rightly deserved kingdom inherited through his father. But by definition the women of Lemnos could not have believed in patrilineal descent because they probably did not know the names of and certainly had no long-term connection with the overnight visitors who fathered their children. Patriliny in this circumstance was impossible. This had to be a matrilineal island. The time, according to the storytellers, is at the beginning of or even before the Dark Age, perhaps before the Trojan War. It is very far back indeed, they say, and at the beginning of the Greeks as a people, when men flew on the backs of rams and women slept with whomever they pleased.

The city in which the Lemnian women lived was called Myrine, after a goddess of that same name whose counterpart in Asia Minor was the Moon-goddess Marian (or Mariamne or Marienna) and whom Homer will later say even the Trojans worshipped as "Leaping Myrine."[4] So the women of Lemnos are not only not patriarchal, but they also live in a city that bears the name of no Olympian goddess at all but rather a goddess of far different associations. Some say that the word *marriage* comes from the practice of joining with Marian—that is, sleeping with the moon goddess or her priestess. The idea is that *marriage* is the act of love with Marian, in a temple, experiencing ecstasy as the divine gift. So the men of the *Argo* "marry" the women of Lemnos in the way of the old religion. They sleep with them. There is some serious distraction

here. Jason and his men are tempted to dawdle and be diverted from their patriarchal mission; loose women are appealing. The Argonauts might have stayed longer had not the primary enforcer of the patriarchy, Heracles, intervened. The old hero forced them to pack up and get back on the ship.

An incident near the beginning of Homer's *Odyssey* presents a problem that resonates with this visit to Lemnos. Odysseus's ship stops over for a visit to the "lotus eaters." It was said that lotus eaters enchanted a sailor, made him lazy and unwilling to go back to work. The lotus is another name for lily, and therefore a suggestion again of sexuality. It could have been places like these or like Lemnos or like the palace at Zakros, which we have described in an earlier chapter, where sailors stopped off and from which they were reluctant to leave. It would be extravagant to assert without question that lotus means lily means sexuality, or that Lemnos was like Zakros, or that Zakros was unquestionably a place of ritual sexuality. But, again, it would be overly cautious to conclude out of hand that what is not certain is not even possible, or in this case even plausible.

In modern times the issue of who can marry whom is something of a hot political issue. An American president has even proposed a constitutional amendment to determine what is a "marriage" and what is not. The question has very old roots. The debate seems to have been raging in the time of Jason. At that time the campaign was waged not by constitutional lawyers but by storytellers. So the next thing we know, the Argonauts are leaving the island of promiscuous women, a matrilineal island, and are on their way to visit a friendly king who was having a marriage feast.

This was a wedding that patriarchs would understand, where the maid is taken by the king—not like Lemnos, where the women take the men. The king in this case, Cyzicus, is a friend to the Argonauts and welcomes them to join his celebration. A real wedding—as opposed to linking up with some moon goddess–worshiping, husband-murdering women—is cause for a grand party. While the banquet is in process, however, they are all attacked by monsters that are described as "sons of Mother Earth." They are brothers to Rhea, clearly a symbolic holdover from a previous religion of the times before Zeus and Cronos. Rhea's monsters are six-handed "Earth-born giants" from the interior of the land, a clue that those hanging on to the old ways did not live on the coasts so much as inland, which is in turn a clue that the raiders who brought the new religion came in part by sea. Rhea's people are not from around the land of Cyzicus, in any case, and they do not honor patriarchal marriage feasts. Jason and his friends overcome these monsters, but all does not end well. Through a tragic misunderstanding the Argonauts also end up killing their host, Cyzicus. The intended wedding is a disaster. At the beginning of Greek patriarchy (probably about 1400 BCE), the very idea of a wedding is repugnant to the Earth Goddess, and not all planned weddings succeed. Perhaps the very survival of the institution is in doubt. That this is a time of transition and uncertainty is then clearly signaled by the fact that the Argonauts nevertheless decide to make penance by sacrificing to Rhea, the very goddess who sent the monsters.

The story presents a vivid picture of religious and political turmoil. Jason's voyage is supposed to be set in approximately the thirteenth century BCE.

It is probably shortly before Mycenae collapsed and residual vestiges of earth worship continued. Rhea, the daughter of Mother Earth, is represented as being on the wrong side of the marriage question. It is her brothers who break up the wedding banquet. The authority of Zeus and Hades, who are more apt to support marriage, is not yet dominant. Jason and his party, who have already slept with the loose women of Lemnos, now sacrifice to Rhea, an earth goddess. They are on a journey to establish patrimony, but at this point they play both sides of the fence.

They next visit a court where Harpies—half-bird, half-human females—are stealing the food of old King Phineus. The poor man is blind and cannot defend himself, and night after night these loathsome bird-women sneak in and steal the his food. Some say it is his wife who is stealing—because wives are not trustworthy either—and blaming it on the Harpies. One way or another women will steal an old king blind, literally. Women who are not married or who are old eat too much while giving nothing in return. Some say that Harpies have hags' faces, clawed talons, hanging breasts, and bears' ears. Some say Poseidon is their lover. He is a god with suspicious old-religion connections. But Jason has supernatural companions of his own, and together they drive the Harpies off. Increasingly, the journey of the Argonauts is beginning to look like a lecture about women.

King Phineus is very grateful for the help against the Harpies and tells the Argonauts how to get through their next adventure, where their ship will be threatened by crashing rocks that hurl together just when anyone tries to pass through. "Trust in Aphrodite," Phineus says. So the man who is being eaten out of house and home by Harpies gives seemingly incredible advice to Jason to trust in another woman, the love goddess, Aphrodite. The simple villagers who were listening to these bards in the eighth century may have been primitive, but now it appears that they were required to hold in their minds at once two equal and opposite concepts of women.

The only way to pass the clashing rocks, explains Phineus, is to send a dove flying through first and then follow the bird, "trusting in Aphrodite." If the dove makes it, the Argonauts can try. So they do as he says. They release a dove that flies bravely through, but these rocks crash together and sheer off its tail. Forewarned, the Argonauts now row their oars desperately and also just make it through, losing the tail of their ship. The dove that preceded them is a regular symbol on Cycladic pottery and is often a symbol of love (fig. 16). The root of its name may in fact mean "love" or "the goddess of love" in pre-Olympian cultures.[5] The Argonauts, the first heroes of Greece, therefore pass through some monstrous, clashing rocks on the way to a jumping-off point for the wilderness (Colchis) by following the symbol of Aphrodite. They lose their tail feathers, just like the dove. But they are not killed. Aphrodite, it seems, will take a man east to the edge of civilization and even back through the lands where women rule by love; it will cost him something, but it will not kill him. The man of course is in search of his patrimony, his claim to his throne, his title, by way of the golden fleece. Aphrodite will show him the way and it will cost him something, but not too much, so long as he keeps moving.

By manning the *Argo* with important names, even sons of gods, the storytellers seem to be referring back to the beginning of Greek culture, to the original heroes. Archaeologists can now date the Trojan War to about 1220 BCE, and because these events involving Jason and Heracles precede that war (but not by much), we can estimate that these events take place sometime in the thirteenth century BCE. Further, by manning the *Argo* with people from Athens and Sparta, a prince from Pherae, a Phocian prince, someone from Samos, someone from Arcadia, someone from Thessaly, someone from Argos, and an Aetolian, plus forty more, they have effectively covered all the land of the Greeks. This was intended to signify that everyone who was anyone was there at the beginning and that this was the beginning of greater Greece. So Jason and all good Greeks are instructed by these bards, these storytellers of the Dark Age, to enjoy but ultimately pass by the free-love Lemnians and to overcome the marriage discouragements of Rhea, and, if they did these things, they would be led through the clashing rocks of misfortune by true love, which would lead a man on to his destiny. There is, after all, a rationale here.

The Argonauts next went to visit another town with yet another name of a moon goddess, Mariandyne, and then on eastward to a town where a woman is said to have resisted rape by Zeus by saying, Well, all right, you can have me, but first grant me one wish. The woman, Sinope, then craftily chose eternal virginity as her gift, a wish that Zeus was bound to honor because premarital virginity in mortal women is close to sacred to patriarchs. The Argonauts seem to have approved of Sinope and then sailed onward past yet another group of women, the Amazons—another race that did not believe in marriage. Flip flop. Flip flop. One after the next, at the dawn of Greek consciousness, the Argonauts are encountering and then passing by women who either embody the patriarchal values of virginity and marriage or are caricatures of the old values of sexuality and license.

There could be a strictly patriarchal rationale for why Jason had to go to the edge of civilization, past all these odd female settlements. Patrimony, or the property system that we call patrilineal, meaning inheritance through a father, could not be achieved with the Lemnians or with the Amazons or with any woman who did not believe in monogamous marriage. Monogamous marriage, on the other hand, was a kind of prison for ancient women. The very institution was disapproved by some of those whom Jason passes and also by the old goddess Rhea. It was probably also disapproved by those religions that engaged in temple sexuality or simply believed that sex was good and that sex led to children and that children were the key to immortality. Rhea sent her monsters to disrupt a patriarchal marriage that was not simply the blissful union of a man and a woman (her kind of marriage), but rather the yoking of a woman (the Olympian kind). She apparently did not care about legitimacy of children and neither did the world she represented. Jason therefore might have had to pass all these temptations just to get back to his patrimonial roots in Colchis, both literally and figuratively.

For many years in the mid–twentieth century CE, there was a theory that the invaders of the second millennium BCE who were Indo-Europeans (some said "Kurgans") had been from Central Asia or from the Caucasus Mountains region. A large number of scholars indulged this theory. Robert Graves, Joseph Campbell, Marija Gimbutas, Riane Eisler, and even the war historian John Keegan all operate on the supposition that the changes that came about in this dramatic transition period were wrought by "invaders" who were originally most probably nomads. Keegan explains how nomads could fight differently from farmers and how they brought the horse as the new technology of war and the composite bow and the chariot, all of which explains their success in sweeping through the Middle East and Greece between 1800 BCE and 1650 BCE.[6] Linguists now say that Indo-European language can be traced back to an area below the Caucasus Mountains, to the east of the Black Sea, and they confirm the timing that the invasions might have come from this region during this period and arrived in Greece about 1600 BCE.[7]

Applied to the issue of patriarchy and the golden fleece, the pieces of the story then fit together in this way: Jason went to Colchis to retrieve the proof of his patrimony. He was told to go back to the area just east of the Black Sea. Scholarship has now pointed toward Armenia—which is just east of the Black Sea—as that land where horses were abundantly raised in the early part of the second millennium and which had the necessary trees from which to construct chariots.[8] It is from this area, therefore, that many scholars think the new kind of warfare originated, and this was the warfare that eventually swept through Asia and Greece in the revolution that Keegan has described. In addition there are linguistic connections between this area below the Caucasus Mountains and the Greeks. Thus there are language and warfare studies to support a conclusion that Jason's ancestors may have come from Colchis. The research now puts the invasion of Greece at about 1600 BCE—that is, approximately two hundred to three hundred years before Jason was sent back to that place to get his bona fides. It makes sense. Colchis is the westernmost port from which these invasions of 1600 BCE would have come if they had come by sea,[9] and Thessaly, from which Jason comes, was a likely first target for these invasions, according to Robert Drews of Princeton University.[10] All of which is to say that there is a plausible reason to explain why Jason, who came from Thessaly, was returning to Colchis to revive his claim to his throne. His forefathers are likely to have come from there in the first place.

Could Jason's training at the hands of a horseman, the Centaur—perhaps the symbol for those nomadic invaders—be tied to the same rationale? The argument fits together: The Centaurs were the last remnants of the old nomadic culture. Jason's patriarchal charter was to be found in the Caucasus region, where many scholars think the Indo-Europeans/nomads, and thus perhaps the Centaurs, originated. This would therefore be where Jason's ancestors came from. The charter of kingly descent, or the fleece, would of course be worth its weight in gold. These are the curious, coded messages in the Jason story. If this was indeed the code, then here is text that supports Graves and Campbell and Eisler and the other scholars who for years have held that the people who came into the country were believers in patriarchy and came from a long way away.

How do we know that the package of beliefs that we today call patriarchal was not extant in Greece all along? It is one thing to say that Jason had to sail past dangerous women who did not believe in marriage; it is another to say that the Argonauts stood, in history, for the clans that brought a whole new way of thinking to the West. It is abundantly clear that the Jason storytellers worried about dangerous women and that such women were scattered from Lemnos to the home of the Amazons along the Black Sea, neither of which was patriarchal. Does that mean that the Argonauts also rejected the deeper meaning of the earth religions, the sense of time as cyclical and humans as immortal? To pursue that question one must go deeper into the stories that were told about the transition by those involved in that transition or those for whom it was still going on. We shall therefore, just below, turn to Homer.

But first, before Homer, and to conclude the story of Jason, a Dublin professor has suggested a direct connection between the Thera cataclysm and the Argonauts. The story suggests a link, that is, between the Argonauts and the Minoans. J. V. Luce puts the Argonauts all the way back as far as 1470 BCE, and although I have posited them somewhat later, the anti-Minoan meaning of the stories is even more likely if Luce's supposition is accurate. Luce makes this earlier connection based upon the myth of a giant named Talos who defended the island of Crete when Jason and his men were sailing past, near the end of their journey. Talos was, according to one source, fashioned by Hephaestos, the god of the fire and forge, and was made entirely of invincible bronze except for a vein near his ankle covered by a thin membrane. Talos threw giant stones at the Argonauts, endangering their ships much as the volcano at Thera might have done. Luce thinks the story may be a residual memory of sailors who were passing by Thera when it exploded.[11] Medea, who was by then married to Jason in the new sense, in the patriarchal way, still, however, possessed the charms or enchantments that the Greeks feared in the old religions. As the now-tamed wife of a Greek, she cast a spell on Talos, dimming his vision so that he accidentally cut himself on his vulnerable ankle and then, the story goes, "the ichor flowed out like molten lead," whereupon the great bronze giant fell over dead with a crash.

Huge rocks flying through the air that endangered passing shipping, the giant's blood flowing "like molten lead," the fact that Hephaestos forged Talos—that is, that he was forged in the hot bowels of the earth—all suggest to Luce some symbolic connection to a volcanic eruption. Further, the Argonauts were near the end of their journey, and the fact that its conclusion was marked by the crash and fall of a great bronze man certainly suggests the end of the Bronze Age and that the storytellers—later writing in the Iron Age—knew very well whereof they spoke. That they chose to place the last bronze giant on Crete and there let him die has undeniable symbolic meaning for later Greek listeners. It is entirely consistent with the sense we have from other myths that these early storytellers were explaining the end of one age and the beginning of another and that the Argonauts also were meant to signify the decline of Minoan culture at a time near the great explosion on Thera.

Odysseus Rejects Calypso

The Greeks built great temples, but they did not endow these temples with priests or any equivalent of mullahs or rabbis who might deliver sermons or discourse on morality. Oracles at Delphi and other places less famous offered to the Greeks specific instruction in response to specific questions, and among the honored were diviners and prophets who foresaw the fates. But it was the poets, or storytellers—sometimes they were called "singers"—who laid down the fundamentals of Greek history and in the eighth century BCE gave to Greeks both their identity and their mission as a people. Within these stories, therefore, could be found roots and justifications for almost all Greek moral values, standards, and disciplines. The singers passed along rules of hospitality, sacrifice, and sexuality.[1] Among them Homer was preeminent. His was the first name to be associated with the stories that had been passed from bard to bard during the preceding four hundred years, and he, or someone on his behalf, wrote them down with breathtaking grace and skill.

Almost certainly Homer did not intend this as literature. Before him there was no such thing as a book. There was therefore also no such thing as a reading public. In all his great work he only refers to a written message once. He himself may have been only a singer and may not have known, personally, anything of writing. There was therefore no such thing as a community of writers and readers or a writing culture.[2] These early poems therefore were more likely political instruction wrapped in colorful and memorable images. The grotesque figures, for example, of Sirens or Scylla or Medusa or Medea were certainly not haphazard or pure fantasy so much as symbols that most listeners were intended to understand and that would certainly be more easily remembered than abstract lectures about hospitality or marriage. The times were tumultuous. Territories were in flux. Religions were in collision; even the gods were at war. Writing in its beginnings was a precious, time-consuming, and labor-intensive art. Both *The Iliad* and *The Odyssey* were originally comprised of twenty-four books apiece, written on rolled papyrus. We don't know if Homer was the poet or the scribe for someone else who was the poet, but in either case it is most likely that the enormous effort was intended not for enjoyment of the idle rich so much as for instruction of those falling under the influence of the spreading Hellenic culture. In this sense these were stories to persuade the undecided. It is more likely, that is, that Homer was weighing in politically than that he wrote or sang to provide a luxury to the elite or as entertainment on a soft summer's evening.

Some Greeks in the classical period, hundreds of years later, were appalled that the poet had given immortal gods such an array of human foibles.[3] He had taken the divine out of the divine. Homer's Hera, the queen of the gods, was constantly angry with her husband, Zeus; Poseidon, god of the seas, was forever maneuvering against Athena, goddess of olives; Hephaestos, the lame smithy, was jealous of Aphrodite, the spinner, because of her love affair with Ares, the god of war; and so on. Commentators in the classical period argued that such tales bred nihilism, helplessness, and a depressing sense of irresistible fate. It is quite likely, however, that these classical commentators did not know as much detail about ancient Mycenae, Thebes, Athens, or Crete as do modern scholars who have the benefit of nearly two centuries of extensive archaeological discovery. Such recent discoveries as the excavations at Knossos or Troy had simply not been done in classical times. Plato and his contemporaries were right that Homer and his ilk were issuing moral instructions; however, Plato and his companions had no specific or archaeological knowledge of the explosion of Thera, the decline of Crete, and the fall of Troy and therefore would not have known the detail of prepatriarchal cultures against which the oral singers of the Dark Age were issuing their warnings. Homer himself, of course, may not have known but was in all probability only passing along those stories that had framed the new patriarchal morality during the early centuries of transition. It is probable that while classical commentators saw in Homer a body of moral instruction, the intent of such instruction was even more a mystery to them than it is to us. They would not have known that it was a turning away from a culture that gave more honor to women and less honor to war, because they would not have known that such a culture had ever existed.

Also, nothing in Homer's stories leads the believer to rely upon the natural order and harmony or beauty of the universe. Hesiod had claimed that the daughters of Zeus were Peace, Justice, and Order, but Hesiod seems to have been spreading the official view of the ruling oligarchs. For common people the gods were more likely symbols for chaos or an explanation for everything in nature that is unpredictable and erratic. There are no full moons, benign dolphins, or kissing swallows in Homer. There are no men bringing gifts of oil or fish to gaily bedecked women. These *had* been the repeated subjects of abundant art in the most important civilization before Homer, portrayed on the walls of Crete and Thera. Clearly, Homer and those antecedent poets from whom he had inherited his lore were turning a cultural corner, describing the natural order as brutish and erratic rather than pastoral and calm. This was a second way in which Homer's instruction escaped unobserved in classical times and probably for the same reason: classical scholars simply did not know of the frescoes and figurines, pots and spirals, and bees and doves of the Minoans. By the time of Plato and Aristotle, Homer's context had disappeared.

To be able to describe the nature of reality was, and is, the central business of both religion and politics. Poets as singers were those who filled the function of historians and teachers in the preliterate world and therefore enjoyed central prominence in both religion and politics. In all likelihood the patriarchal package was easier to sell when cloaked in drama and human struggle because a story has a tendency to hang on in the recesses of the mind. Still today, no doubt for the same reason, more people probably read Homer than Plato. Homer is taught in the eighth grade to nearly everyone; Plato is taught in college to a specialized few. Homer's genius was to bring the new story, with riveting pictures of monsters and demons and heroes and beautiful women gone awry. More people would pay attention.[4]

Homer's two most famous tales, *The Iliad* and *The Odyssey,* (a) glorify war and (b) reject human immortality through the instrument of a woman. The first does not appear in the Minoan material, and the second is everywhere in Minoan material. In each case, therefore, Homer presents a reality that stands the preexisting Minoan world on its head. The case is so deftly crafted and to such an extent with symbols no longer in common usage that to this day the political implications have been mostly ignored. Ancient code words have become obscure and largely irrelevant to today's battles and have escaped today's vocabularies. Marriage, for example, as an institution for the containment of women and their sexuality seems to have been very much an issue in the eighth century BCE. Mythical figures such as the goddess Rhea or the Amazons or Calypso—who did not at all believe in marriage—were no doubt popular among residents of Lemnos, Sparta, Samnos, Crete, Cyprus, Troy, Anatolia, and even possibly Palestine. Those people regarded marriage, which meant yoking a woman to a man, with at least skepticism and perhaps outright hostility. We will see therefore that Homer steers his hero in *The Odyssey* on a slow course through the dangers of places very much like these.

The Odyssey is about a hero of the Trojan War returning to his wife. The man had endured ten years of battle and separation, and during ten more years on his way home he must escape the Sirens, Circe, Scylla, and Charybdis. One after another they have tried to eat him, charm him, woo him, suck him down, and drown him. He has troubles with the Cyclopes and the Lastrygonians and a few others, but repeatedly and profoundly his adversaries are female. We pick up the story when Odysseus has finally made it past them all and is washed up on the shores of a new island. He has been shipwrecked by the last of the feminine dangers, Charybdis, the sucking force of the whirlpool,

which is, importantly, located beside a fig tree. There he lost his ship and his mates and even his clothing before drifting helplessly on the seas until at last he washed up on a lonely island. Here he finds Calypso, lovely and long-haired, "shining among divinities," sitting by a hearth fire, singing. The hearth was, time out of mind, the symbol for home, safety, for protection at last; the fire had to look good to a man who washed up dripping wet and cold. There sat a goddess waiting for him, singing, and looking for all the world like the true woman—beautiful, warm, inviting. She could make a man a little nervous because she was a goddess. Not a famous goddess—more the quiet kind a lonely Greek might meet on a trip and fall in love with against his better judgment. The storyteller would know how to hold the attention of his mostly male audience. When Odysseus walked up the sand, sweetwoods were burning and delicious cedar smells wafted all across her homeland. "Alder was there and black poplar and fragrant cypress and there were birds with spreading wings ... and little owls, and hawks, and birds of the sea, ... vines that ripened with grape clusters. ... even a god who came into that place would have admired what he saw."[5] Noticeably missing from this recitation was an olive tree, the symbol of the goddess Athena, and with her, of the reign of the Olympian king of the gods, Zeus.

Calypso's island is also a place of ambrosia and red nectar. Nectar is alluring but it is also a signal for trouble. Homer's audience would have known that Hera had been the preeminent goddess in Mycenae and Sparta before the Greeks' rise to power, before the Dark Age, before Heracles. It was Hera who, before Zeus, was accustomed to deal in ambrosia and red nectar. Then Hera met Zeus, who put her out of the ambrosia business and made her into a wife. Before Hera's subordination ambrosia was the red life force of a goddess by which she made a man immortal.[6] Ambrosia in Calypso's hands suggests that the reader is being led backwards into some enchanted world of the deep past. Significantly, Calypso also keeps the double-edged axe—the unmistakable symbol of the sacred in the Cretan palace culture. Homer therefore brings his hero, after a series of narrow escapes with seductive women or women who will eat a man alive, to yet one more woman whose sacred association is Cretan and who deals in nectar and ambrosia.

Fig. 44. Odysseus is strapped to the mast to avoid the temptation of the Sirens. These figures combined the image of women and birds and are a representation containing three figures, all of which point back to earlier Minoan images. Sirens are one of a long list of monster women portrayed in early Greek mythology. COPYRIGHT © THE TRUSTEES OF THE BRITISH MUSEUM

Immediately before this episode, Odysseus had been shipwrecked and lost all his crew, all the warriors who had fought with him in the Trojan War. Under the alders, amid the flowers and birds, his fortune at last changes, and the goddess takes him as her lover. The man stays moonstruck in her embrace for seven years. Some say they have three sons.[7] Eventually the hero's passion unravels, and he becomes bored with love. Seven years is enough.[8] In this case seven is probably Homer's symbol of completion for the old Cretan order and of the end of attraction of that order for a great Greek hero. Athena—than whom there is none more Greek or more virgin—is watching from Mount Olympus and decides that it is time for Odysseus to return home to his lawful estate. The Olympian rules are different from the Cretan ones. Athena asks Zeus to send Hermes, the messenger god, to tell Calypso to release her mortal from her sacred embrace.

"I gave him love and cherished him," Calypso pleads. Her plea falls on deaf ears. Homer's *Odyssey* is not a story about the joy of love. Calypso chides Zeus, calls him jealous and hard-hearted, says that the Olympic gods resent goddesses like her who sleep with such men "as each has made her true husband," or, that is, husbands made partners by nothing more than love. Calypso makes it clear that she is describing the joy of union, not of possession. Alexander Pope translates her pleas:

> Ungracious gods! With spite and envy cursed!
> Still to your own ethereal race the worst!
> Ye envy mortal and immortal joy,
> And love, the only sweet of life, destroy.[9]

But Calypso's reliance upon the power of love does not work. Hermes pays her no mind. The goddess then plays her most important card: "I could make him immortal and all his days be endless."[10] Or, as Pope translates:

> Hither this man of miseries I led,
> Received the friendless, and the hungry fed;
> Nay, promised—vainly promised!—to bestow
> Immortal life, exempt from age and wo.[11]

This is a stunning proposition. Here is Odysseus. He lies with the golden goddess on a rich island covered with trees—the universal dream of paradise, the Greek equivalent of the Garden of Eden. Immortality here is not some casual lover's phrase or mortal's whim; it is the central promise of the ancient earth goddess and, as we recall, also of all those Minoan symbols. It is the hopeful core of the message conveyed by combined figurines of women, bees, birds, trees, and the snake. The spiral frieze from Zakros that goes all the way round the room and comes back to the beginning, encircling women's breasts the whole distance, suggests that the cycle of life is endless. Calypso is clearly a pre-Olympian, and as Homer describes her, she is making an offer out of some supernatural world. She is not of the new order of thunderers and earthshakers but is obviously intended by the poet to represent an earlier time. Calypso's love, he has her say, could make Odysseus immortal, like life itself. As Pope translates, it is not merely an offer: it is a promise.

But Athena, the daughter of Zeus, wants Odysseus home with his wife. For Homer, marriage trumps immortality. Calypso relents. "I have no spirit

of iron inside my heart."[12] It is a tender moment. The couple drink ambrosia. Calypso then asks Odysseus if he means to go home, really, rather than become immortal with her. It is a question that might symbolize the quiet choices that Greek men had to make whenever they were in contact with the old culture, the world represented by Lemnian women of the Jason story or other women in similarly scattered villages where remnants of the old culture remained throughout Greece and the islands. It would have been the question set to Samson by Delilah as she tempted him with the old ways. They too were a couple who symbolized the transition from the old women-centered religions. In this case Odysseus makes the correct decision for a would-be patriarch and insists that he must go home. It is the central turning of *The Odyssey*. Again, Alexander Pope's translation is the most lyrical:

> Against Ulysses shall thy anger rise?
> Loved and adored, oh goddess! As thou art,
> Forgive the weakness of a human heart!
> Though well I see thy graces far above
> The dear, though mortal, object of my love;
> Of youth eternal well the difference know,
> And the short date of fading charms below;
> Yet every day, while absent thus I roam,
> I languish to return, and die at home.[13]

Odysseus [Ulysses] does not say that he misses Penelope. Offered "youth eternal" and aware of "the short date of fading charms," he still says he wants to die at home. Reluctantly, Calypso acquiesces and then "they enjoyed themselves in love and stayed all night by each other."

Now Odysseus has made the critical decision in the world ruled by Zeus, the pivotal decision of *The Odyssey*: an Olympian hero rejects immortality offered through the love of a woman.

This story moves from mere fantasy to clear political instruction when we realize that in all the collection of Greek myths that emerged from the Dark Age, all the women who try to make men immortal fail. This is in sharp contrast to the strong suggestion of the earlier Minoan materials that life goes on and on through the agency of women. It is in contrast to the implication that a woman shares with the birds and the snakes, the trees and the bees, the phenomena of disappearance, loss of fertility, and return. In the Minoan materials, a woman, like a bird, like a tree, like the bees, like the snake, or in combination with them, is the symbol of recycling. When female figurines are put into Bronze Age graves, it must be because women will actually be the *vehicle* of recycling. The feminine can make it happen. The spirals around the breasts of Zakros and Knossos say as much in another way. The spirals on the sarcophagus of Hagia Triada surrounding the women who are presiding at a funeral imply the same. These women are ushering the dead man to the next world. Women can bring a man not only to it, but through death. Now Homer gives us Calypso, who is an ancient goddess of the Minoan type who even retains the double-edged axe of Crete and who fails in her attempt to fulfill the promise of the Minoan culture—the promise of immortality. Zeus overrides her, cancels her, denies her power. The audiences of the Dark Age must have known it was a signal defeat and as such it was an instruction.

Other stories in the Greek lore have women failing in the same attempt. It is not necessary to retell every one of those stories in full, but one can at least point to them. The great goddess of grains was Demeter, who tries to make a small boy immortal by putting him into a hearth fire. The spell is interrupted by a mortal Greek queen, and the boy dies. It is a long story, and this is only a small part. The importance here is to note that a great goddess, Demeter, also fails to make a male child immortal. Contrast this to the Cretan material, and the message of the Dark Age storytellers replicates Calypso's futile attempt.

Another famous myth is that of the witch Medea, whom Jason, the leader of the Argonauts, picks up on his adventures in pursuit of his golden fleece. Jason marries Medea, a foreigner from Asia, a land not far from Troy. Medea then tries to kill an evil king who stands in Jason's way to claim his inheritance. That is a good thing. But she does so by falsely promising to make the king immortal. She persuades the king's daughters to help with the first step in the process by killing their father. They do that, and Medea then reneges on her deal and does not use the right potion to make the man immortal. This whole story is brazen patriarchal propaganda. Medea is portrayed as a foreign witch who makes an offer of immortality that she does not ever intend to keep. The story is designed to say to men in the Dark Age, See, these backwoods women promise immortality but do not deliver. The myth therefore intentionally slanders the idea of immortality and makes Medea—like Demeter, like Calypso—another woman who can promise but not deliver or whose promises of immortality are not to be trusted. The three myths are instructional. A woman's promise of immortality will kill a man.

In these stories it is only women who try to make males immortal. Men don't try for it themselves. Women do not try, either, to make other *women* immortal. It is as if they come with the necessary equipment already. They do not need to be put in the fire or changed by a spell. This is all consistent with our reading of the Minoan materials and in a direct way again confirms that reading. It is life that is immortal, not any single individual, and women are the vessel for that life to continue. But, reply the Greeks in Homer's time, it does not work for any single man. In the sense of one immortality for one man, it cannot happen through the agency of a woman. From the number of repetitions of the message, the holdout *against* the patriarchal claim must have been rather extensive. There may have been a great many villagers who still treasured the older doctrine of women as the agency of continuation and rebirth or of what we loosely translate as immortality.

The patriarchs do not only disparage, they ridicule any idea of female-enhanced immortality. Eos, goddess of the dawn, for example, was a daughter of the older gods, the Titans. That puts her origins before the Dark Age, pre-Olympian. She was the goddess of the first morning light. Her divinity suggests that before the Dark Age, people used to rejoice at the return of the sun, the pale streaks in the eastern sky marking the return of the day. It would be a cause for universal joy. And so they named the dawn Eos—rosy fingered and seductive. She came every morning; she was lovely. They said she was also promiscuous; maybe it was because, like a whore, to the bed she brought her pleasures every day, to every man.

Eos, according to the Greek mythmakers—that is, according to the next generation of religions after

the Titans—has a flaw: she repeatedly falls in love with young mortals.[14] One after another, she finds a man, falls desperately in love with him, and then cannot hold him. Finally, Eos finds a bright-looking young swain, Tithonos, and once again falls head over heels in love. Because women have acquired a bad reputation for making men immortal, Eos asks Zeus to make Tithonos immortal for her pleasure. Zeus has by now shown his ability to "do childbirth" just as well as any woman. He can give birth through his head (Athena) or his thigh (Dionysus), and so now he takes on the immortality challenge. Those promoting the new patriarchal religion are not modest. The king of the Olympians can birth gods and kill humans or keep them alive forever. Accordingly, he agrees to make poor Tithonos immortal.

Fig. 45. Eos, goddess of the dawn, chasing a youth. Greek black vase from about fifth century BCE. PERMISSION OF GOULANDRIS MUSEUM, ATHENS.

Unfortunately, Eos neglects to ask Zeus to also keep Tithonos *young*. It is a fateful mistake. Tithonos lives on and on but gets older and older and shrivels and withers down to the size of a crusty little cicada. Eos finally has to keep her lover in a small cage and never gets to make love to him because, as everyone who has ever lived in cicada country knows, cicadas only sing the mating song when the sun is up and the day is hot. But when the sun is up, the dawn is gone. In Zeus's time a woman has to be very, very clever to fool around with immortality.

Immortality is highly valued among Christians and Islamists, even today, and believers go to great lengths to explain how to achieve eternal life. Christian hymns, broadcasts, and sermons offer life without end as the central promise of the religion. The Greeks, however, were making a repeated effort to explain how immortality could *not* be achieved. The reason for iterating on these pages so many of these myths, each with negative results, is to note that the constant running through them all is that women were inept and ineffective at bringing off this greatest and most important, *potentially death-redeeming* idea. In all probability for most humans, as the example of Christians and Muslims signifies, neither riches, nor fame, nor power would compare with the gift of forever. But in each story addressing the issue of forever, the patriarchs say that the constant is *women's* ineffectiveness to bring it about. Calypso cannot overcome the will of Zeus. Demeter fails to overcome the will of a mortal queen. Medea's promise to keep a king alive is a ruse. Eos's effort is ridiculous.

It is probable that had we been only looking at the archaeological materials, we might not have suspected that women in the Minoan culture had borne this promise—the promise of forever, the promise of continuity. A great many scholars have speculated that that is indeed what the artifacts do mean, but the conclusions are always to some degree uncertain. The pots and walls themselves are silent. Interpretations might always be subjective, willed by the researcher's own predisposition. What drives the immortality point home, however, and what seems to confirm the speculation that that is indeed what these artifacts do mean is that the later Greek myths are oppositional. Some action overcoming conflict is woven through them all. The Greeks spent a huge amount of mythological effort trying to refute *someone*. The very number of repetitions tells us that there was some ideological question in the air, something to teach about, and the most likely candidate is a contrary political or religious belief in their immediate past. Because the Cretan civilization was the most important and most highly developed of those civilizations most nearly adjacent to them, and because Minoan influence had spread all around the Greek mainland to places such as Mycenae and Thebes and Delphi—perhaps even to Sparta—the likelihood is that Minoans are the ones being displaced or disparaged. Minoans and their cultural descendants may very well have been the mysterious, never clearly identified enemy in these stories. It is at that point, when we suspect that the rejection is of someone specific, that we look to the Minoan archaeological materials and the coincidence of themes leaps out. The written word spells out opposition to themes that immediately become evident in the Minoan archaeology. Further, the very oppositional nature of the stories seems to confirm that the stories were intended to reinforce a transition away from the culture on those quiet pots and walls. When seen

together, therefore, the artifacts such as the seal ring that combines a woman, bird, and a beehive and the mythology deprecating Stymphalian birds or Sirens or Harpies point to opposite views of the feminine. The spirals around female breasts and the mythology deprecating immortality point to opposite views of regeneration. The archaeology gives us ample evidence to *assert* the themes; the mythology unequivocally *denies* the same themes. To imagine that this coincidence happens through pure chance stretches credulity. The Greeks, in sum, rebutted the idea of immortality achieved through the vehicle of women and most probably did so precisely because the Minoans had asserted exactly the opposite.

The subtext of women's ineffectiveness is sexuality's ineffectiveness. To make that specific point, in still another story Heracles, the earliest of the Greek heroes and one who traces back to the very beginning of the Dark Age (if not before), went to the underworld to steal the apple of immortality. This would be like going to hell to get the gift of eternal life. There is a vase in the British Museum that shows the hero taking the apple from Eros, the little love god who usually goes around and shoots mortals with arrows of passion. Something is wrong with this picture. Why is Eros in it at all? Heracles is not the kind of lover who woos or loses his head in passion. When he wants a woman, he takes her; there is no Eros involved. Heracles slays beasts and steals the Amazon queen's chastity belt—acts of bravery and courage. So why is he here, in his most significant labor of all, stealing a little apple of immortality from a little love god?

The evident answer is that the old symbol of sexual pleasure was an apple, and sexual pleasure resulted in children, and children kept the family

going. If this went on and on, like the spirals at Zakros, or the spirals on all those Cretan pots, or the spirals on the famous sarcophagus from Hagia Triada, sexuality and immortality were linked. That is, until Heracles came and took it away. The storytellers must have been saying that sex and immortality were linked in the old religion but not in the new Olympian religion. So they made up this story that Heracles went at the beginning of (their) time and stole the apple back from Eros—or some say it was from the snake—and that proved the point that there is no such thing anymore as sex-based immortality. From that time forward, the symbol of the hero who gains immortality through exploits trumps the symbol of immortality through feminine sexuality.

In sum, descriptive writing from those who actually made the pots or the women's figurines does not exist, but the Heracles story and Homer's tales give us writing from the next culture that rejected these antecedents unequivocally. Logically, one might assume that they made these assertions about overcoming, or rejecting, sex-based immortality because someone before them was being overcome or rejected. Greeks repeated the message multiple times, perhaps initiating a practice mimicked by today's TV ads in a political campaign. It is also logical to assume that the opposition to be overcome or rejected must at least have included the very prominent, very influential, and very nearby Cretans and the island women of Thera.

There is evidence, of course, that the culture that modern scholars have abundantly uncovered on Crete and Thera was spread much farther across the eastern Aegean. Feminine symbols were widespread. A great many figurines of women were placed in graves. They have been found in the Cycladic islands

Fig. 46. Heracles stealing the apple of eternity from Eros.

beginning in the middle of the third millennium BCE and scattered widely throughout Asia Minor, Greece, and Crete. They were found at Knossos and Akrotiri, two of the prominent sites illustrating the culture before the Dark Age, and in Thebes on mainland Greece, and at Mycenae to the south in the Peloponnesus. They stretch from Ugarit and Anatolia to Italy. They are ubiquitous. In some way they may have been expected to lessen the effect of death, or why else put them in the graves? The most obvious assumption is that they were shorthand for an expected rebirth.

The extensive findings of these small figurines are a plausible basis for saying that women as an aid to rebirth was a belief not limited to Crete and Thera but one that was widely held, spread generally around the Aegean world. These figurines disappeared, further, at the same time as did the pots with the combined symbols of women, birds, and the tree, or the women and the bees, or women and snakes. They all disappeared with the decline of Crete and Thera and their civilization. After the destruction of 1200 BCE and after the Dark Age, a whole new point of view was explained by stories of Eos and Heracles, Medea and Calypso. Immortality for men at the hands of women, or through the love of a woman, was no longer an option.

Greeks did not say that immortality was not an option at all. Heroes in war could become immortal. The patriarchal objection therefore was not simply the practical one that immortality is unrealistic or not in accord with the known facts. They did not reject immortality the concept. They simply changed the way in which it was to be achieved. Instead of through regeneration or reproduction or children or sexuality, it would for them be only achieved through male heroics in battle. Heracles would become immortal. Theseus perhaps. Odysseus perhaps. Not many. Even Achilles did not make it. A man had to be an awfully good warrior, and just sleeping with a goddess would not do it anymore. Which probably means that sleeping with temple priestesses would not do it anymore either. Which probably means that sexuality would not do it anymore. Some combination of war and trade or war and empire had become the new way to promote one's reputation through time, as close as anyone would get to immortality. War had not just replaced peace: it had replaced the idea that there was a connection between sex and the divine. Without its holy meaning, its promise of communal survival, from these days forward, sex would become banal and trivial.

Homer Poses the Choice between Love and Property

The Greeks explained the beginnings of their history in their myth about Jason. Most of the legendary founders of their culture were aboard the *Argo*. They had had to go somewhere far distant to get the symbolic fleece that would guarantee a young man his kingdom. Thus, at the beginning of their story, the first problem of their civilization was to establish a male's claim to his kingdom. *Entitlement* was the foundation question. Civilization was not, that is, founded on gold or trade or iron or weapons or building a great city: it was founded upon a man's claim to his inheritance. It is a signal lesson. Signal in the sense that it points to all the other lessons of Greek mythology. Civilization, say the storytellers, begins with the answer to the question, How does a man lay claim to his property?

The answer is that he goes to the place of his nomadic roots, obtains the fleece of a sheep, which was the staple of the nomadic life, and gets a wife. To do this he must pass by numerous opportunities to join with women who do not marry, because he must pursue not casual sex but marriage. His patrimony will not pass on unless he has a wife, a *continuous* wife, and the way to get her is to bring a wild women from the edges of culture to within the institution of monogamy. Jason finds this woman in Colchis. She is foreign; she has the powers of enchantment and witchcraft. She is Medea. She helps him win the fleece, and he marries her. The history of mortals begins with a claim to patrimony and a marriage to keep the patrimony safe. In the end the story of this marriage is a tragic one. Jason and Medea eventually quarrel over

Jason's desire to take a new wife who would bring their children into the line of kings of Corinth. Jason has made a decision to establish a firm patriarchal claim for his children, which he could not do with Medea. The decision makes sense when the primary cultural value is a male's claim to property. The decision does not make sense to Medea, who thinks like the women of the frontier, like the old enchantress. In a fury Medea kills Jason's intended new bride and her own children. It is a horrendous act. Her fury knows no bounds, and the moral of the story is that when a man like Jason goes out to find one of those wild women, intending to bring her into the patriarchal fold, he should expect trouble.

Other instructions from the earliest storytellers of those early years also point toward women. Calypso, as we have seen, offered immortality that seemed benign or even—according to Homer—positively glorious, and yet Odysseus rejected her. She was a little like the women of Lemnos, having no interest in marriage and only interest in love. For Jason there were also women who were just brutal and a nuisance, such as the Harpies, or who would threaten marriage, such as Rhea, or disregard it, such as the Amazons and the Lemnians. Now it is appropriate to return to the hero Odysseus on his way home from the Trojan War. The story begins again just after the hero has turned down Calypso's offer of immortality.

The whole *Odyssey* story, if it is a morality lesson, is surely about more than women, but the messages prescribing a man's relationship to women are the most pointed. Penelope, the wife in question for Odysseus, is the model for Greeks of the patient and chaste woman. She waits twenty years for her man, who is off to war. She does not sleep with any of the suitors who come for her, even though her husband is thought by all to be lost in his return from the war. He is, after all, a pirate. The chances for a pirate to be killed must have been fairly high. So the suitors come to Penelope in large numbers and eat at her table, consuming her goats and pigs. She treats them with courtesy and guile. She pretends to be interested but is not and quietly pines for her true husband.

Odysseus, on the other hand, is not monogamous. He meets several women on his way home and at least three of them would like to make him her husband. The first is an "enchantress" named Circe, who can turn men into pigs. The god Hermes, with assistance from Athena and Zeus, brings Odysseus a magic potion to ward off her enchantment, and Odysseus successfully resists Circe's spell. The message is that a woman can make a beast out of a man forever or turn him into nothing more than a breeding pig, but this can be successfully avoided if he takes the remedies offered by Zeus, the new king of the gods. One does not have to be a poor villager in the eighth century BCE to get this lesson.

Circe is not as angry as she might be, however, and agrees not to harm Odysseus and to restore all his men that she had already turned into pigs. She then takes Odysseus to bed in the manner of the old goddesses, offering to make him her permanent husband. Thus Calypso—about whom we read earlier—was not the first who proposed a different kind of husbandry. Before her had been Circe. Odysseus enjoys Circe's charms, and some say even has three sons by her, but

eventually he wearies and desires to go home to Ithaca. He does not say that he desires to go home to Penelope so much as to go home to Ithaca, where his "legitimate" son is. The son's name is Telemachus. The emphasis more on the son than the wife is the norm for patriarchy. Penelope is also there, but the reader learns more about the island and Telemachus than about the wife. Homer does not say that this is a love match. The second message of the Circe episode is therefore that an enchantress can be enjoyed temporarily but not for marriage, and a marriage has some purpose other than mere enjoyment or the fulfillment of love.

As Odysseus is about to leave, Circe warns him that he must sail past the Sirens. These are female creatures with bird bodies who promise a man knowledge and simply cannot be resisted. Odysseus must therefore order his shipmates to strap him to the mast and stop up his ears so that he can ignore their call. Forever since, Sirens have been identified with seduction. Here it seems to be the seduction of knowledge, the way of knowing, or the promise of knowing that is even more seductive than the flesh. It is certainly not the flesh, because these women have bird bodies, complete with wings and talons. But they sing, and their song is irresistible. The storytellers are warning of the temptation of the idea that through women will come some deep knowing, like Eve seeking the fruit from the tree of knowledge of good and evil in the Garden of Eden. All that knowledge that a seductive woman offers is but an illusion, says Homer; if a man falls for it, he will end up dead on the rocks, his bones putrid and black.

If he gets past the Sirens, Circe explains, Odysseus will also have to sail between Scylla and

Charybdis. The former is a six-headed monster who lives on a cliff and snatches sailors who happen to sail past. She has an unquenchable appetite, but it is better, says Circe, to sail close to Scylla and lose only six men than to sail on the other side of the channel nearer to Charybdis and lose the whole enterprise. There is, significantly, a great fig tree beside Charybdis. The fig was a sacred symbol in many traditions, though probably not among the Olympians. So here is this sacred—but not Greek—emblem associated once again with an irresistible feminine pulling power that will turn out to be very, very dangerous. Charybdis is a whirlpool of black water. It may be no coincidence that among some ancient traditions, diving into deep water was a metaphor for making love.[1] Charybdis is deep water that would take a man down and never let him go; she was beside a fig tree and would not only take six of Odysseus's men but would suck his whole ship down.

On the other side of this channel is the dangerous monster Scylla. She had an earlier incarnation as a mortal woman, beautiful and tempting. The great sea god, Poseidon, saw her and became infatuated. Unfortunately he was already married, and his wife became jealous. To solve the problem Poseidon's wife changed Scylla into a barking monster with six heads and twelve feet. Later on in the fifth century, playwrights such as Euripides would still refer to Scylla in her earlier incarnation as a seductress, but Homer had fashioned her into a combined image and turned the seductress into a monster. She would not actually kill the whole enterprise but just nibble away at it, weaken it (take part of his crew), and drive a man to distraction.

Thus Odysseus must first steer past the temptation of knowledge from those bird-women, the Sirens (women who, pointedly, have bodies like the female figurines at Knossos and Thebes and Mycenae), and second, he must somehow guide between two great dangers of female attraction. On the one side is the seductress who will eat and chew and rip a little here and there. This has the earmarks of the unfulfilled casual romance. On the other is the craving, sucking black hole of obsession, which is much worse because it will take all of a man—his life, his boat, his livelihood, his whole enterprise. Charybdis is more than temptation: she bears all the indicia of sexual addiction. The message resonates with the anecdote from the journey of the Argonauts when Heracles must warn Jason and his companions to leave behind the passions of the Lemnians. But in *The Odyssey*, Homer's case is much stronger and much more convincing.

The need for the instruction arises from the reality that in the period immediately after the decline of Crete, quite a number of cultures were still unconcerned with the institution of marriage. These were scattered through Lydia and Phrygia, Scythia and Lycia, perhaps Cyprus, Samos, Lesbos, and Lemnos. A mainland example was Sparta, where as late as the fourth century women would be expected to take more than one husband and children might be raised communally. In Homer's time there would have been many such pockets of nonmarrying cultures scattered all around the Aegean. Both Jason and Odysseus sailed past one land after the next in which women were neither subjugated nor tamed nor sexually restrained by laws of monogamy. Such women might, warned Homer, appear harmless, but by degrees they will lure a man to descend at first into attraction, then into the middle territory of temptation or maybe even possession, and then finally into outright obsession.

Obsession is the great, sucking Charybdis beside the fig tree. She will make a slave of a man, drag him down into a whirlpool from which there is no escape. A little bit of passion outside the marriage, Scylla (Poseidon's temptress), might consume something in a man, take part of his crew, weaken him, which is bad enough. But *obsession*, Charybdis, can destroy a man absolutely. Certainly in the earlier Minoan days of freer sexuality, or temple sexuality, such obsession might indeed have been a social problem. Some scholars report that multitudes of men were all lined up outside the temples awaiting their turn. The Old Testament warned Samson to beware of Delilah, probably for the same reason. Temple sexuality could be addictive.

Homer's stories consequently lead his listeners through the descent into hell: first a woman will enchant a man and turn him into a breeding pig (Circe); then she will offer him deep knowledge (Sirens); if he escapes these, she will eat him alive (Scylla); finally (and worst of all), she will suck him and everyone who depends upon him (his shipmates) down into the black hole of death (Charybdis). Today such a progression is described in detail by twelve-step addiction programs, including sex and love addiction, at the end of which is obsession and self-destruction.

Homer warned of this same obsession in *The Iliad*. There he has Achilles nearly prostrate with grief and frustration because his commander, Agamemnon, has taken his slave girl.

> The maid, the black-ey'd maid, he forc'd away,
> Due to the toils of many a well-fought day;
> Due to my conquest of her father's reign;

> Due to the votes of all the Grecian train.
> From me he forc'd her, me the bold and brave;
> Disgrac'd, dishounour'd, like the meanest
>   slave.[2]

Poor Achilles collapses in grief over a lost woman and sends his best friend off to do battle in his place. This is a kind of desperate obsession and, although Homer does not say it explicitly, the kind of sucking whirlpool into which Charybdis draws a man.

In *The Odyssey* it is Circe who describes these dangers in detail. In the actual event, of all the males in his crew, only Odysseus escapes. Scylla eats six of his sailors, and Charybdis sucks all the rest down to their destruction. Exhausted, Odysseus finally and much later washes up alone on the shores of Calypso's island. It is a land of alders and flowers that Homer tells us "even a god would enjoy." It is here that, as we have seen, she offers to him immortality and here that he becomes bored with that prospect, won only through love. This is not an island of seduction nor a false promise of knowledge. Neither is this an island of enchantment like that of Circe, where potions can make a man turn into a farm beast, an animal, never to be human again. Calypso, to the contrary, is a glorious, shining goddess. Only—and here is the point for the patriarchy—she is not Odysseus's wife and does not offer to him property or legitimate sons, and he has a need to set his feet on more-solid ground. Earlier we saw that Calypso pleaded with Zeus's messenger, Hermes, to allow her hero to remain with her. She failed to persuade Hermes, and so she and Odysseus made love. The message is not against cheap seduction, as in the case of Scylla or Charybdis. It is about immortality through love.

Fortunately for the patriarchy, it did not work and Odysseus resolved to be on his way.

Calypso, who could have given him immortality, instead gives him wood from which to make a raft on which to sail home to his son and his estates.

> It was the fourth day and all his work was finished. Then on
> the fifth day shining Kalypso saw him off from the island
> when she had bathed him and put fragrant clothing upon him.[3]

After seven years, finely dressed in Calypso's "fragrant clothing," Odysseus at last departs from her island. He has been afloat for eighteen days when Poseidon finds him and sends waves to toss him from his tiny raft, dropping him into the stormy sea. There he suffers greatly, clambers back aboard, and is fit to perish, overcome with despair, when a sea nymph appears and tells him to shed the clothes that Calypso gave to him and go naked into the sea.

> "Take off these clothes," [said the nymph]
> […]
> … [and] now Odysseus,
> sat astride one beam, like a man riding on horseback
> and stripped off the clothing which the divine Kalypso had given him.[4]

The sea nymph then gives Odysseus a veil to fasten around his chest. It is a veil of "immortality" that will keep him alive while he floats in the sea. He is to keep it wrapped around himself until he comes to land.

> "But when with both your hands you have taken hold of the mainland,
> untie the veil and throw it out in the wine-blue water
> far from the land; and turn your face away as you do so."[5]

The instruction is unequivocal: When you get to solid ground, let immortality go. Do not look back. Turn your face away.

Having shed Calypso's clothes, exhausted and near to death, Odysseus then floats naked, adrift for three days. Finally he sights land and crawls ashore. Here live a king and queen, their beautiful daughter, and a city with laws and fortifications. Most importantly, after Sirens and Scylla, Circe and Calypso, here at last is a young woman who acts normal (for the patriarchy). At the very opening of this chapter, Athena has appeared to this young girl, Nausicaa, in a dream and told her that she should wash her wedding garments and prepare for marriage. A wedding, says the goddess to the mortal virgin, is near at hand for you; not a feast, not an athletic party, not a summer festival, but a wedding. Nausicaa can think of nothing better and happily asks her father's permission to go to the shore and wash her wedding garments. She has no expected or known husband, and so far as Homer tells us, she never gets one. Still, the talk of this island is weddings. The young girl, now for the first time in Odysseus's travels, has a responsible father. There were no fathers around the Sirens, Circe, or Calypso. Nausicaa must ask permission of the father to leave the palace. He says all right, and Nausicaa goes to the shore with her serving maids.

There, after the washing of the wedding

garments is completed, Nausicaa discovers Odysseus naked, exhausted, and prostrate upon the sand. He hastily covers himself with an olive branch, gets down on his knees, and makes a most extraordinary speech. His mood has changed considerably since he left Calypso's arms:

> "I am at your knees, O queen. But are you
>   mortal or goddess?
> If indeed you are one of the gods who hold
>   wide heaven,
> then I must find in you the nearest likeness to
>   Artemis
> the daughter of great Zeus, for beauty, figure,
>   and stature."[6]

Artemis! She is like Artemis, the beautiful virgin goddess who rides in the hunt, who protects womanhood and shelters chaste young damsels from all harm. Artemis is the model *virgin*. Nausicaa is a mirror, says the naked Odysseus (as if he had just appeared from some foreign embassy) of the image of the pure and perfect *marriageable* woman:

> "He is indeed most blessed in heart, above
>   others distinguished,
> Who will prevail with his courtship presents
>   and lead you homeward,
> Since with my eyes I never have seen such
>   another as you are."[7]

He has already forgotten the goddess Calypso, with whom, only twenty-one days before, he had just concluded seven luxurious years. He says he knows that Nausicaa is thinking about marriage:

> "Then may the gods grant you what you in your
>   spirit are wishing;
> may they endow you with blessings, a husband
>   and house, and a noble
> concord of mind: for than this there is no gift
>   better or greater,
> when both husband and wife in concord of
>   mind and of counsel
> peacefully dwell in a house—to their enemies
>   greatest affliction,
> joy to benevolent friends, but especially known
>   to their own hearts."[8]

Nausicaa, enchanted, gives Odysseus olive oil with which to anoint his naked body. Some say she anointed him. Either way it is a solemn welcome, nearly sacred. Then she gives him new clothes too, clothes suitable for a man who gives speeches about marriage, and he puts them on. As they leave the beach to go together into town and to her home, Homer says that Odysseus now has the look of a young god. He has passed from the world of the fantastic, washed up as detritus on the beach, and been transformed and welcomed to a world of normal people where the talk is about marriage. For twenty-eight hundred years readers have been able at last to breathe a sigh of relief. The hero has returned to solid ground.

This is an adventure replete with hidden messages. Odysseus has by now been through a series of encounters with women who cared nothing for marriage and rather more for passion, who embodied the worst of seduction and the great sucking dangers of female sexuality. His last experience with shining Calypso was the best, but he at last became bored with her love. What man would not want to stay forever in the arms of the glorious goddess? Replies Homer, An Olympian hero, that's who. Calypso at last graciously lets him go and then even outfits him with bright new clothes. Eighteen days into the journey, he is capsized by Poseidon and visited by a sea nymph who tells him to take off the goddess's clothes. It is to be remembered that Calypso was herself a goddess daughter of the old Titan religion. Get rid of that old cloak, says the nymph. Odysseus does so and floats stark naked and cold for three days.

Three days is the time that the moon disappears from human sight each month. It is simply gone. No matter where on the planet one is, for three nights of each twenty-eight-day cycle the moon cannot be seen in the night sky. In those ancient times everyone lived under the stars and knew this. It is said by many scholars to have been after this monthly three-day absence that women of the ancient cultures danced and rejoiced at the moon's return, which also meant the return of their own fertility. Three days is therefore the famous crossover time from disappearance to rebirth, from darkness to rebirth. It is the amount of time, in later history, for which Jesus will be gone before the resurrection. It was the symbolic crossover time for all who lived under the thirteen moon cycles, and Odysseus has just gone through this three days of crossover naked at sea. Only after that symbolic period does he float up onto the sand. He transitions from Calypso to Nausicaa after being utterly disrobed and helpless, naked for three days. Now, instead of the moon making the return, as might have been cause for celebration in the cities of the Lemnians (or those named after the old moon goddess), this hero is under the guidance of Athena. Here comes a man of

the new age talking about Artemis and marriage!

He has discarded the clothing of the sensual goddess. The garments of Calypso's old world were cast away immediately preceding the three-day crossover. He is then anointed with oil by a beautiful young woman who is demurely and self-consciously dreaming of marriage. She anoints the naked wretch as if he were the prodigal son! He is not just welcomed with pity; he is given the treatment of ceremonial or ritual adoption, purification. Something sacred is taking place. Odysseus then delivers an opening blessing. Not about how hungry he is, or how tired, or how cold, or how he would really like a small towel, but about how ripe she is for marriage. Marriage has had absolutely nothing to do with his seven years with Calypso or his years with Circe. The imagery is abundantly clear: during the three days through which he floats naked on the sea, he has quite simply crossed over from the land of *no marriage* and returned to the land of *marriage* and now, Homer says, is transformed in his whole being to look and act like a god.

> straightway Athena the offspring of Zeus trans-
>   formed him and made
> him taller to see than before, more mighty; the
>   hair on his head she
> made flow down in thick curls that resembled a
>   hyacinth flower.
> As when a man well-skilled in the task lays gold
>   over silver.[9]

Nausikaa, seeing him, is enchanted:

"How I wish that a man like him could be
    called my husband,

making the land his home, and that it might please him to stay here!"[10]

Calypso, unlike Nausicaa, had never said a word about making Odysseus her husband. She promised immortality, not marriage. But Odysseus had been instructed by the sea nymph to loose the veil of immortality, set it free on the wine-blue sea, and "turn his face away" from immortality. This therefore is the central transition in the whole of this famous book. From dangerous women to women who are looking for good husbands, from singing women or deceptive women to a young virgin who does what her father says. From an island paradise that even a god would love to an island of kings where young women prepare carefully for their weddings. Odysseus, lying naked on the sands, having left the clothes of the promiscuous goddess behind, throws away the veil of immortality and, knowing where he has come, makes a marriage speech. The young maiden gives him olive oil with which to anoint himself, sanctifying his crossover. She gives him new clothes. The symbolism is complete and unmistakable. This is not a love story. Odysseus does not marry Nausicaa. He does not pretend to be in love. He just makes speeches about marriage and she responds in a way appropriate to a marriage culture that is much different from Calypso's culture.

Marriage is of course the foundation of the patriarchy. It is the institution without which patriarchy cannot exist. The central crossover in the whole great epic of *The Odyssey* is therefore the crossover from the lands of monsters and enchantments, of sexual union with goddesses and—as they think—with the sacred, to a return to the lands where marriage, the institution of monogamy for women, is the corner-stone of male power. It is the cornerstone because if women are not married in this new Olympian sense, men, the fathers, cannot know who their sons are. Patriarchy can't work with the Lemnians. It can't work with the Amazons. In all probability it did not work with the Mesopotamians and the women of Lesbos and the women of ancient Crete, and on and on. If men in any of these places did not know which of a woman's sons were their own, they could not know to whom to give their property. Odysseus was a pirate. Homer showed us his ravages along the coast of Asia Minor before and after the Trojan War. He brings home the loot. He is not a farmer. He is not a tiller or a wine keeper, and his wealth will not be expended in a single year. In fact Odysseus has the problem that made the patriarchy necessary: he has more wealth than he can consume in a single year. His stores have fed Penelope and her guests for twenty years. He is not therefore bound to plant and harvest from year to year. His metaphor of success is not replanting in the fall, a little grain coming up in the spring. His metaphor is wealth that is more than he actually needs; it is abundance. A farmer's reward will be contained from year to year by certain natural limits. Some years the rains might be better, but overall a farmer in the Bronze Age is not likely to double or triple his wealth in a single year. A pirate's gains, on the other hand, or a trader's prospects, are unlimited. His gains are not cyclical; his progress is linear, and he is not bound simply to the sun or the moon as were the goddesses of agriculture and the seasons. Odysseus is therefore the new man of the ages. To keep what he has, to preserve the safety of his silos and his fields, no longer bound by the success of a single season, he needs sons. He needs defense. He needs his Telemachus. Further, he needs his wife corralled in monogamous marriage so that when he dies he will not give his inheritance to someone who is not his son. More importantly, so that some young man will not show up and claim that he is a legitimate son and that all Odysseus's abundance belongs to him. An unexpected son can be beaten off now, in the land of marriage, with the defense of legitimacy. In the eighth century BCE, legitimacy is an institution of property, not love, and accordingly, the justification for the institution of marriage is also property, not love. Legitimacy keeps the demands for a man's property down to a minimum. The transition from Calypso to Nausicaa is therefore quite simply all about property. Because in addition, this episode provides the central turning of the story, the crossover from the unnatural to the natural (as a patriarch must see it), the greater point is that *The Odyssey*, as a whole, is all about property.

Clytemnestra Is Sacrificed on the Altar of Marriage

Amazons were symbols among the Greeks to illustrate the opposite of a marriage culture. They did not live by Homer's orthodoxy. They had no use for husbands. They were hostile and a little bit unnatural. Other representatives of former times were portrayed as unnatural too. The earliest men, they said, who fought for the side of mother Rhea against Zeus, lived behind cyclopean walls that only giants could raise. The Greeks even called them Giants, or sometimes they said that they were one-eyed and called them Cyclopes. Storytellers could just say "Cyclopes" and everyone sitting around the fire would know that this was going to be a story about primitive men who had lived in these lands before them and who did not marry and who had no depth perception because they only had one eye in the center of their foreheads. If Greeks were talking about earlier women, sometimes they would say that such women had snakes in their hair or had been turned into dragons. Sometimes such earlier women had six heads, like Scylla, or birds' wings, like the Sirens, or sometimes they put all these images together, like the Sphinx, with a woman's head, a lion's body, and a snake's tail. Sometimes they said that an original woman named Echidna had given birth to monsters such as the Sphinx or the Chimera, and usually these images cast earlier women in a bad light.

In general these early Greeks opined that anybody not from around there, anyone who did not speak Greek, was a Barbarian or an Amazon or a Giant or a Cyclops, and all the people listening to the stories could understand and be grateful for the new civilization that Zeus had brought. Sometimes they told a very particular story, like the one about Odysseus or the one about Clytemnestra. Here was another woman who did not live by the rules, and the storytellers said that she had been a real, mortal, and very bad woman.

The wife of the leader of the Greeks in the Trojan War, Clytemnestra, did not wait for her husband to come home. She was the contrasting figure to Penelope, and together these two frame the morality of the patriarchal world. After Agamemnon had been gone at war for some years, Clytemnestra—who was acting more in the tradition of the old earth religions—chose another man and began to live with him. Helen of Troy had set a tempting example. The Amazon women were fighting on the side of Troy, and they did not take husbands either. So there were many interesting contemporary examples to encourage Clytemnestra to get on with her life.

Tradition relates that both Agamemnon and his brother Menelaos (Helen's husband)—both who were now in Troy fighting to get Helen back—had not been in Greece for very long and that they were the newcomers. Their story was supposed to be set in the thirteenth century BCE, which is not long after some scholars suppose that the Indo-European invaders had begun to take over the palaces of Greece, probably beginning in Thessaly and, in the centuries that followed, working their way down toward the Peloponnesus where Clytemnestra and Helen lived. Agamemnon and Menelaos might have been among those who came and, with their chariots and spears, overpowered the existing earth religions. Scholars disagree on whether there *was* an Indo-European invasion at all, but the traditions here suggest that there were definitely some newcomers from somewhere and that Agamemnon and Menelaos were among them. We have already noticed how Jason may have been part of this invading culture as well, and may have seen from Homer that a part of the new culture was to denigrate women and to corral them in marriage. The (probably new) kings of Mycenae and Sparta were therefore in the Trojan War to enforce the marriage rule against Helen, who had resisted by running off with Paris to Troy. Given her chance for independence, Clytemnestra did not think much of the marriage rule either. Accordingly, Clytemnestra, who was probably of the old order, took another husband, Aegisthus, and they were happily living together when one day in stumbled Agamemnon, home from ten years in the wars. On his arm was the beautiful new slave girl Cassandra.

Cassandra had been a princess, a daughter of Priam, the king of Troy, but now she was a slave/ concubine of Agamemnon's. Clytemnestra therefore had an accumulation of reasons to be angry with Agamemnon. First, there had been the sacrifice of her daughter Iphigenia (to get a fair wind for Agamemnon to go to war), and now the Cassandra affair. The queen was very upset. She invited Agamemnon to have a nice warm bath, and thereupon she killed him with an axe. Nothing in these stories is an accident, and the axe was probably the Cretan symbol of sovereignty— the storytellers linking Clytemnestra's fury to the customs of that ancient island. In the thirteenth century BCE, the influence of Crete is still strong, and the axe comes back to haunt the unwary patriarch. The queen, for her part, must have thought that the old

man was a murderer himself and an adulterer and that she still had the right to choose her own husband. The Greeks were at pains not to notice, but the oral tradition is that before Agamemnon, at the very beginning of her story, Clytemnestra had been married once before. She had been married to yet another king and Agamemnon had come along and murdered that king as well as Clytemnestra's then-infant child and then seized the mother. Agamemnon had brought to her a whole history of weddings, murders, adultery, and perfidy; Clytemnestra had quite a lot to object to. One of her female ancestors was said to be from Crete and another from Sparta, which were places of well-known loose moral conduct, so maybe she could be excused when she finally decided that she had had enough and took the axe to Agamemnon.

While she was at it, she killed Cassandra, the princess from Troy, which was pretty senseless, for the reason that the poor girl was a slave and a prophetess and was not guilty of anything but being carried away as a prize of war. Clytemnestra, in the hands of the apologists of the new order, was therefore a caricature. She was an example of what happens to a woman of the old order when she is in her passion. They said that she felt satisfied after the killings and that she and Aegisthus put on a celebration. The massacre had taken place on the thirteenth day of the month, and Clytemnestra declared the thirteenth day a monthly festival. Thirteen, of course, is the number of months in the moon's annual cycle, and to honor the thirteenth day is a second unmistakable symbol that Clytemnestra's allegiance is more to the moon than to the sun—that is, more to the old order than to the new.

Clytemnestra's son, Orestes, however, was horrified that his mother had killed his father, and so he eventually laid out a plot and killed his mother. He did not concern himself about revenge for the murder of Cassandra, whose killing was more or less routine for young women who happen to be slaves. In the literature of the classical period, Cassandra joins Hecuba, Andromache, and Polyxena as women of Troy who are natural victims. According to Euripides and others, the lucky ones were the slaves.

By this point in the Clytemnestra story there has been a sacrifice/murder of Iphigenia, followed by the murder of Agamemnon and Cassandra, followed by the murder of Clytemnestra. Even bloodthirsty Greeks must have found this all a bit unnerving. Aeschylus's fifth-century drama contrives, therefore, a trial of Orestes for the murder of his mother wherein he is challenged by the Furies. These are the same Furies who were directly descended from the Titans and Mother Earth, representatives of the old order. They are commonly seen on black figure pottery, on vases and amphoras, hostile to patriarchs or their friends. In Aeschylus's play they are the women of the old order chasing the mother-killer Orestes, threatening him with snakes.

Every Greek schoolchild already had to learn the story of Penelope, who stayed faithfully at home for twenty years waiting chastely for Odysseus. Penelope was a model of the married woman. At the same time they had to learn the story of Clytemnestra, who was not so chaste and not waiting around for her husband at all. These two women were therefore the bookend examples of female conduct held up by the storytellers of the eighth century BCE. By the fifth century BCE, three hundred years later, the Greeks had

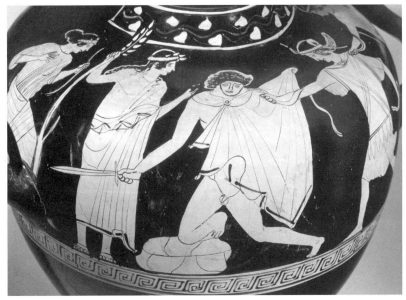

Fig. 47. Orestes being chased by the three Furies, those unhappy women whom Greeks employed to represent displaced women (perhaps the Triple Goddess) and who at least symbolized female anger that resulted from their demotion. PERMISSION OF THE BILDARCHIV PREUSSICHER KULTURBESITZ/ ART RESOURCE, NEW YORK

memorized these stories and made them the bedrock of patriarchal culture. A culminating example is a drama written by the playwright Aeschylus about 452 BCE. Orestes is duly brought to court on trial for the murder of his mother, Clytemnestra. It is the first court in Greek, or maybe Western, history. The god Apollo testifies on behalf of the mother-killer. He says that killing Clytemnestra is not so bad: women are not that important. They are not even really mothers but just temporary carriers of the seed, like the earth, not more.

> Not the true parent is the woman's womb
> That bears the child; she doth but nurse
>   the seed
> New-sown: the male is parent; she for him,
> As stranger for a stranger, hoards the germ
> Of life, unless the god its promise blight.[1]

This is Aeschylus telling us the Olympian view in fifth-century Athens. The mother is not truly a parent. She is a stranger to the child, only a nurse to the seed. The male is parent. Apollo says the proof that a man can give birth to a child is Zeus, who gave birth to Athena. Apollo was not alone in this opinion. There were other serious persons, humans, in fifth-century Athens who were presenting medical and biological theories that women had little to do with parenthood except to hold the seed. Aristotle was among them. It was the sort of Greek equivalent to the Judeo-Christian doctrine of the original sin of Eve. Therefore Eve might be subordinated, the snake driven away in the dust, and the woman forever after to do the will of her husband. For the Athenians in the middle of the fifth century, it served the same purpose: to explain that

women did not really qualify as mothers.

As Orestes' trial progresses, Aeschylus tries to make the drama more balanced and gives us the Furies, who present the case against the mother killer. The Furies are effective in oral argument, and after hearing them the gods cannot make up their minds. For a moment the vote in the assembly of the gods is tied. This is probably another indication of the civil wars that the Greeks imagined had preceded them.

Aeschylus does not talk to the gods any more than anyone else, so he is making all this up. The tie vote in the trial is his device for presenting the Mycenaean world in dramatic transition, teetering in the balance. If feminists today imagine a dramatic paradigm shift from earlier cultures of women symbolized by the Furies arguing against the rules of the patriarchy, they are not alone. Aeschylus was imagining the same thing. The choice the gods were presented was whether it is better to protect the honor of two men or the honor of two women. Finally, to break the tie, the goddess Athena herself weighs in and votes for the two men rather than vindicate the honor of the two women. Athena speaks as if from Mount Olympus:

> "I vouch myself the champion of the man,
> Not of the woman, yea, with all my soul,—
> In heart, as birth, a father's child alone
> Thus will I not too heinously regard
> A woman's death who did her husband slay,
> The guardian of her home; and if the votes
> Equal do fall, Orestes shall prevail."[2]

Athena, the politically correct woman/warrior/patriot, casts the deciding vote for Orestes, who was therefore acquitted of murder. It was an Olympian solution. Athena did what she was put in that position to do. She had once been a fertility goddess in Arcadia; she had once had roots all the way back to Asia Minor. "I vouch myself the champion of the man/Not of the woman, yea, with all my soul." Some translators have her say, "I always side with the man." She breaks the tie in favor of the son and says that she is herself "a father's child alone." Athena was born from the head of Zeus. There was no mother in her case. Of course, mothers were not really mothers, anyway.

The fact that there was a tie to break or that there were two evenly divided sides is probably a reflection of the division in earliest times throughout Greece over the issue of the roles of women. Athena was the protector of Athens, and the trial was held, said Aeschylus, in Athens. Thus from the standpoint of that city, the triumph of the patriarchy was complete. It may not have been so complete over the rest of the Greek mainland, as represented by the Furies, who, according to Aeschylus, had mustered a fair degree of support. Some division is probable, because in any surviving matrilineal society, the idea of motherhood was still key. In any of those villages where property still passed from mother to daughter—perhaps in Lemnos or Chios or Thasos or possibly in the late Bronze Age on the mainland, in places such as Sparta and Mycenae where Hera had ruled, or even in Thebes, where dragons and the Sphinx and Hera had bedeviled the new heroes like Cadmus—motherhood was key. It was the central value. It was the promise of future generations and perhaps the promise of the cycles of the seasons and therefore a natural principle of the universe. To give up on mothers was to give up on a cosmic principle, a norm of society, a fundamental guide to living. To kill a mother in these places

must have been unthinkable. For Orestes to go on trial for matricide was not just, therefore, to go on trial for the killing of the woman Clytemnestra. It was the trial of someone who had violated the foundation principle of the old order. The Greeks had been evenly divided. Athena, the goddess born from the head of a man, weighed in and said it was all right to kill a mother. At least it was all right for Athens, where most people think that dramas such as these were only attended by men.

Every Athenian from then on could be sure that the Furies represented a lust and blood instinct of the past, a kind of woman to be feared but who had neither the blessing of Apollo nor Athena and who had no authority under the law. More than just feared, these women of old, like Clytemnestra, could now be hated. Fear turned into hatred is like mere discrimination turned into misogyny. Because of what we know about the treatment of women in Crete, we can also see it as a regression. For the regression to stick, it was not enough to confine women legally. To allow women caught in adultery to be killed while letting men go free, which was the law in Aeschylus's Athens, was not just legal discrimination; it was across some even greater boundary. It had become misogyny, permission to oppress in general, as a matter of principle. It is the misogyny, not the law of Athens, that has persisted through the ages.

Honoring Orestes the mother-killer while ignoring the father who killed his daughter establishes a new morality. It is of no relevance that Agamemnon had himself taken a concubine, the poor Cassandra, for his pleasure. The key fact is not sexual promiscuity; it is sexual promiscuity *by a wife*. Clytemnestra's act is adultery, "adulterating" Orestes' property line. She had done just what Telemachus was afraid Penelope would do: she had remarried, and Orestes would have lost his estate as a result. So he killed her. When, through these stories, the people understood that the right of a son to secure his property extended to the right to kill an adulterous mother, the triumph of the patriarchy was indeed complete. When Aeschylus was able to write a play about it, imagining the approval of the gods, the dimension was raised from social custom to enforced conduct, from law to religion. The misogyny was not a result therefore of the law so much as a necessary precondition to the law. It was in this sense that the storytellers were playing their biggest role. Without them the soil of Western patriarchy would not have been prepared for the legal planting.

Aeschylus did not make up this story in the fifth century. It was known to Homer and a part of the lexicon of Greek lore at least as early as the eighth century BCE. What those earlier storytellers had done, therefore, was to create the mythological foundation, the necessary precondition, in which fifth-century Athens could approve of killing women caught in adultery; could approve of taking away their property and placing them under complete control of their husbands; could approve of pots, vases, amphoras, and cups in which women were pictured being speared, captured, and routed in battle; and could approve of making them unnatural, like Amazons or Sirens or Furies or companions of snakes and denizens of the underground. This, taken as a whole, was the crucible of Western misogyny. It did not come from the nature of women or even the nature of men; it did not come from economic gains alone. It came from the nature of the stories that were told in order to preserve those economic gains in the hands of the fathers. The drive to control property had led to the drive to control women. Homer and Hesiod, together with those other earliest creators of the Sirens and the Sphinx, Medea and Scylla, Charybdis, Clytemnestra, the Harpies, and the Furies had, further, provided vivid justification, flesh and blood excitement sufficient to make it seem as if the issue were not about property at all but about the evil nature of women.

Marriage Destroys the Mother-Daughter Bond

The last remnants of the women-centered cultures were disappearing throughout the second millennium BCE. In Sumaria and Babylon and in Egypt and among the Hittites in present-day Anatolia, there is evidence that the old centrality of women had been phasing out well before the decline of Crete in 1500 BCE. Far ahead of the islands, the continental lands and their trade-based cultures were turning to patriarchy and the depreciation of women. But on Crete these trends had not taken hold until very late, and we first hear of them as patriarchal after the island is settled by Mycenaeans sometime after 1450 BCE. It is probable, therefore, that Crete and Lemnos and Lesbos and perhaps Cyprus, islands off the mainland shore, were last holdouts of the old order. At such places the package most likely also included a different regard not only for women but for the earth as the prime source of life. These inhabitants may have been primarily agriculturists rather than pirates or warriors.

The growing class of traders of the Mediterranean were, on the other hand, proving that the earth was not the only source of wealth and that one could even possess its copper and bronze and thus, in a way, conquer it. The Bible, written during the latter stages of this same transition, now instructed men to "take dominion" over the earth. That is a radically different concept than that of women arising out of the earth, swaying in the dance, as depicted on the walls of the Spring Fresco; or of woman combined with the doves and bees as on the seal rings of Crete; or as friend to the snake who lives in the earth as retold in the stories of Echidna, the snake woman. "Taking dominion" meant that a traveling man could move the earth's riches, could ship them from Colchis to Pylos to Gibraltar, could increase them. For such long trips a man needed sons who could row and rig sails and defend against pirates without the impediment of pregnancy. They now needed to value boy children and stop leaving them on hills as they had done with Jason. This in turn would bring about a whole new treatment of daughters.

The characterization of women and their daughters in the early stories is no doubt also a metaphor for the characterization of a whole larger package of beliefs. It has been suggested herein that these beliefs would have included ideas of female-based immortality and circular time and therefore rebirth. But immortality is not a perfect equivalent for what women in the old order provided. Women did not plant their seed in the ground, like wheat, and they certainly all died themselves, just like men, so how did they deliver immortality? The answer would have been through their daughters. It was allegory, of course, a way of thinking. Women had to have a few men around long enough to get pregnant (like the women of Lemnos), but they had to have many daughters to keep the village going.

There is a painting of a young woman in an ancient cup found in Crete dating from 1900 BCE.[1] The girl in the cup is rising out of the ground so that the viewer cannot see her feet, and she has no arms, just as a snake has no arms. Rising out of the ground

mimics the seeds of grain that rise out of the ground in the spring and suggests a very early association in Crete between the daughter and the cycles of the seasons and rebirth. Later, there is a long tradition of a public celebration of the daughter, who was simply called *kore,* meaning "daughter." This celebration probably began at least as early as the thirteenth century BCE, and it eventually gave rise to the celebrations held annually in the little city of Eleusis on the mainland of Greece. These were celebrations of the constant and predictable return of the daughter or, by extrapolation, of constant rebirth, of communal immortality. In the earliest renditions of these stories, there was no personal or private name for the daughter, just as the young girls on the wall scenes of Thera are simply young girls without names. But by the time of classical Athens—about the fifth century BCE—the mystery of the daughter or the celebration of constant rebirth had gone completely (literally and figuratively) underground. The ceremony was by this time even labeled a "mystery," and as these celebrations became famous throughout the Mediterranean world, they became known as the Mysteries of Eleusis. The celebrations lasted for more than fourteen hundred years before, in about 350 CE, they finally disappeared.

The requirement to celebrate the mystery of the daughter *in secret* seems to have been a later addition, beginning perhaps only in the sixth century, some several centuries after the ceremonies themselves had become common. In that century a text began to be passed around called the *Homeric Hymn to Demeter,* and this became the basis for the famous Mystery rites celebrated in Eleusis.[2] In the *Hymn* the mother and daughter are at first very close, almost interchangeable, as they might have been when women were represented in a continuous line of fertile breasts, as on the spirals at Zakros. One day, however, at the beginning of Olympian time, the daughter (later called Persephone) is out among the flowers in a beautiful field on a fine spring morning. She is romping with her friends and is the picture of health and independence, looking quite like the bright young women on the walls at Thera. Persephone is about to reach for a narcissus when suddenly the earth opens and an Olympian god seizes her and carries her, screaming, to the underworld, where he "marries" her, whether she will or no.

The girl's mother is Demeter, goddess of grains and agriculture. Demeter is desperate and searches the world for her abducted daughter but cannot find her. In frustration she retires to the small town of Eleusis, where, disguised as a crone, she takes employment in the home of a king and queen who have a first son. Demeter is to become nursemaid to this son. As we have seen earlier, Demeter tries to make the son immortal by burning him in the hearth fire and fails because she is interrupted by the scream of the poor boy's mother. That is the familiar lesson: a woman cannot make a man immortal.

Fig. 48. The fleeing *kore* in the Eleusis Museum.

According, however, to the *Homeric Hymn*, Demeter becomes furious at her failure to make a male child immortal and now allows the seasons to go awry, and thus plants all over the earth cease to grow. The failure with the boy has brought about the death of everything else that grows. The two are therefore linked. Human immortality is understood by the agricultural goddess as connected to cycles of reproduction. Crops and boys follow the same pattern. If immortality fails for the boy, it fails for plants, because the principle is the same. Readers of the *Homeric Hymn* might therefore misestimate that Demeter was simply peeved, angry that she had failed at a simple task. This would severely understate the message. The larger meaning was that the whole concept of immortality, which had been a staple of women-centered cultures, had been defeated. Crops dried up because the *principle* of cyclical immortality had been rejected. Demeter insists that both the boy and the crops are governed by the same principle.

Zeus then pleads with Demeter to start up the seasons again, and the goddess says that she will do that only if she gets her daughter back from Hades. Hades is not only Persephone's husband but also the place we today call hell. Hades has become the principle of *unending* death. By saying, Give me my daughter back, Demeter says, in effect, I *will not* accept this principle. She stands on the ground of the old earth religions, in which daughters are what makes death impermanent. Daughters are the vehicle by which the earth religions, allegorically, defeat death.

Zeus, seeing the need for some compromise between new and old, finally relents and says that the daughter, the *kore*, can come back if Persephone does not eat anything while she is with Hades. Persephone is overjoyed and leaves Hades behind but incautiously takes a bite of a pomegranate, the fruit with hundreds of bright red seeds. This is a fateful mistake. As a penalty for eating the fruit, she must now return, to her "husband," to Hades, for one third of every year.

That is the outline of the traditional story. It is full of symbols, beginning with the flower for which the girl is reaching just at the moment of her abduction. It is not just any flower: it is a narcissus—a bulbous, single-flowered white plant with a crimson and gold corona. It was known in ancient times for its heavy scent that could produce a kind of numbness, or indeed, enchantment. For this enchantment a young girl needed no help; she did not need a companion or a husband. *Narcissism* is derived from *narcissus*. A narcissistic person is quite sufficient in loving himself or herself more than any other. The narcissus of the famous Persephone story is therefore a signal that a young girl is reaching for independent enchantment. Hades, brother to the supreme patriarch Zeus, intervenes, seizes her, and insures that she will not succeed.

Contrast the narcissus to a lily, which we found in Homer and on the walls of the Spring Fresco from Thera. The configuration of the lily suggests the mating of the man and woman. But with the narcissus the enchantment is breathed from a single corona, which has no obvious male symbolism at all. At the critical moment in her story, therefore, Persephone is reaching not for a sexual symbol but for a symbol of solitary enchantment, and is forcefully denied that chance. At the very least this story signals the end of the young girl's independence. More importantly, it also signals the end of her primary role as a daughter, the *kore*, a role that had had critical significance in any society that honored girl children as the promise of continuity.

The word *narcissus* also shares a root with *narcolepsy* and *narcissism*, which point toward death. The sexually ripe daughter, who had represented the promise of rebirth in the old order, is now taken by death. The symbol of the old order is defeated by the symbol of the new order. In the sixth century the old symbol of regeneration transcending death is ripped away and forced to yield by Zeus's command.

This transition is going to lead to marriage whether the woman (Persephone) wants it or not. Her designated husband is Hades, a brother of all-powerful Zeus, whose primary job in all Greek mythology is to insure that death is reckoned awful, unavoidable, and perpetual. He is now one of the three main male gods, as if in earlier religions people had not made enough of a place for death. He is the exact antithesis of eternal life or, that is, of the promise of future life that the daughter represents (if we have been right about the spirals and rebirth thesis of the Minoan pots and vases). The Persephone story was first written down eight hundred years after the Cretans and informs the Greeks of two new developments. First, from this time forward the close relation of a daughter to her mother will at some point be broken by a man who will take a daughter away and marry her, willy nilly. She may like it; she may not, but a man will break the mother-daughter chain. Second, death conquers all, and any previous view of immortality through daughters will be overpowered by the Olympian truth represented by Hades. A man will break the spirals of Zakros and Knossos. The unbroken relationship between Demeter (the goddess of wheat and growth) and her daughter, Persephone (the former symbol of continuation and return), is destroyed by death (Hades). This was the emerging position of the Olympians in about the sixth century BCE. It is one of a great many ways that the Greeks were explaining how civilization, as they saw it, was crossing a great divide.[3]

After the rape of the *kore* by Hades, Demeter, the mother goddess, wanders the world searching for her daughter. She cannot find her anywhere, so she wanders to the small town of Eleusis. As mentioned earlier, at this point she disguises herself as an old lady and the local king and queen invite her to become nursemaid to their only son. In Olympian Greece it appears that sons were by then more important than daughters, and Demeter therefore shifts her attention to the infant prince and tries to make him immortal. She bathes him in ambrosia, a love potion. It is a way of offering motherly love to the boy—a sort of parallel to Calypso's offering Odysseus ambrosia and physical love. Then she puts the babe into the fire to cook. He is burning happily there, on his way to immortality, when the queen enters and screams. The queen commands Demeter, whom she thinks is just a nursemaid, to stop cooking her child, and Demeter does so. Mother Earth, the all-powerful goddess, actually bends her will to that of the mortal wife of a mortal king. Or, put another way, Mother Earth does not rule in this patriarchy. The infant prince, half mortal and by now half immortal, dies. Demeter, goddess that she is, cannot make a male child immortal in the land of kings and queens. Having tried and failed, the result is death. No woman, the storyteller has explained, not even a woman who is a great goddess, can achieve immortality for a man.

It is at this point, after her failure to make the boy immortal, that Demeter becomes petulant and says that she will stop the seasons and all growth and that all the crops will die. She now links all this to retrieving her daughter. In effect, Demeter says to Zeus, Your story is that women cannot make men immortal—you have just foiled my attempt with the infant in the fire—but my story is that you have to have women to achieve immortality. If you don't bring back the daughter, everything that you hope for, all your crops and all your plans for earthly power, will fail. This is a head-on contest between two different ways to explain how the world works. Demeter's is the only story in all of ancient Greek mythology in which another Olympian god openly disobeys Zeus.[4] Two mighty paradigms are head to head. The old religion with women at the center had probably been relayed down through generations of farmers who associated the fertility of women and that of grain, just as the Therans had graphically painted wheat sheaves on their nippled pots. Scholars are generally of the opinion that the origins of this story most certainly date back to Mycenae and probably before.

Demeter dries up the earth, and even Zeus worries. Eventually, the king of the patriarchs, cowed and making a concession that must have been terribly embarrassing, relents and allows the daughter, the *kore*, to leave her married husband long enough to come back and see her mother. This is a political compromise among those gods who order the cosmos. Demeter then also relents and lets the crops grow again, and the *kore* only has to stay with her husband a short part of each year.

The whole episode seems like a child's tale or a fairy story, but it was far more than entertainment.

Without daughters, the idea of immortality or the continuation of the village was (and is) impossible. Men are more expendable. They can come and go like Jason and his crew, or like bees to the flower, and sometimes they sow their seed and sometimes they do not, but if there are not an ample number of daughters, it would be like having no earth for the planting and the seeds would be useless. Just as important, because it takes women nine months to do their part and it does not take men that long, it is clear that numerically speaking the world needs many more daughters than sons to keep the family or the village going. Any population could lose all but one son and a generation would still be able to reproduce. But lose all but one breeding woman—who can literally reproduce roughly only once every year or so—and the village will soon die. It is an elementary matter to see that, although both are essential, it takes fewer men to keep a village going than it takes women, and so daughters would have been—in the old days when they put women in places of honor on the walls in Crete and Thera—far more critical than sons.

That is why although the Demeter story seems to be about seasons, it is an equally compelling story about daughters and immortality. It is a very old story, indeed, and its origins reach to back before the Olympians were firmly in power. It is consistent with the physical record, because before the Mycenaeans, in the remnants of the Cretan civilization, the archaeological evidence points to women and daughters in a continuing spiral through time.

In Greece the planting of grain occurs in the fall; the long, cold winter months are times of rain and growth; and the grain harvest is in June.[5] However, the celebrations of the Mysteries of Eleusis, which were based entirely upon the story of Demeter and Persephone, were held in the fall. It was the fall that ended the long drying heat of summer. It was also fall when Persephone was allowed by Zeus to come back from Hades to her mother. The great fall mystery celebration at Eleusis is therefore a celebration not of harvest, which was in June, but of planting. It is a celebration not of marriage, which took place in spring, but of the return of the daughter, which, as we have seen, is the principle of the continuation of life.

The story seems to represent a forced merger between old and new explanations of how life works. It did not unequivocally celebrate marriage, and yet marriage (like that of Persephone to Hades) is the bedrock of patriarchy. It is not possible to have a patrilineal line through women who act like temple priestesses or freely sexual women, like the Lemnians or Circe and Calypso, who might have sons from different fathers. The way to insure that this adulteration of the line does not occur is to restrain women in marriage and to label any other kind of sex as adultery, precisely because unaccounted-for sons will adulterate the patrilineal line. The mystery celebrations of Eleusis, therefore, were an uneasy balance between two worlds. They acknowledged the submission of the daughter to the patriarch (Hades), but in the secret dark of night, at the climax of celebration, they honored her escape to her mother, her breakaway and, in effect, her rebirth. This was the return that was celebrated below the eyes of kings for thirteen hundred years.

Daughters Die for Civic Good

At about the same time as these two contrary world views were moving into transition, Agamemnon, the great king of Mycenae, was about to go off to lead the fight in the Trojan War. As we recall, Agamemnon gathered together all his men and all the ships from hundreds of allies and they all got on board and waited for the wind to blow. This was about 1225 BCE. They were headed off to win the fight against adultery and for marriage, the bedrock of patriarchy. Helen of Sparta had run off with another man, not her husband, and settled in Troy in an alliance of passion. She had violated the principle of marriage, had made her own choice and gone for a man younger and far better looking than her husband. She was living out the freedom that Zeus would deny to Persephone, and the story of the Trojan War is the story of how marriage will be enforced against women who pursue their own sexuality.

Agamemnon was one of the first patriarchs, and Menelaos (Helen's husband) was his brother. So Agamemnon rose to the cause to get Helen back, and they all boarded ship and waited for the wind to blow, which it did not do. This was bad for marriage in particular and for patriarchy in general. Thousands of assembled warriors were pacing up and down the ships' decks. The oracle of Apollo was thereupon consulted, and the voice of prophecy commanded that Agamemnon sacrifice his own daughter. Agamemnon's wife, Clytemnestra, was outraged. His daughter, Iphigenia, was shocked, but she dressed in clean white linen and went to the stone, where her father slit her throat with a knife. The wind started to blow, and Agamemnon went off to defend marriage.

The marriage side eventually won the Trojan War. The practical application of this new treatment of daughters became immediately apparent. There were other cities that saw how useful it was to kill young virgins. In effect they were changing the virtue of fruitful daughters from offering the promise of immortality to becoming the source of civic pride, or, rather than being fruitful or bearing children, the model became young virgins who would die for their fathers.

Another story has it that the first king of Athens was losing a war against the neighboring city of Eleusis. The two cities were only about twelve miles distant, and there was no great overarching empire to keep everyone in line. It was probably after the decline of Mycenae, after 1200 BCE, when the whole civilized world started falling apart. Athens would one day be a very great city in Western history, but this was at the very beginning. Eleusis had a good natural harbor and wide agricultural lands, and nobody knew whether Eleusis would be the more important or whether it would be Athens. The king of Athens, Erechtheus, was a principled man and did what the oracle told him to do, which unfortunately was the same instruction that it had given to Agamemnon. To win the war and save his city, the king was required to sacrifice his youngest daughter, Otionia. The Athenians later told everyone that Otionia was quite willing; that is somewhat hard to believe. But they said that not only was the young girl willing, her mother was very willing too, and that she said, Well, men go off to die for the city; why should a mother not give her daughter to save us all? It was a noble sentiment and well remembered by the Athenians for a long time after. Otionia did not die alone. Her two older sisters joined her, setting a new standard of civic duty by offering themselves as well. All three of them died.

Altogether, by this time in these Greek stories, the problem of daughters was being solved in a whole new way. The abstract principle was represented by gods: Demeter would give her daughter to Hades to live in the dark, dank underworld for part of the year—that is, the principle of immortal life would be annually cancelled by the principle of inescapable death. The model for moral or virtuous women would also be changed. Women were to stay virgin until married or to become heroines by dying for the public causes of their fathers.

It seems natural that there may have been some resistance to these roles, especially in the early years as the new civilization was emerging from the Dark Age. Women on the frescoes of Crete and Santorini are not in any way being sacrificed. They are usually at the center, beautifully dressed, and looking as if someone might sacrifice to them. They do not set a civic standard by offering themselves to get a fair wind for some warship. The most likely possibility is that in the older, more agrarian centers of life—in the hills where the wine and wheat were grown or in the islands—both men and women would have expected to celebrate the harvest and hold on for much longer to some of the old dependence upon the women-centered religion. They may even have had a cult of the daughter, Persephone, long before or at least parallel to the cult of Demeter. These country people would be apt to give

thanks to the spirit of the seasons, to the regularity of the return, to the fertility of the soil, and to the presence of as many daughters as possible.

Many of the stories that they told are of what is called a Sacred Marriage, a *heirous gamos*, meaning the special time when a queen or a priestess took a young lover as a consort, seemingly for the purpose of making her pregnant, as if the pregnancy itself were sacred, and the sexual union would itself have been sacred too. If those stories of the sacred union—and there are many repetitions—reflect anything like reality, then they also reflect a wholly different view of the role of women in the years preceding the Greeks. Such women would have been slow, no doubt, to give all this importance up. Perhaps they liked the sexual freedom; perhaps they liked the power; perhaps they liked the honor; perhaps they liked the dancing at the harvest; perhaps they liked standing on the reviewing stand like the women on the frescoes in Thera, being important when the fleet came in. Or perhaps they felt whole, in tune with nature, in their old roles. In all the scenes in which we find them, on Cretan seals or on the walls of Thera or in the dancing figurines, they seem to be full of life and expectation. Surely these women would have come to the Greek idea of civic duty very slowly and with heavy hearts.

There is more than one story explaining the glory of young women being sacrificed, more than one story of the new style of citizenship, more than one exhortation, and the reason for all these repetitions is probably that considerable retraining was required. We don't know how bad it was. If it was like the retraining by the Communists in China and Cambodia in the latter half of the twentieth century, it might have caught up an untold number of lives of villagers, dissenters, thinkers (the slower ones and the faster ones), the extremes, and the creative leaders of their societies. To their service, in the Dark Age the propagandists would have used the stories: "Remember Iphigenia" or "Remember Otionia." There was even a daughter of Heracles, Macaria, whose sacrifice the storytellers used for the public cause.

One of the most tragic stories changing the role of daughters is that of young Polyxena, a beautiful princess of Troy. She was not killed in the collapse of her city; she was killed afterward, ritually. She was sacrificed to honor the warrior Achilles, who had died in that great battle. It was not enough for Zeus that a grand warrior die and be remembered forever in the hall of heroes. A young virgin princess had to die in compensation for his tragic loss. So Polyxena joins Iphigenia and the daughters of Erechtheus on the clay pots and in the stories and in the plays of Euripides. All this was probably necessary to overcome the prejudice of country folk in favor of daughters, and just from the number of repetitions of the theme, anyone can see that the people were not all that easy to persuade.

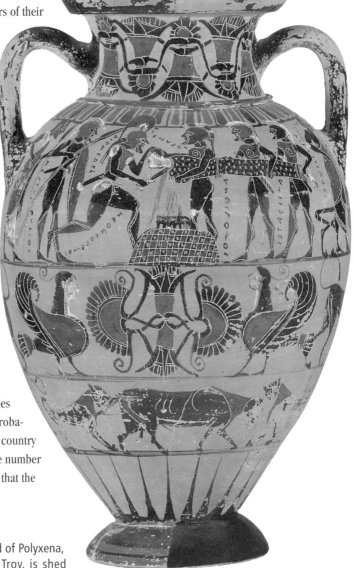

Fig. 49. The blood of Polyxena, princess of Troy, is shed over the grave of the hero Achilles, a signal of the triumph of the masculine over the feminine and, even though they may die, the warrior over the old line of mothers.

Some modern scholars have worried that the Cretans may have sacrificed a boy in the moments when the Minoan temple at Knossos was collapsing, hoping to ward off the last and final earthquake that destroyed that civilization. These scholars get upset when other scholars such as Marija Gimbutas or Riane Eisler, in the face of such evidence, try to make Crete look more benign. There is hard archaeological evidence that a young boy was actually sacrificed just as the walls of Knossos and the cities were all coming down. It is very troubling behavior, and scholars are right to view it with alarm. There is no evidence, however, that the Cretans used human sacrifice—either boys or girls—as a standard of good citizenship. They did not celebrate the event on pots and vases. They did not paint it on their walls or on their burial chambers or on their brightly painted burial boxes. They did not leave evidence seeming to balance the enormity of the deed with the needs of the state. And they did not emphasize the deaths of women in order to soften troubles in the affairs of men.

They did not have to, perhaps because there is nothing in the Cretan materials that suggests that they were overcoming some opposition, some contrary view, some previous religion. The Cretans do not seem to have been a people under attack or in transition.

The Greeks, on the other hand, had to deal with the old prevailing roles of women, which had existed before them and which—if the evidence on the pots, on the walls, and in the stories is any indicator—were roles that simply could not be accommodated in a patriarchy. The Greeks had to wean a whole civilization in the eastern Mediterranean that was still living on islands like those of Calypso and Circe and the Lemnians. They had to create something like a propaganda machine for a role reversal, bringing men up to claim and honor their sons, persuading women after the model of Demeter to give up their connections to their daughters. They had to create morality stories featuring Jason and Odysseus, whose journeys were entirely about establishing sons in their property rather than daughters in their fertility. On the other hand they had to take women once known as beautiful, such as Scylla and Medea, Circe and Calypso, Selene and Semele, and change them to fit new purposes other than immortality or other than love, healing, or weaving. They had to make them into seducers or monsters, or they had to marry them to men who would be certain of, and could claim, their issue. And that, at the dawn of Western civilization, is how the problem of daughters was resolved.

A Multitude of Myths to Tame, Punish, and Disparage Women

In the confusion of the Dark Age, some say that Erechtheus was not the first king of Athens but that a certain man named Cecrops was. Others say that it was the other way around, that Cecrops was the son of Erectheus. Storytellers who passed on the legend probably had some clan purpose or personal loyalty that made them suggest that one or the other was the first king. Claims of descent from kings or gods were used to justify claims to territory. Thus, some said that Heracles came from the area near Mycenae, but the people of Athens said that Heracles was one of theirs. Other towns claimed Heracles as theirs too, and the reason was that all were trying to prove justification to take over, say, Thebes or Mycenae or Athens, or to take property from one of those places and give it to Corinth or to Thessaly or some other place. This is also the reason for putting Heracles on the boat with Jason to go after the golden fleece. Different clans were apt to claim that at the beginning, when Heracles was there and when the first kings took over, their own first clansman was standing alongside. The presence of Heracles signaled the beginning of (Greek) time, and if the clan's own man was there, that meant that their clan had been at the very head of the line. Which is why Jason wanted Heracles on his boat. More accurately, that is why the descendants *claimed* that Heracles was on that boat. If Heracles was there and all those other great heroes of the early patriarchy—such as the Dioscuri from Sparta—were there too, then Jason was in company with a son of Zeus and his claim to the golden fleece would have been a

good one. That is similar to the way title claims are established today. People claim that their ancestors were first in Zion or Armenia or New Mexico and that therefore their descendants have a better claim than the descendants of people who came second. Some Athenians therefore claimed that Erechtheus was the first king of Athens and others claimed that Cecrops was the first king, and the fight was probably between cousins or nephews who were in one family line or the other.

Cecrops was important for a second reason. According to legend he was the king who recognized patrimony and instituted monogamy for women in Athens.[1] Female monogamy would have had to be established in order to determine who should be second in line, or there could be no patriarchy. This Athenian preoccupation with inheritance was the same concern that Telemachus had in *The Odyssey*. If Penelope were not to stay married to Odysseus, then it would be very hard for Telemachus to claim the pigs and goats. Similarly, if his wife was monogamous, then Erechtheus could be sure that Cecrops was his son and give Athens to him. Thus when Cecrops established female monogamy, he was insisting upon the absolutely essential rule that would make him the second king. Patriarchy cannot exist without female monogamy and thus, essentially, Cecrops was known for establishing patriarchy in Athens.

Before female monogamy, property would have been communally owned or else passed down through the mothers, because mothers had the advantage of

always knowing whose children were theirs. Matrilineal descent may still be questioned by some scholars, but it is not at all unusual, historically. It seems to have been the rule among British tribes until the coming of Christianity. The Picts inherited all property, even kingdoms, through the female line.[2] Both Hopi and Navajo tribes in the American Southwest still follow matrilineal rules. An 1894 letter from Hopi clan leaders vividly illustrates what society might have been like in Athens before Cecrops. These same conditions could be imagined among the Minoans, and it seems likely that such conditions were at one time very widespread or perhaps even the antecedents to those matrilineal traditions later traced through to Britain. Said the Hopis:

> The family, the dwelling house, and the field are inseparable, because the woman is the heart of these, and they rest with her. Among us the family traces its kin to the mother, hence all its possession are hers. The man builds the house but the woman is the owner, because she repairs and preserves it; the man cultivates the field, but he renders its harvest into the woman's keeping.[3]

Hopi and Navajo customs demonstrate that patrilineal descent is not part of the human genetic code, which means, in turn, that any suggestion about patriarchy in prehistory must be established by fact, not by assumption. It adds something too that Cecrops the king was legendary precisely for having established female monogamy for Athens. The institution of this rule would not have been necessary if patriarchy had existed all along, because patriarchy simply cannot exist without female monogamy. If patriarchy had been the rule in prehistory, female monogamy therefore would have been established long before Cecrops. On the other hand female monogamy is to patriarchal marriage what a cornerstone is to a temple. There is a corroborating story that Athena became patroness of Athens only after she promised that Athenian boys would stop taking their mothers' names.[4] Thus there are at least two legends that patriliny was new to Athens and that there was a contest about it.

For the Greeks marriage and female suppression went hand in hand. They used the same word for taming a horse as to tame a woman by marrying her.

> A Greek word for "wife," *damar*, apparently meant the "tamed, domesticated one." ... The verb "to tame" ... [was] used of animals, young women, and conquered people.[5]

Livestock, heifers, goats, and horses were tamed, and so were women. One verb served for them all. The wedding of a woman was thus a suppression, a harnessing, a containment. Patriarchs needed to find a way to keep women tamed in the marriage corral, which was meant to keep them from breeding outside the family line. If men did not do that, they could not maintain control of their property.

The overarching purpose of these foundation stories is therefore to establish a property line. Whether it is a clan claiming to descend from the sons of Heracles, the so-called Heraclidai, or another clan claiming to be the sons of Apollo or Zeus or Poseidon, these were important to establish claims to territory. When the dispute was between sons of kings, it was about kingship. When it was between sons of lesser citizens, it was still about patrilineal descent. The fame of Cecrops comes from his rule of monogamy, because at the beginning of Athenian history it had become essential to maintain patrilineal descent.

The nearby city of Thebes provides another illustration of the late–Bronze Age struggle to establish the male line. Thebes had been founded by a man named Cadmus who, legends say, came by sea and may therefore fit the description of those invaders who migrated into Greece sometime after 1600 BCE. Cadmus was said to have come from Phoenicia and brought with him the alphabet. To later generations he was of supreme importance for that reason. For early storytellers, however, it was of greater moment that Cadmus had been required to kill a dragon in order to establish his right to take over Thebes. At that early time dragon slaying was of greater import than the alphabet. Dragon slaying was a common symbolic beginning for those who came as patriarchs to introduce a new religion that would replace the earth religions. Interestingly, at the end of the Cadmus story he and his wife turned into snakes themselves and slid off to lead quiet lives. This may be because invaders have often, throughout history, intermarried and settled down among the people whom they have conquered, adopting many of the local customs. It appears that Cadmus did the same. This was still the Dark Age, and these were the stories that men told to explain how things had happened at the beginning and which, in turn, they told in order to advance themselves politically or militarily.

Dragons and serpents were probably vestigial symbols, carryovers from an earlier age when the women in Crete and perhaps Thebes had serpents coiled around their heads and when they even thought of serpents as friendly. At the start of this whole religious epoch, Apollo is reported to have had a fight with Python and Python's oracular mate, the Pythia, at the shrine at Delphi, which archaeology now tells us was a holy site for Minoans. Both Pythia and Python were snakes who were said to be children of Mother Earth, and it is said that Apollo overcame them and took control of the oracle himself. So snakes and dragons and the Python were common foes of the patriarchs. Sometimes in these stories the early heroes of patriarchy fight the Python, and sometimes they fight Medusa (who is a Gorgon, a woman with snakes in her hair), and sometimes a they fight a Hydra (a many-headed snake), and sometimes the storytellers just say that all the monsters of the worst kind were born of the original snake woman, Echidna.

Snake names were obviously common code in widespread use and were convenient for oral performers who wanted to convey a well-understood meaning. The storyteller could say "Pythia" and his audience would not have to be told the place (Delphi) or the religious affiliation (earth mother). During the Dark Age such connections would have been common lore throughout the land. Unfortunately, the reverse is true for modern audiences. The reader today is completely removed from the particular history, the clans, and the religious struggles that gave rise to these codes. But it is important to recognize the obvious utility of such codes in a time of illiteracy. Snakes and the dragons may confuse readers today, but they were certainly not meant to confuse listeners then. Dragons are therefore of great utility for a storyteller and would be more persuasive than abstract concepts such as "earth mother." Dragons are quite obviously not friendly and just as obviously do not actually exist. It is likely that they were conceived to symbolize women's cultures—or cultures in which women were more prominent than they were in the cultures of the invaders.

Fig. 50. A Gorgon coin from Chios. Numismatic Museum, Athens.

Dragons were commonly waiting in caves, from which the heroes of Greece would be forced to dislodge them. It is likely, therefore, that dragons symbolized some danger embedded in the land or some people who were close to the ground, at one with the earth, before the Olympians. Dragons were larger-than-life snakes, distorted snakes, perhaps meant to symbolize an earlier larger-than-life people, like the Giants or the Cyclopes or perhaps the famous and therefore larger-than-life Minoans who had honored snakes. Such associations would bring to mind the famous so-called "snake goddesses" in the Cretan figurines. The pre-Olympian, prepatriarchal, residents of Thebes and Athens would have shared these beliefs; very likely they were people who followed the fertility religions and very likely they were overcome by invaders such as Heracles, who subdued them all

one by one. Then in order to get in line to lay hold to these territories, the survivors claimed in the years that followed that they were themselves descended from Heracles.

It is said that Heracles killed a Nemean lion, and Nemea is the well-known name of an old village near to Mycenae. Then he killed a Lernean Hydra, and Lerna is another village not far from Mycenae and Nemea. The Hydra was hard to kill and grew seven heads for every one that Heracles cut off. Robert Graves, the scholar who wrote extensively about all these myths in the last century, thought that the seven-headed Hydra was a symbol for rebellion and that every time the early invaders conquered one village like Lerna, there would be seven more villages in revolt, like Nemea. In the end invaders who settled down then claimed that they had gotten their titles through Heracles, who had won these great victories. They said that Heracles finally subdued all the Hydra heads by burning them with a hot stake. This may mean that he burned all these villages to the ground, which is consistent with the historic remains in the area. Archaeological digs give proof of a dozen cities that were destroyed by fire at just this time, about 1200 BCE. It is therefore probably no accident that Heracles was said to have finished off the Hydra with fire. He is also said to have stolen a Cretan bull, which would have been an open insult to the ancient traditions of that Minoan stronghold. He killed a wild bird (Stymphalian), also demeaning Cretan art, which focuses so much on birds. He killed a boar (Erymanthian), a likely fertility symbol in the tradition of agrarian peoples. He stole the girdle (chastity belt) of the Amazon queen, meaning he probably forced the queen to his own sexual will or to give up her sexual independence. He descended to the underworld, demeaning the tradition of death and rebirth. In all these ways Heracles signals the triumph of Olympian patriarchs over a preexisting village life in which people were not only weaker, but in which they honored the ground, cycles, fertility, and even death. If these are thought of as characteristics of the so-called goddess religions, Heracles eliminated them all.

The millennium after the terrible fires and the documented destruction of 1200 BCE were strikingly more tumultuous than the thousand years before. During this period Mycenae made war against Thebes, and then Thebes made war against the city of Gla, and Gla made war against the city of Ochlos, and these all were right next door to Thessaly, where Jason was having trouble with his Uncle Pelias, who would not allow him to claim his patrimony. All in all, there were between seven and eight hundred years of chaos, war, and turmoil, which the storytellers were trying to account for with symbols such as Heracles and his conquest of the Hydra or the Giants, or Jason and his capture of the golden fleece. The stories that moderns call "myths" were apparently made up to give this period some genealogical organization, to explain who came from whom and who was first and who had priority claims to what ground.

This is the storied history that first framed the Western mind and continues to frame that mind even today. Not since that time has there been such a tectonic shift in values, in the placement of women, in the measure of time, in the respect for sexuality. The context was not just political chaos. There was a struggle for power between the gods—that is, among religions. As Greece emerged from the Dark Age, Olympians were shown on all kinds of pots and vases

as fighting the Titans and Giants and Cyclopes. Titans were gods who either birthed the snake figures or protected women (or Mother Earth, depending upon the story). In the beginning, therefore, Greeks saw this as a struggle about earth values and at least the role and status of women in cults that honored those values.

According to legends known to every Greek, there was a famous civilization-beginning battle called the Gigantomachy, or the war against the Giants. Zeus and Athena needed help in this battle from a mortal, the founding warrior of Greece, Heracles. Together, gods and founding hero were said to have vanquished the Giants, who were in turn the children of Rhea, who was in turn the daughter of Mother Earth. The Giants are seen on pots and vases of the sixth century carrying shields shaped like the new moon or shields with snakes on them, clear indications of their identification with Mother Earth and the society of women. On the other hand Zeus, in all his representations, symbolizes a force more erratic, more harsh, more thunderous. He is the descendant of Cronos, who castrated Uranus the Titan. Castration signaled a change not only of religious leaders but also of sexual rules. To castrate the god who consorted with Mother Earth, who had bred children on her without number, was to end the custom of men cavorting with temple priestesses or women who might have had many partners. It was to castrate, and therefore bring to an end, the potency of any male who had bent his knee to women's civilization. Zeus and Heracles were the direct successors of the line that did the castration.

Values were in conflict at every level. That is, not just among the gods, but also among mortals. It was said that early on during this transition, Niobe,

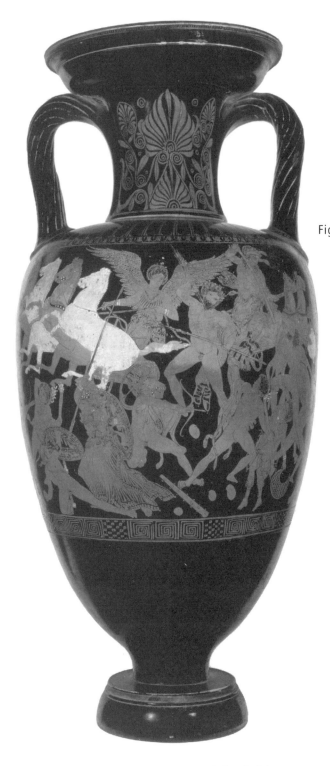

Fig. 51. Zeus and Athena war against the Giants, sons of Mother Earth. These early opponents of the Olympian order carried new-moon shields representing female-centered cultures and were, according to the Greeks themselves, overcome by force, not by natural evolution of culture, as later scholars would have it. PERMISSION OF REUNION DES MUSÉES NATINOAUX/ART RESOURCE, NEW YORK

the queen of Thebes, was inordinately proud of her seven children. She was so fruitful that her success as a mother angered the Olympian goddess Artemis, who was a virgin. Niobe's children were thereupon disposed of by Artemis and her brother Apollo, and the mother's consequent grief was so great that she turned into a rock. The new gods had punished a woman who was fruitful and fulfilled the promise of fertility. Such stories had to have been created by a propagandist of the new order for a purpose that suited that order.

Another young woman, Arachne, was turned into a spider by Athena because she was independent and a very good weaver, so good a weaver that everyone for miles around thought she was the best there ever was. Ever since Penelope in *The Odyssey,* women had been famous as weavers, and Arachne was the best of them. Athena was the goddess of weaving and did not welcome the competition, so she turned Arachne into a spider. This could be a tale of how the first spider came to be or of the origin of spiders. But there are no tales of the first ant or the first cow, and there is no equivalent of Aesop in the ancient Greek legends. More likely, the Arachne tale is another explanation of how authority was being transferred from ordinary women to the gods, how the things women did that they considered fine were not to be considered the result of their own labors so much as gifts from gods who might or might not be dependable. Responsibility for creativity, and credit for it, were being taken over by forces beyond the control of mortals. Quality would come from the gods, not from women, not from the hands of mortals who thought they might rival such gods. These stories are evidence of a prolonged civil argument. They are also signs of a consolidating male power structure.

Some might argue that all these stories are simply a profound warning against hubris. Men should not want to be like gods, because they are not and cannot ever be that grand. These stories are certainly that: they *are* a warning against hubris. But they are also a warning against challenge to all that is symbolized by Mount Olympus and the new gods. Uranus, the earliest of those to be displaced, was not guilty of hubris. He simply did not like the idea of being deposed by his son. The son thereupon castrated him and made sure that the old man had no more families of any kind—that is, made sure that his line came to an awful and final end. Uranus was removed from the chain of title, plain and simple.

Nor was Niobe irrationally proud. Her achievement was to bear children. It would be strange to label this emotion as hubris. Valuing children is honoring life's continuance, the promise of immortality.[6] The subordination and killing of Niobe by Artemis might therefore conceivably be about pride but seems more likely to have been about subordinating her domestic, childbearing values in order that women's roles as a whole would be subordinated and controlled. It was a time of political chaos. Greece was embroiled in a struggle. That the gods were said to be involved makes it clear that it was not only political, but also religious, chaos. That women who bore too many children were involved with the gods and that the Titan god was castrated shows this change in religion was at least about sexuality and reproduction. Heracles' exploits show that it was also about replacing old symbols such as the birds and the Cretan bull, the snake and the boar. Stealing the apple of immortality makes clear that it was also about time and rebirth.

It would be necessary to work a profound change in female sexual conduct in order to cement patriarchal property. One story after the next therefore has to do with men such as Cecrops who set up the rules to make fatherhood certain. Monogamous marriage for women would be the necessary foundation. In the event, marriage had become an institution of suppression. Athena, the goddess who gave up the right of men to bear their mothers' names, thereby confirmed the consolidation of patriarchal power. It should not be a surprise for us to see her enforcing her father's, Zeus's, rules. In civil war, loyalties and symbols are the stuff of propaganda and manipulation. She had become the wise woman who approves of war and does her father's bidding. She would remain herself virgin, subordinate, helpful to war heroes, and the shining example for all Greeks of the tamed woman.

Oedipus, the Lost Son

King Oedipus, the ill-fated ruler of Thebes, tragically killed his father and married his mother and died a stricken man, blinded by his fate. From Sophocles to Sigmund Freud, interpreters have tried to understand. How could fate be so cruel? How could a basically decent man get caught in such a nefarious web?

The story is set before the Trojan War, before 1225 BCE. It was formulated by the bards during the Dark Age, which thereafter is the time during which patriarchy was being permanently established. Laius, the king of Thebes, is told by the Oracle at Delphi that his wife will birth a son who will kill him. Perhaps this father-killing idea was an accurate reflection of the tradition about which Mary Renault wrote so beautifully in *The King Must Die*. Legend had it that every year—or some said every seven years—an old king would be sacrificed and replaced by a new man who would be king for seven years and then himself be sacrificed. In towns all over Bronze Age Greece, celebrants were said to kill the king annually and plow his blood into the soil in order to make the crops grow. The death of kings was therefore holy and sacred and designed to aid the community, but in the long run this is the sort of custom that kings don't like. Robert Graves speculated that kings must have, after a time, objected, and Renault wrote a gripping story about how the tradition was changing in the later years of the women's era. She imagined the young Theseus becoming king of Athens and destroying the old tradition. More correctly, *almost* destroying the tradition, because in the end Theseus became king only after his father died because of Theseus's recklessness. In that sense Theseus was another case of a son causing the death of his father and replacing him. Father-son relationships were on everyone's mind when the Oedipus story first emerged.

A discussion of the rise of patriarchy cannot afford to ignore Oedipus. It is now no longer necessary to show that the first women were dangerous or that marriage is critical to retain property or that daughters are less critical. All those have been established by the stories of Jason, Odysseus, and Persephone. This tale now takes us beyond that bedrock to the consequences of losing track of sons. It begins just as the Jason story did: both these infants were left out on hillsides to die.

Laius, the king of Thebes, had been told by the Oracle at Delphi that if he had a son, the boy would kill him. When the child was born, the king therefore took the babe out of the house and left him on a hillside. A Corinthian shepherd found the lad and took him home to his own king, who took the infant in and in due time made him a prince of Corinth. The child went from prince to wastrel to prince. The losing and finding of foundlings is repeated so often in the first millennium BCE that its occurrence is like a formula, like the rosy-fingered dawn or the wine-dark sea or even the apple. While the apple was code for sexuality and immortality, foundlings were code for patriarchs in trouble, almost always having to do with the claim of a son to his throne.

In the Oedipus story there are two kings and

one prince who thinks he belongs to the kingdom he actually does *not* belong to and thinks he does not belong to the kingdom to which he actually *does* belong. All is well for a short while as Oedipus grows up in Corinth with the blessing of the Corinthian king, whom he thinks to be his real father. Oedipus thinks he is Corinthian, when in fact he is from Thebes. One day, however, the young prince is traveling along the road from Delphi when he accidentally meets the king of Thebes, who is on his way to that same Oracle. It is the Oracle that had earlier told Laius that he would be killed by his son. Laius thinks that that problem had been solved, so he now is on his way to the Oracle to see what to do about a certain evil Sphinx who is terrorizing Thebes. King Laius is in his chariot and, spying the young upstart from Corinth, orders him to get out of the road, to make way for his betters. In the age of heroes this is a personal as well as a governmental insult, and Oedipus resists. They fight, and Oedipus entangles his father in the reigns of the chariot, which he then drives down the road, killing the king. The Oracle has been fulfilled, though neither father nor son knows it.

Not knowing the gravity of his crime, Oedipus then wanders on to Thebes, where he confronts the Sphinx who has been terrorizing that city. A Sphinx is always female. However, she has a lion's body and a snake's tail, which are probably political symbols or symbols of some village or even symbols from Crete. It is a magnificent symbol in some respects, a proud woman with a lion's body and a snake's tail, always sitting on her haunches regally, as if she were somebody, as if the place that was under her protection could be most proud, maybe even arrogant. The Sphinx is more arrogant than the griffins of Crete,

which are often kneeling to women or pulling a chariot or even in one case suckling at the breast of a woman. But there is something in the combination of the women and the animals that is familiar for those who know the Minoan symbols. It could be that the Sphinx is a later variation of feminine symbols and might have been associated with Mycenae, which had a history of wars with Thebes and which showed itself as under the protection of the lion at the famous lion gate. Perhaps the Sphinx meant to all the listeners sitting around the fire in, say, 1000 BCE, that Thebes was still under the dominance of Mycenae, which was again under the dominance of the lion-woman culture or some culture where a woman was gifted with the power of a lion and the earth connection of a snake.

Fig. 52. The Sphinx with her woman's head, lion's body, and snake's tail must have been intended to combine images from some known culture, such as the gods or goddesses or icons of certain villages taken over by Greeks such as Cadmus or King Laius in Thebes. This one is on display at the museum in Corinth.

Whoever this Sphinx woman was, by the time young Oedipus arrives, she is still sitting at the gates of Thebes. Women, to the chagrin of the patriarchs, must have still been powerful in this city, maybe even as rulers or at least as priestesses. Priestesses of Hera had been important at Mycenae before the Olympians squeezed the reigning goddess out of there, and maybe the women of Thebes were akin to them or to some unknown fertility goddess represented by the dragon that Cadmus slew when he founded the town. Men such as Heracles and Cadmus were restless under these feminine figures, and at the time of this story men such as Oedipus who came to Thebes to help get patriarchy established were being devoured by the Sphinx.

In this case, however, her method is most unwarriorlike. The Sphinx puts to Oedipus a question that he must answer correctly. If he does not, he will be eaten alive. It is a curiously unmartial test. The Sirens, whom we recall bedeviled Odysseus by singing to him, filled a man with the promise of knowledge, the hope for it, the yearning for it. Here the Sphinx sits back and does not offer knowledge but instead tests knowledge. For patriarchs this is a riddle itself. In one case a woman will offer knowledge to a man if he just comes closer; in the other a woman will hold a man back with a cold and arrogant gaze and test him to see if he has knowledge already. If he comes to the Sirens' false song, it will kill him, and if he doesn't penetrate the Sphinx's distant glare, she will knock him down. There were other similar stories. The snake woman (Gorgon), Medusa, would turn a man to stone just by looking him in the eye. Scylla or Echidna, the mother of all monsters, would eat a man raw. Now, the Sphinx—haughty, aloof, and beautiful—will put to a

man a simple riddle. In this case she asks, "What being, with only one voice, has sometimes two feet, sometimes three, sometimes four, and is weakest when it has the most." Oedipus answers, "Man." He is right, because an infant crawls on all fours, a youth walks on two legs, and an old man uses a cane. For Oedipus to know what he is talking about is devastating, and the Sphinx of Thebes kills herself by leaping off a cliff. Whether or not a woman can control men with her knowledge or assume her superiority is for her, according to the Greeks, a matter of life and death.

It is not clear whether this story is intended to convey that the right answer for all mysterious questions is man the human or man the male. Most modern interpretations think unconsciously that this is about the growth of the human psyche and that therefore the answer was man the human. It is perhaps more likely in the second millennium BCE that the answer was man the male. The answer to the riddle of the Sphinx would therefore be "a male," which is the answer of the patriarchy to most questions. Given that truth, the Sphinx destroys herself. That is her end and the end to all that she stands for, whatever that might have been. The composite nature-worshipping culture of women, lions, and snakes is over. Oedipus has vanquished the old order with one word, with an idea of the value of the male. Oedipus is welcomed into Thebes as a hero and marries the queen, who happens to be his mother.

It is hard to imagine a worse or stronger condemnation of the easy sexuality of women of the ancient order than to say, first, that they do not even know who are their sons (King Laius), and, second, that they sleep around so much that they may even sleep with their sons (Queen Iocasta). No caricature of the days of free women's sexuality could be more awful than that of this story. Oedipus eventually finds out that his wife is also his mother and is so mortified that he puts his own eyes out and wanders blind throughout the plains of Boetia and Attica. For a long time no one pities him. He had played the game of the old women's religions, had married the queen, the kind of thing that can happen in the land of the priestesses and the Sphinx. Such a society brings confusion into the male line, incest, and blind exile for the offending, but essentially innocent, son. It is reported that eventually the Furies tore poor old blind Oedipus apart. His therefore is the exemplar of the extreme danger in a culture in which the role of marriage is unclear, the boundaries of marriage are not observed, and the order of sons is not known.

It is notable that the old goddess Hera, who before the Olympians had an incarnation as a seasonal goddess, set the Sphinx to control Thebes and set the riddle to which the answer was "man," or "a male." The myths say that Hera was forever furious, for one reason or another, with Zeus, her husband, and apparently had different intentions for Thebes than did Oedipus, who got caught up in this mess about who was his father. The reason that Hera appears in this story is probably to show that the whole danger is caused by those who remain allegiant to the seasonal, or fertility, goddess, who are also the ones who value female sexuality. Fertility goddesses, or women who have many partners in search of fertility, breed sons who don't know their fathers. Sons who don't know their fathers are apt to end up killing them.

This famous story has often been transmogrified, with the help of Sigmund Freud, into a tale about mothers and mystery and fate and blindness. This is vaguely plausible, but it served the nineteenth century of the modern age more than it served the eighth century BCE of Greece or more than it served the chaotic political struggles into which the tale was born. It is very modern to argue that "fate" was the issue when the public context for Sophocles (even by the fifth century) was not blind fate at all. The issue of the times was the consolidation of an Athenian empire, and this presented a contest between real men who were not at all victims of fate but, to the contrary, were attempting to seize their fates, take control. Pericles' famous funeral oration praises the men of Athens for being creative, enthusiastic, and innovative in times of trouble. They are not automatons like the men of some other states, says Pericles in 432 BCE. This is the same context that had created legal systems insuring female virginity and male control of property, a legal and property system that had been at issue for one thousand years, challenged by the Lemnians, the Trojans, the Amazons, the descendants of the goddess Rhea, the Titans, and probably for a time by the Spartans, a system that had been memorialized in such figures as Ariadne, Arachne, and even Antigone. Oedipus's blindness was a moral pronouncement, indeed, but couched in the battle to establish patriarchy far more than a battle with fate. Any Athenian playwright in those times would have to show that the gods adopted the Athenian point of view, and empire could not be justified without the gods' favor. But fundamentally this is a tale that explains why it is critical to be able to answer the foundation question, Who is the father?

The storytellers were at pains to show that poor Oedipus was quite innocent. His was not a fate that

was earned. He did not ever intend to kill his true father and certainly not to marry his mother. When he found out what he had done, he was so full of remorse that he wandered aimlessly around the countryside until he came to Athens, where he was taken in and pitied by Theseus. In the end, however, the moral is not that the gods set him up or that Athenians are forgiving. Rather it is that innocence is of no protection against women of the old order and that they will either sleep with you or tear you apart (as the Furies do at the end, in spite of Theseus's protection). The poor man is, after all, killed by angry women. This is the final ignominy in a long line of ignominies: he upset the male line; he slept with his mother and he got no forgiveness from the Furies. Not knowing one's father is not only bad for the father, it is bad for the son. The story does not dwell upon it, but Iocaste, the queen who married her son, throws herself over the walls to her death. Not knowing who is your son is bad for everybody.

In the scientific method the function of theory is to bring chaos out of disorder or to bring into some order previously disparate or seemingly disorganized facts. Theory is like a new lens that brings chaos into focus. When the lens of a patriarchy in search of its orthodoxy is applied to these Greek foundation stories, as if responding to theory, one after another they make sense. Achilles, the great warrior of the Trojan War, has only one weakness (his heel). After killing the Trojan hero, Hector, he himself is killed because this one heel is vulnerable and his assailant puts a spear there and finishes him off. How did he get this one vulnerable spot? His mother dipped him as a child into a magic potion of invulnerability. The potion worked, except for on that one place where she had

held him by the heel. Wherever a mother holds on to her son, he will be vulnerable. And that, too, is a message that serves patriarchy.

We could return to *The Odyssey* for a similar point. When Odysseus arrives home at last, he kills 102 suitors who have been courting his wife for all those years of his absence. He does not only kill malignant suitors; Homer describes some of them as quite moderate and honorable. They have not, any of them, committed crimes. They have simply been asking Penelope for her hand. Her husband has been gone for twenty years. Most everyone thinks that he is dead. Eligible men come to woo her. Some of them eat too much. Some of them tell lies. But these are not usually offenses warranting death, and Odysseus himself is guilty of telling many lies throughout the tale. Some of the suitors do not tell lies, and some of them are entirely honorable. None of them has slept with Penelope, who has remained faithful, and therefore none of them has committed adultery with her. Even if they had they would not have gone beyond the norm of the late Bronze Age. And yet, Odysseus kills them all with Athena's approval. He then finally, after killing them all, introduces himself to Penelope. They make love and the next day he kills some more neighbors who have not honored his estate. It is clear from Homer's emphasis that the issue here is to establish Odysseus's authority on his island and to preserve his property, which he would have lost had Penelope remarried. Odysseus too, therefore, is a transition figure, because it was still the woman through whom property flowed. It is against this principle that Odysseus's son, Telemachus, has been fighting, and his claim could only be protected if Odysseus came home soon enough. As it turns out, the hero got there just on the day before Penelope was to announce her intention to remarry, and so he saved the day. He killed them all with a great composite bow, the mark of the nomadic invaders about which the war historians write. It is plausible that Homer intended some connection between Odysseus and those old invading nomadic cultures or at least the equipment of their warriors. In that case Penelope, the island queen who controls the property, would have been a symbol of the older age that predated the nomads, and Odysseus would have been the symbol of the new patriarchs who came to enforce the new rules. Saying that it is possible does not make it true, of course, but when so much evidence points in the same direction, a reasonable person would have to wonder.

A final wrenching event in *The Odyssey* solidifies the new rules. It has been little noted in the twenty-eight hundred years during which men and women have lived by these rules, and it is a testament to Homer's craft that this final tragedy has been little remarked. After Odysseus kills all the suitors, he rounds up twelve serving maids who have been caring for his wife for all these years. They are twelve loyal servants, and Odysseus hangs them like a row of pigeons.

> so their heads were all in a line, and each had
>   her neck caught
> fast in a noose, so that their death would be
>   most pitiful.
> They struggled with their feet for a little, not for
>   very long.[1]

Odysseus murders these young women without question or pause in order to make them, as Homer calmly explains, "forget Aphrodite." Telemachus explains quietly, before he assists in hanging them,

> "they have showered abuse on the head of my
>   mother,
> and on my head too, and they have slept with
>   the suitors."[2]

The suitors did not sleep with Penelope, but they had slept with the serving girls, and they were therefore a symbol of sexual promiscuity. Both suitors and serving girls are killed with Zeus's and Athena's approval. These twelve, says Homer in complete explanation, had "taken to immorality."

The Odyssey, like so many of the other tales emerging out of the Dark Age, is a morality tale so repetitious in its themes as actually to become a lecture. It is the first writing of a patriarchy in search of its orthodoxy, and the consequence of the new orthodoxy is that respectable women must be either virgin or married.

A Glorious Monument Enshrining the Subordination of Women

The case is made in these pages that a great paradigm shift occurred in the early part of the first millennium after the fall of Troy and that the shift is reflected in myths, on pots, on vases, on drinking cups, and in tales of rape of some women and evasion of others. There is subordinate evidence in festivals such as the Thesmophoria, through which women were allowed to secret themselves in the mountains and dance and sing or parade about with clay models of male pudenda; or in the Apaturia, a festival held for men of Athens to celebrate the male line. The women's festivals were confined to secret occasions out of sight of the patriarchy, authorized as exceptions to the patriarchal norm. That is, by the time of classical Athens in the fifth century, women had been fully and completely taken off the public stage and their sexuality and ecstasy thoroughly driven from view. I have endeavored further to show how pots, myths, and festivals taken together mean more than pots or myths taken alone or, that is, that the evidence is culture-wide and that conclusions from this evidence are plausible because they are more than a single interpretation that "this picture on this pot means that" or "this myth means that." Rather, when myths, pots, celebrations, history, trade, natural disaster, war, and chaos are all combined, a picture emerges from the whole that may not reliably be deduced from any one element alone. The evidence is, overwhelmingly, that as sons became more treasured because of their ability to make war and to hoist sails on trading ships, as wealth became abundant and men decided

to keep it in their own hands for generations, as women most certainly objected to their systematic demotion, a virulent misogyny grew up to contain and corral the female threat to patrilineal descent. When pots, myths, festivals, and history are combined, the story is not benign or natural but is costly and forced. The final bit of demonstrative evidence in this case, further, is contained in the monuments, in the marble itself of the carvings at Olympia, Bacchae, Delphi, and Athens. The greatest of these was the Parthenon at Athens, built toward the end of the period of classical culture, just before the Athenian empire was destroyed (built no doubt in part to fend off that very result). Pericles of Athens sought to tell his people that their strength and power had come from their rule of women.

Male Olympian gods are sexually active. Zeus is off the charts, fathering children wherever his eye lands. Dionysus sets the standard for bacchanalia (orgies), Hermes is like a traveling salesman, and Poseidon is forever after sea nymphs. Ares sleeps with Aphrodite, Hades rapes Persephone, and Hephaestos makes a try for Athena. But of the six females on Mount Olympus, half (Athena, Artemis, and Hestia) are dedicated virgins, and Hera is cleansed every year to become a virgin again. That makes two thirds of the females on Olympus who intentionally do not reproduce, only one who enjoys sex (Aphrodite), and one who barely gets away with it in order to make the crops grow (Demeter). They all are carved in marble on the Parthenon, where they all celebrate the birth of

Athena and her dominance of the city that takes her name and her protection.

The Parthenon was built at the height of Athenian power and grandeur and is one of the great architectural achievements of humankind. It gleams white and awes the eye even today, despite being half in ruins. It was a temple to Athena, completed in 432 BCE, and its name means "virgin." It does not mean "wisdom" or "courage" or "strength." It advertises sexual restraint for a woman. It was built at a time when Athens and Sparta were already engaged in a military struggle that eventually would determine the fate of the city. Spartan women, often polyandrous (having more than one husband), were not held to standards of virginity like Athenian women were, and they played a different role in their society. Spartan women were also likely to have sexual partners before marriage. Marriage, in Sparta, was an afterthought. They did marriage, but casually. They had not made it a central feature of their social order, nor did they use the subordination of women as a marker of their military strength or as an explanation of their power. Spartans separated young men from women and kept the young men in military barracks, training them for fighting. They trained ad nauseam. But they also expected that the boys would sneak out from time to time to visit their sweethearts, and no one made much of a racket about that. Military leaders expected the boys back in the morning. The children who resulted from these alliances seem to have become part of the communal responsibility. They would be raised to be soldiers if they were boys, dedicated to the polis. Spartan strength might therefore have been said to rely more on the training and containment of men than on the containment of women. Sparta did not go

so far as to exalt women; it seems to have been rather more ambiguous: a little freedom sexually, a little freedom owning property. But the women were not, by the time of the fifth century, ever in control of the city. The goddess Hera had at one time been preeminent here, and she had a definite record as a nature goddess, a seasonal goddess. Helen of Troy of course came from Sparta, and some said that in earlier stories she was a moon goddess, a woman at the center of pre-Olympian religion. The Spartans therefore, all in all, participated in the patriarchy, were driven and controlled by men, but had not made a religion of the evils of female seduction. Misogyny did not have its deepest roots in Sparta.

In the middle of the fifth century BCE, there were growing clouds of impending war between Sparta and Athens. The choice, therefore, of symbols and myths that were put by Pericles on the Parthenon would explain to the people of Athens wherein lay their strength and whereupon they might rely in this struggle. The explanation is made in great detail. In case a visitor missed it on the pediments, he could see it on the metopes. In case he missed it on the metopes, he could see it on Athena's shield. In case he missed it on the shield, he could even see a variation on the inside, high up and hidden, on the frieze.

There were four wars carved above the columns on the outside of the Parthenon, on the metopes. All four feature myths, and in these myths are people or gods who were known universally by citizens of Athens as either believing in marriage or not believing in marriage. In one case, the Trojan War, the battle is in defense of the principle of marriage. That is on the north, facing the largest public space with the most room for observation and awe. On the other side, the south, equally long but with less space to step back and admire, was presented the war against certain unnatural men attempting to break up an actual marriage in progress. This was the war against the Centaurs, who had a great lust for women—usually women protected by Zeus or Heracles. On the east and west of the Parthenon were carved two battles against those who by definition or by popular understanding had absolutely no use for marriage whatsoever. These were the Amazons and the ancestors of Zeus, the Giants. No matter where or on which side a person stood looking up at these metopes, he or she would see a war that highlighted the issue of where women fit into Athena's society.

The other elegant and well-preserved building on the Athenian Acropolis is the Erechtheion, named after the legendary founder of Athens, whom we have already met (King Erechtheus). This building is famous for its marble statues of women dressed in long robes who take the place of columns and who hold upon their heads the whole great weight of a marble porch. The women are called, to this day, Caryatides. The story was told by the Romans that Caryae, a state in the Peloponnesus, sided with the Persian enemies against Greece. Later the Greeks, having gloriously won their freedom by victory in the war (479 BCE), made common cause and declared war against the people of Caryae. They took the town, killed the men, abandoned the city to desolation, and carried off their wives into slavery without permitting them to lay aside the long robes and other marks of their rank as married women. This, according to the famous Roman architect Vetruvius, was "so that they might be obliged not only to march in the triumph but to appear forever after as a type of

Fig. 53. The Erechtheion on the Acropolis, Athens, which depicts the women of Caryae appearing as slaves and forced to bear the burden of the Athenian state.

slavery, burdened with the weight of their shame and so making atonement for their State."[1] The Erechtheum still stands today, held up by the women of insubordinate Caryae.

Higher and larger, fifty yards away on the Acropolis, stands the magnificent Parthenon. It was built less than half a century after the famous Persian wars in which the Greeks defeated the mighty armies from Mesopotamia. Although the Persian wars were so important as to give a permanent place to Athens in world history, there is no depiction of these wars anywhere on this monument. This is a stunning omission, and some argue that the four mythical wars that are on the metopes must be allegories or metaphors for the Persian wars. This is possible, but there is no more factual basis for that than that some people think it ought to be so. There is nothing Persian about any of the adversaries on the metopes. The Persians were patriarchs too: they married, like Athenians; they traced the male line from Darius to Xerxes, from father to son; and they could not have been culturally more removed from the Amazons who are up there on the metopes being defeated. The Persians came from a high civilization and were far from bestial (like, for example, Centaurs); they did not descend—by anyone's account—from the Giants; and they had no stake in the Trojan War. It is an interesting theory that somehow all these wars were stand-ins for the Persian wars, but the evidence is unpersuasive.

There is no depiction, either, of the rise of Athenian democracy against the tyrants of the sixth century. Normally they would be a fitting subject for a grand public building, just as Jefferson and Lincoln are subjects of memorials in Washington, D.C. But on the Parthenon there is no depiction of Psistratus or Pericles, hugely important figures of Athenian political history. The building does not celebrate good leadership, strong warriors, or democracy. It does not celebrate good men at all. It celebrates, rather, wars that ultimately had the effect of radically altering the status of women. That is the carving on the outside, on the metopes. The same is true inside. Within the temple itself stood a huge statue of the virgin goddess Athena. She bore a great shield, and painted on either side, again, were two of these same wars as those carved outside on the metopes, the wars against the Giants and the Amazons. Both were wars fought to defeat mythological and dangerous clans that had inhabited Greece before Zeus and that did not care a whit for marriage. On Athena's sandals was, yet again, the third war, fought to defend marriage against the Centaurs.

At the base of the statue was a depiction of the birth of Pandora. She is the first woman of all humankind, the one whom in the seventh century Hesiod said had "the morals of a bitch" and was the "ruin of mankind." Pandora, the indiscriminate breeder—just as a bitch is indiscriminate—was therefore the symbol of the older morality in which women could have many partners and, most importantly, not know the sire of her pups. Such unknowing would completely destroy the possibility of patrilineal descent. Hesiod's choice of words is therefore no accident. The fault of early women was not that she was not beautiful or useful but that she could breed like a dog. Pandora is therefore the *opposite* of the virgin. Athena stands above her by some thirty cubits, which is about fifty feet. The contrast between the virgin and the promiscuous first woman would have been overwhelming.

The famous Parthenon frieze ringed the outer walls of the inner chamber, which was high up inside a covered area from which a person could look outward through the great marble columns. Out beyond this covered porch, outside the columns and above them, was where the metopes were found, and these metopes carried the carvings of the wars. These would have been outermost and most prominent to the viewer. An Athenian could only see the frieze from inside the portico, or with difficulty, by looking through gaps in the external columns. He or she would be looking way up above his or her head, probably into the dark, and probably only with great difficulty. Nevertheless, this magnificent frieze is still celebrated by everyone in modern times because the carvings are the most well preserved, and they have ended up for the most part in the British Museum. They are some of the best marble sculptures anybody ever did anywhere, anytime. There are horsemen riding naked on lunging mounts and chariots being pulled by horses four abreast, and so good, so skillful, were the carvers that the sixteen feet of the four leaping horses are all discernable. The carver has created the stunning illusion of depth into the marble, although in fact the relief is only a few inches. There is mastery here, and it produces a procession in stone of unmatched grace and excitement.

But the frieze carried a more discreet message than did the metopes that could be clearly seen from the surrounding grounds. It was rather less visible, was high up, not clear from a distance because it was inside the outer columns. This glorious carving must, therefore, have been like some sacred wrap, some necklace that a woman might wear under her gown, near the heart. It was closest of all to the inner chamber where Athena herself stood, but it was not made prominent, not shown off like the wars. It is as if one were moving backward in time, closer to Athena, closer to the origins of Athenian life and power, and here on the inside frieze was this little story.

The frieze presents a grand procession that wraps around all four sides of the temple and finally climaxes over the east entrance in a cluster of five figures who are not gods and about whose significance there is much disagreement.[2] They are a grown man and woman and three young people, probably girls. Some say there are only two girls and the third is a boy. The girl, or boy, has a bare bottom, and some say that such exposure would be uncharacteristic of Greek carvings if it were a girl.[3] Some say the determining factor is the haircut and that this is therefore a girl. Some say that it would just be more likely that a boy would have such a central role in the central

panel of the frieze. Obviously, opinion is divided.

The rest of the frieze does not have any battles or any mortals we might know, such as Heracles, Theseus, Homer, Jason, or some other famous figure, either mythical or real. As a work of art it is all beautiful, but it gives very few clues as to its intended meaning. The procession is alternately joyous and subdued. This scene at the end with the young girl (or boy) is not at all joyous. Here is the climax of the whole frieze. On all sides everyone else is parading, bringing gifts, carrying jugs, riding in speeding chariots coming to this culminating scene. The gods are seated on both sides of this event, which is in the center. They frame it, give it importance. Their presence suggests that the act that is being commemorated is blessed by the twelve most prominent Olympians. It is blessed at the very highest levels.

Many people, perhaps the majority, say this procession is the Panathenaia, an annual ceremony for which young girls spent months weaving a peplos, a woman's gown. The peplos would be presented to a priest who would somehow see to it that it was delivered to the goddess Athena. This happened in a big way every four years, and there is no doubt that there was such a celebration and that Athenians put major effort into it. But other people say it can't be the Panathenaia, because there are too many important people or objects that scholars know were in the Panathenaia but that are not shown anywhere in this whole procession on the Parthenon. For example, there are no hoplites (soldiers), who were supposed to be in the Panathenaia, and no ark to carry the sacred garment to the goddess. Athena, who is supposedly to receive the sacred garment, appears on the frieze immediately *next* to the central scene but with her back turned to it. It would be unusual for the central scene to represent a dramatic gift to her and for her to be sitting with her back turned to the delivery of that gift, apparently uninterested. So some people say whatever it was, it was not the Panathenaia.

In 1996 Joan B. Connelly offered a new idea. She said that if there were myths on the pediments and myths on the metopes and myths in the inner chamber, there was probably also a myth on the frieze, which would mean that it was not the Panathenaia, because that was a real quadrennial event and not a myth. Everything else up there in stone was a myth, so why would the frieze be any exception? There is, however, said Connelly, a myth that fits the images that is more likely and could be seen on the frieze if moderns only had the eyes to see. This myth was, she offered, that of Erechtheus, the first king of Athens, and his unfortunate daughter Otionia.⁴ The daughter's story might have provided a theme for the emerging Athenian democracy, for its origins and its bedrock; it would be both mythical and a cause of civic pride, just as the Trojan War was or the wars against the Giants were. It would be consistent with the rest of the temple.

The story upon which Connelly relies is that of Erechtheus, founder of the city of Athens. The city is at war with neighboring Eleusis and is losing. In order to achieve victory in battle, Erechtheus therefore decides to sacrifice his youngest daughter. The daughter, says Connelly, is the young girl in the central scene of the frieze. She is the one receiving or

Fig. 54. The central, and climactic, scene on the Parthenon frieze in which a man offers a robe to a young woman (or boy). Joan B. Connelly believes that the youth is the girl Otionia receiving the robe in which she will be wrapped for sacrifice to save Athens in its war with Eleusis. Such a construction is consistent with the numerous other themes on the Parthenon that exalt female virginity, sacrifice, and marriage. COPYRIGHT © THE TRUSTEES OF THE BRITISH MUSEUM

passing off the sacrificial robe that will bind her arms tight to her sides at the moment of truth.

Connelly cites a famous contemporary speech by Lycurgus, who in turn quoted the playwright Euripides. Euripides had put patriotism, idealism, honor, and self-sacrifice into the speech of Erechtheus's wife, who—to save Athens—willingly offered her child to the sacrificial knife. It is the sort of civic commitment that seems entirely fitting for the Parthenon, the monument of self-congratulation and the explanation of the city's greatness, its closeness to the virgin goddess, its civic pride, and its willingness to sacrifice its own virgins when the need arose. If the Connelly theory is correct, then the central function of the famous Parthenon frieze is to portray the citizens of Athens in a celebratory mood while coming either to a child sacrifice or to honor such a sacrifice that they believe saved the city from defeat in its first war. The child sacrificed was a girl.

Another scholar has said, No, no, it *was* the Panathenaia, but it was the first Panathenaia as myth and it was the mythical king Cecrops who is receiving the peplos from his son.[5] We have already seen Cecrops was the first ruler to recognize the importance of monogamy for women.[6] To represent him, therefore, would be to enshrine one of the founders of the patriarchy, which is more or less consistent with the message of the rest of the temple. So one way or another this frieze is part of a containment policy for women.

Fig. 55. In this scene on the climactic east front of the Parthenon frieze, Hera raises her wedding veil to Zeus, a scene that is positioned directly beside the central scene with the youth of fig. 54. This is, conclusively, the signification that the Parthenon is a temple honoring the twin requirements within patriarchy for women: virgin or married. Four wars then ring the metopes on the building to show the price paid to establish such a society.

The mildest interpretation of the Parthenon frieze is that it portrays a ceremony to honor Athena, the virgin goddess, by bringing her a warm garment. The next mildest idea is that this is that same ceremony but that it was one of its first performances and featured the king who instituted monogamy for women. The third idea is not mild: it is that in the inner sanctum of the temple the statue of Athena was ringed by this frieze commemorating the highest heroic virtue of an Athenian virgin, the virtue of a daughter of Athens, Otionia, who sacrificed her life for the city. In her case the robe is not a peplos for Athena to wear; it is a shroud to hold her tight when her throat is cut.

Immediately to the left of this scene, Hera raises her veil in the gesture of a bride and is seen turning to Zeus as subject. She is no longer the free, independent queen or the coequal, public woman she was in ancient Mycenaean times. She has been brought into the controlled order through wedlock. The messages on the great Parthenon compound.

In sum the Parthenon is a testament to the glory of Athens, absolutely, but even more to the glory of Athens founded upon the expectation that women in this city should become either wives or heroines. On the metopes of the north the Greeks are shown vanquishing loose-moraled Trojans in a war to restore marriage. On the west the Greeks vanquish the Amazons, who rejected marriage outright.[7] On the south is the war with the Centaurs, whose most significant contribution to mythology is to disrupt a marriage feast.[8] On the east was the first great battle of the new Greek civilization against the Giants, who were sons of the old religion of Mother Earth, Ge. There is no evidence that Ge had any interest in marriage.

Fig. 56. The disruption of a patriarchal marriage and subsequent rape of the Lapith women, pictured here, were the reason for the wars by the Greeks against the Centaurs. This is one of four wars that circled all four sides of the Parthenon, all of which had something to do with the status of women. COPYRIGHT © THE TRUSTEES OF THE BRITISH MUSEUM

Mother Earth bred, but she did not marry. Add to all these wars on the metopes that the west pediment shows Athena gaining mastery over Poseidon, alleged by some to be the former husband to the Triple Goddess. That might be the reason, it is said, that he carries a trident, and therefore Poseidon may not be considered a particular friend of Athens or monogamy. He was anything but a virgin himself.

The east pediment shows Athena being born from the head of Zeus (a male), itself a statement of exaggerated patriarchal pride. Finally, the worst case, in the climactic scene of the frieze, a young virgin is being sacrificed so that her father can win a war. Inside the door below that sad scene, the virgin Athena stands towering over the promiscuous Pandora.

The Parthenon in all its combined parts endorses war's efficacy, virginity or marriage as the only two respectable conditions for women, and the triumph over an old religious order in which none of these values was paramount and none of which, coincidentally, is of primary importance in Sparta, with which Athens is in almost continuous and growing conflict. As if in a signature statement, three times in three different locations there were carved scenes of the sun god rising triumphant and the moon goddess descending into the waves of oblivion.[9]

Everyone since these times who has come to Athens and seen this monument has remarked upon its symmetry, its proportion, and its expert lines, some of which intentionally create optical illusions to draw the eye to believe what is not true. It is a building of grace, but also of careful, consistent calculation. It is impossible that the symbolism of the moon declining on three separate sites could be accidental. It is impossible that the combined visual effects of pillars and sight lines could have been so carefully planned but that the combined effect of the mythology might have been unintended. Even down to the last detail of the moon, the net effect was all a signature statement for the Athenian empire.

The moon had been important for a great many people for a long time and probably in a different way than the sun was important.[10] The sun was abundantly

the life force. When there is no sun, there is no growth. No sun means that winter comes and the leaves die. The moon, on the other hand, was very likely a symbol of both change and constancy, coming and going, giving and taking away. The moon changes sizes from pencil thin to whole and lustrous to ragged and depleted. The sun does not do that. Then the moon wholly disappears for three days. The sun does not do that. Scholars write that when the moon returned, women danced and sang on the hilltops and gave thanks, and some even say that this was the beginning of dance and the lute and drums. Maybe the dancing women on the seal rings of Crete were dancing to the moon. There are moons on some of those dancing rings. Probably women danced because the moon ruled menses and menses ruled fertility and fertility was the key to life.

Fig. 57. Helios's horse (one remaining of an original four) ascending on the east pediment of the Parthenon, full of energy and hope.

By contrast, the sun never changes shape, does not rule menses, is slower—a plodder—and is sometimes dangerously hot and damaging to life. The moon is never damaging to life. The sun moves, but only slowly up and down the horizon; it does not change shape or grow to glory and then decline. Both sun cycles and moon cycles can be seen in a rhythm of death and rebirth, and both were widely worshipped, but the rebirth of the moon was regular occasion for female celebration because it occurred more often and in tune with their bodies. The sun was more likely an intellectual thing, a knowing, a kind of knowledge. We know, men might have said, that it will return. But women did not have to say they knew; they had the experience in themselves, in their bodies, in the return of their own power. It was therefore that women and the moon were so often associated, and it is no surprise that the moon is declining on the Parthenon. Helios, the sun god, with his four-horse chariot is rising (fig. 57); Selene, the moon goddess, is over. Whoever carved the head knew horses, because this one is clearly exhausted and done. She is sinking back into the sea (fig. 58).

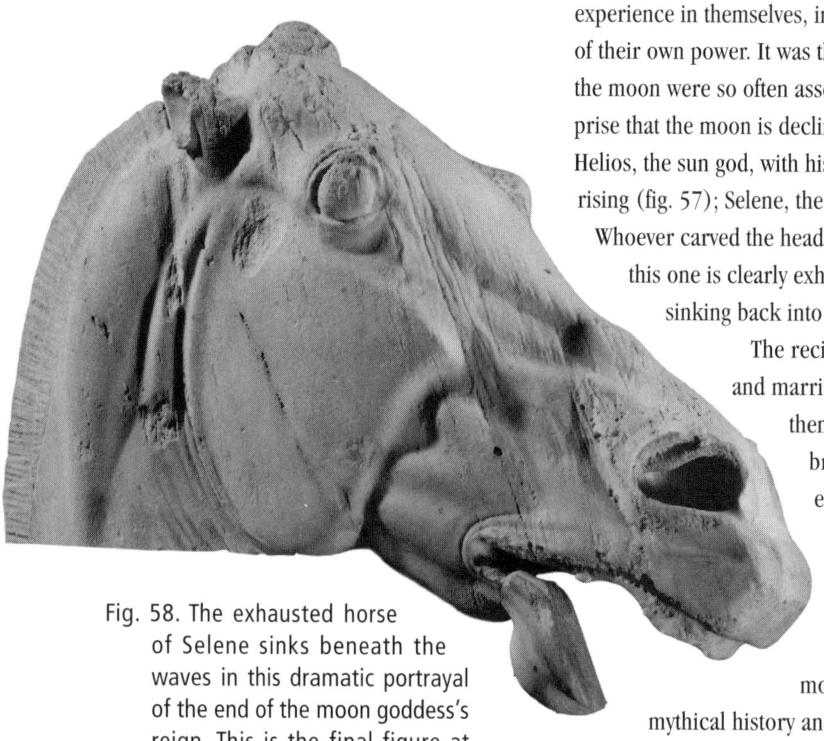

The reciprocal values of virginity and marriage, sanctified by repeated themes and sculpted with brilliance, were therefore enshrined by the fifth century BCE as the central foundation of Athenian strength. They were connected by this glorious monument into Athens's mythical history and held up to the people as the reason for their greatness. The virgin goddess Athena had sprung from the head of Zeus, a male, who had even taken over the powers of regeneration. The replacement of woman's mystery was complete. She was not necessary to the continuation of the line.

This transition seems to be part of a trend over the whole Mediterranean region. Over on the Hebrew side, Eve was said to have been produced from Adam,

Fig. 58. The exhausted horse of Selene sinks beneath the waves in this dramatic portrayal of the end of the moon goddess's reign. This is the final figure at the opposite end of the pediment from where Helios is rising, and the two combined are most certainly a political statement.

a male. Jehovah replaces the progenitrix, and Adam becomes the original mother and father combined. God institutes the new definition of marriage in the first chapters of Genesis. "Thy desire shall be to thy husband, and he shall rule over thee."[11] Sexual restraint becomes the basis for marriage, which becomes the founding institution for the control of women in the new order.[12] In both societies the central mystery of regeneration is explained by a new myth of spontaneous male generation that is even less rational or provable than the old myth of rebirth but that satisfies the new requirements for a male line.

Bad women are now portrayed like sexual Aphrodite, as rising from the depths of the ocean, from the scrotum of Uranus, or from the society of men before Cronos and linear time. Or women are said to be like the Furies and the Maenads, who have power and independent meetings and orgies that are not controlled by men.[13] As late as the sixth century, a male guardian retained the right in Athens to sell into slavery an unmarried woman who had lost her virginity.[14] Over on the Hebrew side, bad women were those like the Philistine Delilah, and the penalty for a virgin having intercourse before marriage was death.[15]

Virginity and marriage, the twin cornerstones of a patriarchal property system, are by these means translated into a new morality underscored by religion. Property becomes key to life after death, its control sanctified. As a practical matter, control of the family property is substituted for rebirth. It is not, therefore, that Athena was wise and active and helpful, and also a virgin, a miracle of purity. It is that she is a virgin, first, above all; her temple is the temple to the virgin, above all, and after that she has other secondary qualities. The temple is not called Sophia. It is not

labeled, in the popular imagination, as courage or strength or androgyny. It is "The Virgin" because that is the value that is most significant and outstanding in Athenian society: the virgin is the cornerstone of patriarchy. Her temple presents her own illustrious statue facing east where it will be illuminated—or impregnated, as it were—by the morning sun. She is surrounded outside by carved scenes of the conquest of the Amazons, to whom a virgin is contrasted; of the Giants, who fought for Mother Earth, who has no identification with virginity; and of the Trojans, who did not respect the marriage of Helen. Nor are there other battle scenes that had only to do with some foreign policy of Athens. The Persians and the Spartans are not here. The battles against Thebes are not there. The battle against Eleusis is not there. Only battles that confirm the twin pillars of marriage and virginity or the demotion of Mother Earth are celebrated. Male power can be traced, lineage forever known and tracked, and the mystery of immortality mooted.

This great monument was a signature statement of the Athenian empire. Unlike Spartans, who did not require their women to come to marriage as virgins and with whom the Athenians were about to do prolonged and fateful battle, Pericles was proclaiming to his countrymen in a gloriously spectacular building that it was their treatment of women that had always been the true source of Athenian power and her hope for favor from the gods in the wars soon to come with Sparta. Since the earliest founding of the city, success in war had been secured by the sacrifice of the female child, by the forced marriage of Hera, and by the virginity of the patron goddess. The city's future success depended upon the continued purity and character of women like these, who, either as virgins or married, secured the future of Greek civilization.

There is a way in which Pericles' motives may have been more admirable. A state that relies entirely upon strength and heroism and that makes no allowance for the deep encouragement of the feminine, as Athens had by that time become, was in danger. It was in danger of losing track of its creative and compassionate self, of the roots of generosity that may at one time have been represented by the ancient goddesses of the hearth (of Hestia), and of the grain (of Demeter), and of the moon goddesses (Selene, Semele, and perhaps Ariadne). It had become so thoroughly a military state that Athens, by the end of the fifth century, was in danger of losing its balance. After generations of studying the stories of Heracles and Achilles, of Agamemnon and Odysseus, it had gone off into empire without compunction or restraint, slaughtering whole populations that might resist Athenian power. There were playwrights, it is true, such as Euripides, who about this time began to write dramas showing some sympathy for the women of Troy (for Hecuba, mother of the sacrificed daughter Polyxena, and for Andromache, the enslaved former wife of Hector). Euripides tried to open the mind to include the suffering of the female of the species and was roundly disapproved by his colleagues, who ridiculed him and mocked him in their own plays. Pericles, in building the Parthenon, may have had some sense of the imbalance of Athenian life. After one thousand years of unbridled male dominion, the state was teetering toward instability. Perhaps he built a monument to the feminine wrapped in the institutions of virginity and marriage. In its beauty and grace, the Parthenon surpassed any building ever built to that time. In its proportion and crisp lines, it could have been a message that beauty counts, that the interior life also counts. Pericles would not have been wrong, of course, to know that these qualities too must be nurtured in order for a civilization to survive.

The benign effect, however, was insufficient and was very like the effect of the cathedrals dedicated to the Virgin Mary in mediaeval Europe. Womanhood was raised by the Parthenon to a heroic level. The image of purity was used to inspire, to lift women to idealism and self sacrifice. The feminine in both the Parthenon and in the cathedrals was, however, still under the domination and control of men. Both in Athens and in Europe the standard of purity was unattainable and could be used not only to inspire but also to oppress.[16]

The Parthenon is one of the last of the great works of architecture in the Athenian cultural explosion. Pericles had proclaimed that patriarchal property, reinforced by the gods, was the basis of Athenian power. The myths that he had chosen to carve into the Parthenon's gleaming marble were not, in the end, myths of fertility or grace or cycles of the seasons or immortality. By this time, one thousand years after Crete, no one would have remembered that it could be any other way.

Biblical Patriarchs Match the Greek Story

There is a remarkable coincidence of symbols employed in Genesis and in some of the Greek myths. The likeness seems too great to be accidental. Genesis is thought to have been written about 1000 BCE, approximately the same time as the rise of the bards who originally sang the myths of Greece. The climate of chaos and contest was similar in both places. "Sea Peoples" ravaged the coasts of Egypt and Asia Minor in about 1200 BCE, and there were also multiple destructions of existing cities in Mycenae, Tiryns, Olkos, and Pylos on the mainland of Greece. Some say the Semites migrated out of Egypt and some say these Semites were early Canaanites themselves who simply arose out of the earlier religious context to adopt a new sky god.[1] Certainly the majority among the Canaanites had earlier worshipped a goddess known by the names of Asherah, Astarte, and Ashtoreth. From the biblical condemnations, we understand that these earlier gods were queens of heaven who were sexual and ecstatic. There was additionally a long subsequent tradition of writing that was both unsanctioned and not included within the Jewish canon but written by Jews honoring the goddess of wisdom, Sophia. The writers within that tradition were unequivocal about the existence of a divine feminine, but when the sacred texts were eventually collected, these works were not among them.[2] Scholars of these traditions say that feminine figures were central to earth religions in other places just as they were in Crete and that others, not just Minoans, believed themselves dependent upon the cycles of the seasons. Others, including residents of Palestine, were riveted by the cycles of the moon and fertility, in awe more of regeneration than of conquest. There is, unfortunately, no detailed and confirming archaeological record of Canaan to match the one that we have found in Crete and Thera. There is no equivalent material record in the artifacts emphasizing women, sexuality, and ecstasy or a belief in immortality and the regenerative quality of death. It is instructive, however, that the early Hebrews systematically reject each of those values that might have been common to both Canaan and the Minoans. Therefore, whereas the values of the earlier Minoan culture have to be extracted from the physical materials, the opposite is true in evaluating early biblical history. There is not the same rich material evidence, but there is direct written testimony. It is as if on one side of the Aegean we had pots and on the other we had writing. The pots tell us what was there in these earth religions before the Greeks. The writing tells us what the first scribes of the patriarchy thought about the Canaanites and the Philistines and therefore what they thought about these earth religions.[3]

At the outset, just as the Greeks had done with Zeus, the new culture of the Hebrews reversed the idea that women were central to birth and regeneration—that is, to the survival of the clan.

> And the Lord God caused a deep sleep to fall upon Adam, and he slept; and he took one of his ribs, and closed up the flesh instead thereof; And the rib, which the

Lord God had taken from man, made he a woman, and brought her unto the man. And Adam said, This is now bone of my bones, and flesh of my flesh: she shall be called Woman, because she was taken out of Man.[4]

Jehovah produces a woman without help from any female. The principle of regeneration—sacred to the earlier worship of the feminine—is taken over by a male god. There would have been no earthly evidence that men can reproduce by themselves or that the males of any species can do that. This is therefore not a belief that naturally evolved from human experience. The validity of everyone's practical experience was fundamentally opposite. In its place was put a story that would lead men away from their dependence upon women, not toward their own practical knowledge but away from it.

What is remarkable about the biblical literature is that it is so explicit. There is no beating around the bush as in *The Odyssey* or in the story of the punishment of Clytemnestra. Genesis takes one chapter to explain the beginning of the world, one to explain the male-generated first woman, and then the third chapter explains the institution of marriage. The new religion is therefore founded first upon a male principle that displaces the female principle and second upon the institution of female subordination. This is not a story of wisdom, or of the earth and the sky parting, or the earth and the sea, or of a Golden Age, or of some rebirth. Rather, here is the story of a formation of woman from man and then his marriage of her. It is more "of" her than "to" her: "thy desire shall be to thy husband, and he shall rule over thee."[5]

Eve, who does not immediately like the idea, then eats of the fruit of the tree by which she shall know good and evil. She seeks knowledge. God has commanded her not to do this. Why he makes this command is mysterious. In a commonsensical and dangerous world, knowledge would always be an aid to survival. Jehovah's is therefore not quite the same message that comes through Homer's Sirens, but it is a similar warning against knowledge in the hands of a female. Women's knowledge is somehow dangerous. This is in the very beginning of the Bible and is therefore not a meandering off on some diversion. It *is* the main point. The founding scribes wanted us to know the order of the universe, the fundamentals of the new religion. Before the wars and the conquests, before the rules of cleanliness or the rules of diet or the justice of the Lord, we are told the foundation principle concerning men and women.

Eve, however, perhaps thinking she was still of the old order when women were at the center, ate the fruit from the tree anyway, in spite of God's warning. This was not pleasing to God who reacted: "I will greatly multiply thy sorrow and thy conception; in sorrow thou shalt bring forth children; and thy desire shall be to thy husband, and he shall rule over thee."[6] Thus the third step in the new religious order, after marriage, is to discredit women's judgment and to punish her for seeking knowledge.

It is difficult to measure the psychological impact of such a pronouncement at the beginning of scripture and at the beginning of recorded history. The punishment is not to be limited to Eve alone. It is a punishment to be suffered by all women through all time. Their lot is hopeless. The Lord God does not say that life is suffering or that pain is inevitable, which might certainly be spiritual wisdom. This is not a wisdom teaching. This is a pronouncement to every mother through time that she (the male is not mentioned) will suffer simply because she is a mother. Her only solace shall be her husband, the man who shall not, as we might hope, love her, but who shall rule her. Suffering and rule by a male is to be borne as an axiom of female life for all time. Who can imagine how many women over the centuries have known these verses, believed them to be right, and went off to sleep weeping?

Snakes do not actually talk, and to think of them as founts of wisdom requires understanding them as symbols. Many people think that they were symbols for the earth religions. The snake lives in the ground, which is the source of agricultural regeneration, and when it sheds its own skin, it is a model for a principle of rebirth. The snake therefore lives where the life force comes from, disappears and returns when the life force returns, and brings with it the magic of transformation. Some snakes are also deadly, and to hold a snake or wrap a snake around one's body required a comfort with the presence of life and death in the same moment. The snake goddesses of ancient Crete—seen on the famous figurines of Knossos—seem to be in some transformed state, almost transfixed, as if straddling two worlds. Even the latterly tamed Greek goddesses Athena and Demeter might often be seen in the presence of snakes—Demeter sometimes, Athena regularly. The snake was not *from* Zeus but *before* Zeus, and it was a symbol of the connection of these goddesses to the older order. The snake was therefore a symbol used by people of the old generations including those who, in all probability, preceded the Hebrews in Canaan. The Bible handled the snake symbol roughly:

> Now the serpent was more subtil [*sic*] than any beast of the field which the LORD God had made. And he said unto the woman, Yea, hath God said, Ye shall not eat of every tree of the garden? And the woman said unto the serpent, We may eat of the fruit of the trees of the garden: But of the fruit of the tree which is in the midst of the garden, God hath said, Ye shall not eat of it neither shall ye touch it, lest ye die. And the serpent said unto the woman, Ye shall not surely die: For God doth know that in the day ye eat thereof, then your eyes shall be opened, and ye shall be as gods, knowing good and evil. And when the woman saw that the tree was good for food, and that it was pleasant to the eyes, and a tree to be desired to make one wise, she took of the fruit thereof, and did eat, and gave also unto her husband with her; and he did eat. And the eyes of them both were opened and they knew that they were naked.[7]

Now the apple, the snake, and the woman, featured in Cretan artifacts and Greek mythology, presumably with resonance in Canaan, are discredited—not singly, nor haphazardly, but as a package. This is at the very beginning of one of the foundation myths of Western history; it will be read and reread even more than Homer, will be more influential than any creation story in Western culture. The reason that the female should be subordinate to the male is that her judgment is flawed, and the reason her judgment is flawed is that she takes advice from creatures of the ground and her knowledge from the fruit of the trees.

> And the LORD God said unto the serpent, Because thou hast done this, thou art cursed above all cattle, and above every beast of the field; upon thy belly shalt thou go, and dust shalt thou eat all the days of thy life: And I will put enmity between thee and the woman, and between thy seed and her seed, it shall bruise thy head, and thou shalt bruise his heel.[8]

Can it be coincidence that the Pythia at Delphi was a snake oracle or that the emblem of the snake, which Jehovah banishes, was also present in Greece? The Pythia was also known as the Sybil, the source of wisdom. Men and women came to climb the steep slopes of Mount Parnassus to sit beside her rock and consult her. Was it this tradition spread across the Mediterranean that Jehovah found in the Levant and now banished? At Delphi the "Oracle" connoted wisdom and clear sight into the future. During all of the Oracle's history, men and women came from all about the Mediterranean world to consult her concerning practical everyday choices and for instructions. Early on, as the patriarchy became established, the Oracle was wise enough to see a change coming and warned everyone about the law of sons. The Oracle, the Pythia, the snake woman, was therefore central to prophecy and was honored as the fount of wisdom by pilgrims from Sicily to Asia. Her early dates approximate the earliest dates when the foundation stories of the Bible were being formulated.

It is no small coincidence, then, when a snake is ordered out of the Garden of Eden. The central promise of the old religion in Crete had been immor-tality and cyclic regeneration for which the snake was famous. In Genesis 3:4 the snake says to Eve, "Thou shalt not die," and she believes the snake. If the earth religion of the ancient Canaanites was similar to that of the Minoans, then the snake was a messenger of the promise of return, a message consistent with the activity of the moon or the seasons. The eternal return is what the snake promises and what woman brings. For an agriculturist the equivalent promise is of the sprout, the full ear and the seed of corn, followed by winter, followed again by spring. That is the eternal order, and the man or woman who knows this order is blessed. But Genesis rejects this promise and reverses the meaning of these symbols. Genesis has both man and woman eat the apple from the tree of knowledge of good and evil, get knowledge, and, because of this violation of the rule, be banished from the Garden of Eden. The tree of life is in the Garden too, and they are thus banished from this tree as well or, that is, from eternal life. The fruit of the tree of knowledge is thereby changed into a symbol of breach of contract, and the fruit that in the older symbolism had borne the promise of sexuality and eternal life now, in the new religion, gets them banished and costs them eternity. The fruit's significance has been reversed, converted into a symbol of the price to be paid for disobedience. Instead of the snake's promise of life, Jehovah now substitutes the threat of death.

Nor was the apple some accidental fruit that fell carelessly or randomly into this story. The golden apple was, as we have already seen, the source of the conflict between the other goddesses and Aphrodite at the outset of the Trojan War. Further, in the earth religions, the so-called goddess cultures, the apple generally was the mythical symbol of immortality:

Eve's fruit of knowledge used to be the Goddess's sacred heart of immortality all over the Indo-European complex. The Goddess's many western paradises grew the apples of eternal life. The Celts called the western paradise Avalon, "Apple-land," a country ruled by Morgan, the queen of the dead. Irish kings received the Goddess's magic apples of immortality and went away to live with her under the sunset. King Arthur was taken to Avalon by the Triple Goddess in person, as three fairy queens.[9]

The Greeks also saw a great symbol in the apple. They opined that originally, before her marriage to Zeus, Mother Hera kept a magic apple garden in the west, where the tree of life was guarded by her sacred serpent. According to the scholar Robert Graves, the whole story of Adam, Eve, and the serpent in the tree was therefore deliberately misinterpreted from icons in common use at the time. These icons had once showed the Great Goddess Hera offering life to her worshippers in the form of an apple with the tree and its serpent in the background.[10]

Now we have a creation story that is not about origins of the religion itself, as in Hesiod's story of the Titans and Zeus, but rather a story that forthrightly rejects certain prehistoric symbols. The existence of such a wide carpet of apple myths across the whole of the ancient Mediterranean world makes it highly likely that the Genesis story is a rejection of some form of the preexisting old religion. It is a morality tale of the new patriarchal order, a designation of good and evil, us and them, and a sanctification of obedience to the new kings. This sanctification

of obedience is of the most profound importance to the rest of Western history.[11]

Genesis does not explicitly speak to sexuality except to say that Adam and Eve were naked and did not notice it. They were innocent of sexuality or, most certainly, of its pitfalls. But Christian interpreters, most especially Augustine, interpreted the passage to mean that the original pair were living in sin, by which he meant living in sexual freedom. It is likely that the unselfconsciousness of Adam and Eve about their nakedness is exactly the metaphor that Augustine thinks it was, i.e., a metaphor for freer sexual conduct in which not only sex in the garden but temple sexuality, "prostitution," was acceptable, as it may have been in ancient "goddess" societies. In any case Jehovah makes clear that this conduct is to end. Accordingly, through much of Western history, freedom of individual choice in matters of sexuality has been seen as "a positive force of evil in history and in ourselves, a force ready to tempt, to corrupt, to infect."[12] To this day the message of the story of Adam and Eve is interpreted as an injunction against sexuality and seductive women.

There is a good deal of practical sense in limiting sexual conduct. Unbridled licentiousness is a downward spiral as addictive as any drug and as corrosive to discipline or responsibility as any drug. It may well have been that temple sexuality, or unbridled sexual freedom, among the early Hebrews or the early Greeks was becoming a social problem. But the restraints in both the myths of Genesis and in the myths of Odysseus, Jason, and Oedipus do not address sexual freedom. They address *female* sexual freedom. Males are as likely as females to become addicted to the sensual life, if not perhaps more so. Despite this, the warnings in Genesis against sex do not apply to them. For males, procreation by any means remains highly important. It is reasonable to conclude that the psychological health of sexual restraint—in itself entirely desirable for both men and women in most situations—was not at the base of these traditions. More likely the issue was, again, property.

The next chapter of Genesis confirms the point. It introduces Cain and Abel and a long line of their offspring, commonly known as the "begats." "And unto Enoch was born Irad: and Irad begat Mehujael; and Mehujael begat Methusael; and Methusael begat Lamech," et cetera. Chapters 5, 10, and 11 are further begats, and so down to Abram. The point now is not marriage but the record of sons. In Chapters 15–17 Abram is without an heir because his wife, Sarai, is barren, and so the solution is at first attempted with Sarai's maid, Hagar, who conceives of Abram a son, Ishmael. But this would create a separate branch in the family line, a potential for contest, and so the Lord made Sarai fertile after all, and she bore Isaac. The "legitimate" family line was thereby assured. Later, in the same line, Lot is attempting to escape from Sodom with his two daughters, but Lot also has no sons. And so his daughters make Lot drunk and sleep with him so "that we may preserve the seed of our father." Over and over, chapter after chapter, whether it is the long lists of begats or the preoccupation of Abram to have a son or the desire of the daughters of Lot to carry the father's seed, Genesis repeatedly returns to the same theme. There are twice as many chapters of begats than there are those that deal with creation or Adam and Eve. In effect Genesis provides these new settlers in Canaan with their first chain of male title, together with a complete, sometimes-riveting story of how it came to be sanctified.

Establishing the begats is apparently of as great importance to God as it is to mortals, and the implication is that establishing the male line is not just Abram's but also God's work. I "will multiply thee exceedingly," says the Lord,[13] and this not only addresses a patriarch's greatest worry but also transfers to a male the promise that before this time could only be fulfilled by a woman. A good deal is accomplished in one short sentence: "I will multiply thee exceedingly" promises (1) a patriarchal line, (2) of unlimited duration, and (3) through the agency of a male god rather than through the feminine principle. The teaching of Genesis is therefore on balance only partially about female monogamy. It is perhaps even more about male propagation and a transfer of power to men, a result, of course, that female monogamy promotes.[14]

All over Canaan and wherever they settled, the new religionists were in a struggle to establish their claims. All the tools of war had come to their command; they came with chariots and fire:

> And it came to pass in the days of Am-ra-phel king of Shi-nar, Ar-I-och king of El-la-sar, Ched-or-la-o-mer king of E-lam, and Ti-dal king of nations; That these made war with Be-ra king of Sodom and with Bir-sha king of Go-morrah, Shi-nab king of Ad-måh, and Shem-e-ber king of Ze-boi-im and the king of Be-la, which is Zoar. … and in the thirteenth year they rebelled. And in the fourteenth year came Ched-or-la-or-mer, and the kings that were with him and smote the Reph-a-ims in Ash-te-roth

Kar-na-im, and the Zu-zims in Ham, and the E-mins in Sha-veh Kir-I-a-tha-im, … [15]

Chapter after chapter in this biblical account relates territories in contest. Ultimately the question would be who could trace back to Abraham and the Lord, and these matters would be determined by the sword. Just as the contestants across the water in Greece were at the same time claiming to trace back to Heracles or to Zeus himself, in the Levant the secret was to trace back to Abraham. The all-important chain of title was now to be recorded in Genesis.

It is tempting to consider that the consequence of these early scriptures might have been limited to the end of the Bronze Age, dying out over time. But in the legislature of the State of New Mexico in February 1999, a bill to ban marriage for gay or lesbian couples was introduced by Sen. Leonard Lee Rawson (R-Las Cruces), imposing criminal penalties upon anyone who performed such marriages. "Marriage," Senator Rawson said, "is more than the union of two people who have strong feelings for one another. It establishes blood lines and kinship. It enables people to pass on property." [16]

It is likely that this has been the essence of the matter for three thousand years. Senator Rawson was correct. With the early Semites as well as the Greeks, marriage was originally not about love at all but was about property.

IV
Objections to the Warrior Civilization

A "root fire" is one that catches among the roots of a tree and burns along or under the surface, rising from time to time to the ground but then returning under or near ground, traveling along again out of sight. In some ways it could be a metaphor for what happened to the values of ancient Crete and Thera. By 1000 BCE and during the early rise of the patriarchs, these values burned mostly underground. During succeeding centuries, elements would flare up from time to time in the mystery celebrations in Eleusis or in the Song of Solomon or in the prophetic tradition of the Hebrews. At Eleusis, celebrations secretly kept alive the hope for life beyond death, as well as for the metaphorical ever-promised return of the feminine, the daughter, and the worship of the grain or the harvest, the natural fruitfulness of the earth. The figure of Persephone returning cyclically from Hades promised eternal springs and a certain triumph of the feminine over death. Female participants were welcomed at Eleusis as well

as men, and goddesses were at the center of the celebration. In all these ways these celebrations seemed to carry forward values more akin to those of the Minoan archaeology than of martial patriarchy.

Sexual rites are also suggested at Eleusis, although these reports come from harshly disparaging Christian sources of the Common Era and are hard to evaluate. Additionally, though we have not discussed them here, in some later forms of the Eleusinian rites the god Dionysus, purveyor of wine and ecstasy, was also celebrated. In the mythology Dionysus was husband to the moon goddess Ariadne, who herself was a princess from Crete. Thus the later mystery celebrations claimed connection with Crete not only through Demeter, who was said to have come from there, but also through Ariadne through Dionysus. The Athenians did not ever quite claim that they had incorporated doctrines from Crete or, that is, from Minoan sexuality and ecstasy, but they did fold

Dionysus neatly into the Eleusinian ceremonies. They told the story that Ariadne, princess of Knossos in Crete, had been saved from her evil father, Minos, by Theseus, and then in turn was abandoned upon the island of Naxos. There the poor girl was left until met and wed by the god Dionysus. Athenians thereby achieved the best of both worlds. After abandoning Ariadne, Theseus came home to build a great patriarchy in Athens. Thereafter the divine feminine in the figure of Ariadne was subjected to the husbandry of the ecstatic god Dionysus, who was honored at Eleusis. But Ariadne herself never came to Eleusis, so in effect the Greeks transferred her feminine qualities to Dionysus, a male wine god, who was—in other stories—regularly given to exaggeration and excess.

Dionysian excess seems not, however, to have occurred at Eleusis, and in that place there was a close approximation of the old Minoan values. Of the five central elements of those values—that is, the celebration of women, their sexuality, ecstasy in general, circular time, and the absence of war—four of these are definitely carried forward. The centrality of the feminine, ecstasy, and circular time are honored here, and this is not a war celebration or a celebration in any sense of heroes. If the later Christian reports are accurate, then there was also sexuality here. All of which strongly suggests that the Eleusinian rites carried forward, albeit secretly, a significant combination of features of the ancient Minoan paradigm. It may have been for this precise reason that they had to be kept secret, under the vision of Olympian orthodoxy, and it is no doubt for that reason that they were known as "Mysteries."

The next undeniable eruption of the root fire was in the teachings of Jesus. I will not write here of Jesus the Christ but rather of the historical Jesus of Nazareth. They are not the same and have different value for different people. Although Jesus the Christ has had a profound impact upon Western history and culture, our effort here will be to excavate from the mountains of Christian tradition those portions of the story that confirm the Eleusinian and Minoan (or Canaanite) package of values. This retelling is interested therefore in Jesus the man. Most of the quotes in the pages that follow are taken from the re-creation of the Jesus story by Henry Burton Sharman, who spent the last forty years of his life teaching, researching, and leading seminars in the pursuit of what he considered to be the most likely core teachings.[1]

Jesus brought the Minoan paradigm to a new level of articulation. Unlike the Eleusinians he took the message with remarkable courage into an open contest with the existing patriarchal authorities. Of the five Minoan values, Jesus gave clear expression, however, to only three: (1) the centrality of natural cycles and indivisibility of the human and the divine that such cycles imply. (These are ways of describing immortality.) (2) the futility or insanity of war, and (3) the equality or dignity of women. In this sense he honored the package that we associate with the divine feminine and can trace back not only to Eleusis but also to Minoan civilization—or in his case, more likely the civilization of ancient Canaan. He did not, on the other hand, give voice to the nonpatriarchal norm for women's sexuality, or particularly to ecstasy, although neither did he condemn these.

Jesus Carries Forward the Eleusinian Symbolism of Grain and Wine

There are direct connections between the celebration that Jesus authored in the communion, or the ceremony of the chalice and the grain, and those that took place at Eleusis. In Jesus' case the teaching is explicit, detailed for the first time, and more directly in confrontation with patriarchal authorities.

At the center of the ceremony in Eleusis, at its height, after nine days of ritual bathing and purification and after a ritual killing of the piglets and the replay of the story of Persephone's return, at the very peak of the experience, a mystical event occurred. Some say it was a sexual performance. Others have also speculated that the ceremony at the center in Eleusis involved a basket with a boy. But most telling of all is the report that a sheaf of *wheat* was held up in the torchlight. Wheat, or grain, was the gift of the goddess Demeter, and the circumstances were meant to inspire awe and reverence. In the dark of night, in a great temple dedicated to initiation, a brilliant light burst forth and a fire blazed up. A sheaf of wheat was held high in the air, and sacred words were spoken. Something was so grand or so moving or so out of the ordinary, perhaps

Fig. 59. Carving of crossed torches that may still be seen today at the entrance to the sacred ceremonies at Eleusis, where secret celebration of grain and rebirth took place annually.

because of its physical nature but more likely because of its emotional impact, that the person who had experienced this moment was thereafter considered "initiated." He or she had entered into the mystery of life, death, and *the return* and been changed by the experience. On this point there is more or less universal agreement: the profound gift of the goddess Demeter was the promise of life beyond the grave, a rebirth, and therefore that "death is not only not evil but is good."[1]

Here, then, is a remarkable carrying forward from the past of the probable meaning of the Minoan pictures and their emphasis on the continuity of life. Minoans celebrated wheat on their pots and jars, frescoes and rings—everywhere in the open. Celebrants at Eleusis put wheat at the center of secret mysteries. Now, fifteen hundred years after the Minoans, Jesus similarly lifts the loaf made from the grain and promises life and death and then the return. Christians would very soon come to treat this ceremony as an initiation.

The chalice had been a central ceremonial object for thousands of years before Jesus. The museum of ancient artifacts at Herakleion, Crete, is filled with multiple examples of elaborate vessels in use by Minoans in the period after 2000 BCE. Colorful decorations and designs make clear that these were used ceremonially. Jesus' use of the same vessel in the center of the ceremony that Christians now describe as communion was not therefore an accident or a new invention but drew from a tradition that traced back to the earth religions much before his time. If Jesus was not intentionally continuing that tradition, it is very curious that he came so close to reproducing the core of it. Rather than a coincidence, it is probable that he intended to point to the theme of agricultural recycling. Further, he is likely to have been pointing to recycling—life, death, and rebirth—as a natural phenomenon of life rather than to his own divinity, a claim which he never seems to have uttered.

It is doubtful that the use of wine in communion was intended to glorify Jesus so much as to glorify the wine itself. Ritual drinking of blood did of course exist in remnants of archaic tradition and have a resonance in *The Odyssey*. Such a rite is, however, substantially inconsistent with the rest of what is known about Jesus, and it is unlikely that he would have used such a ceremony to bring glory to himself, a glorification he opposed in any human anywhere he faced it. When Jesus was asked if he were the Messiah, he would not claim such grand status. He answered only, "If you say that I am." Not only did he not promote the sacrificial tradition from which drinking of blood was taken, he consciously and vocally opposed such practices. He had, in fact, been a scourge in the temple, condemning sacrifice. He was forever pointing the way toward blessings that spring from seeds in the earth (and *not* from sacrifice), or healing from faith in

natural processes (and *not* from magic), or rejection of formulaic ritual as a substitute for inner experience. To be consistent it is therefore highly unlikely that he called for his own remembrance in a ceremony reminiscent of human sacrifice.

The confusion comes because translators in the Christian tradition have reported that Jesus held up a loaf of bread and said, "This is my body." Then he held up the cup and said, "This is my blood." It is far more likely, however, that he held up the bread and said something rather more to the effect of, "My body is *this*." The simple change in the word order entirely reverses the meaning. The words in the new order convey that Jesus is inseparable from the land and its bounty or, more significantly, that *any* human is inseparable from the earth. My body is material; my body, he would be saying, and yours, is part and parcel of the food we eat, the nourishment from the earth, neither less grand nor more grand than that. Such a meaning is directly in accord with the message of the Eleusinian Mysteries and, as important, with the body of the Jesus teachings.

Therefore, if translators or later scribes were given the story of the Last Supper and asked to record it or translate it, they would have had to choose— from those four words—whether to emphasize *Jesus* at the end or the *grain* at the end. In the event, they chose to put Jesus at the end—that is, the words in the order that made Jesus the author of a magic sacrifice. In so doing they chose to step outside the Eleusinian tradition and attempt to create a new tradition. They succeeded, of course. But whether they accorded the true intention of the teacher is another question.

No contemporaneous writing and no writing of

any actual witness to the Last Supper exists. It was spoken in Aramaic and later translated into Greek. Therefore, for all these years, for a reading of this speech we have been dependent upon someone who did not see body language or experience the context. Depending upon how Jesus himself ordered the sentence—that is, depending upon which word he put at the *end* of the sentence—he either said, "I am like the bread" or "The bread is to become like me." In the latter formulation he points toward himself as God. In the former he points to the natural world as divine and finds himself as simply a part of the natural order.

Which did he actually say? In English the last word is typically the most important revelation of the sentence; everything in the sentence leads to that word of conclusion, that finality. Which word to put at the end would have been known in the moment by those who actually heard Jesus speak. But we have no testimony from any such person, and therefore the whole question of the word order would be a matter of some later translator's judgment and intention.

A second-century translator of Aramaic to Greek (and later a translator of Greek to English), in service of the doctrine of the new church, would have *wanted,* or perhaps even been required, to put the emphasis on Jesus rather than upon the grain. Formulating the sentence with emphasis on the natural world would surely diminish the supernatural significance of Jesus. The early church was promoting his divinity. They were not trying to promote his unity with the natural world, and they were certainly not promoting any connection to the ancient earth religions or to the mystery celebrations at Eleusis. There would be references throughout his teaching that could easily point

to Eleusis—as in the pointing to the grain or to the old stories such as the three-day crossover to immortality—and the writers of the Gospels of Matthew, Mark, and Luke could not simply take these references out. They could not delete the stories entirely. But they could materially alter the meaning of a single sentence simply by the way they ordered the four words.

From the life and other sayings of Jesus, it seems far more likely that instead of focusing on himself he was focusing on the simple wonder of a grain of wheat.[2] He was doing much the same as the chief priest in the ceremonies at Eleusis had done. Judging by the humility throughout the body of his work, this self-effacing Jewish reformer would have been far more likely to honor his and his companions' complete dependence upon wheat and wine, his own identification, totally, with the natural fruit of the earth. Perhaps he was of a same mind as environmentalists today, trying to heal the divorce from the earth. He would then have been saying: My body is as natural as this. My blood is as heavenly as wine. Instead of "This is my blood," rather, "My blood is *this.*"

An agrarian's message showing the correspondence between our inner selves and wine makes sense. Wine itself goes through a transformation. The juice of the vine is not good to drink when it first goes into the barrel. The grapes must ferment, and when the wine is ready for consumption it has gone through an inner change and become completely different from when it was harvested. The same can be said for human beings who go quiet and look deeply inward. Or again, wine can free a troubled spirit. The same can be said for inner transformation. Wine's fermenting is therefore a ready metaphor for human change and one that would have been widely understood in the rural area where the teacher, Jesus, lived. In an agrarian world, "*I* in my transformation am like the fermenting *wine*" is a far more understandable preaching than "the *wine* through my own magic turns into my blood and becomes like *me*." The latter describes a process unknown and not actually ever seen by anyone on the planet and therefore requires a new and essentially blind faith. It requires the faithful to sit upon a chair that is not there, and it makes faith itself into a new concept. Faith in this radical sense, that wine turns into blood, requires a leap into the completely unknown.[3] Jesus, on the other hand, if he were truly trying to persuade his agricultural friends, might more likely have been equating human transformation to fermentation, which was a process known to everyone.

One might ask, Would not a rabbi, a teacher of the common people, be far more likely to use metaphors he knew would be understood than to require his listeners to regard as true a phenomenon the likes of which they had never seen?

The church's early founders were still, in the second century, in danger of Roman persecution. An attitude of hopelessness no doubt produced serious arguments between Jesus' followers, and by now some insisted that the only way to salvation would be through a Messiah in whom one could trust totally. Others, including many who had been among the earliest followers of Jesus, vigorously disagreed. But there was more discipline and more security, less personal struggle, in the path of faith in the Messiah than in pursuit of personal, inner transformation.

It is plausible therefore that a simple reversal of sentence order by the scribes of the early church changed the history of the church and diverted it out of the Eleusinian and Minoan streams. Such a change would have resulted in a ceremony that points the finger at the extraordinary and external divinity, Jesus the Christ. Followers would then begin to emphasize Jesus as unnatural rather than natural, once again exporting divinity from the human plane. This exportation of the divine had occurred one thousand years before with the institution of the patriarchal gods in that period between 1500 BCE and 800 BCE. Now it happened again by reversing the significance of the teachings pointing to the lilies of the valley and the birds in the trees. It would come by reversing the meaning of one who seems in most ways to have identified with nature and who may have said, "My body is that … and that … and that … and here … and there … and everywhere." For a thousand years patriarchs had said that heaven, or the divine, was not in here or underfoot but rather out there, in the sky beyond knowing. But according to Jesus, the "kingdom of heaven" was *within and without*, and therefore "communion" would be to understand that it is everywhere.

All this raises, at minimum, the question of how much did Jesus and his cultural circle know about the Mysteries and was there any intentional connection?

He grew up in Nazareth, only about three and a half miles from the major Hellenic city of Sepphoris, a city that might very likely have maintained some variation of the ancient Mysteries of Eleusis or one of the other mystery schools. It would not have been a far walk for a carpenter from the small village to go to find work in the larger town. It is altogether likely, in fact, that Jesus would have often found himself in Sepphoris. If, in turn, he were exposed to the Mystery cults as they were practiced in that town, it is not unlikely that these teachings had an impact on his own teachings about resurrection, the Last Supper, equality as to possessions and as between the sexes, perhaps even as to adultery and to the linearity or cyclical nature of time. There is a surprising consistency, that is, between Jesus' teaching and the teaching inherent within the stories that underlay the Mysteries, and, in turn, the values that underlay Minoan culture, from which we assume the Mysteries originated. This does not answer the question of whether Jesus intended to make a link between his teaching and the Greek Mysteries. But there is enough here to make it a remarkable coincidence of messages if he did not.

Finally, by Jesus' era there had been nearly fifteen hundred years in which wars were being fought to eliminate the culture of circular time and immortality, the symbols for which were the grain and its harvest. According to Barbara Walker, shibboleth, against which the Bible rails, literally translated to mean "ear of corn," which seems to have been the mystical object displayed as the ultimate revelation in temples of Demeter and Astarte. Old Testament writers, says Walker, supposed that the shibboleth was Astarte's dying-and-reborn god, Baal. "Patriarchal opposition to the symbol later made it synonymous with a false deity, a meaning that remains up to the present time."[4] The evil of the shibboleth was not therefore the evil of some person but rather some object, and the object of scorn was not a golden calf or false idol but simply a sheaf of wheat or an ear of corn. There was therefore more than sexuality in the forbidden Jewish past. Cain had been a farmer and was despised while Abel had been a nomad and honored. All these traditions lay in the fifteen-hundred-year rich history of the reformer from Nazareth. From the very beginning wheat somehow had been at the

center of the controversy, and at the height of his spiritual and intellectual powers, Jesus elected to wade in and take a side.

At the Last Supper when Jesus reached for the bread and wine, he held up symbols that connected him both to the underground tradition of the mystery cults of Greece and perhaps to the long-suppressed practices of his Canaanite ancestors. At Eleusis such open expression of the mysteries had been punishable by exile or death. Jesus went the next step and spoke openly of a communion with the divine (reflected in all of nature) and with that an implication of immortality. Or perhaps more accurately, he spoke of the indivisibility between the human and all that sustains us, which, as the web of life is indivisible and not bound by time, is immortal. Today moderns say, We are one or All things are one. The simplicity of the principle is similar to that expressed on pots and walls or even on the sarcophagi of Crete and Thera, where there seems to have been little fear of death. Perhaps Jesus feared death as little as they did because he shared their view in cyclical time and the continuity of life.

Although there is not direct evidence, beyond these similarities, to connect the historical Jesus to the Mysteries of Eleusis, there is considerable evidence that the Palestinian culture in which he lived had been substantially influenced by Greek philosophy. Throughout the Mediterranean there had been a flowering of views in some ways consistent with the ancient earth religions that had built additional sophistication into these early cult practices. In the first century BCE, apparently both before and after Jesus, there had arisen a large number of cults that today are generally grouped together and thought of as "Gnostics." Today, looking back, it is not clear whether Jesus' teachings gave rise to Gnosticism or whether a widespread and prevalent Gnosticism gave rise to the myths of Jesus. And while we cannot tell for certain that Jesus was influenced by the Greeks, it is abundantly clear that the Gnostics were. One of these, a writer by the name of Lucius Apuleius, described his experience of initiation into Gnosticism by direct reference to the Greek goddess Persephone, famous from the Mysteries of Eleusis. He claimed that this (Christian) initiation was modeled after that older Greek one. Another early writer, Hippolytus, attacked Apuleius and others because, as he said, they were relying directly on Eleusinian rites.[5] Finally, in the fourth century, St. Augustine, the bishop of Hippo, who had himself been a Manichean Gnostic, wrote:

> That which is called the Christian religion existed among the ancients, and never did not exist, from the beginnings of the human race until Christ came in the flesh, at which time the true religion, which already existed, began to be called Christianity.[6]

These testimonies are further support for the conclusion that Jesus himself may have been strongly influenced by Greek traditions, especially the traditions of the Mysteries, and may even have intended a continuation of that tradition.

Jesus and his followers carried forward the underground tradition as well in the position that he and they gave to women. The Gnostics were often led by women who taught at their ceremonies and partnered with men all over the Mediterranean world for two hundred years. This was a flowering of feminine leadership that had not been experienced anywhere in the Western world since the decline of Crete and

Thera in 1500 BCE. In that sense the Jesus teachings propagated a dignity for women reminiscent of Eleusis, where women were equally admitted.

There is nothing to suggest, however, that Jesus or any of his immediate followers advocated a return to the earlier sexual freedom that we have imagined in these pages to have been original features of the goddess traditions a thousand years before. Jesus is not known to have advocated sexual freedom. He did make a friend of and include within a beloved circle Mary Magdalene, who may well have been a prostitute and certainly was guilty of adultery. He did not condemn her but welcomed her into his following. In another case he stopped the stoning of a harlot. In this regard he was radically different from his contemporaries. He did also counsel against divorce, which in those times was an institution that aided procreation and maintenance of the male line but that was wholly unfair to females. By claiming that a man should not, under any circumstances, divorce his wife, Jesus was not increasing the pressure on women; their desperate condition remained the same. Women had never had, in any case, any realistic power to divorce their husbands. Rather, he was limiting the freedom of men to cast a woman out onto the street, to abandon her, for any cause the most likely of which would be that she was barren. This was a radical left turn from the traditional teaching and was a pronouncement that certainly worked more to the benefit of women than men. But there is nothing in this teaching that frees women to sexual equality. Jesus did not go back that far. While therefore this is a parting of the clouds of oppression for women, it is probably no more than that. And it is not permanent.

Jesus Takes On the Threat of Military Destruction

One other connection to the ancient Minoan stream of consciousness warrants mention. Jesus seems to have come to a conclusion about war similar to that suggested by the Minoan materials. Conquest simply did not profit a man much. "He who lives by the sword dies by the sword," of course, but more than that, the agricultural principle is that what goes around comes around, that the seasons in a culture's life are inexorable. From this principle one would conclude—much as modern scholars such as Arnold Toynbee have done—that empires too are seasonal. Even death is temporal. The dead seed in the autumn becomes the green shoot in the spring. All these verities reflect badly on the utility of war, and Jesus spoke these verities in many ways.

Seeing that Jewish culture was threatened with extinction if it revolted against the Roman Empire, he urged a less aggressive approach. If his fellow countrymen, known in the debates of the day as Zealots, prevailed over the popular mind and if Jews rose in armed rebellion against the Romans, the handwriting was on the wall. They would lose.

> In that day, he which shall be on the housetop, and his goods in the house, let him not go down to take them away: and let him that is in the field likewise not return back. In that night there shall be two men on one bed and the one shall be taken, and the other shall be left: there shall be two women grinding together the one shall be

taken, and the other shall be left.[1]

As events proved in 70 CE, Jesus' intimations of the Day of Desolation were specific and accurate. Jerusalem was eventually destroyed by the very zealotry against which he had warned.

For a thousand years before his time, unremitting warfare raged throughout the whole of the Mediterranean world. In the course of these years, the Jews were removed by force of arms to Babylon and returned again to their homeland. Through centuries of destruction, ten of the original twelve tribes were wiped out, lost to history. In short order the collapse of the Athenian Empire at the end of the fourth century BCE was followed by the rise of Rome and a new order was imposed by Roman legions. War had become the standard of power, and heroics the measure of a man. Even during the centuries of the Roman Republic, leaders came to power by dint of their military successes.[2] To gain leadership at home, Roman generals indulged in conquests from the Black Sea to Israel to Egypt to Carthage to Gaul. Armed by the liquidation of gold and treasure from these victories, by the beginning of the first century BCE, the Romans were virtually unstoppable. Against them no group of Israeli nationalists stood a chance. By the time of Jesus' coming, rebellion meant destruction not only for the few Jews who rose in arms but for all Judaism. Nevertheless, there was a group of Jews in Israel who sought to throw the Romans out by force of arms. They were called Zealots and were loud and insistent, vying for public consent at the time when Jesus began his teaching.

The great divide to patriarchy, which had been crossed in the years between 1200 BCE and 800 BCE in Greece, had been crossed even earlier in the Middle East. The last of the pure earth religions had been displaced in at least the two or three millennia before the final collapse of Minoan civilization. There were thus at least three thousand years of conquest and reconquest in Jewish tradition—war for so long a period that no one knew to the contrary. It would not have required a sage to look around and see that the consequences had repeatedly included untold suffering and destruction. It would not have required a direct connection to the earth religions carried on through Greeks in the Mystery schools of Eleusis. It would not have required much more than common sense. The times were ripe in and of themselves for an upwelling of some alternative. Any view of human dignity and universal communion would include acknowledgement that all war was civil.

As a practical matter Jesus apparently had the distance from the nationalists to be able to see this equation. Perhaps most compelling of all, however, was his teaching that peace may be not an oppression but a release, a freedom. This would be an internal matter. Peace for an individual would not be won by treaty or by a power balance or by sovereignty or dominion. If peace is a bowing down to oppression, it is a canker. If it is a humbling or a humiliation, there is no joy in it. Better to die with heroic dignity than obsequiousness. The inspiration, rather, of Jesus' teaching was his pointing to an internal transformation that dignifies restraint in the face of anger, that recognizes difference as a positive rather than a cause

for battle, that allows forbearance to be an act of love.

> The lamp of thy body is thine eye: when thine eye is single, thy whole body also is full of light; but when it is evil, thy body also is full of darkness. Look therefore whether the light that is in thee be not darkness. If the light that is in thee be darkness, how great is the darkness![3]

Looking to thine own eye is taking personal responsibility. This can be more of a release, more freeing, than getting wound up in the Gordian knot of justice and revenge. The message is that the promise and richness of life is not dominance but to become oneself a person of light. Focus on this one thing, "that thine eye be single," and the result will be a treasure beyond all reckoning. Wars at that time were fought substantially for territory, for pillage and loot, or, in short, for property. The way to freedom—according to this radical teaching—was not that way.

> Lay not up for yourselves treasures upon the earth, where moth and rust doth consume, and where thieves break through and steal: but lay up for yourselves treasure in [the Kingdom of] heaven, where neither moth nor rust doth consume, and where thieves do not break through nor steal: for where thy treasure is, there will thy heart be also.[4]

This brings any similar teaching—which might have existed in the Mystery cults of Eleusis or the earth religions of the past—to new heights. What was inarticulate on the Minoan pots with their singing swallows and leaping dolphins is now articulate. What is implied in the spirals of life and the promise of immortality in those symbols is stated straight out.

> Be not anxious for your life, what ye shall eat, or what ye shall drink; nor yet for your body, what ye shall put on. Is not the life more than the food, and the body than the raiment?

> Behold the birds of the heaven that they sow not, neither do they reap, nor gather into barns; and God feedeth them. Are not ye of much more value than they? …

> … Consider the lilies of the field, how they grow; they toil not, neither do they spin: yet I say unto you, that even Solomon in all his glory was not arrayed like one of these. But if God doth so clothe the grass of the field which to-day is, and to-morrow is cast into the oven, shall he not much more clothe you, O ye of little faith?[5]

This teaching goes well beyond the imagined meanings of the Minoan materials but is fully consistent. Either such teachings were derived from some underground tradition, such as that inherited through the Mystery schools of the Greeks and therefore traceable all the way back to Crete, or else these teachings arose from some perennial fire in the human heart that catches life spontaneously in times of reflection and reverence. In either case Jesus brings us closer to a doctrine that might accompany and explain the Minoan material more than any writing had done to that time. This is true not only in the obvious reverence for nature and the simplicities of the natural world but also in the reflection of that spirit of nonviolence that pervades the earlier, prepatriarchal Minoan culture. There was no war on the Minoan walls, and there was no war in Jesus' teaching.

In the face of conflict, one should turn the other cheek and, if necessary, offer one's shirt to the man who has already taken one's cloak. When taken out of context the sayings are naïve. When in the context of personal transformation, however, the adversary becomes irrelevant. The sayings are the capstone, the explanation of the freedom that comes from giving up any preoccupation with evil. This freedom would lead a man or a woman to become a person of light. Persons of light would have little use for war, because killing stamps out the light somewhere, in someone else, and in oneself as well. In this sense Jesus the Jew had, at the beginning of the Common Era, brought the innate wisdom of the ancient island cultures to the surface. He had brought the messages of kissing swallows and swinging monkeys, of the joy of the dance, to a brilliant new articulation.

Here also is the likely meaning of the famous parables of the Kingdom of God, an alternative to kingdoms of kings, empires, and high priests. Because of the dangers he faced from the Pharisees, the safest course for Jesus would be to put the proposed solution into parables, or code, for willing listeners. Most interpreters in the centuries since have understood that he spoke of a kingdom in heaven, literally, after death. The concept makes more sense, however, as a description of a successful and nonviolent way to deal with conflict here on earth.

The Kingdom of God, he said, is like a mustard seed. It begins small, with this person and that person and not with armies. The kingdom is not nourished in stony ground, but in your hearts, again, not in your arms. In the kingdom the wheat and the tares grow together, as you will always live among dissent and with disagreement. Rather than rooting out the tares, lest ye root up the wheat with them or pull out the good with the bad, let them be. Moderation works better to turn the mind of dissidents than to conquer them. "The earth beareth fruit of herself, first the blade, then the ear, then the full corn in the ear." Progress is gradual, and the model is again taken from nature rather than the institutions of empire or war. This kingdom is like the leaven in the loaf, and the work of one person will spread to two more who will become three until the whole loaf is leavened. All of this, he said, pointing to the bounty of the earth, is worth more than riches, for the rich man is less apt to pass into the kingdom of such bounty than a camel shall pass through the eye of a needle. Further, all of this is immediately available to the man or woman who turns within instead of following the Zealots toward armed revolution.

The messianic tradition had significant followers among the Israelites, and they earnestly sought some man who would appear and take the Chosen to an afterlife, leaving bad people behind. But the kingdom Jesus described was not like a heaven or an afterlife in the sky. It was like a seed in the ground. It was like the leaven in the loaf. It was *more* valuable than kingdoms (political) and heavens (religious). The idea was not easy for his followers, or anyone else, to grasp. Finally, in frustration, he said, Either you get it, or you don't. "For whosoever hath, to him shall be given; and whosoever hath not, from him shall be taken away even that which he thinketh he hath."[6]

The majority of Jesus' listeners sought justice, freedom, and political independence from the Romans. His teachings, on the other hand, urged a left turn from that majority view, an orthogonal change of direction, with the promise to find abundance in the midst of tyranny, an encouragement to find an internal life in the midst of persecution.

> Behold, the sower went forth to sow: and it came to pass, as he sowed, some seed fell by the way side, and the birds came and devoured it. And other fell on the rocky ground, where it had not much earth; and straightway it sprang up, because it had no deepness of earth: and when the sun was risen, it was scorched; and because it had no root, it withered away. And other fell among the thorns, and the thorns grew up, and choked it, and it yielded no fruit. And other fell into the good ground, and yielded fruit, growing up and increasing; and brought forth, thirtyfold, and sixtyfold, and a hundredfold.[7]

Prepare yourself, be like the fertile ground awaiting the seed. To make this preparation, dig deep, beneath the patriarchal menu, beneath the claims and the rules of Deuteronomy and Leviticus, beneath the Sabbath and the salvation, dig into Isaiah, dig into the deeper meaning of faith and find more. And if a person is looking for riches, then these are true riches, this internal knowledge of life, this reverence for life (one might almost say, this reverence for the feminine). *This* is the pearl of great price.

This teaching was heretical. In all probability it was therefore for this reason that Jesus at first spoke in agricultural parables, avoiding outright contradiction with religious authorities on the one hand or the wrath of politically motivated Zealots on the other. Within the parables would be the moderate message (in other words, revolution will not work) and also the heretical message (in other words, hollow sacrifice at the temple does not work either). "He who hath ears to hear, let him hear," he said, but in the glitter of conquest and clash of arms that eventually brought down the Roman Empire, this part of the message was a hard sell.

As years passed, among those most disturbed by the implications of the agricultural parables was a group of Christian leaders (not Gnostics) who were beginning to winnow out "true" teachings. They assembled a canon and systematically began to brand as heretical those stories and writers who did not serve the purpose of centralization and control. Gnostic writers and teachers who touted the individual experience of divinity were among the first to be attacked. Gospels that the new leaders selected as "true" were now those that required absolute faith in the external God and, by extension, faith in his true representatives here on earth. The adopted "true" canon had the effect of facilitating a patriarchal discipline upon which organizers could build a united church. This canon emerged in the second and third centuries of the Common Era and was decisively different from the gospel conveying the idea that each man or woman had within himself or herself the power to become whole, to gain personal freedom, or to survive spiritually without blessing of leadership. The Kingdom of God was therefore shifted from a doctrine of internal transformation in the manner of the Eleusinian Mysteries to a doctrine of heavenly salvation for those who believed in the Christ. Initiation

into a consciousness of death's redemption and continuation through new life was transmogrified into an initiation for the chosen believers, who would follow an evolving code of conduct to be perpetrated by the church fathers.

The ensuing struggle between Gnostics (who thought they had the original message more in its true form) and the new church authorities was furious and, in the end, brutal. The Gnostics were increasingly opposed by doctrine claiming that the central meaning of the Christian myth was salvation through a male savior. Now church fathers, even the most liberal among them, began to revive the original story of Adam and Eve and with it the complete and total subordination of women. Ephesians, attributed (probably falsely) to the evangelist Paul, made the critical link between subordination and religion, seeming to justify hierarchy as from the word of God:

> For the husband is the head of the wife, as Christ is the head of the church. … as the church is subject to Christ, so let the wives also be subject in everything to their husbands.[8]

In the same vein, I Timothy (also probably falsely attributed to Paul) recalls Eve's sin and commands that women must

> learn in silence with all subjection. I [supposedly Paul] suffer not a woman to teach nor to usurp authority over the man; but to be in silence. For Adam was first formed, then Eve; And Adam was not deceived, but the woman being deceived and was in the transgression.[9]

Sexuality, especially in women, became the subject of Christian opprobrium. Clement of Alexandria (150–215 CE), who was himself among the more liberal of these new leaders, nevertheless regarded sexuality as highly dangerous.[10] Similarly, the bishop of Lyon, Irenaeus (130–202 CE), wrote a massive work condemning the passion of Adam and Eve as an expression of adolescent lack of discipline. These two writers were to be of monumental importance in the history of the church. Biblical scholar Elaine Pagels writes that "Clement and Irenaeus ... set the standard of Christian behavior for centuries—indeed, for nearly two thousand years."[11] We are told therefore that although the two of them disagreed on many things, they did not disagree on sexuality. They did not imagine anything like union with the divine through sexual communion. These two agreed with the authors of I Timothy and Ephesians about the status of women. That status had for a brief moment in historical time (with the Gnostics for about two hundred years) improved. But if the waters of the Red Sea had momentarily parted on the issue of female oppression, by the end of the second century, the sea of the patriarchal order was already closing in again.

Ancient Beliefs Spring Up among the Celts

Out beyond the far reaches of the Roman Empire, beyond the immediate interest of the lords of Rome or the early bishops of the Holy Roman Church, there arose in Ireland a Christianity that blended Gnosticism and worship of natural creation. The prayers and art of the early Celtic church wove together the spiritual and the material, heaven and earth, time and eternity. A hymn attributed to St. Patrick says that God's healing and restoring powers are found in the goodness of the earth. This sounds like an ancient earth religion wrapped in new vocabulary. Here again is a tearing down of boundaries, a sense of connection, as they put it, to the starlit heaven, the sun's life rays, the whirling wind, and even to the rocks.[1]

It did not take long for the Holy Roman Church to respond. When a Celtic Christian by the name of Pelagius began to teach that God was in all creatures, the Celt found himself embroiled in a furious dispute with Augustine, the bishop of Hippo. At this time Augustine was maturing after the riotous, promiscuous lifestyle of his youth. Women were therefore for him the ultimate source of temptation. Pelagius on the other hand taught women to read the scriptures. Augustine saw evil in every woman and man. Pelagius wrote that the image of God is in every child. Augustine held that original sin could only be cured through baptism. Pelagius saw God in everything, with or without baptism.

Women were naturally attracted to Pelagius's tolerant teachings about them and to the teaching that humans were basically good. The Celt wrote, further, that Jesus did not teach doctrine, primarily, but action. A person who does alms (charity) is more blessed than he who goes to church and does not do alms. Augustine, the bishop of Hippo, hearing of all this, was appalled. Augustine had come to blame his youthful, riotous life on the sin of Eve. Because of *her* he had explanation for what he considered to be his own innate and irremediable bad character. Much the way Hesiod had done in blaming Pandora, Augustine blamed his own early temptations and tortures on the first woman, only this time her name was Eve.

Pelagius's teaching cut to the core of Augustine's attack on women. The bishop of Hippo thereupon sought to have Pelagius silenced, enlisting the aid of the His Holiness Pope Innocent I of Rome. The pope at first refused and told Augustine to "love thy neighbor as thyself." Augustine would not, however, relent. He rallied his supporters outside the capitol and then appealed to the Roman emperor. The emperor was, like him, interested in discipline and order. The emperor therefore agreed to quiet the disturbance and banished Pelagius from Rome. The year was 418 CE. A year later the pope reversed himself and also condemned the Celtic monk, who was now not only banished but also excommunicated from the Holy Roman Church. The root fire that had sprung up through Celtic spirituality was being driven underground again. No matter whether in the Mysteries of Eleusis or in the teachings of the Gnostics or those of the Irish, no such threat to patriarchal control could be tolerated. The church fathers were once again chopping at the roots, trying to put out the flames of nature-based spirituality.

Before the Greek poet Homer, the tales of Jason and the golden fleece had been used to disparage women-centered culture, and after Christian canon was established in the third century, Christian/Hebraic myth could be used to the same effect. Now it was the story of Jesus as God and the claim that his church was the only way to immortality. Thus, it is not surprising that in 664 CE the leader of a Celtic religious community, Abbess Hilda, was called before a council in Whitby, England, to answer charges that she and her abbey had followed doctrines of the evangelist John rather than submitting to the authority of the line through Peter. The council was attended by representatives of the Holy Roman Church who insisted upon the preeminence of Peter, not John. Hilda said that they followed John because he had been the disciple at the Last Supper who had leaned on the breast of Jesus. Ever since, she said, this image of John and Jesus had provided Celts with a metaphor of spiritual life. They were to go about with ears to the wind and an eye to the earth, "listening for the heartbeat of God."[2] The emphasis on the natural world was of course pre-Christian Celtic and was part of the underground tradition tracing back to Pelagius. Keeping one's eyes and ears open for all the messages of the earth could even have harkened back to the Minoans. Taking one's cues from earth, however, rather than from government and its administrators, including its tax collectors, would loosen the strict controls of Rome and eventually drain her coffers. The Roman response was therefore a council convened for the purpose of closing down Hilda, her abbey, and her followers of the strong earth messages. The meeting was called the Synod of Whitby.

The decision was similar to the decision of the Roman emperor in 418 CE to ban Pelagius. The king who made the decision at Whitby opted in favor of spirituality mediated through Peter's line and not through John's openheartedness. Peter's line, all male, had by this time ossified into something like the lineage of the begats in Genesis. By the end of the seventh century, therefore, wherever the Holy Roman Church could extend its reach, earthbound spirituality was again scourged or cast out to the secret fringes.

A Short-Lived Islamic Challenge

By the seventh century CE no peace had come to the world through the teachings of the prophets Jesus, Moses, and Abraham. The Christian/Byzantine Empire was engaged in a centuries-old war with Zoroastrians in Persia

> which was to bleed them both white. In the Arabian peninsula, dependent on the diminishing caravan trade between South and North, tribal wars, anarchy, economic decline and increasing camel-nomadism were the rule.[1]

It was into this uncertain situation that Muhammad was born in the late sixth century CE. When he grew to manhood, he married an older woman, Khadija, whose encouragement eventually helped to birth Islam. At that time Judaism, Manicheism, and Christianity, together with polytheism and goddess worship, were spread widely in South Arabia. At a little temple called Ka'ba, near Muhammad's home in Mecca, all the gods were honored, but Allah especially. Muhammad's tribe, the Quraysh, ruled the area. It was their custom to practice religious exercises for a month of every year, Ramadan, including walking around the Ka'ba seven times and other such practices still honored today. It was in one of these Ramadan months when Muhammad was visited in the night by the angel Gabriel. He thought he had been possessed and was disgusted, withdrawing at first to the mountain and then finally in despair to his wife, Khadija, confessing that he had gone quite mad. He was known

in the community as a fair and just man, but he was only a caravan manager, a step above a camel driver. Khadija comforted her husband and said to him, "Rejoice! … for you are a good man and will therefore become a prophet." From then on Muhammad started to teach.

At the heart of the original message of Muhammad's Qu'ran was the principle that God is One, and there is *only* One. In its highest form this is a restatement of the principle of the unity of all, the complete interdependence and nonseverability of everyone and everything. It is the first and most important of the five pillars of the Islamic faith, even today. Obedience to the One God is the heart of Islam. It is not unlike the Jewish command to love God with all one's soul, mind, heart, and strength, which Jesus also stressed as the first commandment. But while the unity principle could be used to unify the nations, it could also be used to divide and separate. As between Jews, Christians, and finally Muslims, the issue would eventually become *whose* God was *the* One. The Jews had also said that there was only one God, but it was *theirs*. The Christians would say that there was only one way, or path, to God, and it was through Jesus. These claims of superior right spawned wars. The wars in turn spawned—as they always had done—a premium on sons and after a period, once again the suppression of women.

In the early years of Islam, women were accorded far more dignity than anywhere in Europe or the Middle East. They were neither treated as property nor traded as chattels. They were allowed, to the contrary, to own their own property and even to divorce. If a husband divorced a woman, he was required to afford to her some maintenance. The Qu'ran said that men and women were equal before God and should therefore work in partnership and harmony together. Most certainly a woman was not to be simply a sex object.

Muhammad by his example had made his wife, Khadija, a companion in the spiritual path. Women were therefore not helpless, and they were to have legal rights. Scattered through the Qu'ran were various lines that spelled all this out, and for several generations it appears that the Prophet's followers attempted to comply and to elevate women to the status that these lines promised. Women were allowed to work and appear in public. They could be educated and they often pursued that opportunity. But the society into which these reforms were introduced had for centuries been thoroughly patriarchal and was highly resistant. What one verse of the Qu'ran gave, another might take away:

> Your women are a tillage for you; so come
>> unto your tillage as you wish, and forward
>> for your souls.[2]
> There was no mercy for adultery for either
>> male or female:
> The fornicatress and the fornicator—
>> scourge each one of them a hundred
>> stripes, and in the matter of God's religion
>> let no tenderness for them seize you
>> if you believe in God and the last Day. …[3]

It is not revulsion against women that is the source of Islam. This is nothing like the contemptuous disrespect of Hesiod for the first woman, Pandora, nor like the monsters of Homer's *Odyssey,* Scylla and Charybdis. This is nothing like the biblical foundation in Genesis, which, by chapter 3, relegates women to the eternal requirement of obedience and submission. The Qu'ran did not arise centrally out of the effort to control women or their sexuality. Islam does not therefore begin where the Greek myths do or where Genesis does, with the need to bring women into the corral of marriage.

That is probably because by the seventh century of the Common Era, patriarchal controls were already bedrock and practically universal in the Western world. Islam did not arise, therefore, as a challenge to the superiority of men in religious and political matters; its reform sprang from a different source. Here was an attempt to overcome sinfulness of other kinds—of drink, of greed, of idolatry. The danger lay in false gods and idols or nonbelievers who do not understand or bend to the will of the prophets, including Moses and Jesus. Marriage was by then assumed, and the subordinate role of women was routine and established. Early Islam was not as brutal to women as Middle Eastern culture had been a thousand years earlier. Muhammad's wife was his first convert and most loyal supporter, and without her Islam might never have come into being. Khadija gave him courage to be a prophet, to follow his path, and she gave him financial assistance. So the story of Islam does not start out vilifying women. But it is assumed that she will come to marriage sexually pure and that all the rules of patriarchy will be observed. By 635 CE female suppression is not necessary; it has already been accomplished.

The fact that women were allowed to own property in Islam might have given them a ticket to independence. Control of property had been the original justification for rules of marriage and virginity both in Greece and among the Hebrews. But in this culture there was never the corresponding respect for mothers and daughters that had been extant among the Minoans, and there was not any such revival of mother-daughter worship as had occurred in secret at Eleusis. Muhammad's code was to establish morality through compliance with rules of prayer, rules of tithing, and rules of Ramadan, all of which tend in their effect to promote not only purity but also hierarchy. In the end it was the hierarchy, and the power that hierarchy purchased, that eventually triumphed over the early reforms for women.

Islamic architecture and design avoid any direct representation of Allah or any association with God of any person. There is therefore no nature or any creature of the live earth represented in Islamic mosques. Some of this architecture—as well as many Islamic palaces—are among the most exquisite building construction in the world. One need only mention the Blue Mosque in Istanbul and the Alhambra of Granada. Little in the world outshines these dramatic and lovely structures. The Alhambra celebrates water and design, but still, all in all, Islam is not a nature worship of any kind. While Muhammad was a reformer, he was not searching back among the earth religions of his past for a revival of its views of immortality or fertility or ecstasy or of the futility of war. Instead, like prophets of ancient Israel, he sought to tighten the code, increase the discipline, straighten out the wicked, and praise an external God. For a time, women benefited. But there never was less war

in the mainstream of Islam or a return to the cultures with women at the center. Unlike even the Gnostics, women in Islam never played a major role as leaders and teachers and were never equal partners in shaping the values and direction of the new codes.

Outside the mainstream, Islamic mystical Sufism was something of an exception. This offshoot bloomed in the eleventh and twelfth centuries and was as full of the spirit of wholeness and communion as anything produced before or since in Europe. Mystics in all religions share a part of the Minoan paradigm as we have imagined it—that is, the sense of unity and ecstasy in the communion with the ever-present, ever-surrounding divine. Sufis too, like students of the Jewish Kabbalah and Christian mystics, discovered their own path to an imminent God. They went to God by reaching both outward and inward at once. They rejected the projection of divinity outward to a male figure—mediated by a male hierarchy—and found God in the world around them, altogether unmediated by anybody. Sufi writers included both men and women; famous poets Hafiz and Rumi were men, but Lalla was a woman. They all found joy in the ecstasy of sexuality. They were not prudish about that. But the ecstasy they sought was beyond sensuousness; it was to unite with the divine, not to milk it. In the last thirty years, Sufism is for the first time becoming something of an inspiration in the West. In the centuries since its origins, however, Sufism never managed to take its place among the central wellsprings of Western culture. Its arrival did not bring surcease to the Western oppression of women or the raging wars of the Middle Ages. When the fields of the Western mind were being trampled by war horses, Sufism was unfortunately only a flower on the far edge of the meadow.[4]

The Metaphor of the Holy Grail

Throughout the early years of the Common Era, the repeated experience was that whenever individual freedom or personal enlightenment began to break the bounds of established knowledge, hierarchy was threatened. Whenever hierarchy was threatened, the mysteries of science or the heart were driven underground and Jesus was crucified, the Gnostics were branded as heretics, Pelagius was excommunicated, or the Sufis were condemned. This pattern was dramatically repeated in the experience of those who engaged in the search for the Holy Grail.

Some say that the search for the Grail leads back through Leonardo da Vinci all the way to Mary Magdalene and her lover, Jesus, and that a clandestine brotherhood passed the secret along for centuries, just below the eye of the church, escaping danger at every turn.[1] But others say, No, the Grail is a black stone, indeed, a fine gem, hidden at rest on a mountain in the Grail Castle, and some say that this is the very same stone that was in the Ka'ba, which is at the center of Islam. Still others say that originally, before all the fuss, the Grail was a flat platter or dish that was carried by the descendants of Joseph of Arimathaea to France and inherited by his family. Still others say that the Grail is not a thing at all but is a certain wisdom beyond description, the inner knowing that comes to only the pure of heart after a life of suffering. But most say that the Grail is a cup or a chalice, the vessel that holds the promise of rebirth. The rich cup is famous in Western lore because its use is said to date back to Jesus, and some say that at one time this cup con-

tained his blood from the crucifixion—that is, the blood that promises rebirth.

The chalice of course had been in use fifteen hundred years before Jesus and twenty-five hundred years before the story of the Holy Grail swept through Europe.[2] Nor of course does the central idea of human rebirth begin with Jesus; it, too, more than likely traces back to the spirals and symbols of ancient Crete. Most probably, faith in rebirth traces back to before and outside the Minoan culture, but that culture is the strongest and probably the best evidence of a woman-honoring, regeneration-loving culture of ancient times, and Minoans certainly made extensive use of the chalice. When the story of the Holy Grail swept through Europe in the eleventh century of the Middle Ages, it was another example of the root fire resurfacing, the flame once again of a very old myth linking a chalice with the feminine and rebirth.

Some say the Grail is the cup, the stone, the mystical container of the feminine, the vessel of alchemical wisdom, or all these together, and that even when it is found, it is not found. The Grail is therefore an *idea* of transformation that is never a physical thing. Whatever it is, the legend of the Holy Grail is that, in the beginning King Arthur's Knights of the Round Table set out to find the cup, as if it were a concrete thing. More than a dozen went off into the woods and forests to find this object, but in the end only three of those many knights who originally set out actually found it. They were, quite improbably, a simpleton (Parsifal), a good man (Bors), and a pure man (Galahad). These three and these three alone made it past evils and demons, dangers and frustration, all the way to the Grail Castle to see the Grail itself. But the storytellers never tell us *what* they saw. Their experience, as it turns out, is *in* them, not out in front of them. It is an internal experience after all: not a thing, maybe not even a cup but, rather, more the *idea* of a cup.

Along the way these three successful searchers had to pass by the castle of a certain "Fisher King," where the land at that time lay wasted and dry because the Fisher King had suffered a wound in his genitals. Now this is a very strange metaphor; it reminds one of the castration of Uranus, about which the Greeks were so concerned at the outset of patriarchal time. It certainly suggests some dangers inherent in maleness, perhaps in male sexuality or even in the foundation of patriarchy. All about the Fisher King's castle, his crops lay dead. The king's plight reminds us also of those earliest tales of Eleusis in which Demeter's daughter Persephone had been raped and taken away by the mighty patriarch Hades. The misuse of male sexuality had caused the great goddess of agriculture, Demeter, to dry up the land. Now, two thousand years later, a similar story arises in the midst of Catholic Europe. Some flaw in a king's maleness is a problem. The flaw resides in the genitals, which might be a symbol for patriarchy itself, and the king, the chief patriarch, *cannot resolve his own pain*. The king needs someone to come and ask a right question. This again is strange. The king did not need some knight to come fight for him or to wage war or to build a cathedral or to write his law codes. He did not need someone to tell him how to become civilized or how to do anything. He needed someone to come from afar and *ask a right question*.

Long ago a question lay at the heart of the story of Oedipus and the Sphinx, and now again a question lies at the heart of the mystery of the blight upon the land of the Fisher King. When Oedipus in his turn answered the question correctly, the symbol of feminine power was destroyed, and those were times of transition out of feminine influence or even feminine control in ancient Greece. By the time of the Grail story, two thousand years later, feminine control is no longer in issue. Feminine control has been completely banished, blotted out, the lands of all of Europe ruled by kings and very subordinate queens. Women are close to chattel and have been so for a very long time. Wars ravage the countryside. The mysteries of life and death are so institutionalized, so lacquered in Latin and filtered through the holy cloth of black-clad priests, that joy has been all but extinguished, and the feminine raised in the figure of Mary the Virgin is so artificial, so pure, so beyond passion or emulation that more than a few must have felt she was distant and untouchable, even alien.

Now into this environment comes the Grail story, which is told by dissenters, by some of those who may have felt that a blight had settled upon Europe, and these may even have been those trying to rebirth the power of regeneration or the mystery of fertility, not only literally but creatively or even spiritually. In the Grail story if some knight could ask a right question, then and only then would feminine power, the power of fertility, be restored, and the lands of the Fisher King would bloom again.

Questions, it seems, dissolve power. In the ancient Oedipus story, during the last of the Bronze Age, women had been in positions of significant control of property and perhaps even were co-rulers of

Thebes. Two thousand years later the reverse is true; kings are in full ascendance without contest or dispute, except that peace never settles upon any realm. In the earlier time Oedipus had to answer the question of the Sphinx, and when he did that, the symbol of feminine power was permanently destroyed. Now, during the Middle Ages in Europe, another riddle must be answered. But this time it is in order to dissolve a patriarch's hold, or perhaps it is to dissolve the certainty of the patriarchal mind. The result will be that the lands of the patriarch will be not destroyed but restored. Believers in the Grail are now therefore spiritual rebels. They have seen the metaphor of the dry land. They believe that such blight is caused by the failure to ask the right questions or even a single right question. The dried-up earth can only be cured, the waters will only flow again, says the legend, when someone correctly answers "Whom does the Grail serve?"

The Grail was magic; it carried a message of transformation, something about the freedom of being. Whom would this magic serve? The story does not tell us specifically but points to only three who were able to understand even the significance of the question. Only these three could penetrate all the way to the Grail Castle. After years of journeys, jousts, pilgrimages, and consultations with oracles and omens, of all the Knights of the Round Table, not Lancelot, not any of the fighters, the lovers, the seekers reached the goal. The secret of life and death was therefore only seen by these three: a simpleton, a good man, and a pure man. That would have excluded popes and kings, barons and priests, traders and usurers, most of those who thought that they had a corner on the power and the property of the Middle Ages.

This message swept Europe in the tenth and eleventh centuries. It mesmerized generations. The times were warlike and feudal, but within this tale was an unwarlike message, a way to understand what might have gone wrong within the feudal hierarchical system. The Grail did not serve the Fisher King or any kingly hierarchy; it could not therefore serve patriarchy alone, nor could it be measured in any way as to whether it did or did not serve property. It served the simple, the good, and the pure. To these alone it offered the promise of rebirth.

The earliest texts mentioning the Holy Grail were from the late 1100s. They offered a quest for a cup or a dish that had been brought to Europe by Joseph of Arimathaea, who knew certain teachings not revealed even to the apostle Peter. Escaping from persecution, Joseph had founded a secret church, perhaps in Glastonbury, England, and for some centuries this Glastonbury cult flourished alongside the established church, though not sanctioned by it. The cup of course was supposed to have originally contained the sacred blood of Jesus, but as the centuries evolved, the focus centered on the mysterious chalice itself. It had deep historical antecedents, as we have seen. There was a formulation at the Mysteries of Eleusis in which the initiate took a drink of a liquid called *kykeon*, mixed from barley and pennyroyal. "Initiation" at Eleusis meant that a person passed in trance from this life into another world, a world of delight and healing. Both at Eleusis and Glastonbury the experience—and it appears to have been more an experience than an idea—was certainly rebirth.

The vessel also had a soul connection in the Celtic tradition, where it was conceived not as a cup but as a *cauldron* of rebirth. Celtic legend held that in hell a man could be dipped into this cauldron head first and be restored to life.[3] The experience would, again, offer the promise of immortality. Now, this is not inconsistent with the Jesus myths in that the chalice is in that instance also a vehicle for eternal life, but in the Celtic case, the rebirth came through being dipped into inspiration, into the center of the circle of life. This message was not inconsistent with the original meaning of the Jesus communion, but it was definitely inconsistent with official dogma. In the sanctioned Catholic myth, it was God, and God alone, who produced salvation. The Holy Roman Church set down elaborate rules to determine who was qualified to receive this God. At ancient Eleusis, by contrast, the initiation had been available to any man or woman who spoke Greek and was not a murderer. Fifteen hundred years later, the official church held that it was only those who adhered to their sacraments—which they would themselves prescribe—that one might come to God. The Grail dissidents did not totally disagree. They said that true initiation, the passage, the healing and transformation, was limited to the fool, the good man, and the pure virginal knight. This alone, however, this permission for the individual saint as opposed to the saint determined by the hierarchy of the church, was sufficient to eventually incur the wrath of the pope.

The quest for the Holy Grail did not include women. Rather, they were enjoined to be like the Virgin Mary: pure, holy, and otherworldly, giving birth as required, submitting to the rule of heaven explained to them by men. Worship of the figure of Mary had become by the eleventh century a matter of astounding proportions. There were therefore these two major currents swirling through Europe throughout the course of several centuries. The stories of the Grail were very popular and circulating all throughout the continent and in England. For men, they were exhortations to goodness and purity. At the same time there were exhortations for women to be like the Virgin—pure and heavenly. Clearly, many men and women were inspired by each. Magnificent cathedrals were dedicated to the Virgin. Armed knights went about dedicating themselves to virginal, pure love for courtly ladies, mimicking the knights who had gone off in the stories in the search for the Holy Grail. The new knights sought to heal the sick and care for the poor and be more like Jesus than Jesus.

Finally, modeling themselves on these Grail knights, a group arose in France who called themselves "Cathars." They soon gathered thousands of followers. Perhaps the corruption and rich display of the Roman Church was repugnant, or perhaps it was the perennial search for some passage or initiation that could promise a glimpse into, or some hold onto, immortality. Like Gnostics before them Cathars believed that every man was responsible for his own soul. But taking personal responsibility once again undermined the authority of the priesthood and especially its rules of conduct. Just as, three centuries earlier, the central powers of church and state had collaborated to eliminate the instability caused by Celtic spirituality, once again the central authorities determined to overcome the erosion of control caused by freethinking Cathars. In 1208 CE Pope Innocent III, acting more like a king than a spiritual leader, launched a holy war against Cathars in Languedoc and Provence, both in France. He destroyed their castles, rounded them up, and burned at the stake hundreds of their followers along with their leaders and priests.

Some have called it the first European genocide, so horrible and unearned was the fury of the pope.[4] When it was done, those who had tried to tell a new story of salvation, this time personally embodying the ideals of the knights of the Holy Grail, had once again been eliminated.

One of the last of the Cathar strongholds was a castle in southern France, Montségur. Its governor was a woman of great spirituality and goodness, one Esclamonde de Foix. Her prominence was in itself a sign of irregularity, of deviance from the male hierarchy in Rome, and it carried within it a threat to established order. The siege had come; the pope's armies had arrived to wipe out this one last outpost of heresy. Then, in the midst of the pope's siege of Esclamonde's castle, high on her castle wall appeared a single Cathar wearing a suit of gleaming white armor, the brilliant appearance of a knight of the Holy Grail. The pope and his armies looked up, stunned.

At this dramatic moment the white knight on the ramparts and the immaculate pope below represented two entirely conflicting world views. On the ramparts was a figure who embodied the story that power comes from personal responsibility and transformation, represented by one man. Down below was a figure who embodied the story of original sin that must be controlled and disciplined, represented by an army. As the soldiers below gasped and gazed at the white-armored figure on the castle wall, these two historically significant stories hung in the air, vying for supremacy. For a shining moment the Grail story suddenly triumphed, and the besiegers turned and fled.

It was some time before the pope could rally his supporters to his other story, the patriarchal choice between good and evil and the benediction of power. Eventually, however, he was able to do so. He renewed his siege, the governing lady Esclamonde de Foix died, and the castle fell. Legends say that after her death, a great treasure of that fortress, a certain "rich cup," was smuggled out of the castle, and to this day no one knows where that cup has gone.[5] From these roots we have the continuing mystery of the Holy Grail.

The last of those who tried to put the ancient story of transformation and rebirth into daily practice had been quelled, and its symbol, the "rich cup," vanished. On the other hand if the Grail was not just a chalice, but if rather the meaning of the circular rim was the transformation that comes from heading into the cauldron, the fires of life, then the Grail would always be here and there and everywhere. The imminent spirit once portrayed in the frescoes of leaping dolphins and dancing ladies under the moons of Knossos had now been imagined again in the very center of a chalice. The paintings on the walls of Crete and Thera were taken down by earthquake or perhaps by Indo-European invaders who brought with them the patriarchal norm. The Grail Castle and its mysteriously similar message had been destroyed by invaders again, and then again on behalf of a decidedly patriarchal hierarchy.

In the earliest years of patriarchy, during and after the Bronze Age, suppression of women had been an effective means to establish a male line and thereby to claim and control rapidly increasing gains from trade and piracy. To create a cosmology and religious sanction for property had been at least one function of *The Iliad*, *The Odyssey*, and Genesis. Two thousand years later, by the time the Cathars were destroyed in France, the patriarchal system had become so widespread, so powerful, so fully established in its hierarchies that no ordinary men or women could challenge its dominion. But throughout that whole two thousand years, patriarchy had failed to provide any replacement for the simple joy in the art of the Minoan frescoes, or in the celebration of the daughter's return at Eleusis, or even in the wondrous birth as it emerged in the story of the miracle at Bethlehem (later converted to patriarchal purposes). Patriarchy had not imagined any replacement for the singing faces of the men on the famous harvester vase in Crete. Nor had it found some culture of openhearted communion with birds and the fish of the sea and the moon in the sky. To the contrary, it had suppressed these cults whenever they arose, as in Jerusalem or Ireland or the castle at Montségur.[6] Nor had the patriarchs found a way to bring women back into the center, to honor their passion and miraculous powers of regeneration. They were honored for their sexual restraint, but never for their sexual miracle. Nor, profoundly, had patriarchs found some reverence for life, some experience of the cycles of rebirth, that would

make killing a useless act. Kill a man and he will simply come back, the oldest beliefs had said. Nay, kill a warrior and banish him forever to Hades, the Greek patriarchs had rejoined. Patriarchy had not, in two thousand years thereafter, found a causal connection between death and new life. Patriarchs promised heaven in another, removed world. They had no theory of heaven on earth.

By 1200 CE and the extinction of the Cathars, patriarchy had been at war so long that it had proved, again and again, the point of the Greek story of dragons' teeth: warriors planted in the ground only to breed more warriors. King would fight king again and again, and those who raised question about Zeus's mythological progeny—Peace, Order, and Justice— were themselves cut down in the general melee that tolerated dissent not at all. By the Middle Ages the power of patriarchal armies had combined with the orthodox mythology of both Christianity and Islam, and these powers had become untrammeled, everywhere ascendant, and uncontested.

Devil Talk and Witch Burnings

The worst of the patriarchal catastrophes, however, was not the suppression of the Cathars or the Gnostics, and not Greeks "taming" women and turning them into chattels, and not even the crucifixion of Jesus. In a perfect world one would be tempted, certainly, to put King Agamemnon on trial for the murder of his daughter, the sweet Iphigenia, or perhaps it should be Erechtheus for the sacrifice of his daughter Otionia. But none of these represents the worst of the consequences of patriarchal misogyny. If, in a moment of justice, one were to put the patriarchs on trial, one would have to conclude the case, sum up the evidence, and make as a final argument the absolute and unmitigated horror of the burning of the witches.

The trial of Joan of Arc in 1431 was manually recorded as it was taking place, and its transcripts are available to us today. A simple farm maid had gone off from her village to lead a war to restore the king of France to his throne. She had led armies with great courage and flown about in battle with her banner waving, driving the English in front of her. She had developed an aura, a mystical quality, and she said she went into battle having been commanded by voices of her angels, St. Margaret and St. Michael. She had become a living example of the power of woman and the ecstatic combined. Then, in a sudden turn of fate, she was captured by disloyal French and ransomed over to the English. They put her in prison in Orleans and put her on trial, not for political offenses, not for revolt, but for heresy and witchcraft. The charge read that she should be denounced and declared

a sorceress, diviner, pseudo-prophetess, invoker of evil spirits, conspiratrix, superstitious, implicated in and given to the practice of magic, wrong-headed as to our Catholic faith ... mischievous, blasphemous towards God and His saints, scandalous, seditious disturber of the peace, inciter of war, ... having completely and shamelessly abandoned the decencies proper to her sex. ... [1]

She was tried before bishops and clergy, the assembled principals and scholars of the Holy Roman Church. She appeared before them completely alone. Although she could neither read nor write, she maintained her wit and intelligence, matching point by point first one interrogator and then another. One asked if St. Margaret spoke to her in English. "Why should she," replied Joan, "since she is not on the English side?"

She denied that she was a witch, claiming only that she had been visited by angels and commanded by them to leave her village and save France. Why had she not married, they asked, and had children like any other woman? She meant no harm to the church, she replied, but loved her country more than any man she had yet met. Why, then, they wanted to know, had she *dressed* like a man? Why so careless with the symbols of her female purity? It is safer, she replied reasonably, when riding and moving among common soldiers to dress like a man and so not to attract their attention.

The bishops shifted ground. Did she not know that for a farm maid to talk directly to God was not credible, that such connection to the Almighty could only be had through learned priests and bishops? Yes, she said, she did know, but St. Margaret and St. Michael had come to her nonetheless, and she could not pretend that she did not hear them. She loved her angels more than anyone, more even than these lord bishops who were asking her questions.

Responding to some such ecstatic impulse, women had once been portrayed dancing on the golden seal rings from the fabled Minoan palace at Knossos. A thousand years thereafter, in classical Athens, in some such manner, women must have explained to their husbands why they attended three days of women's dancing and keening on the mountains outside the city at the festival they called the Thesmophoria. In some such manner, Gnostics and medieval mystics must have exalted their own direct communion with God; in some such language, Jesus and Pelagius and seekers for the Holy Grail had sought and explained their connection with the One, or the Source, or the Father and Mother of us all. In some such experience, beyond all naming, men and women over the centuries had given witness to the ecstatic, and since that earliest beginning, in some manner, over the course of nearly three thousand years, with gradually increasing severity, patriarchal powers had crushed them.

The bishops probed for a weakness. The nineteen-year-old girl fought for her life, and the hierarchy sought to maintain its authority, the source of its power. Through it all, out of the righteousness and condemnation, out of the mists of accusation and scholasticism, slowly emerged a remarkable,

outwardly untrained but inwardly elegant young woman.

Trials such as Joan's had been going on, dating from about 1100, all over western Europe and continued throughout the course of six centuries. Women like Joan who acted with unusual independence—midwives, healers, women who drove hard bargains in the sale of eggs or a cow, women whose husbands were impotent, women who were themselves barren or were in contact with others who were barren—were throughout the course of this period charged as witches. A man charged that during a certain transaction a woman had said to him, "You will be sorry for this," and that simple female shopkeeper was accused of being a witch. The man testified that when he turned around to look at the woman, his mouth had gone out of shape and had not gone back to its right shape for three days, and that this was proof that he had been bewitched.

In time Pope Innocent VIII became fully alarmed and issued a papal bull in 1484 saying that witches were hindering men from begetting and women from conceiving. The fields were dying, calves were not being born, men were being tortured by the devil. The pope commissioned two Dominican priests to instruct judges how to track down more witches. Two years later these two Dominicans issued the famous *Malleus Maleficarum* ("The Hammer of Witches") explaining, as they thought, the whole phenomenon. The very word *woman*, they wrote, "is used to mean carnal lust."

I had rather dwell with a lion and a dragon than to keep house with a wicked woman.
  … All wickedness is but little to the

wickedness of a woman. … What else is woman but a foe to friendship, an unescapable punishment, a necessary evil, a natural temptation, a desirable calamity, a domestic danger, a delectable detriment, an evil of nature, painted with fair colours! … When a woman thinks alone, she thinks evil.[2]

Neither the Dominicans nor the pope, of course, knew anything of the Minoans. They had, however, inherited the biblical and Greek mythology, which had arisen in response to Minoans and to confound Canaanite followers of Astarte, and which had from its very beginnings identified and suppressed the central values of the prepatriarchal world. The female, her ecstasy, and her sexuality had always been condemned. Now, in 1486, they summed up two thousand years of misogynist history: "When a woman thinks alone, she thinks evil." If the poor creature were to think independently, she might make her own connection to God. If, further, what is meant by God is some essence that lives forever, is immutable, then this is the experience through which human connects to the *immortal*. Immortality, as we have seen, was the final piece of the Minoan, prepatriarchal world view. Immortality in the hands of a woman was the very offer that Calypso made to Odysseus and that Zeus commanded the Bronze Age hero to reject. Joan of Arc was participating in an ancient mystic ritual with the inner divine, which was in a way her claim to connect with that same immortality. Like Calypso and Eve and all her sisters over the millennia, she posed too great a threat to be tolerated.

Some scholars have found in Eve a symbol of wholeness. For some that may be true. But for the Dominicans who wrote *Malleus Maleficarum*, Eve was not a metaphor for human growth or for completion. To the contrary, she was the first and primary example of godless wickedness. A woman, they said, any woman, is quicker to waver in her faith and consequently to abjure her faith, and this wavering "is the root of witchcraft." Further, if the Bible stories were not enough, *Malleus* also relied on Greek myth. Woman is the Chimera, an image straight out of Hesiod from the eighth century BCE:

> [The Chimera's] face was that of a radiant and noble lion, it had the filthy belly of a goat, and it was armed with the virulent tail of a viper. … [It] means that a woman is beautiful to look upon, contaminating to the touch, and deadly to keep.
>
> Let us consider another property of hers, the voice. For as she is a liar by nature, so in her speech she stings while she delights us. Wherefore her voice is like the song of the Sirens, who with their sweet melody entice the passer-by and kill them. For they kill them by emptying their purses, consuming their strength, and causing them to forsake God.[3]

Accused women were under suspicion of copulating with the devil and then of shamefully denying that they had done so. The denial itself, said the Dominicans, was heresy. Protecting a woman who denied that she had slept with the devil was therefore protecting the devil and was also heresy. The practical effect was that a defender of an accused witch could only protect her if he was willing to "protect heresy."

The Dominicans warned that any such man should know that he was at risk of being excommunicated or even being accused himself. Under these conditions no man could safely defend a witch, or certainly not defend a witch with the effect of having her acquitted, because to do so was to risk being condemned himself. Few ever did defend them, and almost all those accused of witchcraft were therefore convicted. Finally, as a result, the accused discovered over the years that they had no hope to defend themselves with logic or reason. Many therefore chose to remain silent. The Dominicans then devised a way to catch them even if they did not talk.

A woman's silence, they said, would be evidence of the devil's hold upon her soul. She should therefore be tortured for her own sake, to gain a confession, to break the devil's hold upon her. This was a delicate decision, the Dominicans admitted. Many would not ever confess. "The torture step," as they called it, was tantamount to a death sentence. The Dominicans explained what to do:

> Now a surgeon cuts off rotten limbs; and mangy sheep are isolated from the healthy; but a prudent Judge will not consider it safe to bind himself down to one invariable rule in his method of dealing with a prisoner who is endowed with a witch's power of taciturnity and whose silence he is unable to overcome. …
>
> If he wishes to find out whether she is endowed with a witch's power of preserving silence, let him take note whether she is able to shed tears when standing in his presence, or when being tortured. For we are taught both by the words of worthy men of old and by our own experience that this is a most certain sign, and it has been found that even if she be urged to and exhorted by solemn conjurations to shed tears, if she be a witch she will not be able to weep: although she will assume a tearful aspect and smear her cheeks and eyes with spittle to make appear that she is weeping.[4]

It was under these conditions and within the collective body of this patriarchal mind that Joan of Arc was brought to trial.[5]

Estimates of the numbers of witches killed during these six hundred years range in the literature from seventy thousand to millions. One television program ran on public stations in America for years claiming that the number was as high as 9 million, nearly all of them women. The witch burnings were patriarchy run beyond its moorings, completely amuck. Centrally, these horrendous events were not just patriarchy wallowing in its evil, an analysis that suggests that the problem is merely bad men. The scourge that was harrowing Western Christendom was a combination of fantasies of the late Bronze Age carried along and amplified through the centuries until they were actually overpowering the rational mind. Scylla and Charybdis, Circe and Calypso, and Eve and Medea were the forerunners of this scourge, and without such predecessors in Greek story and biblical myth it is unlikely that any two Dominicans or a single pope could have brought their world into such a convulsion of accusation and hatred.

Stories organize the mind. They can be beneficial, but they can also be perfidious instruments. No

one had ever seen Satan, but the very word, the mythical idea, conjured up a power stronger than anyone's actual experience, and untold numbers began to imagine that they had seen him or his works. No one had ever made a compact with Satan, signed a document, inked the paper, or produced some such paper in court for cross-examination, but the stories of such compacts overpowered common sense and convinced otherwise rational men that just such a contract had actually been made. Patriarchy had originally been grounded in stories of evil and sexual women, and those stories had, after two thousand years, become reality, overpowering anything anyone had actually experienced. Ideology and imagination, story and myth, substituted for evidence and carried the day for six hundred years. The authors of *Malleus Maleficarum* put a cap on the tale and wove a web of conviction entirely consistent with Hesiod's original description of Pandora, whom the old Greek said had been the ruin of mankind.

Men under the spell of these stories at last led Joan of Arc from her stone cell in Orleans, took her into the grand courtroom, and pronounced her a sorceress and a witch. The executioner and his cart stood waiting for all to see. A crowd of citizens watched the defendant, all eyes glued to her face. Joan of Arc, the Maid of Orleans, who had sought to restore the French king to his rightful throne, who had flown about the battlefield on behalf of France, now was accused by French patriarchs and had not had one person to defend her, not one word of advice or assistance or any evidence presented on her behalf. Then it was done, the sentence pronounced. After months of prosecution and humiliation, days when she had been examined to determine if she were

virgin, days when all the great minds of Europe had been united to outsmart her, the little girl who had grown up tending cows and ducks collapsed. She fell at last on the floor, shaking and sobbing, surrendered her pride, her denials, her direct connection to her voices. She gave them all away. She *would* recant all her conversations with St. Margaret and St. Michael. She would do, from now on, only what the church told her to do. She said it again and again. She *would* recant.[6] The French bishops and the English soldiers went into a frenzy. The surprised judges did not know what to do next. They asked Joan to sign a document. She made a mark, for she could neither read nor write, this woman who had stood the church and all of Europe on its head these many months. She was led away, safe for a moment.

It was not over. The English were furious. They conspired then to force the French to reverse their acceptance of the Maid's recantation. The French thereupon sent a gentle bishop to interview her one more time. He found the girl alone, weeping in her cell. "Had she heard the voices since her recantation?" the bishop asked. "Yes," she said, fatally, she had heard them again, just now. Then she said, "I consented in making the abjuration and revocation to save my life, and in saving my life I was damning myself. ... I did very wrong. ... It was fear of the fire which made me say that which I said. ... "[7] There on the floor of the cell, before the old bishop, the trembling young woman recanted her recantation.

On Wednesday, May 30, 1431, in Orleans, Joan the Maid, probably more pure of heart than any of her persecutors, was burned alive for witchcraft and sorcery.

Burning a live human being is beyond imagination. Burning thousands or millions of them is quite beyond comprehension. Every single one of them must have gone through some experience equivalent to that of Joan, though not of course in such grand circumstances or with such a parade of bishops. The ending, however, must have been always somehow the same: collapse, tears, disbelief, horror, and sometimes a willingness to accept death itself rather than be untrue to the inner voice.

A story had been found to divide the human mind from reality, to give women's character an existence unaffected by the evidence. It was the story of the natural inferiority of the female and the natural right of men to manage, subordinate, intimidate, and impregnate them. If ever, in an abundance of justice and righting of the wrongs of history, there were a trial of the patriarchal storytellers, of Hesiod and Homer and the author of Genesis, the burning of witches would be the first itemization of consequential damages in the long criminal complaint. Women of decency and passion, women who were healers, women of character and strength who might have offended someone or made a man grimace—as the record says—for three days, women who cared for the elderly and helped birth the young, women who spoke out with bold courage like Joan of Arc, and women who remained timidly silent, all were rounded up in village after village and led away to the fire.

Closing the Book on the Patriarchy

When Heinrich Schliemann first excavated Troy in the late 1800s, he did so on the hypothesis—then widely questioned—that the Trojan War was history and not fiction. Until Sir Arthur Evans began digging in Crete in the early part of the twentieth century, the record of that island civilization—which was supposed to have existed even before the Trojans—was largely unavailable. What we knew was limited to the disparaging and damaging images in the stories of the Greeks. There were no collections of pots, not a single wall fresco, no rooms of lilies and dolphins, no lustral basins upon which to judge the reality of Crete. It was even later after that, 1952, when we were first able to translate the written language called Linear B, which gave some clue to Bronze Age Greek bookkeeping. Even more recently, the 1960s produced the wall paintings from Thera that show the elegant women gathering flowers, the monkeys swinging, and the swallows kissing under the moon, a message in stark contrast to all the Greek art about which we already knew. Then again, in 2003, scientists revisited the Theran explosion and reported revised conclusions, that the volcano blew up at about the same time as Minoan culture had abruptly declined.[1] With a high degree of probability it can now be said that the Theran explosion created not only an agricultural and political crisis but also, without question, a spiritual one. The Earth Mother had literally exploded in the faces of those who believed in planting, in the recycling of life by reseeding, in the centrality of flowers and spring, in the beauty of women and their powers to give birth, and in women's power to mimic the earth and redeem death. Earth had discredited herself.

Within three hundred years after the Theran explosion, the Aegean had fallen into civil war. It is highly probable that the underlying issue was the policy question of whether a woman should be kept in a monogamous marriage or could choose for herself or could choose no marriage at all. As a practical matter it boiled down to controlling women's sexuality. Ultimately, the flash point was over the issue of who would inherit and keep property. The Mycenaeans led this war because theirs was the dominant kingdom of mainland Greece and because no warlike kingdom could survive without identifiable male heirs. The increasingly preeminent value of sons and therefore the sanctity of the male line and the ultimate control of countries was at issue. On the other side of this war were the Trojans and their allies, a scattering of cities across the Aegean and Anatolia who shared a view that women might choose monogamy or any of the alternatives. Trojan roots were deeper into the mainland, more agricultural, less nomadic. They do not appear to have been descendant from the so-called Sea Peoples or raiders, nor were they apparently a recent migration, as the Greeks may have been. Trojans were neither the dominant sea nor land power. They seem to have been a trading center on the way to Colchis or to inner Anatolia or to Phrygia and the Hittite empire. As trading increased, the value of sons who could more easily travel would also have increased, and they may have been a culture in transition. They lay on the periphery of earlier empires that had by then rendered the center of Mesopotamia thoroughly patriarchal. By their acceptance of Helen as the meandering queen from Sparta, they apparently accepted the central value of women and their daughters, the communal responsibility for children, and the divine blessing of birth, no matter who the father.

Agamemnon and his assembled tribal chiefs won this war, claimed to their benefit the assistance of the suborned goddesses Hera and Athena, and established for all time the centrality of marriage for women, reinforced by divine order. The rest is history.

This dismal Olympian view of the role of women was in dramatic contrast to the traditions of Crete and Thera and probably many cultures extending through Canaan, across Anatolia and Lydia, and down to Babylon. Women who did not agree with the hegemony of Zeus and men who agreed with their women were forcefully converted. Women were vilified, portrayed as snakes, demons, monsters, maneaters, seductresses, and enchantresses. Here in these portrayals are the origins of misogyny, which does not come from trade or conquest or riches or even the supposed natural dominance of powerful males. There is nothing in this collection of images that arises naturally, or necessarily, out of the conditions of the times, neither from increasing Mediterranean trade nor improved techniques of war nor natural disaster of the Theran volcano. Misogyny, rather, is a concoction that comes directly from the stories. Women, Hesiod wrote in a phrase that was entirely gratuitous and not required by any of these other causes of patriarchy, had been the ruin of mankind. Greek schoolchildren thereafter were required to memorize his words. The option for women who did

not agree with this rampant misogyny was to take the agricultural ceremonies underground at Eleusis, to separate out from men at the female-only fertility celebration of Thesmophoria, to make secret the magic of perpetual rebirth. A practical political compromise was therefore reached in which the women of Greece remained in the back rooms except at these secret celebrations, while on public monuments such as the Parthenon, the victory of the marriage culture was rendered glorious and as the foundation of Athenian power.

Someone needed convincing, probably including those who had until then traded icons of women with wings and laid these icons in graves as a part of their faith in the feminine principle. To discredit women and communal property, the mythmakers named the monster Echidna; others who did not honor marriage were demonized as Centaurs, Amazons, Cyclopes, Lemnians, and opponents of Heracles. Persuasion was then backed by force, and the tales they told were of opposition and conquest, not ever of peaceful assimilation or love or nature's harmonious balance. We now know that what was being extinguished had been more benign, more hopeful, more focused on the cycles of life and death leading to new life, and less preoccupied with endless death.

In sum, five major themes are found in the older frescoes, the seal rings, on the pots, and in the friezes and figurines, and each is later contradicted by the Greeks:

1. The first is the idea of rebirth, and this is in turn a pointer toward immortality. Throughout the artifacts, honor is given by the Minoans to life-forms that die or disappear and are then in some sense reborn (the tree, the bee, the snake), subjects that create an

implication of life as sufficient to perpetuate itself indefinitely. Death is therefore not portrayed anywhere as evil but rather as a link between cycles and therefore as a *cause* of life that goes on continuously and—before individualism—is a way of imagining human immortality. Time is imagined as circular, cyclical, seasonal, and revolving indefinitely, which creates a greater sense of presence in the moment because every moment is both past and future. Progress, which is a function of linear time, is not a fixation.

The symbols that suggest these values are gradually replaced in the Greek archaeology. Birds, bees, trees, butterflies, et cetera, are replaced by pictures of awful death: conquest over gods of the old order; spearing of Amazons; killing of Giants, Cyclopes, a Gorgon (Medusa), or Centaurs; and finally, the arrival of Hades as the all-powerful brother of Zeus. Death comes with agony and is final, not any part of a cycle. Immortality is exported to Elysian Fields, for heroes only. Demeter, Eos, Medea, and others are portrayed as having misused the power to make men immortal; Heracles ultimately steals the belt of immortality, ending the female promise of eternal continuation. Seasons can now be interrupted by Hades; Zeus can even make Helios, the sun, reverse directions; Hades controls Persephone and therefore has ultimate control over her. The eternal order is rendered not dependable but intemperate and erratic.

2. A second major Minoan theme is that the feminine principle is honored and portrayed at the center. Images of women vastly outnumber men and are central to iconography, painting, ceremony, and public life. Women are dressed elegantly and are honored on reviewing stands and mountaintops while men bring them gifts, and never once are men seen harming them.

In the Greek pictures to follow, by contrast, women are vilified, distrusted, portrayed as Sirens, Harpies, Furies, Scylla, or Charybdis, all of whom are dangerous, untrustworthy, niggling, and at best a necessary evil.

3. Third, it is apparent from Minoan archaeology that sexuality (including women's) is celebrated in symbol, in dance, in bare-breasted statuettes, and encoded in the symbols of lilies, dolphins, fish, and snakes.

In the Greek materials the contrast is again obvious. Female sexuality is dangerous (Circe and Charybdis), corrupting (the serving maids hung by Odysseus), arrogant (Semele, who wants to look upon Zeus), a source of hubris (Niobe, who loves her children), purchased at war (Cassandra, daughter of the fallen king of Troy), traded for as chattel (Achilles' slave girl, Briesis), and ultimately degraded on numerous scenes of bacchanalia, with obscene men intent upon rape, chasing terrified women.

4. The Minoans seem to have no fear of ecstasy or joy or grace. These are celebrated in paintings, seal rings, and figurines of bull leapers, women dancing on the mountain, dolphins leaping above the waves, swallows kissing in midair, and gentle, obeisant griffins, and there is a graceful elegance in some pottery vessels as fine as any ever produced.

The Greeks who come after and reject all this do not celebrate joy but exaggerate its worship in the excesses of Dionysus. They warn against the dangers of wine or of women, who will eat a man alive and replace the ecstasy of natural order with the ecstasy of battle.

5. Finally, in the Minoan materials there is one remarkable omission:

War is absent.

In the Greek myths, to the contrary, war is ubiquitous and is everywhere celebrated, heroes of war are rewarded by immortal life, and carvings of war are on every major temple. Pots, vases, and jars portray men killing women or Centaurs or Giants or Cyclopes or Trojans.

And here is one of the central points of this comparison: it is the very extraordinary coincidence between these later myths and the predominant values represented in the Minoan artifacts that makes it most likely that the latter were related directly to the former. The five themes of Minoan materials are not just any five themes; they are five major themes. The focus and concentration of the subsequent Greek culture on these same five themes is too extraordinary to be coincidence. It seems clear that the subsequent stories are therefore a rejection; that the turning point in Homer, for example—the rejection of Calypso and all her kind—was pointed directly at the Minoans and their cosmic paradigm with its cluster of feminine principles. The same must be said of Jason and his rejection of the Lemnians and the Amazons or of the killing of the Amazon queens by Heracles and Theseus. They are all too related to earlier cultures to be fairy tales, and they are all too violent to signal a benign transition. Rather, they signal that the culture of cyclic time—women-centered, indulging in female ecstasy and joy, the culture without war—was violently suppressed and that a dramatic mythology was used to sanctify the conquest.

Many have construed these ancient Greek myths as stories of human maturation, transformation, or individuation. In some cases they have been turned successfully by modern psychologists and scholars to

these ends. Persephone, it is said, might have been an example of the sexually maturing woman. Odysseus was seemingly on a journey to his true home, the return of the soul to itself. These efforts do have the redeeming value of transforming stories of pain into something useful and sometimes therapeutic. It is probably, and unfortunately, a good deal more likely that in the chaotic and hotly contested centuries in which they were written, these stories were not intended to redeem the psyche so much as to control the estate.

The method followed in these pages has been that of the trial lawyer. It has been to combine evidence from different disciplines and therefore point to both myths and monuments, to themes from some myths but not all, to carvings on friezes and tales from Lycurgus in court, from the earthquake to the absence of pictures of war. No single one of these disciplines alone would make the case. The artifacts alone, for example, might not make the case about ancient Crete were there not so many written stories aimed at the very obvious values raised by these artifacts. The monument of the Parthenon would not make the case for virginity and marriage by itself, but combined with the constant themes of mythology its conclusions are irresistible.

In support of this radical charge against patriarchal misogyny, a trial lawyer might fairly bring to the surface the combination of these myths, monuments such as the Parthenon, and distinctly different wall frescoes (like women arising out of the ground in Thera or swallows kissing, dolphins leaping, and monkeys swinging). It is appropriate to combine with these the evidence of celebrations such as the Mysteries at Eleusis and the Thesmophoria, which pointed backwards a thousand years toward a more benign and women-centered age. In ancient Crete and Thera, women were possibly in political control, although that cannot yet be proven. But it was an age in which women were most certainly celebrated, and that can be proven. We now have a vast accumulation of paintings, artifacts, stories, monuments, and surviving ceremonies that point over and over to this conclusion. Women were not only celebrated but also played a central role in the ceremonies of living and dying. There is no evidence that they were sexually contained in marriage, and they seemed to have played their sexual roles at the expense of a male's ability to hold and accumulate his property. The first great property revolution in Western history was not therefore the one advocated by Karl Marx. It was advocated by Homer and Hesiod and the author of Genesis. They were taking property *away* from either feminine control or communal control.

If this were a trial of, say, Father Zeus, in a court of common opinion, the evidence would show that invaders rode into Greece and the Middle East on horses, with composite bows, and in lust for property accumulated from trade and piracy, frantic to hold the accumulation for their sons. The evidence would show that storytellers picked up their cause and immediately began to malign women and women's views of immortality, views that had long been held in Crete but that made the accumulation of male property impossible. The evidence would show that under the banner of the first completely patriarchal gods, Zeus and Jehovah, the conquerors raped and pillaged these people, depended upon men such as Heracles to cut down Nemea and Lerna, violated the sexual customs of the Amazon queen, and ridiculed the idea of rebirth. All this was made glorious. In a case against these propagandists, one would show that Homer and Hesiod had enlisted their talents on the winning side, had come to the aid of the powers that swept Greece and occupied the psychological chasm left by the horrific explosion on Thera. One would show that the consequences for Western history have been to make war seem desirable at any cost; to make women undesirable so far as they could be made, at any time, undesirable; and to make the future seem grim because life is less important than the way one dies or the property one leaves behind to his sons. Finally, one would show three millennia of consequences and changes in the lives and psyches of women and men of ancient Greece, the Middle East, and, subsequently, all of Europe. One might conclude by saying that the trial and political murder of Joan of Arc and thousands, or perhaps millions, of other women was not merely the overflowing of some natural ignorance or even of some innate evil in the hearts of men so much as the triumph of story over intelligence, of minds encrusted by story and deadened by it. And all these stories were already, by the time of the witch burnings, two thousand years out of date.

History as a Choice of Stories

The president of the United States, the planet's most powerful military machine, led his country to war in Iraq in March 2003. The strike was preemptive, the cause or justification for the conflict was fashioned to meet changing American election cycles, and the war's warriors were deemed heroes. There is no doubt that since the days of the first mythology justifying war and heroics—more than three thousand years ago—the pattern has been the same. The temptation that accompanies great political and military power is to act like Heracles or Agamemnon and to use it. In the United States the supporting role of the publicists once played by Homer and Hesiod is now less artfully played by raucous commentators. No matter that the cost of war might be a whole city of civilians—the modern-day equivalent of a chieftain's daughter—the temptation is still today to justify the sacrifice. Substitute Fallujah for Iphigenia, and the principle is the same; presidents are not different from Agamemnon and his chieftains sailing off to Troy.

The resistance, on the other hand, to these powerful temptations has over the generations been from those who urged a different model for the spread of civilization, contending that on the whole, civilization spreads more abundantly and more successfully through civil means. That is to say that the meaning of the "civil" in "civilization" is particular and resides in values and methods that are more apt to be life-preserving, more apt to continue the cycles of human evolution, more apt to foster the feminine in every man and woman than the military option. Some of these values are clearly Minoan, and there is inspiration in the realization that for a thousand years a culture existed that did not indulge the temptation to become a war culture. That they had weapons and experienced conflict with their neighbors seems inescapable. That their response, however, was to emphasize and glorify a military culture or naval power is decisively *not* borne out by the evidence. There is simply no record in the artifacts. Harkening back to an earlier time, therefore, can give hope. There has been at least one civilization that was more civil than our own. It lasted five times longer than ours so far has done.

Today the consensus is that general nuclear war is not survivable.[1] In the nuclear age, therefore, the consequence of continued military adventure, of gradual overextension and certain ultimate retaliation, is so great that life on the planet is threatened. This single fact alone dictates that the "civil" in "civilization" must now be realized and broadened to revive the applicable elements of a Minoan mentality: faith in the cycles and reverence for regeneration of life in all its forms. If we do not do this—because war is no longer sustainable and its natural eventual outcome is certain to be catastrophic—a return to a primitive dark age is probable. Civilization is therefore at a crossroads.

Women Coming Home to Dignity

Looking back over these three millennia, it appears that wave upon wave of challenges to patriarchy have forever, and seemingly futilely, washed hard against the rock of patriarchal hierarchy, its control of knowledge, its harsh reliance upon power and dominion, its authority over the imagined consequence of death and prospects for immortality. Challenges emerged in France, Ireland, Jerusalem, and Eleusis, but none of these storied movements alone has brought down the fortress. And yet the memory of the goddess—call her Demeter, call her Sybil, call her Sophia—or the memory of Jesus, Pelagius, Esclamonde de Foix, and a hundred other extraordinary personalities has lingered in the Western mind.

Stories such as that of Agamemnon and Helen of Troy, Odysseus and Penelope, and Eve and the Garden of Eden were at first passed along orally by professional singers or bards. Sometime later they were written on papyrus or wood or carved in clay tablets. In the Christian tradition, the biblical stories were copied slowly by monks in monasteries, embroidered in gold and crimson, and made into wondrous works of art. All this copying was so labor intensive that for fifteen hundred years after Homer only the most powerful could afford to make books or to purchase them. Those who controlled economic or political resources could therefore control the story of humankind. It was because patriarchs controlled the story of Odysseus and Heracles that we never heard the sides of Calypso and Scylla.[1] It was because a male hierarchy controlled the story of Adam and Eve that

untold numbers of women could be burned at the stake in the Middle Ages. But when in 1430 the printing press was invented, patriarchy would gradually and increasingly be confronted with that same problem with which it began and against which it countered in the early myths: the spread of knowledge.

Female knowledge, as Homer surmised, would be a danger to power, so Odysseus was therefore advised to beware the Sirens' call. Female knowledge, as Jehovah commanded, would be a danger to authority, so Eve was ordered not to eat from the tree of the knowledge of good and evil. When, however, after nearly twenty-five centuries the press was invented and knowledge in books became widely available, those whose power was hierarchical and not practical or lay in glory and not wisdom began to lose control, precisely as Homer and Genesis predicted. Knowledge was going to prove more powerful than armies.

The unraveling began slowly. In the thirteenth century Thomas Aquinas was still able to pronounce that "woman is defective and misbegotten." He, in turn, was following Aristotle, who had held that women were "weaker and colder by nature, and we should look upon the female state as being as it were a deformity. ..." Aquinas concluded that when a male child was born, it was perfect but when a female child was born, it was because of a "defect in the active force."[2] This was two centuries, more or less, before the printing press. Over the next five centuries, after the printing press, the story of humankind began to change. That new story is still emerging. In its broad outlines we are beginning to see new thinking as a forest emerges from a fog. The old patriarchal story has been that when kings lead, the people follow. The new story is emerging that when the people lead, governments follow. The old story has been that chaos yields to militarization. The new story is emerging that chaos yields to civilization, to books, poetry, and music. The old story was that glory matters foremost and leads to immortality. The new story is emerging that life is most important, and life's continuance is the meaning of immortality. The old story would feature heroes in combat. The new story would remember rebels of the heart, such as Jesus and the Gnostics, who acknowledged the futility of combat. The old goal was victory over all challengers. The new goal of the Gnostics, Celts, Cathars, Sufis, and searchers for the Holy Grail would be victory internally, within the soul. The old story had been that women should learn neither to read nor write. The new story would be that an illiterate village maiden named Joan had more dignity and grace than all the learned bishops combined.

Some will say that the old story is still so loud and told so repetitively that these ingredients of a new story are practically inaudible. Without question progress is brutally slow. Still, emerging from the centuries there is change that is not entirely consistent with the old patriarchal paradigm and that over six hundred years begins to have the inexorable force of a tectonic shift.

The bedrock of patriarchy began crumbling gradually. In sixteenth-century England, King Henry VIII was such an old-fashioned patriarch that he accused his wife, Anne Boleyn, of adultery and chopped off her head. The real reason was not so much adultery—never satisfactorily proven—but was more fundamental to a patriarch: she had not borne Henry a son. To the dismay of the pope and all of Europe, Henry's throne was taken soon after his death by Anne Boleyn's precocious and brilliant *daughter*, Elizabeth. Beginning in 1558, this flaming-red-haired woman of dance and song ruled—and united—England more effectively than had any man before, probably more effectively than any crowned head in Europe of her time, and ruled for forty-five years. Elizabeth, along with other women in her court, could read Latin, Greek, French, and Spanish. Her maid of honor, Mary Sidney, left the court to found the first literary salon in England and patronized playwrights, poets, translators, and actors. Some reasonably argue that Sidney authored the works attributed to William Shakespeare.[3] Elizabethan England saw a birth of literature in Marlowe, Shakespeare (or Sidney), Jonson, Bacon, and a score of others. No one yet believed in democracy, but books and the spread of literature necessarily presaged the unraveling of absolute monarchy. Elizabeth had unknowingly sponsored all the tools that would unleash revolution in the generation after her death.[4]

It was in that next generation that Anne Hutchinson of the Massachusetts Bay Colony rediscovered the principles of grace, which she said lay within every human being. Humans shared in the divine naturally, not just through works, which was another way of saying not just through wealth or power or kings, which is another way of saying not just through patriarchy. All people, she said, including women, could be the chosen of God, and their numbers included not just the leaders of politics, hierarchy, and commerce. Here was a woman entering into the world of the Puritan fathers, wading into fire and brimstone and pointing to a gentler theology. At first she rallied the support of men who were leaders in the church in Boston, but one by one they each were surrounded and intimidated. They all eventually recanted their support or were driven out from Boston. At last Anne Hutchinson herself was ordered to stand trial for sedition and contempt. Sedition, as if to speak one's own theology were disloyal to the king. She was a sixteenth-century American Joan of Arc, having spoken her mind, followed her own voices, and threatened to loosen the chains of human discipline upon which patriarchy depended. After an ecclesiastical trial she was excommunicated and banished from Massachusetts. At first she settled in Rhode Island but then started her own colony where, in 1643, she and all her family (but one daughter) were murdered by Indians. Anne Hutchinson could not have known of the ancient Minoan civilization. But her principles—defying hierarchy, drawing God down to a presence in all things—would not have led her to quarrel with the Minoans. She would have been less a threat to the Cretans than she was to the Bostonians. She may have been the last public figure in American history to suffer banishment from society for not following the rules of patriarchy. The rules would stay in place, but information and knowledge had already begun to erode their authority.

By the eighteenth century books were more apt to migrate to the backwaters and small towns of the American frontier than priests from Rome or governors from London. Books were cheaper and traveled more easily. With no preachers to tell them what to think, men and women could fall back on their native wit. It is ironic that in the first centuries of writing, in Homer's time and in the time of Genesis, books had *solidified* the stories and therefore the powers of those who owned property. That, however, was to be true only when there were not many books. Three thousand years later, when there were a great many books, the effect was reversed, and the bonds of patriarchal control were gradually loosened. The frontier settlers now took with them more than the Bible or the classics; they took Shakespeare and Voltaire, Locke and Coke. In the small cabins in which they lived, these volumes could be picked up and read by anyone, including women. It is said by the modern Shakespearean scholar Harold Bloom that Shakespeare "invented the human," and these American settlers took these volumes with them and went on inventing. In the Shakespeare plays readers for the first time since Euripides had their eyes opened to the exaltation and tragedies of women such as Juliet, Ophelia, Queen Margaret, Lady Macbeth, Cleopatra, and Desdemona or to the triumphs of brilliant women such as Portia and Rosalind. Women burst forth onto the Shakespearean stage in full glory—beautiful, intelligent, crafty, and scheming, the whole range. Shakespeare wrote for the popular audience, and the plays are probably today the most widely read in world literature.

The eighteenth, nineteenth, and twentieth centuries then produced dramatic breakthroughs in all areas of the Minoan world view, always accidentally of course, never by intention, because no one knew about Minoan Crete or Thera. The world view was, however, proving itself ubiquitous, perhaps because elements of respect for women, for nature, for non-military solutions, for internal transformation had been passed down—sometimes secretly, sometimes openly—from one culture to the next. While in the nineteenth century women did not quite come to the center as they had in Crete, they rose out of the ranks of obscurity in politics, literature, and medicine. The names Susan B. Anthony, Emily Dickinson, and Florence Nightingale became metaphors for change. (Other areas of the old world view, circular time, honoring the process of rebirth and the cycles of the earth, honoring the peacemakers, honoring ecstasy, were not as quick to surface in the nineteenth century, but by the late twentieth century they too were coming to the forefront.)

In some ways the current generation in both America and Europe, and perhaps globally, has seen the most remarkable explosion of women's rights and opportunities in three thousand years. In educational opportunity, in the possibility to own property and to move into professions that until recently were forbidden to them, the last fifty years have brought an extraordinary, indeed almost revolutionary, return to dignity. In their choices to marry or not to marry, in their choices to have children or not, in their choices to pursue science and engineering, to dress as they like, appear on stage, become heads of corporations, or to start their own businesses, they have made history-changing progress. Women have now entered the political and visible professions, are into journalism and television, and altogether have exploded onto the stage of the Western world.[5] Within the realm of women's economics, the bonds of patriarchy are unmistakably loosening. Whether truly equal opportunities will become available at the top remains to be seen, but the trend is in the right direction. Considering that most of the change has happened in only the last fifty years, the progress is electric.

But if there has been progress in women's wages, other effects of the long history of misogyny are still tragically in evidence. Two thousand eight hundred years of glorifying heroes who hang serving maids and kings who barter slave girls has had its indelible effects. In the Middle Ages French, English, and Italian codes all discussed wife beating and when it was to be authorized and when it was not. A thirteenth-century French law code stated: "In a number of cases men may be excused for the injuries they inflict on their wives, nor should the law intervene. Provided he neither kills nor maims her, it is legal for a man to beat his wife when she wrongs him."[6] That is to say that intimidation and minor injuries, rule by force, was to be expected. Physical and mental intimidation, ruling by fear, which would have been far and away most common, does not even warrant a caution. The fifteenth-century Sienese *Rules of Marriage* instructed kindness to women, in general, but within limits:

> But if your wife is of a servile disposition and has a crude and shifty spirit, so that pleasant words have no effect, scold her sharply, bully, and terrify her. And if this still doesn't work ... take up a stick and beat her soundly ... not in rage, but out of charity and concern for her soul. ... [7]

The continuing effects of such history persist to this day. In 1998 in the United States alone there were nine hundred thousand reports to police by women reporting assault by male partners. Twenty-two to 35 percent of women who seek emergency relief at American hospitals are there because of domestic violence. Twenty-five to 30 percent of women in Britain say that they have experienced physical abuse by a male intimate. In Armenia 32 percent of women think it is acceptable for a husband to beat his wife for one or more specific reasons, including burning his food, arguing with him, going out without telling him, neglecting the children, or refusing sex.[8] Throughout history the persecuted have been apt to personalize the blame, take the guilt for their condition upon themselves, as these women of Armenia have done, and accept the beatings as if it were their own fault. This means that 900,000 American abuse reports, 570,000 more in the United Kingdom, and 25,000 more in Argentina, et cetera, are probably understated numbers.

Western civilization has a distance to travel to retrieve not just wages but dignity and honor for women, and equally important, dignity and honor for the concept of fertility and survival of life over the long term. The respect for women in Minoan times was unequivocally a respect for life's continuation. One is not talking, therefore, about some moral superiority of women or moral inferiority of men. Such a limited interpretation would be a disservice to the Minoan-Eleusis-Jesus-Grail tradition and misses its central point. The case is not made that the world should be ruled by women, substituting one form of domination for another. Such a change would not transform the governing political model at all. The case is rather made for a revival of the respect for life of which the feminine is some symbol, of the respect for continuation of the species of which rebirth is some symbol, and respect for balance between the outer and inner lives, seeing that hierarchy, dominion, and heroics are contrary to ancient symbols of the lily, the dolphin, the wheat, and the chalice.

Depreciation of women has had the effect that we now value property above any passion for ongoing life. The concept that Minoans represented with spirals we might today call sustainability of life or now again, at last, valuing life above property. The spiral of ancient Zakros was wrapped around breasts. Our new spiral might wrap around daughters and trees and grasses and the rain, or even again, quite simply the lily, the dolphin, the wheat, and the chalice, symbols of richness and fertility and exuberance rather than symbols of domination. In some way these are all sacred symbols of the return, the ever-revolving continuity of life, which is both a dream and an absolute necessity for long-term balance and stability.

The Declining Utility of War

A measure of the declining utility of patriarchal norms has been the surprising number of occasions during the last fifty years that power has changed, or boundaries of great states have changed, without war. These last years are in this regard distinctly different from the preceding two thousand years. Over and over during this recent period, the world balance of power has changed, or governments have changed, without a shot being fired. The heroic Heraclean myth was repeatedly not followed; war has become increasingly impractical.

During the height of the Cold War, Russian generals—who were not so practical—were heard to admit that no one, not even the Russians, could survive the nuclear winter that would certainly follow their first-strike nuclear attack against the West. Still, they said, a first-strike nuclear attack would be "successful" because, even though they would all be dead, "they would have won."[1] This absurd calculation makes no logical sense but makes complete sense within the patriarchal story. Successful death as an idea arises from the ancient Greek story that gave us the word *hero* when it meant "to die too soon," to die before one's season was over, and to be remembered forever. The Russian generals who were willing to die and still "win" were like Achilles and Hector before Troy, giving all for the glory in their names, living for the immortality of their reputations and the reputation of their country. In the patriarchal story of which they were a part, heroism is more important than survival, dying with honor more important than surviving

unnoticed. The Russian generals did not seem to care that by the 1980s the story was morally troglodytic. Unlike Achilles and Hector, who would die singly in hand-to-hand combat and be remembered forever, a nuclear exchange would kill untold millions and might destroy all records and all memory of anyone on earth. The stakes are dramatically greater today, and there is no honor, glory, or morality in extinction. Yet the generals surely knew the ancient story of Achilles and continued to play the old story as if it were applicable today. For them the Americans were playing Hector, and they would be Achilles. The Americans of course played the same game, following an announced policy of Mutual Assured Destruction or, rather, assured death for all who would challenge them, including of course all Americans too. A nuclear winter, they knew, would not just settle over Russia and destroy Russian agriculture. It would reduce and threaten the agricultural productivity of every continent on the planet. The official American position was therefore that it would be better for all to die than for Communism to win. This was patriarchy as virulent and mad in modern times as it had been in the Trojan War.

Whether a new story will emerge to replace the patriarchal narrative will probably turn upon our ability to redefine the utility of war and with it the sense of heroism that drives it. The picture in modern times is mixed, and the return to the more practical point of view of 1500 BCE is by no means likely. Yet there are signs here of remarkable changes within only the last century that run parallel to the changes in the lives of women and that may be even more profound in their long-term consequences.

In the 1940s the British Empire was dissolved without a war between the colonies and the English. In the 1980s the Russian Empire was dissolved without a shot. The South African apartheid regime was displaced without a civil war, and in the end the process was accomplished largely as a peaceful transition. In the 1980s Eastern Europe was reorganized and Germany was reunited without a general war. In the 1990s the Cold War was resolved without a military exchange, which had been threatened between the two greatest military powers on the planet for almost half a century.

Expansion of international trade and global networks of corporate enterprise have made war an impractical solution for most of the problems that industrialized or commercialized nations might face, including finally the United States and the Soviet Union. In the 1940s Japan went to war to create the Greater Southeast Asian Co-Prosperity Sphere, with the goal of expanding economically. Today the Japanese build cars in the United States and could not attack the United States without destroying their own assets. The same is true for the Germans and the Italians. None of these countries achieved economic expansion militarily but have done so very successfully nonmilitarily. War between France and Germany is today unthinkable; their linkages are too great, their interdependence too obvious, and the costs beyond any gains that could be won economically. War between advanced, industrial states has become obsolete. Sensing this and responding to it, the Vietnam War—a proxy war between industrialized

states—was largely ended by an upwelling of popular resistance. It may have been the first war in history ended by the people, some of whom had even fought in it, ended because of widespread horror and resistance to the war's costs and the American people's calculation that the gains were not sufficient to offset the losses.

On the other hand, in the last fifty years since the end of World War II, the United States has been at war in Korea, Lebanon, Vietnam, Nicaragua, Grenada, Panama, Haiti, Somalia, Bosnia, Afghanistan, and Iraq, and our military bases encircle the planet. We have increasingly and unabashedly defined ourselves as a military power. In 2004, in its public pronouncements, an American administration began to define the United States as an imperial power. From year to year the United States spends approximately 49 percent, or virtually half, of its discretionary federal budget on war.

It was the mythmakers of Greece who first prepared the mind to think of war as good. Heraclitus claimed it as the father of civilization. In those times, Pericles built the Parthenon to reaffirm that war works and that patriarchy, the suppression of women and the control of property by men, is a system that can afford war. In the last part of the twentieth century, the United States has done all that the Greeks did except to build the Parthenon. We are, however, also witness to contrasting successes: the end of the Cold War without a shot, the transformation of Europe, et cetera, and the growing number of cases where civil means worked more effectively than military means. Americans have, therefore, again, two competing streams in their recent history: one that augurs toward ever-greater use of the military, living out the heroism of the patriarchal norms, and another, recently emerged, that counts the costs of war and finds it contraindicated for human survival. Whichever of these two stories that in the end captures the public's attention and becomes the popular narrative will determine the course of Western civilization.

Another Story All Along

Stories give humans their orientation, provide sign-posts in the storm, a sense of direction in times of trouble. Stories direct a culture's attention and the use of its treasure. The first Greek poets told one kind of story, and subsequent generations spent their money and time on the subjects that these stories dictated: property, patriarchy, and war. Initiates at Eleusis or Cathars at Montségur oriented themselves in accord with quite a different story and spent their money and time in quite a different way. Today, looking back at these comparisons, it appears that there is more leverage in story than in wealth because the story determines when, where, and how the wealth shall be used. There is more power in narrative than in military arms, because the story determines whether and why men will fight. There is more power in story than from statistics or scientific data, because it is story that authorizes or condemns the search for truth. The power of story comes from its motion, its momentum, its sense of awe, and its magnetic attempt to explain life's yearning for itself. If we are trying to find the lever to move the world, the lever is story. Homer knew that. The authors of the Jason sagas knew that. The author(s) of Genesis knew that. Winston Churchill knew that. George W. Bush, with his exhortations to engage evil all over the world, wherever it may be, knows that. Story is as binding and motivating today as it was twenty-eight hundred years ago.

Even what we *see* or do not *see* is dictated by story. When we are looking for an eagle in the sky, we don't see the warblers in the bushes, or when we are looking for a red puzzle piece, we don't see the blue puzzle pieces. We see, most often, what we are looking for and do not see what we are not looking for. This well-known phenomenon probably keeps us from going crazy. If we could not filter out and organize the noise and confusion that comes in upon us, the world would seem like chaos. We don't try to keep track of everything—of the ants and the flies and the birds and the dogs barking in the distance and when the kids are coming home and when the president will make peace in some foreign war—all at once. It is too much to keep track of. We have to filter and focus just to stay sane.

The effect of this filtering is that the muscles that focus and reinforce what we already see get all the work, and the muscles that might see other things go to sleep or atrophy or get lazy. This is not only true for those who defend patriarchy or its children; it is equally, and tragically, true for those who could change the story but instead live in despair and ignore the facts that work in their favor. If we get proficient at seeing all the suffering and being compassionate, we may not see the things that are not suffering.

If we cannot see what is not suffering, we cannot see the Minoan paradigm. If we cannot see it, we cannot revive any part of it. We do not have the tools in the brain. We need not even try. Thus we must be prepared to see anew. That, I believe, was the original intention of the parables of the Kingdom of God: to persuade people in Israel to see anew or with new eyes. That, I believe, was the intention of the story of the Fisher King and the barren land and of the search for the Holy Grail—to lure people in the midst of knighthood and clashing of arms into thinking in new ways about goodness and simplicity. Homer and Hesiod and a hundred others had lured a whole civilization into thinking that war was heroic, women were evil, ecstasy was dangerous, and death was endless and dark. Since then we have not worked the brain enough to see more than this suffering and therefore do not have the nerve endings, the muscle, the habit, to even see the possibility of joy.

The restraint against building the new way of thinking is not therefore from outside or from afar or held by the conspirators who run a patriarchal world. Rather, the problem is that when we look at history in a traditional way, we see the sorts of things that we have always seen and do not see the sorts of things that we don't have words or even concepts for. We do not see, for example, that the long evolution of democracy is really an evolution of techniques of nonviolence replacing war or that there is a long history of innovators, adventurers, and courageous dissenters who have already staked out the alternatives to patriarchal domination and who are equally our ancestors, equally in our line. If we want to see the future anew, we must build a new story out of these antecedents, claim them, and give them a modern voice.

The language we develop to shape the new story is also important. We do not really have any word for a nonwar culture, and we do not yet know what to call it. If we don't know what to call this new condition, we won't learn how to see it or practice it. We need a better word than "peace," because there is never peace. The conditions of life are always changing and conflicting, and there is turmoil in the atoms when the rain hits the rock. Peace, the absence of conflict, is not what we are looking for, but we don't have another word, so we don't know just what instructions to send along the nerve channels. And if we don't know what to call this more enlightened condition, we don't see it and, worse, we don't experience it—the nerve cells don't send the message to the body. We not only need a new name, therefore, for peace, but we also need a new story and a new vocabulary for peacemakers, their history, their lineage, their successes, and their courage; and a new story for women, their beauty, their grace, their intelligence, and their toughness; for fertility and sexuality and mystical union; and for the earth, for its nurturing properties and its power. Without this new, comprehensive story tying all these together, it will not be possible for us to believe that they ever existed or to see the reality of the Minoan experience or the centrality of all those who carried forward these values through the centuries. It will not be possible to believe that society today can be of this civilized, delicate, and nurturing mind.

We do not, that is, today have a narrative to match Homer's war story in *The Iliad*, we do not have a story to match Julius Caesar crossing the Rubicon, El Cid defending Spain against the Moors, or Charlemagne. "Once more unto the breach!" cried Henry V of England in Shakespeare's glorious language of four hundred years ago. We do not yet have a narrative explanation, an answer to Homer, that says that these are *not* all of our story or even the most important parts of the story of Western history. We do not yet have the narrative to say that these blunders and failures—for every war is an abysmal failure—are not nearly so inspiring as the stories of the wheat held up in the flame at Eleusis or the young Jewish reformer who gave his life or Pelagius or the Cathars or the Maid of Orleans, all of whom connected with something deeper and more wonderful than war, more complex and more magical than simple peace. When we see that *these* are the bright names who have, after all, cast light on the path through Western history, who have brought us closer to civilization than any massacres or village burnings, then we might begin finally to call the whole story of Western progress by a different name.

In modern times when a person undertakes a course of personal therapy, the work is often for that person to uncover the story or to reconstruct the story of his or her life or even to put the pieces of a personal story together in a completely new way. Therapists help individuals do this one-on-one. Now the overriding issue for Western civilization is whether this same reconstruction can be done for a whole culture and for the same purpose: to make us healthy again.

When, as now, the fabric of community has been shredded or become confused, when the social consensus threatens to unravel, there is a tendency for all sides to dig into old doctrines and intensify old debates. Something like this has been happening recently in American presidential elections. The country digs into red and blue molds while the paradigm of civil society and constitutional progress slowly is shredded in claims and counterclaims of righteous indignation. Do we not then have a primary job— those no longer afraid to eat from the tree of knowledge or to trust the feminine impulse or to value life above property—to recollect the pieces, to reweave the tale of who we are and where we came from?

Until we do, can we expect to gather any passion or momentum or concentrated purpose? Until we do that, in turn, can we elect any person here or in any country with a mandate or a substantially new moral authority? There is talent enough, in excess, in today's politicians. We do not lack talent. But there is not a sufficient story. Can we object if the president of the United States gallops off to war in a reenactment of the Lone Ranger story if we who value the civilian tradition have not created a new, more glorious, more ennobling story? We have not, in the United States in recent years, produced the noble purpose in any narrative form to focus our energy and enthusiasm to any greater purpose than cowboys chasing terrorists. We have moved to economic prosperity but at the same time continued on the path to moral confusion, even degradation. We suffer a confusion about the poor, about materialism, about sexuality, about death. Is that not because we do not know what story we as a people are living or what story we intend to fulfill?

Today the species flirts with extinction because we have become careless with our soil, careless with our water, careless with our future, careless with our nuclear knowledge. Misogyny and militarism from our foundation patriarchal myths are not the cure, however, with which to address this comprehensive carelessness. The storytellers of old who made Oedipus an example of a man blinded by carelessness about marriage and an example of a culture careless of its sons did not intend a solution to problems such as those we face today. Loss of sons or failure of the family property line is not the blindness that threatens civilization today. The storytellers of old created a Jason who was blind to the dangers of a strong woman (Medea), but blindness to the dangers of the strong feminine is not the blindness that threatens civilization today. Hades took away Persephone to put daughters in their subordinate place as wives. Subordination of women is not the change that will make civilization strong today. Jehovah commanded Eve to be subordinate, to end her quest for knowledge, to not seek the divine except through her husband. Turning our backs on knowledge and divorcing ourselves from direct connection to the divine will not make civilization stronger today. Unlike that desperate time three thousand years ago, these old myths do not contain the stories or include the reforms that will keep us alive. And yet, unmistakably, all these stories are still with us and still substantially guide us. The Lone Ranger story that has taken the United States through the world on a posse raid in pursuit of terrorism is only a modern version of Agamemnon rallying the ships to pursue Helen of Troy. Today these old stories, in all their new versions, breed anachronistic values that are irrelevant to cure any of those great challenges that we can see and to which today we must not be blind.

The poet laureate Archibald McLeish once wrote, "An age ends when its metaphor has died." The metaphors of patriarchy have died. To survive over the long run, Americans must be ready to choose a new metaphor for a new age. We might choose to identify with the underground school of initiates who streamed through Eleusis, with the rebels and dissenters from the power struggles of Rome and the Roman empire, or with the mystics and the masters of the Middle Ages. We might remember those ancestors of the spirit who for three thousand years have tended a fire on a different hearth—those such as Anne Hutchinson and the Maid of Orleans, who followed their own voices, and those such as Pelagius, who nourished the spirit of compassion for both men and women. Those who carried the torch at Eleusis were also our ancestors, the ancestors of what is "civil" in "civilization." We did not just come from Heracles or Odysseus or Adam. Those who sang on the harvester's vase and those who danced under the moons of Crete were also our ancestors. They too are a part of our story. Indeed, they are the part of our story that is benign, and for that reason they alone nourish our future. All the rest that is not benign and is not of compassion or for the survival of life has shortened life and cut down our ancestors and is not in our line.

In this age of books and knowledge, Internet and global communications, we are privileged to choose the stories that we will follow and the symbols that will give us meaning. We may consciously choose now, after thirty-five hundred years, to line up and claim our ancestry from those women and men who danced in the light of the moon or, alternately, with those heroes who danced at the funeral pyre of Hector singing the praises of the warrior Achilles. We can make our metaphors for the feminine from golden lilies or from fire-breathing dragons, choose anew the pursuit of fertility and rich natural abundance, or stay with demonization of the great earth religions. We can pursue the path of personal salvation as if inspired by the pursuit of the Grail, or we can continue the pursuit of fame, hierarchy, dominion, and empire. We have the power to consciously choose to line up with either Jason, Heracles, kings, and patriarchs or with Calypso, Medea, Parsifal, and Esclamonde of Montségur. We may for the first time in human history, fully informed and aware of the possibilities, consciously claim the feminine principle, or we can subdue it once again as was done in the stories of Iphigenia and on the carvings on the Parthenon. We may choose now, when selecting and living out our story—which is to say, when deciding where to put our resources and our attention—to learn from the cycles of earth how to die and go on living, how to appreciate anew ecstasy, fertility, beauty, and civility, or we may choose again how to simply die, join Hades, and be done.

To bend one's back in the great effort to continue the evolution of civilization is to reencounter the meaning of faith, which in turn is the willingness to advance with an open mind and full heart into an uncharted world. Looking back, we can see that Anne Hutchison did that; Joan of Arc did that; Pelagius, perhaps; and Jesus, for sure. The pursuit of the Grail was about finding a new path in a time of seemingly eternal conflict. Even Mohammed should be included in the list of those who tried to straighten us up, to make us more righteous, more honest, more in connection with the One. He too, persuaded by his good wife, Khadija, acted out his calling in faith without knowing the outcome. These, along with a thousand others whose names we will never know, are the forbearers of the "civil" in "civilization," those who attempted to carry the light in the belief that we can do better. Enlightened, finally, by a fuller knowledge of where we have come from, we may seize the understanding that we are at the close of one historic epoch and the beginning of another. The Minoan times are over, gone forever. Patriarchy is most assuredly unraveling. It is up to us now to select the threads and do the weaving to create a new tapestry that celebrates the best we have in our past rather than the meanest or most desperate. Heracles, Jason, Achilles, Caesar, Charlemagne, and Napoleon are names to associate with failures of civilization, not its advances. Now, at last, after thirty-five hundred years, we have the archaeology, the widespread distribution of learning, the experience of democratic institutions, the taste of nonviolent successes, and the return of dignity to the feminine that will allow us to celebrate civilization as we have never done before, to give it a name, and to give it a try.

Appendix
Success and Failure in Women's Wages and Employment in America

In the 1970s I tried a lawsuit on behalf of Denver's nurses, attempting to achieve for them equal wages for equal skill, effort, and responsibility. It was labeled at the time a "comparable worth" case and was the first of its kind in the country. The trial judge, as I noted in the introduction to this book, ruled against the nurses. So did the Court of Appeals for the Tenth Circuit, and the Supreme Court of the United States refused to hear the appeal. At the end of that case, after some five years of effort, the nurses and I were exhausted and discouraged. We had tried to break the boundaries of a patriarchal consciousness and had failed. Still, the matter was not done. I felt I owed it to those nurses, who had contributed thousands of hours of intense labor and research into that case, to explain how that defeat could have happened. This book has, after all these years, been an attempt to do that. Now, also for the record, a brief attempt to bring the wage and discrimination facts up to date.

Thirty years ago women earned approximately two thirds as much as men do, and today they earn approximately three quarters, a gain from 67 percent to about 75 percent.[1] Some of the continuing disadvantage can be attributed to the greater tendency for women to come and go from the marketplace more frequently than their male counterparts. A larger proportion of women consider caring for their children, as their job or must have flexible work schedules to allow them to care for their children, or for school pickups, or doctors' visits. These proportions are changing, and more men are now providing child care, but the greater burden is still borne by women, and they pay a price in the marketplace.

But not all of the wage gap is explained by child care or childbearing. A residue of the patriarchal past hangs on. Even with child care discounted, women still make approximately 10 percent less than men. Contrary to what might be expected, increased education does not always help. In 2001 in the United States women with doctorates holding full-time, year-round jobs were paid only 60 percent of what men with doctorates were paid. That gap was greater than it had been ten years earlier.[2] Part of the explanation for the overall gap is that women's jobs, if they are known to be occupied primarily by women, have for generations been less valued. Women are also often crowded into low-paying fields. They are expected to be less ambitious or aggressive and therefore have been less likely to gain access to higher-paying promotional tracks. Stereotypes do not go away just because legislation makes them illegal, and they are equally as likely to go underground. Courts have been reluctant or even unwilling to literally enforce the legislation and have narrowly limited what is meant by "equal pay for equal skill, effort, responsibility and working conditions."[3] In addition studies show that stereotypes do matter and that both women and men tend to value less those professions in which they see other women in the majority. This can be true not only when the profession is traditionally female, as in nursing, but in other professions as they become female dominated. As the change occurs, both men and women value these jobs less.[4] This is, again, a carryover of historic expectations, fashioned in the centuries of patriarchal misogyny. Whether it will continue to be true in a modern age when women are advancing into engineering, computer technology, law, and medicine in dramatic new numbers remains to be seen. The employment doors have been opened today as never before, but not everyone has yet passed through.

Unfortunately, there are professional pockets that resist change. Nutritionists, physical therapists, nurses, secretaries, librarians, and to some extent even schoolteachers, for example, do not fully benefit from free-market competition. A nursing supervisor with a substantial budget and hundreds of employees will likely not be paid equally to a supervisor of equal qualifications in a male-dominated field. An employer who claims to "simply follow the market" ignores that "the market" has been depressed by three thousand years of discriminatory history. The pay rate in a field affected by gender discrimination is cheaper at every skill level. There has not, until now, *ever* been a fully fair market for traditionally female professions. It is the story of this book to show why that has been the case. Tragically, it is this knowledge that also prepares women to expect less and that keeps wage demands lower.[5]

Women who are not in traditional "women's professions" also have problems getting out of the mid-range. They still hold only a minimal number of top jobs in Fortune 500 companies and hold only about 10 percent of board seats of those companies. They do hold a small, perhaps increasing, number of CEO positions in large companies,[6] but the numbers are so small that their presence is still remarked as extraordinary. The reality of this "glass ceiling" is denied by a few but belied by the numbers. There are only sixty-seven women in administrative positions in the United States for every one hundred males. Even more significantly, *95 percent* of senior-level managers in Fortune 1000 industries and Fortune 500 companies are men.[7] The biggest companies, those that dominate world markets and make critical decisions about the direction of global trade, are directed overwhelmingly by men. Nor is the picture entirely promising among lower wage levels. In 2004 a U.S. federal judge certified a class of 1.8 million female employees of Wal-Mart who alleged that they had been systematically discriminated against in pay and promotions. Wal-Mart employs more women and more workers than any other employer in the United States. The case is therefore the largest employment discrimination lawsuit against a company in U.S. history. A portion of the evidence offered to support the complaint was that while 65 percent of Wal-Mart employees were women, only 33 percent of store managers were women. In addition female store managers made, on the average, $16,400 a year less than male store managers, a whopping difference. Upon certifying the class, the judge held that there were "substantial legal and factual issues" concerning gender stereotyping,[8] a signal to Wal-Mart that as a practical matter, the burden of proof would shift to the company to show that these numbers were not correct.

The long history of misogyny is not over.

Endnotes

Introduction

1. The judge in that case, who had been on the federal bench for many years, told the author at the end of the trial that it "was the best-tried case he had ever seen," and then he ruled against our plaintiffs. See *Lemons v City and County of Denver*, 620 F.2d 228 (CA10), cert. denied, 449 US 888 (1980), and *Pay Equity: Equal Pay for Work of Comparable Value*, Joint Hearings before the House Subcommittees on Human Resources Civil Service Compensation and Employee Benefits of the Committee on Post Office and Civil Service, 97th Cong., 2d sess., Sept. 16, 21, 30 and Dec. 2, 1982, Part I, esp. 597 et seq.

2. M. L. West, *The East Face of Helicon: West Asiatic Elements in Greek Poetry and Myth* (Oxford: Clarendon Paperbacks, 1997).

3. Ibid., 408 et seq. Professor West believes that there are Eastern antecedents for Circe and Calypso but couches his persuasion in words such as "conceivable" and "possible," and while such possibilities do exist, I do not find the "possibility" at all convincing in the case of these two divinities, whom he lumps together as "doublets." They are far from that. The function of each in *The Odyssey* is entirely different, as will be made clear in later chapters. West does not cite any Near Eastern equivalents that fit the purposes for which Homer seems to have intended these two. A few situational similarities do not make an equation, and to treat all seductive women as the same, or "doublets," is to fall victim to the patriarchal predisposition.

4. See, e.g., Rosemary Radford Reuther, *Gaia and God: An Ecofeminist Theology of Earth Healing* (New York: HarperCollins, 1992).

5. See, e.g. Lucy Goodison and Christine Morris, eds., *Ancient Goddesses: The Myths and the Evidence* (Madison: Univ. of Wisconsin Press, 1998), or Cynthia Eller, *The Myth of Matriarchal Prehistory: Why an Invented Past Won't Give Women a Future* (Boston: Beacon Press, 2000).

Part I

1. For an excellent treatment of these early religious systems on the mainland, see Walter Wink, *Engaging the Powers: Discernment and Resistance in a World of Domination* (Minneapolis: Augsburg Fortress, 1992).

The Mystery of Minoan Civilization

1. Most current scholarship imagines this connection, and there is rather a uniform consensus that women in the center of seal rings or on Minoan frescoes are goddesses. For example, "On the interpretation all are agreed: here amid the whirling dance of the votaries, the goddess herself appears." Walter Burkert, *Greek Religion* (Cambridge: Harvard Univ. Press, 1985), 40. A woman dancing, however, may simply be a woman dancing. To conclude otherwise is to remove ordinary women from their ecstasy. To insist, that is, that women who are dignified and at the center of rings or frescoes are goddesses is to assume that ordinary women were neither at the center nor dignified.

2. Sara A. Immerwahr, *Aegean Painting in the Bronze Age* (University Park, PA: Penn State Univ. Press, 1990), 44–46. "The floral pieces are especially attractive: sinuous sprays of ivy with leaves on the same stalk alternatively sky blue or olive green which give the impression of filtered light, mauve pink and light blue dwarf iris, a pink wild rose, blue papyrus with orange florets and white madonna and pancratium lilies against a coral red ground. ... Surely these paintings are more than mere decoration. ... [I]f we think of 'sheer joy' in the beauty of nature as part of a mystic communion with the great Minoan Goddess of Nature ... we shall not be wide of the mark."

3. It is reasonable to assume that a wall painting of kissing swallows followed a convention of some sort. See, e.g., Nanno Marinatos, *Art and Religion in Thera: Reconstructing a Bronze Age Society* (Athens: Mathiolakis, 1984), 33–34. "I believe that there is a definite intention behind a group of paintings designed to give a message or to relate the pictures to the activities which took place in the room."

4. See, e.g., exhibit in the Goulandris Museum of

Cycladic Art, Athens, for dramatic presentations of original Cretan pottery copied in Italy, Syria, Lebanon, and Mycenae.

5. It is because it is so recent that we are only in the last few years beginning to explore the implications, and it is also true that in the last thirty years the eyes with which we see have changed. We are seeing things from a perspective that may allow us for the first time since those ancient times to appreciate what they had. Such eyes would include new appreciation for women's dignity and revived awareness of our connections to and dependence upon Mother Earth.

An Expectation of Rebirth or Immortality

1. There is also a young woman who seems to be rising out of the ground drawn upon a cup that was found at the palace at Phaistos. She has no arms, almost like a snake. See Ann Suter, *The Narcissus and the Pomegranate: An Archaeology of the Homeric Hymn to Demeter* (Ann Arbor: Univ. of Michigan Press, 2002), 174.

2. A "seal" was literally a small engraved stone that was sometimes on a ring and sometimes in round form and was used to mark clay and probably seal containers or documents. Hundreds and perhaps thousands of these have been recovered, bearing witness to many different facets of recreation, hunting, dancing, and decoration.

3. Six meters of this spiral have been reconstructed in the Herakleion Museum. "Of all the decorative friezes preserved in Minoan palaces, villas, and mansions, this is the longest and most characteristic, providing a vivid impression of the way large ceremonial halls were adorned." Nicholas Platon, *Zakros: The Discovery of a Lost Palace of Ancient Crete* (New York: Scribner's, 1971), 173.

4. At least one scholar believes that the spiral is one of the most ancient symbols of eternity, having manifestations in many ancient cultures. Jill Purce, *The Mystic Spiral: Journey of the Soul* (London: Thames and Hudson, 1974), 11, passim.

5. See Joan V. O'Brien, *The Transformation of Hera: A Study of Ritual, Hero, and the Goddess in The Iliad* (Lanham, MD: Rowman and Littlefield, 1993).

Time as a Circle Rather Than a Line

1. Some scholars think that there was a whole culture of rituals built around the phases of the moon. See, e.g., Demetra George, *Mysteries of the Dark Moon: The Healing Power of the Dark Goddess* (San Francisco: Harper Collins, 1992), 31–33: "As the moon turned from new, to full, to dark, it was worshipped as an embodiment of each of these three phases; hence the Triple Moon Goddess, who displayed herself on many levels as sets of three. … Her triple nature was woven into the beliefs about the nature of reality. In the realm of the Triple Goddess, the concept of time was cyclical rather than linear, and the cycle of the seasons, with its phases of waxing and waning, or life and death and revival, was the basic pattern of thought."

2. The so-called Dark Age in Greek prehistory was that period between about 1200 BCE and 800 BCE, a period of chaos and confusion in which there was no writing. It was a period of storytelling and bards like Homer but was before their tales were written down.

3. Dorothy D. Lee, "Lineal and Nonlineal Codifications of Reality," In *Symbolic Anthropology*, ed. Kemnitzer Dolgin and David M. Schneider (New York: Columbia Univ. Press, 1977), 161.

4. "In the real life of these preconquest people, feeling and awareness are focused on at-the-moment, point-blank sensory experience—as if the nub of life lay within that complex flux of collective sentient immediacy. Into that flux individuals thrust their inner thoughts and aspirations for all to see, appreciate, and relate to. This unabashed open honesty is the foundation on which their highly honed integrative empathy and rapport become possible. When that openness gives way, empathy and rapport shrivel. Where deceit becomes a common practice, they disintegrate." Richard E. Sorenson, "Preconquest Consciousness," in *Tribal Epistemologies*, ed. Helmut Wautischer (Aldershot, England: Ashgate Publishing, 1998), 79–115. A reviewer commenting on this consciousness says: "Individuals in such societies are highly sensitive to changes in muscle tension in others indicating shifts in mood. If others feel good, they feel good; if others feel bad, they feel bad. … In other words, the entire thrust and motivation of this form of consciousness is to optimize feelings of well-being in the community. What is 'real' or 'right' (we might call it 'true') is what feels good. In such cultures, the 'right' or the 'true' or the 'real' is a question of value, not a correspondence between some pattern of abstract concepts and

empirical fact." From a comment on Sorenson's book by Christian de Quincey, "Consciousness: Truth or Wisdom?" *IONS Noetic Science Review* 51 (March–June 2000): 8.

5. Riane Eisler sees these tombs as womblike and the small opening as vagina-like, thus increasing the imagery of fertilization. Riane Eisler, *Sacred Pleasure* (New York: HarperCollins, 1996), 64–65.

6. Lucy Goodison, *Death, Women, and the Sun: Symbolism of Regeneration in Early Aegean Religion* (London: Univ. of London, Institute of Classical Studies, 1989). See also Goodison and Morris, *Ancient Goddesses*, 119: "The construction of the tomb [at Koumasa] was apparently geared towards … not the worship of a personified deity, but alignment to the cycles of the natural world. The twentieth century's preoccupation with human and emotional affairs may have overfed the search for anthropomorphic divinity."

7. Found near Phaistos, Crete, dated about 1500–1300 BC. Now in the museum at Heraklion, Crete.

8. "The picture speaks for itself; it is the passing of winter and the coming of spring, the passing of the Old Year, the incoming of the New, it is the Death and Resurrection of Nature, her New Birth." Jane Ellen Harrison, *Epilegomena to the Study of Greek Religion and Themis* (New Hyde Park, NY: University Books, 1966), 178.

9. Sakellarakis, J. A., *Herakleion Museum: Illustrated Guide* (Athens: Ekdotike Athenon S. A., 1995), 65.

10. O'Brien, *Transformation of Hera*. Similarly, though much later, Hera, the goddess of fertility, is widely worshipped although she brings with her both death and life.

11. Marinatos, *Art and Religion*, 80.

12. Brian Browne Walker, trans., *Tao Te Ching of Lao Tzu* (New York: St. Martin's Griffin, 1996), 50.

13. T. S. Eliot, *Little Gidding*, in *Four Quartets* (New York: Harcourt Brace, 1943), 58.

14. According to Henry Burton Sharman, the addition of the phrase "for my sake" was an unlikely addition of later Christian church builders. In his study of the teachings he omits that phrase. See Henry Burton Sharman, *Jesus as Teacher* (Palo Alto, CA: Sequoia Seminar Foundation, 1935), 68.

15. Hesiod, *Works and Days* (New York: Penguin Classics, 1984), 1.111–118.

16. Robert Graves, *The Greek Myths*, vol. I, rev. ed. (New York: Penguin Books, 1960), 36.

17. "Crete has left us with a unique vision of life as a celebration of being alive and an image of death as the same, so that life and death are experienced as one sacred whole. It is as though life were lived on the intake of a breath of wonder and delight, where, as in childhood moments of epiphany, nature and the divine ground of being are one. Can it be coincidence that for thousands of years the people of Crete lived in harmony with the rhythms of nature experienced as a great goddess and also lived in peace?" Anne Baring and Jules Cashford, *The Myth of the Goddess* (New York: Penguin Books, 1993), 144.

18. Drawing from Goodison and Morris, *Ancient Goddesses*, 127.

19. Lord William Taylour, *The Mycenaeans* (London: Thames and Hudson, 1983), 46.

20. I know of no scholar who would agree with this point. Uniformly, scholars are apt to look at these pictures of women in Crete or Thera and announce that they are "goddesses." But if one applies the test of scholarship itself, which is to ask what is the factual basis for such conclusion, one uniformly finds that we have become accustomed to make an assumption. The assumption, further, may be based upon the fact that these would be goddesses in other cultures or perhaps upon the fact that such honor would be unnatural for women if they were not goddesses. Such an assumption is evidence of a patriarchal mindset, but it is not evidence from statements or words on the paintings themselves or, that is, from the Minoans themselves. The Minoan evidence, without the patriarchal predisposition, is simply that these were honored women, at the center, certainly special, possibly in charge, possibly goddesses, but also possibly simply honored because they were women.

21. Semele has a later incarnation as a mortal. But some scholars seem to think she was originally a moon goddess from Crete. See e.g., Arthur Evans, *The God of Ecstasy: Sex Roles and the Madness of Dionysus* (New York: St. Martin's Press, 1988).

22. Miriam Robbins Dexter, *Whence the Goddesses: A Source Book* (New York: Pergamon Press, 1990), 41–42.

23. One theory of the coming of the Greeks is that they were part of an Indo-European migration

that originated in either southern Russia or in the broad swath of territory stretching all the way from Hungary to Central Asia. They might have brought the word for earth, *zemleye*, and this might have translated at some point into the moon-goddess Semele.

The Troubling Question of War

1. There is a seal in the British Museum that is identified as "perhaps Minoan" that has two men definitely in combat (GR 1874.4–5.5) (1500–1400 BCE), and this is placed beside a seal of men fighting, which is unequivocally attributed to the Mycenaeans. The Museum's wall posting makes this disclaimer: "In the late Bronze Age it is often impossible to distinguish between seals of Minoan or Mycenaean manufacture." The "perhaps Minoan" seal is therefore the only one I have seen that arguably fits the category of men at war. Making the determination that this is Minoan rather than Mycenaean is problematic. There are a few other seals on display in the museum at Herakleion that are blurred and indistinct and could conceivably be scenes of men fighting. In none of these, and there may be three or four out of many hundred, is the action distinct enough to say for sure what is going on. There are two seals now in the Ashmolean at Oxford, one that shows two men fighting (1910 196) and another that shows a man chasing a woman across the body of another fallen man (1938 1122), but the author of the most famous study of these seals believes that neither is authentic by reason of their motif, style, and technique. That is, he thinks they are forgeries. See V. E. G. Kenna, *Cretan Seals* (Oxford: Clarendon Press, 1960), 154 et seq. Altogether the picture therefore is that while there may be a few among hundreds of these rings that do portray combat, there is not one that I have seen that is unequivocally Minoan and only one that is even "perhaps" Minoan. On the other hand, I have not seen all that there are, and there may be some out there. What is incontestable is not that there are none, but that wherever they might be they are in such a small minority as to be inconsequential.

2. It is perhaps corroborative that Minoan feasts seem not to have especially emphasized hierarchy, a social feature that necessarily accompanies warfare. Elisabetta Borgna's chapter in *The Mycenaean Feast* examines evidence for Minoan feasting and concludes that in Minoan Crete, feasts could be either elite and exclusive or more communal affairs in which social identity rather than power relations were primarily at stake. Borgna notes that this presents a stark contrast to hierarchical Mycenaean feasting. See Seth Button, review of *The Mycenaean Feast*, ed. James C. Wright, *Bryn Mawr Classical Review* 4, no. 49 (2005).

3. I am indebted to Barbara Ehrenreich for the origins of this argument. Barbara Ehrenreich, *Blood Rites: Origins and History of the Passions of War* (New York: Henry Holt, 1997).

4. Dave Grossman, *On Killing: The Psychological Cost of Learning to Kill in War and Society* (New York: Little Brown and Company, 1995), 250.

5. Reuther, *Gaia and God*, 143 et seq.

Crete and the Issue of Female Sexuality

1. "Ritual prostitution by devotees of the Moon-goddess was practiced in Crete, Cyprus, Syria, Asia Minor, and Palestine." Graves, *Greek Myths*, vol. I, 100. Or see Burkert, *Greek Religion*, 108.

2. Amos 9:7 AV.

3. Most scholars today take it as certain that Kaphtor is Crete, but there are other possibilities. See Manuel Robbins, *Collapse of the Bronze Age: The Story of Greece, Troy, Israel, Egypt, and the Peoples of the Sea* (Lincoln, NE: Author's Choice Press, 2001), 315.

4. Jeremiah 47:2, 4 AV.

5. A detailed description and mapping of each of these rooms is beyond the scope of this book but is covered marvelously in Nicholas Platon's *Zakros*, 1971.

6. See Platon, *Zakros*, 94.

7. See, e.g., Eisler, *Sacred Pleasure*, and George, *Mysteries of the Dark Moon*, ch. 2.

8. Rodney Castleden, *Minoans: Life in Bronze Age Crete* (London and New York: Routledge, 1993), 13.

9. "The dolphin possesses a womb and breasts so it became one of Aphrodite's special symbols." Buffie Johnson, *Lady of the Beasts: Ancient Images of the Goddess and Her Sacred Animals* (San Francisco: Harper and Row, 1988), 239–240. There is a marble sculpture of Aphrodite with a dolphin in the Getty Museum in Santa Monica, California, and Johnson refers to Aphrodite in an early Greek form "standing on a dolphin."

10. See, e.g, Marija Gimbutas, *The Language of the Goddess* (New York: HarperCollins, 1991), 263.

11. Johnson, *Lady of the Beasts*, 240.

12. Baring and Cashford, *Myth of the Goddess*, 358.

Five Values Dramatically at Odds with Patriarchy

1. "Ritual prostitution by devotees of the Moon-goddess was practiced in Crete, Cyprus, Syria, Asia Minor, and Palestine." Graves, *Greek Myths*, vol. I, 100. See also the works listed in the bibliography hereto, including especially Eisler, Gimbutas, George, Sjoo and Moore, Johnson, Neumann, and Redmond.

Part II

The Invasions of 1600 BCE

1. John Keegan, *A History of Warfare* (New York: Vintage Books, 1994), 155.

2. "This constant fight against [the existing] religion and custom is the primary theme of the Old Testament. It begins in Genesis, with the takeover of the Goddess's Garden of Immortality by a male God, and the inversion of all her sacred symbols—tree, serpent, moon fruit, woman—into icons of evil. Of the two sons of Eve and Adam, Cain was made the 'evil brother' because he chose settled agriculture (matriarchal)—the 'good brother' Abel was a nomadic pastoralist (patriarchal). The war against the Goddess is carried on by the prophet's rantings against the 'golden calf,' the 'brazen serpents,' the 'great harlot' and 'Whore of Babylon' (the Babylonian Goddess Ishtar), against enchantresses, pythonic diviners, and those who practice witchcraft. It is in the prophets' war against the Canaanite worship of 'stone idols'—the Triple Moon Goddess worshipped as three horned pillars or menhirs. One of her shrines was on Mount Sinai, which means 'Mountain of the Moon.' Moses was commanded by 'the Lord' to go forth and destroy these 'idols'—who all had breasts." Monica Sjoo and Barbara Moore, *The Great Cosmic Mother: Rediscovering the Religion of the Earth* (San Francisco: Harper and Row, 1987), 264–265. The present author distances himself from the use of the word *matriarchal*, which may be more than the evidence supports. To say that women were influential in ceremonies is unquestionably accurate. They seem to have supervised burials and even assemblies and were often in public attendance on high stages. But to go the next step and assert that

they controlled the power, were in charge of government, and ruled and decided issues of land and taxes simply cannot be certainly deduced from pictures of them being honored.

3. Exodus 32:26–28 AV.

4. Robert Drews, *The Coming of the Greeks* (Princeton: Princeton Univ. Press, 1988).

The Theran Explosion

1. Immerwahr, *Aegean Painting*, 44–46.

2. J. V. Luce, *Lost Atlantis: New Light on an Old Legend* (New York: McGraw Hill, 1969), 150.

3. For a systematic analysis of the force of the explosion and the earthquake, tidal wave, and ash destruction that followed see Ibid., 145 et seq. Luce supports his hypothesis that the Thera explosion destroyed Minoan civilization, in part by noting reference to myths of floods from Attica, the Argolid, Troezen and the Saronic Gulf, Lycia, the Troad, Rhodes, and Samothrace. In all these locations early stories portray mighty Poseidon avenging himself on helpless populations by flooding their lands, and all such myths occur early in mythic history when the gods are said to be struggling among themselves for dominance. Luce believes that Poseidon's floods may be a memory of great and widespread flooding from Thera's explosion and the subsequent tidal wave.

4. Although Herodotus does relate a tale from a little village of Praisos in eastern Crete near Zakros, which explains that Crete was one time, at least three generations before the Trojan War, "depopulated." Herodotus, *The History*, trans. David Grene (Chicago: Univ. of Chicago Press, 1987), 170–171.

5. "Mycenaean iconography suggests that the principal deity in the Argolic plain during the palace period was the *potnia*, 'lady', whether she was called Hera or another name. Much other evidence—archaeological and linguistic—suggests that the *potnia* was already called Hera in the Mycenaean period or at least had cultic continuity with the Hera of the Archaic period." O'Brien, *Transformation of Hera*, 120. As late as the fourth century BCE one of the earliest extant allegorical manuscripts, the Derveni Papyrus, equates Hera, as well as Ge, Rhea, Meter, and Demeter, as symbols for the earth: "The poet [meaning Homer and those of his ilk] ... is aware of this and conveys his knowledge of hidden connections in a

code, which lies waiting for the perceptive interpreter to restore and reassemble." Peter T. Struck, *Birth of the Symbol: Ancient Readers at the Limits of Their Texts* (Princeton: Princeton Univ. Press, 2004), 38. Thus the writer of the Derveni Papyrus in the fourth century shared the conviction of the current writer that ancient poets intentionally conveyed allegorical meanings or meanings embedded in the language that are not apparent to average readers of a later age. The Derveni commentator also makes the equation between Hera and Mother Earth that is advanced in these pages.

The Growth of Trade

1. Robert Morkot, *The Penguin Historical Atlas of Ancient Greece* (New York: Penguin Books, 1996), 28–29.

2. Homer, *The Odyssey*, trans. Richmond Lattimore (New York: HarperCollins, 1991), 1.215–216. In Alexander Pope's translation of *The Odyssey* (Hartford, CT: Silas Andrus and Son, 1849), Odysseus states the problem straight out: "To prove a genuine birth, the prince replies/ On female truth assenting faith relies;/ Thus manifest of right, I build my claim/ Sure founded on a fair maternal fame,/ Ulysses' son" (1.275–79). In other words, man can only know his father depending upon his faith in "female truth," or a woman's word.

3. Homer, *The Odyssey*, trans. Lattimore, 1.106–112.

The Great Civil War over Marriage

1. Hermann Kinder and Werner Hilgemann, *The Anchor Atlas of World History: From the Stone Age to the Eve of the French Revolution*, vol. I (Garden City, NY: Anchor Books, 1974), 35. These authors indicate that Phrygians celebrated the "orgiastic cult of the 'Great Mother' (Cybele)" down until at least 800 BCE.

2. Burkert, *Greek Religion*, 24.

3. A plausible exception to this generalization might be the continued existence and prosperity of the Etruscans, who were not subdued until nearly the middle of the next millennium. From what we can see of Etruscan art, they were apt to emphasize the partnership between men and women more than the patriarchal domination of men. Unfortunately, the Romans thoroughly destroyed Etruscan civilization, so a generalization of equivalence between that civilization and the Minoans is still highly speculative.

4. As this is written, my grandson is reading Homer's *Odyssey* in the ninth grade. In the 1940s, when I was a child, I got it (probably in a simpler version) in the fifth grade.

5. Scholars have differing opinions concerning Homer's identity. Some argue that there were many Homers and the handed-down version of his poetry represents the condensation of an oral tradition. Others say he was more than one person or that *The Iliad* was written by a man and *The Odyssey* by a woman. These debates, while perhaps important, do not materially impact the analysis that follows, which applies whether he was several people or one, man or woman.

6. O'Brien, *Transformation of Hera*.

7. Gilbert Murray thinks that the story of Helen may be a variation on the ritual of the Spartan marriage goddess. "The marriage ceremony in Sparta involved carrying off of the bride, and Helen's chief function is to be carried off." From *The Literature of Ancient Greece*, 3d ed. (Chicago: Univ. of Chicago Press, 1956), xiii. That Spartan women practiced polyandry well into the fourth century BCE and were free to bear children with more than one man, see Sarah B. Pomeroy's *Goddesses, Whores, Wives, and Slaves: Women in Classical Antiquity* (New York: Schocken Books, 1975), 39, 117. Sparta at one time was a favored citadel of Hera in her days before becoming Zeus's wife, which is another reason why Helen may have thought she had license to wed whomever she wished for as long, or short, as she wished.

8. Graves, *Greek Myths*, vol. II, 271–272.

9. It may help to explain the willingness of others in Asia to join in this dispute to note that even as late as the sixth century BCE, Herodotus reported a practice of free female sexuality in adjacent Lydia. "All the daughters of the common people of Lydia practice as whores to collect dowries for themselves until, by doing so, they set up house with their man." Herodotus, *History*, 1.93. Troy and Sardis, capital of Lydia, were less than 150 miles separate. Additionally, both seem to have shared in an older Ionian culture that had earlier emigrated from the Greek mainland at a time when the fertility religions or primary worship of the principle of regeneration was dominant. The earliest religious unions also are known to have occurred among these Ionians, by this time as worshipers of Poseidon. Morkot, *Historical Atlas*, 45. There

was thus a history of religious solidarity among these settlements and by common report a view of female sexuality that differed strongly from that of the mainland Greeks. While Poseidon's role in *The Iliad* is mixed, his position in *The Odyssey* is decisively against that of Athena and his connection with the Ionian religious unions is therefore a pointer toward an earlier religion that seemed to have been different from that of the mainland after the Dark Age.

10. Homer, *The Iliad*, trans. Pope, 48–49, note 28. Robert Drews thinks the *Catalogue of Ships* is the oldest part of *The Iliad* text. Drews, *Coming of the Greeks*, 193–194.

11. Hermann Kinder and Werner Hilgemann, *The Anchor Atlas of World History: From the Stone Age to the Eve of the French Revolution*, vol. I (Garden City, NY: Anchor Books, 1974), 35.

12. Graves, *Greek Myths*, vol. II, 259, 265.

13. Martin P. Nilsson demonstrates that Helen was at some time a goddess figure in Sparta connected with a tree cult, and Isocrates expressly states that the Spartans sacrificed to her and Menelaos not as heroes but as gods. Helen had two temples at Sparta, and there is evidence that she was also associated with the lotus, which we have seen, above, associates with sexuality. Nilsson, *The Minoan-Mycenaean Religion* (New York: Biblo and Tannen, 1949), 530. It is not beyond conjecture that during the upheavals that accompanied the invasions of the Dorians and the decline of Mycenaean power that Phrygians may have come to Sparta to reclaim Helen or, that is, reclaim some aspect of her cult. The tree and lotus cult may have been sacred to Phrygia and in need of protection against invading Greek kings such as Menelaos. Nilsson concludes that there is some probability, additionally, that "the Minoan tree cult survives in the cult of Helen" (531) and also that there is some correspondence between snake feeding vessels used in Crete and Sparta (541–542). So while it cannot be positively proven that the Trojan War had to do with extirpating Minoan values, there is scholarly support for that conclusion.

14. Barbara G. Walker, *The Woman's Encyclopedia of Myths and Secrets* (San Francisco: Harper and Row, 1983), 48–49. Graves, *Greek Myths*, vol. II, 145, 151.

15. Homer, *The Iliad*, trans. Alexander Pope (London: Bell and Daldy, 1865), 5.417–423.

16. O'Brien argues that the words *hero* and *Hera* are etymologically linked as portrayed here. *Transformation*, 113 et seq.

17. Homer, *The Odyssey*, trans. Lattimore, 6.488–491.

18. Even after the Greeks came, the goddess Hera was thought to be made virgin each year by bathing in the river. It was a story that identified the goddess with the floods of spring and tied her, as the archetypal woman, to seasons and renewed fertility in the land. That much of the old concept hung on in the new mythology. O'Brien, *Transformation*, ch. 6.

19. See, e.g., Michael Wood, *In Search of the Trojan War* (Berkeley and Los Angeles: Univ. of California Press, 1998), 250. Or see Taylour, *Mycenaeans*, 159: "We do not know what was the cause of the Trojan War, for the abduction of Helen by a prince of Troy was merely used as an excuse."

20. The women of Lemnos, as we will see, did not honor marriage. The women of Lesbos are also highly suspect. I do not know what sexual practices may have existed on Pedassos and Lynressos.

21. Homer, *The Iliad*, trans. Pope, 2.180–219.

22. Ibid., 2.974–975.

Part III

Four Hundred Years of Chaos Sets the Stage

1. The "Dark Age" of the years between 1200 BCE and 800 BCE is not to be confused with the so-called "Dark Ages" of European History, also called the Middle Ages, roughly from 600 CE (Common Era) to about 1300 CE. Both periods unfortunately are widely known by these confusingly similar labels.

2. Goethe, Johann Wolfgang, *Faust: Erster und Zweiter Teil* (München: Deutscher Taschenbuch Verlag, 1977), 351.

> Das Unbeschreibliche
> Hier ist's getan;
> Das Ewigweibliche
> Zieht uns hinan.

The indescribable
Here it is done
The eternal feminine
Pulls us on.

Values Shaped by Storytellers

1. See, e.g., Purce, *Mystic Spiral*.

2. Professor Peter Struck points out that no doubt there was more than one meaning and that from place to place dragons might have had numerous connotations (from private correspondence with the author). Struck is most certainly correct. What we are searching for here is not the meaning of the dragon in all cultures but rather a likely meaning for its presence in repeated Greek myths of transition or conquest. It is extremely common, that is, for myths to have numerous variations, including the myths about the golden fleece. We ought not assert a sort of iron-clad interpretation. On the other hand, in that most of the myths chosen for analysis in this book are pan-Hellenic, their utility and understanding across all of Greece must have been more or less to the same point. Myths were intended, no doubt, to be instructional and were effective to the extent that they were instructional across a broad band of popular culture.

3. One is reminded of the modern story that circulated in Russia following the ascendance of Mikhail Gorbachev to first secretary of the Communist Party in 1985. It was popularly reported in Moscow at the time that Andrei Gromyko had persuaded old-line Communists in the Politburo to support the young Gorbachev because, although he had a nice smile, "he had steel teeth."

4. Luc Brisson, *Plato the Myth Maker* (Chicago: Univ. of Chicago Press, 1998), 7–8, referring to *Republic* II and III. Plato, says Luc, often disagreed with the values conveyed by the myths. "[S]uch a will to modify mass behavior immediately poses an ethical problem. … Any poet, and in particular Homer, can be considered as a true educator because he wants to transform the behavior of his audience by offering them the beings he is summoning as models. … The poet wants to mold the souls of his public in the name of a community which seeks to assure, through persuasion, the obedience of its members to a system of values."

5. Ibid., 9. "For both the community and the individual, these myths fix the reference points in every essential area of existence, and even propose explanations concerning the origin of the gods, the world, human beings, and the society in which they live."

6. Minstrel poets still sing hours-long songs, making them up as they go, in Central Asia. In the old days, says a modern Kyrgyz singer, they were "extemporaneous preachers who lectured in sung verse on the political and moral issues of the day, adapting old legends or codes for the country's latest ruler." This is an apt description of the style and purpose of storytellers such as Homer. See Peter Finn, *The Washington Post*, reported in *The New Mexican*, March 7, 2005, sec. A, p. 5.

7. Compare, e.g., the vestiges or remnants of Near Eastern myth contained in the Greek tales as presented by M. L. West in *East Face of Helicon* with the detail about Lerna, Nemea, Crete, Hera, snakes, et cetera, contained in the many Heraclean myths. While the later stories undoubtedly borrow themes from the Near East and undoubtedly also some meanings, there is no example of simple replication, or outright copying, of such myths and therefore no adoption wholesale of Near Eastern struggles. The struggles portrayed in Greek myths are too local and detailed to be interchangeable.

8. Nor is there evidence that the mythological figures of Greek religion can be traced back to Crete as if directly imported from Minoans. Rather, the names of the Greek gods and goddesses emerge for the first time in Linear B after Minoan civilization is either in decline or completely destroyed, and therefore the gods and goddesses had to have been molded by the Greeks for whatever political purpose they may have had after Crete. See Burkert, *Greek Religion*, 23–24. "It is hazardous to project Greek tradition directly into the Bronze Age."

9. In modern times Mary Renault has given us a splendid but perfectly patriarchal amplification of this adventure in her novel *The King Must Die*.

10. Professor Peter Struck accurately points out (in a note to the author) that there was no foundation in archaeology, either, for stories of Achilles or Hector or Heracles. All these figures, as well as King Minos, must have been made up, conjured, or partial representations of famous ancestors half-remembered, tailored in time to the political, territorial, or religious (perhaps the same thing) needs of the storytellers.

An Exaggerated Feminine Is Made Monstrous

1. No one else calls them "Siren figures," and the appellation is not the general view of scholars, none of whom (so far as I know) has made the same connection. I simply call them that because they are ubiquitous and so widespread as to have been a likely symbol of the earlier age, the values of which would have been in contest during the latter years of the Bronze Age, the time about which Homer was writing when he found so many ways to disparage the old culture.

2. Hesiod, *Theogony*, In *Hesiod and Theognis,* trans. Dorothea Wender (New York: Penguin Books, 1984), 39–43.

3. Ibid., 87–94.

4. Maria Leach, ed. *Funk and Wagnalls Standard Dictionary of Folklore, Mythology, and Legend*, vol. II (New York: Funk and Wagnalls, 1950), 1147.

5. Hesiod, *Theogony*, In *Hesiod and Theognis,* trans. Dorothea Wender, 299.

6. Hesiod, *Theogony*, 822 et seq.

7. Graves, *Greek Myths*, vol. I, 134.

8. Hesiod, *Theogony*, 841 et seq.

9. The defeat is not found in Hesiod, but according to later sources. See Hesiod, *Theogony*, 822 et seq., and Graves, *Greek Myths*, vol. I, 134.

10. Hesiod, *Theogony*, 858.

11. Mary E. Voyatzis, "From Athena to Zeus," in Goodison and Morris, *Ancient Goddesses*, 143.

Mother Earth is Overthrown

1. In the Cratylus, Plato acknowledges that certain readers of Homer equated the goddess Hera with air and Athena with mind and thought. Plato therefore recognized that there was a school of ancient thinkers who believed that Homer intended certain undermeanings that were encoded in his poetic text. Those thinkers, whose names included Metrodorus of Lampsacus and Stesimbrotus of Thasos, thought Homer was actually replete with allegory. See Struck, *Birth of the Symbol*, 43. Plato, however, disapproved of such reading of Homer, as did Aristotle, and eventually these two became much the more significant voices of the age, with the result that Metrodorus and Stes-

imbrotus have long been ignored. It is, however, precisely such allegorical reading that is revived in the analysis of this book.

2. See especially the Derveni Papyrus of the fourth century BCE in which the position taken is that the poetic texts were repositories of great and even sacred hidden truths "conveyed in riddles through the whole poem, in a manner that resembles the semantically dense language of oracular speech, esoteric philosophy, and cultic practice and so requires an expansive interpretation to unpack the significance of each word. ... For the Derveni commentator—and a whole line of allegorical readers after him—the poem is a riddle to be solved." Struck, *Birth of the Symbol*, 38. These readers in the classical ages would have not have had access to any of the details of that Minoan culture that had preceded them by more than a thousand years and that lay buried under ash or was destroyed by later invasions. They would not have known any culture that had ever included such dramatically different values as those represented upon the Minoan artifacts (which we know about today), and the mysteries of the poetic texts would therefore have appeared to them as "riddles." From the perspective of the twenty-first century CE, however, we can now see for the first time that the poetic texts arose out of a culture-shaping conflict between civilizations and property systems and that the meanings that were riddles to later populations had had the earlier purpose of political and religious propaganda. Such stories were no doubt first told by sages or priests or those entrusted with the sacred messages of the new culture, told as poems for easy memorization. The word *propaganda* may seem to demean them. But sacred propaganda is not really a contradiction in terms.

3. This is supposing a mixing together of Hesiod's *Theogony* and his *Works and Days*.

4. Deuteronomy 8:7–8 AV.

Jason Resists the Many Shapes of Seductive Women

1. One time on my brother's cattle ranch in the rugged Arizona mountains, I rode for hours behind a young cowboy as he worked his horse up and down narrow canyons, around and between greasewood and saguaro, darting after cows and their calves. The

cowboy and his mount sailed over cactus and boulders at a full run or across miles of desert with such graceful combined purpose that I thought I had never seen anything more beautiful. He might have been a modern Centaur.

2. I have seen this same cowboy (note 1) seeking escape from the blistering sun, crawl under and prop up against a leg of his horse and nod off to sleep in the shade of the animal's belly. The horse rested standing while the cowboy lay against him. It was an arrangement that would not work if each did not completely understand the other or if either were to move suddenly, which neither ever did.

3. The Dioscuri were two brothers in the early legends of Sparta and were Sparta's pride. Castor was a famous soldier and tamer of horses, and Polydeuces was the best boxer of the day; both won prizes at the Olympic Games. Graves, *Greek Myths*, vol. I, 246.

4. Graves, *Greek Myths*, vol. II, 227, 235.

5. From a conversation with George Tassoulas, curator of Goulandris Museum of Cycladic Art, Athens, who, while observing a dove ceremonial vase on exhibit in the museum, explained that the Greek word for dove traces back through words for Ishtar, Astarte, and Aphrodite.

6. Keegan, *History of Warfare*, 155 et seq, esp. 161.

7. Drews, *The Coming of the Greeks*, 194.

8. Ibid., 148.

9. Which Drews believes is exactly how the invaders did come. Ibid., ch. 8.

10. Ibid. Drews also notes that Thessaly, from which Jason comes, was the source of the greatest number of ships and warriors to contribute to the Trojan War (according to the Catalogue of Ships), indicating that it was the area to which the invaders may first have come and would have been the most populated by Indo-Europeans at about 1200 BCE.

11. Luce, *Lost Atlantis*, 148 et seq.

Odysseus Rejects Calypso

1. Barry Powell, *Homer* (Oxford and Australia: Blackwell Publishing, 2004), 28.

2. Ibid., 33.

3. Ibid., 9.

4. Political persuasion is still done in much the same way. A similar combination of monsters, demons, and heroes was used to justify the American vendetta against Saddam Hussein and the invasion of Iraq in 2003. The failure, further, of Democrats in 2004 to create an alternative story, any sustained narrative of alternative heroes and demons, explains in part their failure to capture the public imagination in that election. In both 2000 and 2004 Democrats offered facts, analyses, claims, and assertions while George W. Bush reminded Americans of their cowboy stories, their narratives of heroism and sacrifice. What one side analyzed as rash and intemperate the other acted out as mythical and bold, even visionary.

5. Homer, *The Odyssey*, trans. Lattimore, 5.64–74. Pope translates: "A scene where, if a god should cast his sight/ A god might gaze, and wander with delight!" (5.95–96).

6. Walker, *Myths and Secrets*, 27.

7. Homer does not tell us about the three sons, but the story was a part of a more common lore, and other versions fill in this detail.

8. Seven has all sorts of ancient connotations. In this case it will not be coincidence that the elaborate, ornamental dress of the famous snake goddess from Knossos contains exactly seven layers. The meanings of seven are manifold. Seven is the number of stars in the constellation Pleiades by which sailors steered. The best sailors of those pre-Homeric times had been the Cretans. The Pleiades were each named after seven weeping moon goddesses. One of the goddesses' names was derived from Halcyon, which marked the fourteen halcyon days before and after the winter solstice of the sun. Seven days is exactly one quarter of the moon's cycle, et cetera. Sun and moon cycles are therefore both woven into a pattern of beginnings and endings. Here it means an end.

9. Homer, *The Odyssey*, trans. Pope, 5.149–152.

10. It is sometimes objected that we cannot know the meaning of the old symbols, such as spirals and apples (of immortality), because we do not have any contemporary text or writing that explains such meaning. Here, however, in Homer we have a direct reference to a pre-Olympian goddess, a daughter of the Titans, who offers immortality to a man. Homer is telling us directly what, in his view, the old religion offered. We do therefore have text, not from the Titans or the Cretans themselves, but from the first literature to recall them.

11. Homer, *The Odyssey*, trans. Pope, 5.171–73. Calypso repeats the offer in line 267.

12. Homer, *The Odyssey*, trans. Lattimore, 5.190–91. There is a double meaning here, for iron is the discovery of the new age after the Bronze Age of Crete, and she is also saying that she has not the spirit of the Iron Age in which the Olympians rule.

13. Homer, *The Odyssey*, trans. Pope, 5.274–282.

14. Aphrodite was once vexed to find Ares in Eos's bed and cursed her with a constant longing for young mortals, whom Eos thereupon secretly and shamefacedly began to seduce, one after the other. First Orion; next Cephalus; then Cleitus, et cetera. Graves, *Greek Myths*, vol. I, 149.

Homer Poses the Choice between Love and Property

1. Walker, *Myths and Secrets*, 821. "All Asia called water a female element. … To dive into such water was a symbol of sexual intercourse."

2. Homer, *The Iliad*, trans. Pope, 16.76–81.

3. Homer, *The Odyssey*, trans. Lattimore, 5.262–264.

4. Ibid., 5.344, 5.370.

5. Ibid., 5.348.

6. Ibid., 6.149.

7. Homer, *The Odyssey*, trans. Rodney Merrill (Ann Arbor: Univ. of Michigan Press, 2002), 6.158.

8. Ibid., 6.180.

9. Ibid., 6.229.

10. Ibid., 6.244.

Clytemnestra is Sacrificed on the Altar of Marriage

1. Aeschylus, *The Eumenides*, trans. E. D. A. Morshead, in *The Complete Greek Drama*, vol. I, ed. Whitney J. Oates and Eugene Gladstone O'Neill (New York: Random House, 1938), 658–652.

2. Ibid., 738.

Marriage Destroys the Mother-Daughter Bond

1. A picture of the cup is reproduced in Suter, *Narcissus and the Pomegranate*, 174.

2. The name Eleusis "refers to the underworld in the favorable sense and may be translated as 'the place of happy arrival. … [It] is related … to Elysion, the realm of the blessed." Carl Kerényi, *Eleusis: Archetypal Image of Mother and Daughter*, trans. Ralph Manheim (Princeton: Princeton Univ. Press), 23. Thus, in the thesis of this book, the place of happy arrival of some important or divine influence from outside. "According to the sacred history of Eleusis, the first to 'arrive' was Demeter herself. The Homeric hymn tells us that she came from Crete (V 123), but this does not absolutely mean that the Mysteries themselves were of Cretan origin. The goddess was the first initiate and also the founder of the Mysteries; her initiation was the finding of her daughter. This did not happen in Crete. Nevertheless, as with so many of the characteristic elements of Greek cultural history, there are indications pointing to an origin in Crete, the great island whose advanced civilization had been shared by Greeks since the fifteenth century B.C." Ibid., 23–24.

3. Some may have objected that they were on the wrong side of that divide. There is a coin from the island city of Thasos that portrays a rape in process. It may have been that the Thasians thought of themselves as rapists, or, perhaps more likely, because they had been defeated in war by the Athenians in 465 BCE, they may have considered themselves the ones who had been raped. Thasos is not so far from Lemnos, where we learn from legend that women did not believe in or practice marriage. Those island cultures seem to have been slower to move toward male predominance. Thasian coins were silver, and Thasos had been an exporter of silver. By printing such coins after the Athenian conquest, they seem to have been saying to the world that rape is the lot of the weak and that the weak are represented by women and by little Thasos. The same thing had happened to them as had happened to Persephone. In the classical story that every Thasian and every Athenian knew by heart, Demeter, the mother, had been devastated by the loss of her daughter and then went into mourning. So, too, the Thasians might have been saying with their coins, We are the ones of the old world, akin to the *kore*, mourning our life before the rape by Athens/Hades.

4. Prometheus certainly defied Zeus and was himself a son of the Titans, so he might qualify as

another who ran counter to the Olympians. He came to no good end, of course, chained to a rock where vultures ate out his liver every day. He was never, however, strictly an Olympian, never one of the twelve who ruled. Demeter's role and her importance as a source of life to be worshipped was much more prominent.

5. Grapes and olives were harvested in the fall, but grain was planted in the fall and harvested in early summer. Demeter, who was central to the Eleusian ceremonies, was goddess of the grains but not olives or grapes.

A Multitude of Myths to Tame, Punish, and Disparage Women

1. Graves, *Greek Myths*, vol. I, 97.

2. Walker, *Myths and Secrets*, 620, citing Merlin Stone's *When God Was a Woman* and Elise Boulding's *The Underside of History*.

3. Letter to "Washington Chiefs" by 123 Hopi clan and village leaders, March 1894, posted on National Park Service sign, Coyote Village, Far View Sites, Mesa Verde, CO.

4. Graves, *Greek Myths*, vol. I, 60.

5. O'Brien, *Transformation*, 184. "In his study of female choruses in Archaic cult, Claude Calame has shown that the most pervasive metaphor for marriage is the taming of the filly or heifer, the woman being seen as a wild, undomesticated animal, who becomes acculturated and civilized by being broken like a young beast."

6. These values were those of Niobe, a queen of Thebes whose predecessors are from Phoenicia and Phrygia, where it was quite likely that there were residual elements of the older religion.

Oedipus, the Lost Son

1. Homer, *The Odyssey*, trans. Lattimore, 12.470.

2. Ibid., 12.463.

A Glorious Monument Enshrining the Subordination of Women

1. Vitruvius, *The Ten Books on Architecture*, trans. Morris Hickey Morgan (New York: Dover Publications, 1960), 6.

2. For recent examples, see Jeffrey M. Hurwit, *The Acropolis in the Age of Pericles* (Cambridge: Cambridge Univ. Press, 2004), 227–228; Jenifer Neils, *The Parthenon Frieze* (Cambridge: Cambridge Univ. Press, 2001); and Margaretha Rossholm Lagerlöf, *The Sculptures of the Parthenon: Aesthetics and Interpretation* (New Haven, CT: Yale Univ. Press, 2000).

3. In dispute of those who say that women's bottoms are never bare in ancient Greek sculpture, e.g. Hurwit, see to the contrary an undeniably female *kore* in the museum at Eleusis holding an apple (third–fourth century BCE, #5137). This *kore* has a bottom half covered in much the same way as that on the figure of the Parthenon frieze. It cannot therefore be accurately maintained that only boys' bottoms were revealed in this way.

4. Joan B. Connelly, "Parthenon and Parthenoi," *American Journal of Archaeology* 100, no. 1:53 et seq.

5. Chrysoula Kardara, cited in Neils, *Parthenon Frieze*, 175, says that the bare bottom has to be that of a male. The argument is based upon a picture of Erechthonios on a red-figure cup of about 460–450 BCE in the Acropolis museum. To the contrary, however, see the full figure of a female at Eleusis, referred to in note 3 above.

6. Graves, *Greek Myths*, vol. I, 97.

7. Lillian E. Doherty, *Gender and Interpretation of Classical Myth* (London: Duckworth Publishing, 2001), 137.

8. The marriage feast was of the Lapiths. Heracles had to be brought in to drive the Centaurs off.

9. Jane Henle, *Greek Myths: A Vase Painter's Notebook* (Bloomington, IN: Indiana Univ. Press, 1973), 54–55. See also Janet Burnett Grossman in her review of Brunilde Ridgway's *Prayers in Stone: Greek Architectural Sculpture*, carried on owner-bmcr-1@brynmawr.edu, 2/28/00: "Ridgway demonstrates that the primary purpose of the sculptures on architectural monuments was religious. ... Architecture was the means of visually communicating and transmitting epics and mythology in a society where just a small elite was literate."

10. "In its dual rhythm of constancy and change, it provided not only a point of orientation from which differences could be measured, patterns conceived and connections made, but also, in its perpetual return to its own beginnings, it unified what had

apparently been broken asunder." Baring and Cashford, *Myth of the Goddess*, 21. To the same point: "The ancients perceived the moon, which displayed the ebb and flow of birth, life, and death, to be feminine, and they personified her as the Great Goddess who ruled over these three great mysteries. As the moon turned from new to full to dark, it was worshiped as an embodiment of each of these three phases; hence the Triple Moon Goddess, who displayed herself on many levels as sets of three." George, *Mysteries*, 31–32.

11. Genesis 3:16.

12. Elaine Pagels places the timing of Genesis between 900–1000 BCE, more or less coincident with the complete victory of the patriarchies. Pagels, *Adam, Eve, and the Serpent* (New York: Random House, 1988), xxii.

13. "There is a marked tendency in Greek mythological representations to divide powerful women up into the sexually active but hostile, and the virginal but helpful." Sue Blundell, *Women in Ancient Greece* (Cambridge: Harvard Univ. Press, 1995), 43.

14. Pomeroy, *Goddesses*, 57.

15. Deuteronomy 22:21. "The latter rule was to invalidate the pagan custom of premarital defloration by a stranger, lest someone other than the husband might have a claim on the bride's property." Walker, *Myths and Secrets*, 11.

16. "The Virgin Mary was permitted to exist as a kind of bowdlerized version of Isis, resolutely unacquainted with the biological, emotional and spiritual imperatives of real women, a makeshift goddess created by misogynists for misogynists." Lynn Picknett and Clive Prince, *The Templar Revelation: Secret Guardians of the True Identity of Christ* (New York: Simon and Schuster, 1997), 78.

Biblical Patriarchs Match the Greek Story

1. Robbins, *Collapse*, ch. 13, 14.

2. Timothy Freke and Peter Gandy, *Jesus and the Lost Goddess* (New York: Random House, 2001), 23 et seq.

3. The prophet Amos noted that the Philistines originally came from Crete, and the subsequent Hebrew rejection of Philistines therefore was again in all probability a rejection of old Cretan values. This is made even more plausible by the reference in Amos—at the same place where he mentions the Philistines—to the willingness of the Hebrew God to touch the land and make it melt or to make the sea rise up like a flood. At the time of these prophecies, the most recent example of such enormous godly power would have been the volcanic explosion on the island of Thera, which in turn was what had caused the Philistines to migrate to Canaan. There is thus biblical text that may plausibly have reference to the Theran explosion.

4. Genesis 2:21, 22, 23 AV.

5. Genesis 3:16 AV.

6. Ibid.

7. Genesis 3:1–7 AV.

8. Genesis 3:14, 15 AV.

9. Walker, *Myths and Secrets*, 48.

10. Ibid., 49.

11. "The harm that has been done to souls, during the centuries of Christianity, first by the literal interpretation of the story of Adam, and then by the confusion of this myth, treated as history, with later speculations, principally Augustinian, about original sin, will never be adequately told." Paul Ricoeur, *The Symbolism of Evil*, quoted in Roger Shattuck, *Forbidden Knowledge: From Prometheus to Pornography* (New York: Harcourt Brace, 1996), 53.

12. Ibid. This is the view of Shattuck, not Ricoeur.

13. Genesis 17:2 AV.

14. "Both polygamy and divorce ... increased opportunities for reproduction—not for women, but for the men who wrote the laws and benefited from them." Pagels, *Adam, Eve*, 11.

15. Genesis 14:1–5 AV.

16. Karen Peterson, "Panel Favors Ban on Same Sex Marriage," *Santa Fe New Mexican*, Feb. 13, 1999, A–5. Similar laws, said the newspaper, had already been adopted in twenty-nine other states.

Part IV

1. Sharman, *Jesus as Teacher*, and Henry Burton Sharman, *Records of the Life of Jesus* (Palo Alto, CA: Sequoia Seminar Foundation, 1917). Sharman's work bears a remarkable similarity to Thomas Jefferson's

The Life and Morals of Jesus of Nazareth (New York: Wilfred Funk, 1904), originally written between 1803–1816. See also Stephen Mitchell, *The Gospel According to Jesus: A New Translation and Guide to His Essential Teachings for Believers and Unbelievers* (New York: Harper Collins, 1991); James Breech, *The Silence of Jesus: The Authentic Voice of the Historical Man* (Philadelphia: Fortress Press, 1983); Michael Grant, *Jesus: An Historian's Review of the Gospels* (New York: Scribner's, 1977).

Jesus Carries Forward the Eleusinian Symbolism of Grain and Wine

1. Walter Burkert, *Ancient Mystery Cults* (Cambridge: Harvard Univ. Press, 1987), 21.

2. For an analysis of how later translators may have bowed to the will of King James for what were then his current political purposes, see Walter Wink, *Violence and Nonviolence in South Africa: Jesus' Third Way* (Philadephia: New Society Publishers, 1987).

3. Judging from his other teaching about the curing power of faith and the usefulness of faith in practical situations, it is perhaps far more likely that when Jesus used the word *faith*, he might have been speaking of an attitude that a human can intentionally adopt of benign expectation, a hopefulness, a willingness to rely on the implicate order of the universe. This would be a meaning of faith that might in itself cure the sick or heal the heart and is something that a person can see in others and find in himself or herself. Faith as an attitude of this kind is much different than faith as a requirement to believe what does not make sense.

4. Walker, *Myths and Secrets*, 933, citing Count Goblet d'Alviella, *The Migration of Symbols* (New York: University Books, 1956), 2.

5. For a fuller discussion of the many Gnostic antecedents to Jesus within the Greek tradition, see Freke and Gandy, *Jesus and the Lost Goddess*, especially ch. 2.

6. Ibid., 37.

Jesus Takes On the Threat of Military Destruction

1. Sharman, *Jesus as Teacher*, 125. Sharman's text arises out of seminars that took place over a generation during which he sought to excavate from the King James version of the synoptic gospels those teachings most likely to have been authentic out of the mouth of Jesus of Nazareth. In general his method and that of his students was to seek those phrases and that meaning that was internally consistent with the approach of the whole teacher and to be wary of that language that had the obvious purpose to build a following for the adherents in the new church or that was otherwise contrary to the sense of the whole.

2. Tom Holland, *Rubicon: The Last Years of the Roman Republic* (New York: Doubleday, 2003). The fierce rivalry of Marius and Sulla in the first century BCE is illustrative.

3. Sharman, *Jesus as Teacher*, 83.

4. Ibid.

5. Ibid., 84–85.

6. Ibid., 51.

7. Ibid.

8. Ephesians 5:23–24.

9. I Timothy 2:11–15.

10. Pagels, *Adam, Eve*, ch. 1.

11. Ibid., 28.

Ancient Beliefs Spring Up among the Celts

1. Philip Newell, *Listening for the Heartbeat of God: A Celtic Spirituality* (London: SPCK, Holy Trinity Church, 1997), 25.

2. Ibid., 1–2.

A Short-Lived Islamic Challenge

1. John Alden Williams, ed., *Islam* (New York: Braziller, 1962), 60.

2. *The Qur'an*, in *Islam*, ed. Williams, 49.

3. Ibid., 50

4. An exception to this broad statement may lie in the influence of Sufis upon the Cathars, who for a brief time exercised mighty influence in Provence and Languedoc, which were for a time perhaps culturally the most advanced areas in the Western world. John Mathews thinks that Sufi teachings may have come to France from the East via Spain and the Pyrenees. Mathews, *The Grail: Quest for the Eternal* (New York:

Thames and Hudson, 1981), 22.

The Metaphor of the Holy Grail

1. See, e.g., Picknett and Prince, *Templar Revelation*.

2. See especially Riane Eisler, *The Chalice and the Blade: Our History, Our Future* (San Francisco: Harper and Row, 1987).

3. Mathews, *The Grail*, 9.

4. See Picknett and Prince, *Templar Revelation*, ch. 4.

5. Mathews, *The Grail*, 21–22.

6. While it may be argued that from time to time the church tolerated unusual figures such as Francis of Assisi, it is abundantly true that it never encouraged any of them.

Devil Talk and Witch Burnings

1. Vita Sackville-West, *Saint Joan of Arc* (New York: Grove Press, 1936), 304–305.

2. Alan Kors and Edward Peters, *Witchcraft in Europe: A Documentary History* (Philadelphia: Univ. of Pennsylvania Press, 1972), 117.

3. Ibid., 126.

4. Ibid., 169.

5. Joan's trial was before *Malleus Maleficarum* was written but within the same century and same general climate.

6. Sackville-West, *Saint Joan*, 326.

7. Ibid., 335–336.

Closing the Book on the Patriarchy

1. William J. Broad, "It Swallowed a Civilization," *New York Times*, 21 October 2003, sec. F, p. 1.

Part V

1. Anatoly Gromyko and Martin Hellman, *Breakthrough: Emerging New Thinking* (New York: Walker Publishing, 1987). A successful first strike by one side or the other in the Cold War would result in such a dust and ash cloud covering both hemispheres of the planet that temperatures would drop by 6–10 degrees, crippling the world's agricultural production.

Women Coming Home to Dignity

1. The Greek playwrights Euripides and Aristophanes are exceptions. Euripides' Hecuba and portrayal of Polyxena and Andromache are quite sympathetic. He was, however, ridiculed by other playwrights. Aristophanes' *Lysistrata* perhaps took the side of women opposing the war of Athens against Sparta, but there are grounds to think Aristophanes was quietly ridiculing them. There are other examples. But the general principle is accurate that the overwhelming resources and powers were on the side of those who defended patriarchy.

2. Both quotes are in Frances Gies and Joseph Gies, *Women in the Middle Ages* (New York: Barnes and Noble, 1978).

3. For my own dramatization of the thesis that Mary Sidney was the true author of the Shakespearean works, see the full-length stage play *King's Yellow* by Craig S. Barnes, which may be found at www.craig-barnes.com. The leading advocate of this theory is Robin Williams, *Sweet Swan of Avon: Did a Woman Write Shakespeare?* Wilton Circle Press, 2006.

4. Elizabeth I of England died in 1603. Her successor was James I, the son of Mary Queen of Scots. In 1625 James was succeeded by his son Charles I, who was deposed in a civil war and beheaded in 1649.

5. For a more detailed analysis of progress and failures in the last fifty years in the United States in women's wages and employment, see Appendix.

6. A. Salmon, ed., *Coutumes de Beauvaisis* (Paris: Picard, 1899), 355, quoted in Gies and Gies, *Women in the Middle Ages*, 46. The full *Coutumes* has been republished by Picard in 1970–74, including the analysis of A. Salmon but I have been unable to reverify the page cited by Gies in the more recent printing.

7. Cherubino de Siena, *Regole della vita matrimoniale* (n.p., 1888), 12–14, reproduced in Julia O'Faolain, ed., *Not in God's Image: Women in History from the Greeks to the Victorians* (London: Temple Smith, 1973), 177.

8. Joni Seager, ed., *The Penguin Atlas of Women in the World* (New York: Penguin Books, 2003), 26–27. This writer once was stranded in a Moscow airport for some five hours awaiting the arrival of a late plane. Falling into conversation with a middle-aged Armenian woman who happened to be standing at the

counter, I discovered that the woman was there with her brother and his family, who played about on the floor in the lobby. After an hour or two of conversation, the woman confessed that she had never in her life been so long out from under the direct control of her brother and had only once in her life had such an conversation with a male who was not a family member. The other conversation had also been accidental, in an airport, some years before. Until that confession, this writer had not realized that the conversation was unusual or in the least bit intimate. The woman had been leading a life closer to the backroom confinement of ancient Greece than to that of modern Western Europe.

The Declining Utility of War

1. Ales Adamovich, "Problems with the New Way of Thinking," in *Breakthrough: Emerging New Thinking* (New York: Walker Publishing, 1987), 121. These specific comments were related to the author by Adamovich in extended conversations in Moscow in 1986. Adamovich said that he had confronted the generals for taking this position and ridiculed them in his writing.

Appendix

1. U.S. Census Bureau, Historical Income Tables—People, Table P-40, *Woman's Earnings as a Percentage of Men's Earnings by Race and Hispanic Origin: 1960 to 2001*. For all races the percent was 76.3. Based on median earnings of full-time, year-round workers fifteen years old and over.

2. U.S. Census Bureau, Historical Income Tables—People, Table P-24, *Educational Attainment—Full-Time, Year-Round Workers 25 Years Old and Over by Median Earnings and Sex: 1991 to 2001*.

3. Fair Pay Act legislation (US, 1963).

4. Hilary M. Lips, "Women, Education, and Economic Participation," keynote address at the Northern Regional Seminar of National Council of Women in New Zealand, Auckland, New Zealand, March 1999.

5. For a more in-depth discussion of comparable

worth, including graphs and charts that demonstrate the effects of historic discrimination in the market and in the City of Denver's employment system, see *Lemons v. City and County of Denver*, 620 F.2d 228 (CA10), cert. denied, 449 US 888 (1980) and *Pay Equity: Equal Pay for Work of Comparable Value*, Joint Hearings before the House Subcommittees on Human Resources Civil Service Compensation and Employee Benefits of the Committee on Post Office and Civil Service, 97th Cong., 2d Sess., Sept. 16, 21, 30 and Dec. 2, 1982, Part I, esp. 597 et seq. The author was trial counsel in the Lemons case, and the congressional hearings reflect his explanation to Congress of the ways in which discrimination goes underground but maintains its continuing effects on pay for women in historically female professions.

6. Lips, "Women, Education, and Economic Participation."

7. Ibid. Citing the U.S. Government's Glass Ceiling Commission report in 1995.

8. Steven Greenhouse and Constance L. Hays, "Wal-Mart Sex-Bias Suit Given Class-Action Status," *New York Times*, 23 June 2004, sec. A, p. 1, late edition.

Bibliography

Aeschylus. *The Eumenides*. Trans. E.D.A. Morshead, in *The Complete Greek Drama*, vol. I. Ed. Whitney J. Oates and Eugene Gladstone O'Neill. New York: Random House, 1938.

Alexander, Caroline. "Echoes of the Heroic Age." *National Geographic* 196, no. 6 (December 1999): 55.

Baillie, Allan, and Suzanne Ostro. "The Lotus." *Tricycle: The Buddhist Review* 9, no. 3 (Spring 1999): 57.

Baring, Anne, and Jules Cashford. *The Myth of the Goddess: Evolution of an Image*. New York: Penguin Books, 1993.

Barret, André. *Greece Observed*. Trans. Stephen Hardman. London: Kaye and Ward, 1974.

Bernall, Martin. *Black Athena*. 2 vols. Piscataway, NJ: Rutgers Univ. Press, 1991.

Blundell, Sue. *Women in Ancient Greece*. Cambridge: Harvard Univ. Press, 1995.

Bolen, Jean Shimoda. *Gods in Everyman: A New Psychology of Men's Lives and Loves*. New York: HarperPerennial, 1990.

Borgna, Elisabetta. "Aegean Feasting: A Minoan Perspective." Ch. 6 of *The Mycenaean Feast*. Ed. James Wright. Princeton: The American School of Classical Studies at Athens, 2004.

Breech, James. *The Silence of Jesus: The Authentic Voice of the Historical Man*. Philadelphia: Fortress Press, 1983.

Brisson, Luc. *Plato the Myth Maker*. Trans. Gerard Naddaf. Chicago: Univ. of Chicago Press, 1998.

Broad, William J. "It Swallowed a Civilization." *New York Times*, 21 October 2003, sec. F, p. 1.

Brown, Dale M., ed. *Wondrous Realms of the Aegean*. Alexandria, VA: Time-Life Books, 1993.

Bullfinch, Thomas. *Myths of Greece and Rome*. New York: Penguin Books, 1979.

Burkert, Walter. *Ancient Mystery Cults*. Cambridge: Harvard Univ. Press, 1987.

————. *Greek Religion*. Cambridge: Harvard Univ. Press, 1985.

Button, Seth. Review of *The Mycenaean Feast*, ed. by James C. Wright. *Bryn Mawr Classical Review* 4, no. 49 (2005).

Buxton, Richard. *The Complete World of Greek Mythology*. London: Thames and Hudson, 2004.

Cahill, Thomas. *The Gifts of the Jews*. New York: Anchor Books, 1999.

Campbell, Joseph. "Part I: The Sacrifice." In *The Way of the Seeded Earth*. Vol. 2 of *Historical Atlas of World Mythology*. San Francisco: Harper and Row, 1988.

Campbell, Joseph, with Bill Moyers. *The Power of Myth*. New York: Doubleday, 1988.

Carpenter, Thomas, and Christopher Faraone. *Masks of Dionysus*. Ithaca, NY: Cornell Univ. Press, 1993.

Castleden, Rodney. *Minoans: Life in Bronze Age Crete*. London and New York: Routledge, 1993.

Connelly, Joan B. "Parthenon and Parthenoi." *American Journal of Archaeology* 100, no. 1: 56 et seq.

Cook, B F. *The Elgin Marbles*. London: British Museum Press, 1984.

Crossan, John Dominic. *Who Killed Jesus?* New York: HarperCollins,1996.

Davaras, Costis. *Phaistos, Hagia Triada—Gortyn: A Brief Illustrated Archaeological Guide*. Athens: Editions Hannibal, 1987.

Demakopoulou, Kaie, and Dora Konsola. *Archaeological Museum of Thebes: Guide*. Athens: General Direction of Antiquities and Restoration, 1981.

de Quincey, Christian. "Consciousness: Truth or Wisdom?" *IONS Noetic Science Review* 51 (March–June 2000): 8.

Dexter, Miriam Robbins. *Whence the Goddesses: A Source Book*. New York: Pergamon Press, 1990.

Diamond, Jared. *Guns, Germs, and Steel: The Fates of Human Societies*. New York: W. W. Norton and Co., 1999.

Diehl, Paul. *Symbolism in Greek Mythology*. Boulder, CO: Shambhala, 1980.

Dodds, E. R. *The Greeks and the Irrational*. Berkeley and Los Angeles: Univ. of California Press, 1951.

Doherty, Lillian E. *Gender and the Interpretation of Classical Myth*. London: Duckworth Publishing, 2001.

Doumas, Christos G. *Early Cycladic Culture: The N.P. Goulandris Collection*. Athens: N.P. Goulandris Foundation; Museum of Cycladic Art, 2000.

Drews, Robert. *The Coming of the Greeks*. Princeton: Princeton Univ. Press, 1988.

———. *Early Riders: The Beginnings of Mounted Warfare in Asia and Europe*. London and New York: Routledge, 2004.

du Bois, Page. *Centaurs and Amazons: Women and the Pre-History of the Great Chain of Being*. Ann Arbor: Univ. of Michigan Press, 1991.

Edmunds, Lowell, ed. *Approaches to Greek Myth*. Baltimore: Johns Hopkins Univ. Press, 1990.

Ehrenreich, Barbara. *Blood Rites: Origins and History of the Passions of War*. New York: Henry Holt, 1997.

Eisler, Riane. *Sacred Pleasure*. San Francisco: Harper and Row, 1996.

———. *The Chalice and the Blade: Our History, Our Future*. San Francisco: Harper and Row, 1987.

Eliade, Mircea. *Myth and Reality*. Trans. W. Trask. San Francisco: Harper and Row, 1963.

Eliot, T. S. *Little Gidding*. In *Four Quartets*. New York: Harcourt Brace, 1943.

Eller, Cynthia. *The Myth of Matriarchal Prehistory: Why an Invented Past Won't Give Women a Future*. Boston: Beacon Press, 2000.

Errico, Rocco. *Setting a Trap for God*. Unity Village, MO: Unity Books, 1997.

Euripides. *Electra*. In *Euripides V: Electra, The Phoenician Women, The Bacchae*. Chicago: Univ. of Chicago Press, 1959.

Evans, Arthur. *The God of Ecstasy: Sex Roles and the Madness of Dionysus*. New York: St. Martin's Press, 1988.

Evans, Ivor H. *Brewer's Dictionary of Phrase and Fable*. San Francisco: Harper and Row, 1981.

Fewell, Donna Nolan, and David Gunn. *Gender, Power, and Promise: The Subject of the Bible's First Story*. Nashville: Abingdon Press, 1993.

Frazer, Sir James G. *The Golden Bough*. Abridged ed. New York: Macmillan, 1922.

Freke, Timothy, and Peter Gandy. *Jesus and the Lost Goddess: The Secret Teachings of the Original Christians*. New York: Random House, 2001.

Frymer-Kensky, Tikva. *In the Wake of the Goddesses: Women, Culture, and the Biblical Transformation of Pagan Myth*. New York: Ballantine Books, 1993.

Gardner, Joseph L., ed. *Atlas of the Bible*. New York: Readers Digest Association, 1981.

George, Demetra. *Mysteries of the Dark Moon: The Healing Power of the Dark Goddess*. New York: HarperCollins, 1992.

Gies, Frances, and Joseph Gies. *Women in the Middle Ages*. New York: Barnes and Noble, 1978.

Gimbutas, Marija. *The Language of the Goddess*. New York: HarperCollins, 1989.

———. *The Living Goddesses*. Berkeley and Los Angeles: Univ. of California Press, 2001.

Goethe, Johann Wolfgang. *Faust: Erster und Zweiter Teil*. München: Deutscher Taschenbuch Verlag, 1977.

Goodison, Lucy. *Death, Women, and the Sun: Symbolism of Regeneration in Early Aegean Religion*. London: Univ. of London, Institute of Classical Studies, 1989.

Goodison, Lucy, and Christine Morris, eds. *Ancient Goddesses: The Myths and the Evidence*. Madison: Univ. of Wisconsin Press, 1998.

Gospel According to Thomas, [The]. Trans. A. Guillaumont, H.-Ch. Puech, G. Quispel, W. Till and Yassah 'Abd Al Masih. San Francisco: Harper and Row, 1959.

Göttner-Abendroth, Heide. *The Dancing Goddess: Principles of a Matriarchal Aesthetic*. Trans. Maureen T. Krause. Boston: Beacon Press, 1991.

Grant, Michael. *Jesus: An Historian's Review of the Gospels*. New York: Scribner's, 1977.

———. *Myths of the Greeks and Romans*. New York: Meridian Books, 1995.

Graves, Robert. *The Greek Myths*. 2 vols. New York: Penguin Books, 1960.

———. *Homer's Daughter*. Garden City, NY: Doubleday, 1955.

———. *The White Goddess: A Historical Grammar of Poetic Myth*. Amended and enlarged ed. New York: Farrar, Straus and Giroux, 1966.

Greenhouse, Steven, and Constance L. Hays. "Wal-Mart Sex-Bias Suit Given Class-Action Status." *New York Times*, 23 June 2004, sec. A, p. 1, late edition.

Gromyko, Anatoly, and Martin Hellman. *Breakthrough: Emerging New Thinking*. New York: Walker Press, 1987.

Grossman, Dave. *On Killing: The Psychological Cost of Learning to Kill in War and Society*. New York: Little, Brown and Company, 1995.

Gutiérrez, Ramón. *When Jesus Came, the Corn Mothers Went Away: Marriage, Sexuality, and Power in New Mexico, 1500–1846*. Palo Alto, CA: Stanford Univ. Press, 1991.

Hamilton, Edith. *The Greek Way*. New York: W. W. Norton and Co., 1983.

Harrison, Jane Ellen. *Epilegomena to the Study of Greek Religion and Themis: A Study of the Social Origins of Greek Religion*. New Hyde Park, NY: University Books, 1962.

———. *Mythology*. London: Harbinger, 1924.

Henle, Jane. *Greek Myths: A Vase Painter's Notebook*. Bloomington: Indiana Univ. Press, 1973.

Herodotus. *The History*. Trans. David Grene. Chicago: Univ. of Chicago Press, 1987.

Hesiod. *Theogony*. In *Hesiod and Theognis*. Trans. Dorothea Wender. New York: Penguin Books, 1984.

Hesiod. *Works and Days*. In *Hesiod and Theognis*. Trans. Dorothea Wender. New York: Penguin Classics, 1984.

Holland, Tom. *Rubicon: The Last Years of the Roman Republic*. New York: Doubleday, 2003.

Homer. *The Iliad*. Trans. Alexander Pope. London: Bell and Daldy, 1865.

———. *The Odyssey*. Trans. Robert Fagels. New York: Penguin Books, 1996.

———. *The Odyssey*. Trans. Richmond Lattimore. New York: HarperCollins, 1991.

———. *The Odyssey*. Trans. Rodney Merrill. Ann Arbor: Univ. of Michigan Press, 2002.

———. *The Odyssey*. Trans. Alexander Pope. Hartford, CT: Silas Andrus and Son, 1849.

Houston, Jean. *The Hero and the Goddess: The Odyssey as Mystery and Initiation*. New York: Ballantine Books, 1992.

Huffington, Arianna, and Françoise Gilot. *The Gods of Greece*. New York: Atlantic Monthly Press, 1993.

Hurwit, Jeffrey M. *The Acropolis in the Age of Pericles*. Cambridge: Cambridge Univ. Press, 2004.

Immerwahr, Sara A. *Aegean Painting in the Bronze Age*. University Park, PA: Penn State Univ. Press, 1990.

Jacobs, Jay, ed. *The Horizon Book of Great Cathedrals*. New York: American Heritage Publishing, 1968.

Jefferson, Thomas. *The Life and Morals of Jesus of Nazareth*. New York: Wilfred Funk, 1904.

Johnson, Buffie. *Lady of the Beasts: Ancient Images of the Goddess and Her Sacred Animals*. San Francisco: Harper and Row, 1988.

Johnson, Robert A. *Ecstasy: Understanding the Psychology of Joy*. San Francisco: Harper and Row, 1987.

Jung, C. G., and C. Kerényi. *The Myth of the Divine Child and the Mysteries of Eleusis*. Princeton: Princeton Univ. Press, 1949.

Kaltsas, Nikolaos. *Sculpture in the National Archaeological Museum, Athens*. Los Angeles: J. Paul Getty, 2002.

Keegan, John. *A History of Warfare*. New York: Vintage Books, 1994.

Kenna, V. E. G. *Cretan Seals, with a Catalogue of the Minoan Gems in the Ashmolean Museum*. Oxford: Clarendon Press, 1960.

Kerényi, Carl. *Eleusis: Archetypal Image of Mother and Daughter*. Princeton: Princeton Univ. Press, 1991.

Kinder, Hermann, and Werner Hilgemann. *The Anchor Atlas of World History: From the Stone Age to the Eve of the French Revolution*, vol. I. Garden City, NY: Anchor Books, 1974.

Koiv Mait. *Ancient Tradition and Early Greek History: The Origins of States in Early-Archaic Sparta, Argos, and Corinth*. Tallinn, Estonia: Avita Publishers, 2003.

Kors, Alan, and Edward Peters. *Witchcraft in Europe: A Documentary History*. Philadelphia: Univ. of Pennsylvania Press, 1972.

Lagerlöf, Margaretha Rossholm. *The Sculptures of the Parthenon: Aesthetics and Interpretation*. New Haven, CT: Yale Univ. Press, 2000.

Leach, Maria, ed. *Funk and Wagnalls Standard Dictionary of Folklore, Mythology, and Legend*. 2 vols. New York: Funk and Wagnalls, 1949 and 1950.

Lee, Dorothy D. "Lineal and Nonlineal Codifications of Reality." In *Symbolic Anthropology*. Ed. Kemnitzer Dolgin and David M. Schneider. New York: Columbia Univ. Press, 1977.

Leeming, David, and Jake Page. *Myths of the Female Divine Goddess*. New York: Oxford Univ. Press, 1994.

Lefkowitz, Mary R. *Women in Greek Myth*. Baltimore: Johns Hopkins Univ. Press, 1986.

Lefkowitz, Mary R., and Maureen B. Fant. *Women's Life in Greece and Rome: A Source Book in Translation*. 2d ed. Baltimore: Johns Hopkins Univ. Press, 1992.

Lips, Hilary M. "Women, Education, and Economic Participation." Keynote address at the Northern Regional Seminar of National Council of Women in New Zealand, Auckland, New Zealand, March 1999.

Lissarrague, Francoise. *Greek Vases: The Athenians and Their Images*. Trans. Kim Allen. New York: Riverside Book Co., 2001.

Luce, J. V. *Celebrating Homer's Landscapes*. New Haven, CT: Yale Univ. Press, 1998.

———. *Lost Atlantis: New Light on an Old Legend*. New York: McGraw Hill, 1969.

Macqueen, J. G. *The Hittites: And Their Contemporaries in Asia Minor*. London: Thames and Hudson, 1986.

Manuel, Frank E., and Fritzie P. Manuel "Sketch for a Natural History of Paradise." *Daedalus* 101, no. 1 (Winter 1972).

Marangou, Lila I. *Ancient Greek Art*. N.P. Goulandris Collection, Athens: N.P. Goulandris Foundation; Museum of Cycladic Art, 1996.

Marazov, Ivan, Aleksandur Fol, Margarita Tacheva-Khitova, and Ivan Venedikov, eds. *Ancient Gold: The Wealth of the Thracians*. New York: Harry N. Abrams, 1998.

Marinatos, Nanno. *Art and Religion in Thera: Reconstructing a Bronze Age Society*. Athens: Mathiolakis, 1984.

Matarasso, Pauline M., trans. *The Quest of the Holy Grail*. New York: Penguin Books, 1969.

Matthews, John. *The Grail: Quest for the Eternal*. London: Thames and Hudson, 1981.

McClure, Laura K., ed. *Sexuality and Gender in the Classical World: Readings and Sources*. Oxford and Australia: Blackwell Publishing, 2002.

Meier, John P. *A Marginal Jew: Rethinking the Historical Jesus*. New York: Doubleday, 1991.

Meyer, Marvin W., ed. *The Ancient Mysteries: A Sourcebook*. Philadelphia: Univ. of Pennsylvania Press, 1987.

Miles, Christopher, with John Julius Norwich. *Love in the Ancient World*. New York: St. Martin's Press, 1997.

Mitchell, Stephen. *The Gospel According to Jesus: A New Translation and Guide to His Essential Teachings for Believers and Unbelievers*. New York: HarperCollins, 1991.

Morkot, Robert. *The Penguin Historical Atlas of Ancient Greece*. New York: Penguin Books, 1996.

Motz, Lotte. *The Faces of the Goddess*. New York: Oxford Univ. Press, 1997.

Moyers, Bill. *Genesis: A Living Conversation*. New York: Doubleday, 1996.

Murray, Gilbert. *Five Stages of Greek Religion*. London: Oxford Univ. Press, 1930.

———. *The Literature of Ancient Greece*. 3d ed. Chicago: Univ. of Chicago Press, 1956.

Mylonas, George E. *Eleusis and the Eleusinian Mysteries*. Princeton: Princeton Univ. Press, 1961.

Neils, Jenifer. *The Parthenon Frieze*. Cambridge: Cambridge Univ. Press, 2001.

Neumann, Erich. *The Great Mother*. Princeton: Princeton Univ. Press, 1974.

Newell, J. Philip. *Listening for the Heartbeat of God: A Celtic Spirituality*. London: SPCK, Holy Trinity Church, 1997.

Nilsson, Martin P. *Greek Folk Religion*. Philadelphia: Univ. of Pennsylvania Press, 1940.

———. *The Minoan-Mycenaean Religion and Its Survival in Greek Religion*. 2d rev. ed. New York: Biblo and Tannen, 1949.

O'Brien, Joan V. *The Transformation of Hera: A Study of Ritual, Hero, and the Goddess in* The Iliad. Lanham, MD: Rowman and Littlefield, 1993.

O'Faolain, Julia, ed. *Not in God's Image: Women in History from the Greeks to the Victorians*. London: Temple Smith, 1973.

Pagels, Elaine. *Adam, Eve, and the Serpent*. New York: Random House, 1988.

———. *Beyond Belief: The Secret Gospel of Thomas*. New York: Random House, 2003.

———. *The Gnostic Gospels*. New York: Random House, 1979.

———. *The Origin of Satan*. New York: Random House, 1995.

Parke, H. W. *Festivals of the Athenians: Aspects of Greek and Roman Life*. Ithaca, NY: Cornell Univ. Press, 1977.

Pelikan, Jaroslav. *Jesus Through the Centuries: His Place in the History of Culture*. San Francisco: Harper and Row, 1987.

Peterson, Karen. "Panel Favors Ban on Same Sex Marriage." *Santa Fe New Mexican*, 13 February 1999.

Petrakos, Basil. *Delphi*. Athens: CLIO Editions, 1977.

Picknett, Lynn, and Clive Prince. *The Templar Revelation: Secret Guardians of the True Identity of Christ*. New York: Simon and Schuster, 1997.

Platon, Nicholas. *Zakros: The Discovery of a Lost Palace of Ancient Crete*. New York: Scribner's, 1971.

Pomeroy, Sarah B. *Goddesses, Whores, Wives, and Slaves: Women in Classical Antiquity*. New York: Schocken Books, 1995.

Powell, Barry B. *Homer*. Oxford and Australia: Blackwell Publishing, 2004.

———. *A Short Introduction to Classical Myth*. Upper Saddle River, NJ: Prentice Hall, 2002.

Purce, Jill. *The Mystic Spiral: Journey of the Soul*. London: Thames and Hudson, 1974.

Redmond, Layne. *When the Drummers Were Women: A Spiritual History of Rhythm*. New York: Three Rivers Press, 1997.

Renault, Mary. *The King Must Die*. New York: Bantam Books, 1958.

Reuther, Rosemary Radford. *Gaia and God: An Ecofeminist Theology of Earth Healing*. New York: HarperCollins, 1994.

———. *Sexism and God-Talk: Toward A Feminist Theology*. Boston: Beacon Press, 1983.

Robbins, Manuel. *Collapse of the Bronze Age: The Story of Greece, Troy, Israel, Egypt, and the Peoples of the Sea*. Lincoln, NE: Author's Choice Press, 2001.

Sackville-West, Vita. *Saint Joan of Arc*. New York: Grove Press, 1936.

Sakellarakis, J. A. *Herakleion Museum: Illustrated Guide*. Athens: Ekdotike Athenon S. A., 1995.

Sanford, John A. *Fate, Love, and Ecstasy: Wisdom from the Lessser-Known Goddesses of the Greeks*. Willmette, IL: Chiron Publications, 1995.

Schein, Seth L. *Reading The Odyssey: Selected Interpretative Essays*. Princeton: Princeton Univ. Press, 1996.

Seager, Joni. *The Penguin Atlas of Women in the World*. New York: Penguin Books, 2003.

Segal, Charles. Introduction to *The Theban Plays*. New York: Alfred A. Knopf, 1994.

Sharman, Henry Burton. *Jesus as Teacher*. Palo Alto, CA: Sequoia Seminar Foundation, 1935.

———. *Records of the Life of Jesus*. Palo Alto, CA: Sequoia Seminar Foundation, 1917.

Shattuck, Roger. *Forbidden Knowledge: From Prometheus to Pornography*. New York: Harcourt Brace, 1996.

Shlain, Leonard. *The Alphabet Versus the Goddess: The Conflict between Word and Image*. New York: Viking, 1998.

———. *Sex, Time, and Power: How Women's Sexuality Shaped Human Evolution*. New York: Viking, 2003.

Sjoo, Monica, and Barbara Mor. *The Great Cosmic Mother: Rediscovering the Religion of the Earth*. San Francisco: Harper and Row, 1987.

Sorenson, Richard E. "Preconquest Consciousness." In *Tribal Epistemologies*. Ed. Helmut Wautischer. Aldershot, England: Ashgate Publishing, 1998.

Spathari, Elsie. *Mycenae: A Guide to the History and Archaeology*. Athens: Hisperos Editions, 2001.

Struck, Peter T. *Birth of the Symbol: Ancient Readers at the Limits of Their Texts*. Princeton: Princeton Univ. Press, 2004.

Suhr, Elmer G. *The Spinning Aphrodite: The Evolution of the Goddess from Earliest Pre-Hellenic Symbolism through Late Classical Times*. New York: Helios Books, 1969.

Suter, Ann. *The Narcissus and the Pomegranate: An Archaeology of the Homeric Hymn to Demeter*. Ann Arbor: Univ. of Michigan Press, 2002.

Taylour, Lord William. *The Mycenaeans*. London: Thames and Hudson, 1983.

Tyldesley, Joyce. *Daughters of Isis: Women of Ancient Egypt*. New York: Penguin Books, 1995.

Tzu, Lao. *Tao Te Ching of Lao Tzu*. Trans. Brian Browne Walker. New York: St. Martin's Griffin, 1996.

Van Andel, Tjeerd H., and Curtis N. Runnels. *Beyond the Acropolis: A Rural Greek Past*. Palo Alto, CA: Stanford Univ. Press, 1987.

Vickery, John B. *Robert Graves and the White Goddess*. Lincoln: Univ. of Nebraska Press, 1972.

Vitruvius. *The Ten Books on Architecture*. Trans. Morris Hickey Morgan. New York: Dover Publications, 1960.

Walker, Barbara G. *The Woman's Encyclopedia of Myths and Secrets*. San Francisco: Harper and Row, 1983.

Warner, Marina. *Alone of All Her Sex: The Myth and Cult of the Virgin Mary*. New York: Vintage Books, 1983.

Weems, Renita J. *Battered Love: Marriage, Sex, and Violence in the Hebrew Prophets*. Minneapolis: Augsburg Fortress, 1995.

West, M. L. *The East Face of Helicon: West Asiatic Elements in Greek Poetry and Myth*. Oxford: Clarendon Paperbacks, 1997.

Williams, John Alden, ed. *Islam*. New York: Braziller, 1962.

Williams, Robin P. *Sweet Swan of Avon: Did A Woman Write Shakespeare?* N.p.: Wilton Circle Press, 2006.

Wink, Walter. *Engaging the Powers: Discernment and Resistance in a World of Domination*. Minneapolis: Augsburg Fortress, 1992.

———. *Violence and Nonviolence in South Africa: Jesus' Third Way*. Philadelphia: New Society Publishers, 1987.

Wood, Michael. *In Search of the Trojan War*. Berkeley and Los Angeles: Univ. of California Press, 1996.

Woodford, Susan. *Images of Myths in Classical Antiquity*. Cambridge: Cambridge Univ. Press, 2003.

Index

* *Italics* indicate illustrations

A

Abel, 192, 201; fight with Cain, 113–114

Abraham, 193, 211

Abram, 192

Achilles, 51, 135, 186, 238, 244, 245; Agamemnon and, 139; Amazons and, 44; bravery of, 100; Cheiron and, 114; combat and, 44; death of, 87, 173; death of Polyxena and, 159, *159*; murder of Penthelesia, 49, *49*; Odysseus and, 87–88; at Troy, 83, 92, 98

Acropolis, 177

Adam, 184

Adam and Eve, 8, 81, 184, 191, 207, 208

adultery, 146, 150, 156, 157, 202

Aegisthus, 146

Aeschylus, 147, 148, 149, 150

Agamemnon, king of Mycenae, 47–48, 81, 92, 186, 231, 233; Achilles and, 139; Cassandra and, 146, 148–150; glory of, 98; in *The Iliad*, 88, 90; murder of, 146, 147; sacrifice of Iphigenia, 157, 159, 220; Trojan War and, 83, 85, 89, 145–146, 157, 227, 244

Ai, 91

Akrotiri, 33, 72; frescoes of, *14, 15,* 33–34, 38, 39, 42, 45, *45,* 46–47, *70,* 135, 151, 153

Alhambra (Granada), 213

allegiance, 100

altars, 44

Amazon women, 66, 126, 150, 172; Achilles and, 44; depiction of, on Partheon, 177, 182; Heracles and, 49, *49, 50,* 164–165; Jason and, 117, 120–121, 122, 136; marriage and, 227; as symbol, 145; Trojan War and, 89, 99

ambrosia, 126–127, 129, 154

Amnisos, 53

Amos, 52

Anatolia, 3, 11, 91, 92, 135, 151, 226, 227; Thera explosion and, 72

Andromache, 147, 186

animal sacrifices, 30, 38, 39

Antaeus, 77, *78*

Anthony, Susan B., 236

Apaturia, 107, 175

Aphrodite (love goddess), 69, 70, 86, 87, 89, 108, 185; affair with Ares, 85, 124, 175; apple with, as symbol for sex, 114; dolphin as symbol of, 57, *57,* 59, 60; Jason and, 120; patriarchy and, 84; Trojan War and, 87, 89, 90

Aphrodite *pandemos,* 59

Apollo, 3, 36, 88, 101, 111; accoutrements of, 39, 40; fight with Python and Pythia, 163; Jason and, 117; oracle of, 157; testimony at trial of Orestes, 148

apples, 66; in Garden of Eden, 190–191; golden, 85, 86–87; Sirens and, 94; as symbol, 96, 189–190; as symbol of immortality, 34, 167–168, 169; as symbol of sexual pleasure, 114, 133, 169; theft of, by Heracles, 34–35, *35,* 40, 86–87, 133, *134,* 135

Apuleius, Lucius, 202

Aquinas, Thomas, 233–234

Arachne, change of, into spider, 167

Arcadia, 108

archetypal conflict, 84

Ares, 47, 79, 101, 109; affair with Aphrodite, 124, 175; Jason and, 117

Argolid, 11

Argo (boat), 117, 118, 120, 136

Argonauts: Jason and, 113, 118, 119, 120–121, 122, 123, 130, 138

Argos, 66, 75, 99, 101

Ariadne, 186, 195, 196

Aristotle, 7, 233

Armenia, 6, 92, 115, 121

art: as labor intensive, 23; similiarity between Minoan and Mycenaean, 73. *See also* Minoan art

Artemis, 69, 100, 101, 108, 109, 167, 175; accoutrements of, 39, 40

Arthur, King. and Knights of the Round Table, 214–215, 216

artifacts: assigning meaning to, 23; Minoan, and inevitability of patriarchy, 9–12

Aryan invaders, 68

Asclepius, 114

Asherah, 187

Ashtoreth, 187

Assyrians, 6, 10

Astarte, 187, 222

Atalanta, Jason and, 117

Athena, 69, 75, 80, 85, 86, 101, 108, 111, 227; appearance to Nausikaa, 140–141; birth of, 109, 131, 137, 149, 175–176, 182–183; in combat, 44; depiction of, on Partheon, 178, 179–180, 182–183; as fertility goddess, 79, 106; helmet as symbol for, 99, 114; Jason and, 117; marriage and, 128–129; murder of Clytemnestra and, 148–149; Odysseus and, 128; olive tree as symbol of, 100, 124126; as patroness of Athens, 162; Poseidon and, 44, 182; temple to, 176; Trojan War and, 87; Zeus and, 137

Athens, 25, 49, 75, 98, 101, 175; war and, 98

Atlantis, 73

Augustine, 74, 191; bishop of Hippo, 209; St. Augustine, 202

axe, 53; double-edged, 37, 46, 52, 82, 104, 126; as symbol of sovereignty, 146

Azerbaijan, 115

Azeris, 6

B

Baal, 201

Babylon, 4, 6, 11, 227; removal of Jews to, 203; women in, 151

Bacchae, 175

bacchanalia, 175, 228

Bacon, 234

bards, 98, 100, 169, 187, 233

bare-breasted women, 21, *22,* 29, *29,* 32, *41,* 56, *56,* 72

beauty, principle of, 65

beehives, 24

bee master, 117

bees, *20,* 30, *30,* 33–34, 46, 64, 155

begats, 59, 192

Bible, 151; patriarchs in, 187–193

Biblical stories, 4–5, 9, 10, 66, 233. *See also* Genesis

Biblos, 91, 92

birds, 14, 37, 44, 46; beak of, *76;* blue, *13,* 16. *See also* doves; partridges; raven; swallows

bird/woman figurines, *25, 26,* 93

bird-woman-tree combined figures, 16, 24–25, *25,* 27, *27*

blood, ritual drinking of, 198

Bloom, Harold, 235

blue birds, *13,* 16

Blue Mosque (Istanbul), 213

Boetia, 89–90

Bolyn, Anne, 234

Boulding, Elise, 7

boy children, value of, 151

Briesis, 228

Brisson, Luc, 98

British Empire, dissolving of, 239

"Bronchos," 115

Bronze Age, 10, 40, 50, 79, 80, 123, 143, 169, 173, 215–216, 226

bronze swords, 46

bull leapers, 17, 27, 44, *44,* 60, 62, *62,* 64, 102, 104, 228

bulls, 53–54, 65; Cretan, 34, 66; sacrifice of, 30, 38, 65

Bush, George W., 48, 241

butterflies, 52, 53, *53,* 54

C

Cadmus, 66, 104, 105, 106, 107, 149, 163, 171

Caesar, 245

Cain, 192, 201; fight with Abel, 113–114

Calypso, 99, 222, 223, 244; in Homer's writings, 51, 93, 136; island of, 139; love of, 61; offer of immortality and, 136, 140, 143, 154; Odysseus' rejection of, 81, 124–135, 137, 141–142, 143, 160

Campbell, Joseph, 7–8, 68, 69, 121, 122

Campbell-Gimbutas theory of invasions, 8

Canaan, 91, 110, 187, 189, 227; archaeological record of, 187

Caryae, 177

Caryatides, 177

Cassandra, 228; Agamemnon and, 149–150; murder of, 146, 147

castration, 110, 111, 112, 165

catastrophes, 73–74

Cathars, 217, 218–219, 220, 234, 241, 243

cause of life, 64

Cecrops, 161, 162, 163, 168, 181

Celts, 234; ancient beliefs of, 209–210

Centaurs, 44, 49, 66, 114–115, 122, 177, 178, 227; depiction of, on Partheon, 182, *182*; marriage and, 178

Cerebrus, 103

chalice, 197–198, 214

change, metaphors for, 236

Charlemagne, 245

Charybdis, 6, 66, 126, 138, 139, 212, 223, 228

Cheiron, 114

Chimera, 103, 107, 145, 222

Chios, 4, 149

Christianity, 211, 219; Great Paradox and, 39

chrysalis, 54

Churchill, Winston, 48, 241

cicadas, 132

Circe, 93, 99, 126, 160, 223, 228; Odysseus and, 137, 139, 140

circular concept of time, 33–43, 64, 151, 201, 228, 236

civic duty, Greek idea of, 158

civic good, death of daughters for, 157–160

civil war over marriage, 82–90

classical period, 124–125

Clement of Alexandria, 208

Cleopatra, 235

Clytemnestra, 6, 83, 157, 188; murder of, 147; murder of Agamemnon by, 146; sacrifice of, on altar of marriage, 145–150

coastal raids, 90

coded phrases, 114–115. *See also* symbols

Coke, 235

Colchis, 96, 97, 115, 117, 121–122, 136, 151, 226; dragon in, 103; route to, *116*

Cold War, 238, 239

combination images, 23, 24–28, *25*, *26*, 33–34, 128; bird-woman figure, *25*, *26*, 93; bird-woman-tree, 16, 24–25, *25*, 27, *27*; griffins, 14; lilies sprouting from stones, 33; Minotaur, 17; sphinx, 6, 103, 105, 107, 112, 145, 150, *170*, 170–171, 215, 216; woman-snake, 26; women sprouting from ground, 37; women-wheat, 31, *31*

Common Era, beginning of, 6

communion, use of wine in, 198

comparison, 36

cone as stage of womanhood, 15

Connelly, Joan B., 180, 181

continuity of life, *76*, 132, 156

Corinth, 49, 75, 97, 99, 102

counting cycles, 79

creation: stories of, 110, 191

Cretan bull, 34, 66

Crete, 4, 11, 32, 230; as center of influence, 22; decline of, 151; excavation of, 226; impact of tidal wave on, 72–73; inability to translate writing, 17; palaces in, 17; Thebes abd, 104–105; trade and, 19; wall paintings of, 125

crocuses, *23*, 30

crone, 152

Cronos, 100, 103, 107, 110, 111, 119, 165

crown: doves in, *27*; snakes in, *28*

cultural persuasion, 99

Cycladic islands, 133–134

cycle of life and death, 28–29, 32, 34, 36, 38, 39, 59, 94, 112, 187, 227, 236

cyclical immortality, 153

cyclic time, 229

Cyclops, 99, 103, 126, 145, 165, 227

Cyprus, 4, 138; Thera explosion and, 72

Cyzicus, King, 119

D

daily life, 44

dancing, 46, 62, *63*; satyrs, *20*; women, 13, *16*, 24, 33, 60,

62, 64, 183, 228

Dante, 74

Darius, 178

Dark Age, 34, 82–83, 92, 93, 96, 98, 109, 125, 129, 158; storytellers of, 120

daughters: death of, for civic good, 157–160; diminishment of, 79–81

da Vinci, Leonardo, 214

death, 51, 59, 112; association of women with, 31; of bulls, 30, 38, 65; of daughters, for civic good, 157–160; nonportrayal of, in Minoan art, 228; pomegrantes as symbol for, 97, 114; principle of inescapable, 158; procreative power of, 39

Debir, 91

Delilah, 54, 59, 129, 139, 185

Delphi, 3, 97, 101, 102, 175; oracles at, 124

Demeter: control of seasons and, 100, 155; cult of, 158; as goddess of grains, 79, 152–153, 186; as goddess of growth, 31, 32; immortality and, 130, 132, 155; myth of Hades, Persephone and, 8, 153–154, 155, 156, 158, 215; origin of, 69–70, 109; wheat sheaf as gift of, 197; Zeus and, 155

descent: claims of, 161; matrilineal, 80, 118, 161–162; patrilineal, 83, 118, 121, 156, 162

Desdemona, 235

Deuteronomy, 81, 206

Dickinson, Emily, 236

Dionysian orgies of Greece, 21, 61

Dionysus, 100, 195, 228; bacchanalia and, 175; birth of, 131

Dioscuri, 117, 161

divine, relation with ecstatic, 60–66

divine feminine, 94

dolphin(s): leaping, 13, 16, 36–37, 46, 51, 57, 59, 60, 63, 64, 71, *71, 74*, 125, 204–205, 228, 229; as symbol of aphrodite, 57, *57*, 59, 60

domestic violence, 236–237

dominance, 36

Dominicans, 221, 222–223

Dorians, 92

double-edged axe, 37, 46, 52, 82, 104, 126

doves, *27*, 59; as symbol of love, 120

dragonfly, 71

dragons, 66, 97, 98–99, 163–164, *164*; slaying of, 104; teeth of, 3, 97–98, 107; as vestigial symbol, 163

Drews, Robert, 122

E

Earth-born giants, 119

Earth Goddess, 119

Earth Mother, 226

earth religions, 122

Earthshaker, 108, 109, 112

Eastern Mediterranean, end of women-centered societies in, 82–90

Echidna, 104, 105, 106, 107, 145, 151, 227; bestial offspring of, 103

ectasy, 64, 65; relation with divine, 60–66

Eglon Hebron, 91

Egypt, 4, 6, 11; Thera explosion and, 72; women in, 151

Eisler, Riane, 7, 121, 122, 159

El Cid, 242

Electra, 6

Eleusinian symbolism of grain and wine, 197–202

Eleusis, 154, 157, 195, 196, 241, 243, 244; battle against, 185; Mysteries of, 2, 152, 155–156, 197, *197*, 200–201, 202, 204, 207, 209, 216, 229–230

Eliot, T. S., 38–39

Elizabeth I, 234

Elysian Fields, 228

embedded riddles, 110

entitlement, 136

envelope concept, 34–35, 40

Eos, 108, 109, 130–131, *131*, 132, 228

Ephesians, 207, 208

The Epic of Gilgamesh, 6–7

epic stories, 82

Erechtheion, 177, *177*, 220

Erechtheus, 157, 161, 177, *180*, 180–181; sacrifice of daughters of, 158, 159

Eros, 85, 133, *134*

Erymanthian, 164

Esclamonde de Foix, 218, 233

Eternal Feminine, 94–95

Euboea, 90

Euripedes, 138, 147, 159, 181, 186, 235

Evans, Sir Arthur, 17, 226

Eve, 184, 188–189, 222, 223, 233; original sin of, 148

ewers, 25, *26,* 71, *71, 76*

exaggerated feminine, 102–107

Exclamonde of Montségur, 244

Exodus, 69

F

faith, loss of, in Mother Earth, 71–77

father-killing, 169

Father Sky, 106

father-son stories, 7

Father Time, 110

female disparagement, 6

female ectasy, neglect of, 1

female knowlege, 233

female monogramy, 161–162, 181, 192

female sexuality, 52–59, 208

female suppression, marriage and, 162

feminine, blindness to dangers of strong, 243–244

feminine figurines, shapes of, 21, *21*

feminine principle, 64, 65, 227, 228

fertility, 27–28, 42, 79; pomegranates as symbol for, 114

fertility worship, 99, 172

figs, as symbol, 138

fig tree, 138, 139; as symbol, 96–97

figure-eight shields, 46, 104

Fira, 71

I Timothy, 207, 208

fish, 64

Fisher king, 215, 216, 242

fishing, 46

flaming sun, 24

flowers, 37

flying swallows, 51, 71, *71*

foundation stories, 113, 115, 117, 120, 122, 136, 150, 188; purpose of, 162–164

Four Quartets (Eliot), 38–39

Freud, Sigmund, 169, 172

funeral ceremony, 37, *37*

Furies of Greece, 111, 147, 148, 149, 150, 172, 175, 185, 228

G

Garden of Eden, 9, 51, 128, 137, 190, 233

Ge, 182. *See also* Mother Earth

Genesis: author of, 2, 6; stories in, 64, 102, 109, 185, 188, 191, 192, 212, 218, 230, 233, 235, 241; symbols used in, 187

genetic code, 1

Georgia, 115

Giants, 44, 98, 100, 165, 177, 178; war against, *166*

Gibbon, Edward, 10, 74

Gibraltar, 151

Gimbutas, Marija, 7, 8, 121, 159

Gla, war and, 165

Glastonbury cult, 216

Gnostics, 202, 207, 209, 213, 214, 217, 220, 221, 234; teachings of, 2

goddess cultures, 190–191

goddess figures, subordination of, 70

goddess movement, 8

goddess religions, 68, 211; characteristics of, 165

Goethe, Johann Wolfgang von, 38, 60–61, 62, 94–95

Golden Age, 9, 10, 110–111

golden apple, 85, 86–87

golden calf, 201

golden fleece: Jason's pursuit of, 96–98, 115, *116,* 117–123, 130, 136, 161, 165, 210; as symbol, 97

Gordian knot of justice and revenge, 204

grace, 64

Grail Castle, 214, 215, 216, 218

grain: Demeter as goddess of, 79, 152–153, 186; Eleusinian symbolism of, 197–202

grapes, 71, *71*

graphic symbols, use of, 96–97

Graves, Robert, 4, 7, 39, 84, 121, 122, 164, 169, 191

Great Divide, 42, 43

Greater Southeast Asian Co-Prosperity Sphere, 239

Great Paradox, 39

Greece, 4

Greek mythology, 4, 7, 9

Greek patriarchy, 117, 119

Greek pictography, 6

Greek rationalism, 36

griffins, 6, 14, 17, 37, 39, 64, 228

H

Hades, 73, 83, 105–106, 112, 195, 244; abduction and rape of Persephone, 8, 76, 153–154, 155, 156, 158, 175, 186, 215; authority of, 119; brutalities of, 113; Demeter and, 158; origin of, 111; rape of the *kore*, 154

Hafiz, 213

Hagar, 192

Hagia triada, sarcophagus of, 14, 37, *37*, 39, 104

Harpies, 93, 119–120, 136, 150, 228

Hebrews, 6, 187–188

Hector, 238, 244; murder of, 173

Hecuba, 147, 186

Helen (goddess), 60–61

Helen of Troy, 83–84, 145, 157, 176, 227, 233; seizure of, 84, 88, 90

Helios, 108, *183*, 184

Hellenes, 47, 48, 85

helmet as symbol for Athena, 99, 114

Henry V, King of England, 242

Henry VIII, King of England, 234

Hephaestos, 101, 122, 123, 124, 175; temple of, 115

Hera, 31, 32, 69, 75, 76–77, 82, 85, 87, 108, 110, 227; annual cleansing of, 175; apples and, 191; depiction of, on Parthenon, *181*, 182; Hercules and, 109; marriage to Zeus, 70, 76–77, 107, 124, 126–127, 172, 186; priestesses of,

171; seasons and, 100, 172

Heracles, 6, 44, 47, 66, *78*, 84, 100, 171, 186, 231, 244, 245; claims involving, 161; exploits of, 75, 79, 82; illegitimacy of, 76–77; immortality and, 135; Jason and, 117, 138; killing of Amazon warrior, *50*; killing of Centaur, 49; killing of Lernean Hydra, 164, 165, 230; killing of Nemean lion by, 164, 230; opponents of, 227; patriarchy and, 118; symbols for, 99; theft of apple (immortality), 34–35, *35*, 40, 86–87, 133, *134*, 135

Heraclidai, 162

Heraclitus, 48, 239

Herakleion, 46

heresy, 214, 220, 222–223

Hermes, 128, 137, 139, 175; Jason and, 117

Herodotus, 10, 22, 74

heroes, pastoral, 113

heroism, 48, 238

Hesiod: story of creation and, 110; values of, 113; writings of, 1, 6, 9–10, 74, 92, 102–103, 105, 106, 107, 109–111, 125, 178, 209, 212, 222, 224, 225, 227, 230, 231

Hestia, 69, 175, 186

hierarchy, 1, 36; of patriarchy, 233

Hilda, Abbess, 210

Hippolytus, 202

history, as choice of stories, 231–232

Hittites, 6, 10, 11, 79, 92, 226

Hittite women, 151

Holy Grail, 221; metaphor of, 214–219; search for, 242, 244

Holy Roman Church, 209–210, 217, 220

Homer: choice between love, property and, 136–144; imagination of, 115; writings of, 1, 6, 51, 64, 74, 80, 82, 83, 84, 87–88, 90, 93, 96–97, 102, 103, 118, 122, 124–126, 129, 136, 138, 143, 150, 173, 210, 212, 225, 230, 231, 233, 241, 242. *See also The Iliad; The Odyssey*

Homeric Hymn to Demeter, 109, 152–153

honeycombs, 30

Hopi tribe, 162

horns of consecration, 82

horse(s), 44, *44*; of Selene, *184*; warfare and, 121; wisdom of, 114

hubris, 60, 167, 228

human sacrifice, 157–158, 159, *159*

hunting, 46

Huntingdon, Sam, 5

Hutchinson, Anne, 234–235, 244, 245

Hydra, 34, 66, 77, 107; conquest of Lernean, 164, 165, 230

Hyperion, 107

Hyksos, 11, 68

I

The Iliad, 4, 83, 88, 89, 90, 124, 125–126, 139, 218, 242

Ilium, 87

immortality, 32, 48, 64, 228; apple as symbol of, 34, 86–87, 167–168, 169; Calypso's offer of, to Odysseus, 124–135, 136, 140, 141–142, 143; communal, 152; concept of human, 153; cyclical, 153; Demeter and, 154–155; evidence on question of, 38; expectation of, 23–32; female-based, 151–152; Garden of Eden and, 128; Heracles' theft of, 34–35, *35,* 40, 86–87, 133, *134,* 135; love and, 139–140; marriage and, 128–129; principle of, 158; prognosis, 217; promise of, 132, 157, 222; rejection of, through instrument of a woman, 125–126; Tithonos and, 131–132; women as key to, 34, 125–126

impotence, 110

individualism, 228

Indo-European invaders, 11, 69–70, 75, 77, 121, 122, 145–146, 218

Indo-European language, 121

inescapable death, principle of, 158

inheritance: Athenian preoccupation of, 161. *See also* matrilineal descent; patrilineal descent

Innocent I, 209

Innocent III, 217

Innocent VIII, 221

Invasions, 82

Iocasta, 172

Iolcus, 96

Iphigenia, 7, 146, 147, 231, 245; sacrifice of, 157, 159, 220

Irenaeus, 208

Iron Age, 123

Ishmael, 192

Ishtar-Astarte, 52

Islam, 214, 219; women in, 211–213

Israelites, 52, 54, 59

Ithaca, 80, 137

ivy, 64

J

Japan, efforts to create Greater Southeast Asian Co-Prosperity Sphere, 239

Jason, 3, 6, 7, 66, 81, 82, 155, 160, 229, 241, 244, 245; Argonauts and, 113; education of, 114; Heracles and, 138; Lemnian women and, 117–118, 119, 121, 129; marriage to Medea, 122–123, 130, 136, 243; pursuit of golden fleece, 96–98, 115, *116,* 117–123, 130, 136, 161, 165, 210; resistance of seductive women, 113–123; shepherds and, 113, 114; value of boy children and, 151

Jehovah, 8, 30, 40, 42, 101, 103, 185, 188, 244; patriarchy of, 52; rules for life set down by, 3

Jeremiah, 52

Jericho, 91

Jerusalem, zealotry in destruction of, 203

Jesus, 2, 211, 214, 233, 234; childhood of, in Nazareth, 200; crucifixion of, 220; Eleusinian symbolism of grain and wine and, 197–202; Last Supper of, 198–199, 200; parables of, 205–207; teachings of, 196, 197, 202; threat of military destruction and, 203–208

Jewish Kabbalah, 213

Jews, removal of, to Babylon, 203

Joan of Arc, 220–221, 223, 224–225, 230, 243, 245

John (evangelist), doctrines of, 210

Jonson, Ben, 234

Joseph of Arimathaea, 214, 216

joy, 64

Judaism, 211

Juliet, 235

Julius Caesar, 242

Jungian psychologists, 99

Justice, 110, 125, 219

K

Ka'ba, 211, 214

Kaphtor, 52

Kazakhstan, 6

Keegan, John, 50–51, 68, 121

Khadija, 211, 212, 245

King, Martin, Luther, Jr., 2

Kingdom of God, parables of, 205–207

The King Must Die (Renault), 169

kissing swallows, 13, *14,* 33, 64, 74, 101, 125, 228, 229

Knossos, palace at, 19, 40, 53, 54, 55, 59, 74, 101, 125, 135, 138; Linear B writing uncovered at, 108, 226; ruins of, 17; walls of, *13,* 14, 15, 38

kore, 152, *152,* 153–154, 155; rape of, by Hades, 154

Koumasa, tombs found at, 37

Kryghistan, 6

Kurgans, 121

L

Lachish, 91

The Lady, 40

Laius, 169–170, 171

Lamech, 192

Lapith women, rape of, *182*

Lastrygonians, 126

Last Supper, 198–199, 200, 210

leaping dolphins, 13, 16, 36–37, 46, 51, 57, 59, 60, 63, 64, 71, *71, 74,* 125, 204–205, 228, 229

Lee, Dorothy, 33, 35–36

legitimacy, 144

Lemnians, 136, 142, 156, 172, 227

Lemnos, 4, 66, 88, 138, 149, 151; Jason and, 117–118, 119, 121, 129

Lenin, Vladimir Ilyich, 2

Lerna, 75, 77, 91, 164, 230

Lernean Hydra, Heracles killing of, 164, 165, 230

Lesbos, 88, 138, 151

Levant, 3, 9, 42, 193

Leviticus, 81, 206

Libnah, 91

life-forms, honor given to, 64

lilies, *15,* 33–34, 53, 54, 64, 97, 101, 108, 153

lily room of Thera, 108

Linear B writing, 108, 226

linear thinking, 35

linear time, 40, 65, 110, 111, 185

lions, 105; Nemean, 34, 103, 164, 230

lion-woman culture, 170

literature, first introduction of, 4

Locke, John, 235

Lot, 192

lotus, 97

lotus eaters, 118

love: choice between property and, 136–144; diving into deep as metaphor for making, 138; doves as symbol of, 120; immortality and, 139–140

Luce, J. V., 122, 123

lustral basin, 52, 54

lustral chamber, 52

Lycia, 66, 97, 138

Lycurgus, 181, 229

Lydia, 66, 97, 138, 227

Lyrnessos, 88

M

Macaria, 159

Macbeth, Lady, 235

Maenads, 185

maid as stage of womanhood, 15

Malleus Maleficarum (Hammer of Witches), 221–222, 224

Mallia, palace at, 17, 59, 72, 98

Manicheism, 211

Marathan, 3

Marco Polo, 115

Margaret, Queen, 235

Marian (Moon-goddess), 118

Marian-dyne, 120

Marinatos, Nanno, 38, 39

Marlowe, 234

marriage: Amazon women and, 227; Athena and, 128–129; Centaurs and, 178; centrality of, 227; destruction of mother-daughter bond and, 151–156; female suppression and, 162; great civil war over, 82–90; immortality and, 128–129; institution of, 90, 138; monogamous, 84, 86, 121, 136, 137, 138, 144, 168, 192; patriarchal, 82, 83, 119, 121, 122–123, 136, 143, 248; as political issue, 118–119; reciprocal value of virginity and, 176, 184–185, 186; sacrifice of Clytemnestra on altar of, 145–150; in Sparta, 176; Trojan War and, 157, 176

marriageable women, 141

marriage rule, enforcement of, 146

Marx, Karl, 230

Mary Magdalene, 202, 214

Massachusetts Bay Colony, 234

mating swallows, 56–57

matriarchy, 21, 51, 66, 68

matricide, 149

matrilineal descent, 80, 118, 161–162

McLeish, Archibald, 244

Medea, 6, 124, 132, 150, 160, 223, 228, 244; enchantments of, 60; marriage to Jason, 122–123, 130, 136, 243

Medusa, 124, 171; hair of, 98

Mehujael, 192

men: depiction of, 42; lack of pictures at war, 44–51; in song, 17, 18

Menelaos, 83, 84, 85, 145–146, 157

Mesopotamia, 68

metamorphosis, 53

Methusael, 192

militarism, 1, 243

military destruction, Jesus and the threat of, 203–208

Minoan art, 13–14; inevitability of patriarchy and, 9–12; on seal rings, 21, 24, 44, 52, 56, 60, 102, 108, 133, 151, 183; similarity between Mycenaean art and, 73; themes of: absence of war, 228–229; feminine principle, 227, 228; lack of fear of ecstasy, 228; rebirth, 227–228; sexuality, 228

Minoan civilization, 10–12; achievements of, 10; alternate values of, 1; buried archaeology of, 2; decline of, 5, 12, 67, 73, 104; influence of, 6; mystery of, 13–22; primitive, 22; rediscovery of, 10–11; suppression of, 12; women in religion in, 88

Minos, King, 17, 74, 101

Minotaur, 17, 101

misogyny, 1, 67, 149, 175, 176, 222, 243; discrimination and, 149; effects of history of, 236; mythology and, 67; origins of, 7–8, 227; patriarchal, 229–230; virulent, 175

Mohammed, 245

monarchy, 1

monkeys, 17, 23, 36–37, 39, 44, 57, 64, 74; swinging, 229

monogamous marriage, 84, 86, 121, 136, 137, 138, 144, 168, 192

monogamy, female, 161–162, 181, 192

Montségur, 218, 219, 241

moon(s), 27, 33, 34, 74, 125; cycles of, 142, 184, 187; importance of, 183–184

moral instruction, 125

morality stories, 160

Moses, 211

mother as stage of womanhood, 15

mother-daughter bond, marriage and destruction of, 151–156

Mother Earth, 103, 106, 107, 113, 119, 147, 154, 182, 185; children of, 163; inheritance from, 87; loss of faith in, 71–77; nature of, 82; overthrow of, 108–112

mother goddess, 40

Mount Aetna, 104

Mount Olympus, 108, 128

Mount Parnassus, 190

Muhammad, 211–213

Muses, 102–103

"Mustangs," 115

Mutual Assured Destruction, 238

Mycenae, 25, 75, 77, 91, 101, 138; art of, 73; collapse of, 10, 11, 79, 105; decline of, 82, 157; fall of, 6; fortress of, 19; war and, 98, 165

Myrine, 118

myrtle, 51; branches of, 71

Mysteries of Eleusis, 2, 152, 155–156, 200–201, 202, 204,

207, 209, 216, 229–230

myths, 5, 6, 99–100; in taming, punishing, and disparaging women, 161–168; values conveyed by ancient, 98. *See also* stories

N

Napoleon, 245

narcissism, 153

narcissus, 153, 154

narcolepsy, 154

natural causes, 67

natural regeneration, 94

Nausicaa, 140–141; Odysseus and, 141, 142–144

Navajo tribe, 162

naval fleet fresco, Akrotiri, 45, *45, 46–47, 70*

Nazareth, 200, 201

nectar, 126

Nemea, 75, 77, 164

Nemean lion, 34, 103; Heracles killing of, 164, 230

Nightingale, Florence, 236

Niobe, 165, 167, 228

nomads, need for sons, 80

nomad theory, 8

nuclear winter, 238

O

obsession, 139

Ochlos, war and, 165

octopuses, 14, 24, *24,* 27, 46

Odysseus, 25, 80–81, 82, 92, *127,* 160, 186; Achilles and, 87–88; bards on, 100, 233; Calypso's offering of ambrosia to, 154; journey of, 6, 229; marriage to Penelope, 80, 137, 147; Nausikaa and, 141, 142–144; rejection of Calypso, 81, 124–135, 137, 141–142, 143, 160; temptation of Sirens and, 126, *127,* 139, 140. 171

The Odyssey, 4, 80–81, 87–88, 118, 124, 125–126, 136–137, 139, 144, 161, 167, 173–174, 188, 198, 212, 218

Oedipus, 6, 7, 107, 215, 243; as lost son, 169–174; shepherds and, 114

oils, 53

olive trees, 37; branches of, 16, 141; leaves of, 71; as symbol of Athena, 100, 124, 126

Olympia, 49

Odysseus, rejection of Calypso, 81, 124–135, 137, 141–142, 143, 160

Ophelia, 235

opium pods, 60, *61, 62, 63*

order, 110, 125, 219; patriarchal, 93, 99, 102

ordinary creatures, portray of, 64–65

Orestes, *147*; murder of Clytemnestra by, 146–147, 149; trial of, 147, 148, 149

orgiastic cult, 82

original sin of Eve, 148

Otionia, sacrifice of, 7, 157–158, 159, *180,* 180–181, 182, 220

P

Pagels, Elaine, 208

Palestine, 11, 53

Panathenaia, 179–180, 181

Pandora, 92, 102, 178

parables, 241

Paris, 83, 86, 90

Parsifal, 244

Parthenon, 3, 175, 186, 229, 239; depiction of Zeus on, *181, 182*; subordination of women on frieze of, 175–186, *180, 181, 182, 183, 184*

partridges, 16, 17, *19,* 36–37

Pasiphaë, 101

Pastoral heroes, 113

patriarchal order, 93; propagandists of, 99, 102

patriarchy, 81, 151; ascendance and, 113; beliefs associated with, 122; Biblical, 187–193; challenges to, 233; closing the book on, 226–230; consolidation of power in, 168; conversion to, 68; crumbling of, 234; declining utility of war and, 238–240; establishment of, 111; foundation of Greek, 117, 119; golden fleece and, 121; gradual takeover of, 112; great divide to, 204; hierarchy of, 233; history of, 96; loosing of bonds of, 236; marriage and, 82, 83, 119, 121, 122–123, 136, 143, 157, 248; metaphors of, 244; Minoan artifacts and inevitability of, 9–12; misogyny and,

229–230; norms of, 2; principle of, 86; property and, 185; rationalization of, 2; rise of, 169; suppression of women and, 218–219; underlying cause of, 79–80; values at odds with, 64–66; values of virginity, 120–121; wealth and, 143

patrilineal descent, 83, 118, 121, 156, 162

patrimony, 121; recognition of, 161

Paul, 207

Pausanias, 74

Peace, 110, 125, 219

Pedassos, 88

Pelagius, 209, 210, 233, 243, 244, 245

Pelias (uncle), 165; Jason and, 113, 115

Peloponnesus, 75, 102

Penelope, 6, 80–81, 83, 129, 137, 167, 173, 174, 233; marriage of, 143, 145, 147

Penthelesia, 49, *49*

Pericles, 48, 172, 175, 176, 178, 185, 186, 239; funeral oration of, 48

Persephone, 3, 31, 100, 195, 197, 229, 244; cult of, 158; Demeter and, 152, 153–154, 156; eating of pomegranates, 153; Hades abduction and rape of, 8, 76, 153–154, 155, 156, 158, 175, 215; origin of, 109; Zeus and, 157

Persia, 6

Persian wars, 177–178

Phaistos, palace at, 17, *46*, 54, 59

Philistines, 52–53, 54, 91, 18

Phineus, King, 119, 120

Phoenicia, 90, 97, 106, 163

Phrygia, 66, 82, 85, 138, 226

Picts, 162

pirate raiding, 88–89, 90, 92–93

Pireaeus, 96

Plato, 7, 22, 73, 98, 99, 125

poets, as singers, 124, 125. *See also* bards

political persuasion, 99

politics, 100

polytheism, 211

Polyxena, 7, 147; sacrifice of, 159, *159*, 186

pomegranates, 31, 96; eating of, by Persephone, 153; as fertility symbol, 97, 114

Pope, Alexander, 74, 89, 128, 129

poppies, 64

Portia, 235

Poseidon, 73, 75, 100, 104, 108, 112, 124; Athena and, 44, 182; brutalities of, 113; Harpies and, 119; Odysseus and, 140, 142; origin of, 111; Scylla and, 138, 139; sexual activity of, 175; trident as code for, 114. *See also* Earthshaker

post-Dark Age stories, 34

Potnia, 40

Potnia Athena, 40

Potnia Hera, 40

power, 100; changes in world balance of, 238

preconquest consciousness, 36

pregnancy, 158

prehistory, 4

premarital virginity, 120

Priam, King of Troy, 146

printing press, 233–234

progenitrix, 185

property: choice between love and, 136–144; inheritance of, 161–162; legitimacy and, 144

prostitution, 52, 59, 191

Psistratus, 81, 178

public places, 65

purification, 142

Puritanism, 234–235

Pylos, 40, 90, 91, 101, 151

Pythia, 107, 190; Apollo's fight with, 163

Python, 36; Apollo's fight with, 163

Q

Qu'ran, 211, 212

Quraysh, 211

R

Ramadan, 211, 213

raven, 37

Rawon, Leonard Lee, 193

rebirth, 38, 54, 227–228, 230, 236; expectation of, 23–32;

idea of, 227–228

recycling, woman as symbol of, 129

reductionist research, 3

regeneration, 30, 31, 215; principle of, 188

relevance, principle of, 65

Renault, Mary, 169

Reuther, Rosemary Radford, 51

Rhea, 103, 107, 110, 111, 113, 121, 126, 136, 165, 172; marriage discouragement of, 120, 136; monsters of, 119; Zeus and, 145

rhyta, 52

ritual sexuality, 52

role reversal, 160

Rome, 4

root fire, 195, 196

Rosalind, 235

Rules of Marriage, 236

Rumi, 213

S

Sacred Marriage, 158

sacred trees, 44

sacrifice(s): animal, 30, 38, 39, 65; human, 157–158, 159, *159, 180,* 182, 186, 220; to Zeus, 117

St. Margaret, 220, 221, 224

St. Michael, 220, 221, 224

St. Patrick, 209

Salamis, naval battle at, 48

Samos, 66, 91, 96, 138

Samothrace, 66

Samson, 52, 54, 59, 129, 139

sanctification of obedience, 191

Santorini, 33, 38, 74; frescoes from, 16

Sarai, 192

satyrs, dancing, *20*

Schliemann, Heinrich, 226

Scylla, 6, 66, 93, 124, 126, 137–138, 140, 145, 150, 160, 171, 212, 223, 228; Poseidon and, 138, 139

Scythia, 138

seal rings, art on, 21, 24, 44, 52, 56, 60, 102, 108, 133, 151, 183

Sea Peoples, 79, 92, 187, 226

Selene, 184, 186; horse of, *184*

self-sacrifice, 117

Selige Sebnsucht (Goethe), 38

Semele, 41–42, 100, 160, 186, 228

Semites, 187

sensuality, 36

Sepphoris, 200

serpents, as vestigial symbol, 163

sexual irresponsibility, principle of, 86, 133

sexuality, 51, 64, 111; apple as symbol of, 114, 133, 169; celebration of, in Minoan art, 228; ecstasy and, 60; female, 52–59, 208; ineffectiveness of, 133; lotus as symbol for, 118; ritual, 52; symbols of, 96–97; temple, 139; as theme in Minoan art, 228

sexual promiscuity, 149–150

sexual rites, 195–196

Shakespeare, William, 234, 235, 242

Sharman, Henry Burton, 196

shibboleth, evil of, 201

shield, figure-eight, 46, 104

Sicily, 11

Sidney, Mary, 234

Silver Age, 10

Singers, poets as, 124, 125

singing swallows, 204–205

Sinope, 120

Sirens: Odysseus and, 126, *127,* 137, 139, 140, 145, 150, 171, 228; symbolism of, 94, 98–99, 102, 124

snake goddesses, 55, 97, 103, 108, 164

snakes, 14, 17, *28,* 46, 64, 66, 77, 97, 103; names of, 163–164; portrayal of women with, 26; as symbol, 189, 19041

Sodom, 102

Solon, 81

solstice, 114

Song of Solomon, 195

sons, value of, 175, 226

Sophia, 187

Sophocles, 169, 172

sovereignty, axe as symbol of, 146

Sparta, 49, 70, 75, 84, 90, 117, 172; Dioscuri from, 161; marriage in, 176

Sphinx, 6, 103, 105, 107, 112, 145, 150, *170,* 170–171, 215, 216

spider, change of Arachne into, 167

spirals, 24, 29, *41,* 52, 53, 54, *76,* 97, 104, 128, 129, 133, 152

Spring Fresco, Akrotiri, *14, 15,* 33–34, 42, 151, 153

stories: Biblical, 4–5, 9, 10, 66, 233; creation, 110, 191; epic, 82; father-son, 7; foundation, 113, 115, 117, 120, 122, 136, 150, 162–164, 188; history, as choice of, 231–232; language in shaping, 242; morality, 160; post-Dark Age, 34; purpose of, 241–245; rewriting, for Western civilization, 1–8. *See also* myths

storytelling, 124, 230; biblical, 4–5, 9, 10, 66, 233; Cyclopes in, 145; of Dark Age, 120; emergence of the new in, 234–234; history as choice of, 231–232; shaping of values by, 96–101, 113. *See also* Genesis; Hesiod; Homer

strife, 85

Stymphalian, 133, 164

Sufism, 213, 234

Sumeria, 4, 6; women in, 151

sun, 27; importance of, 183, 184

Sunion, 3

swallows: flying, 51, 71, *71;* kissing, 13, *14, 33,* 64, 74, 101, 125, 228, 229; mating, 56–57; singing, 204–205

swans, 44

swinging monkeys, 229

swords, bronze, 46

symbols, 114–115; Amazons as, 145; apples as, 34, 96, 133, 167–168, 169, 189–190; axe as, 146; correlation between, 15; doves as, 120; dragons as, 163; figs as, 138; fig tree as, 96–97; in Genesis, 187; golden fleece as, 97; graphic, 96–97; for Hercules, 99; helmet as, 100, 124, 126; olive trees as, 100, 124, 126; pomegranates as, 97, 114; of sexuality, 96–97, 114, 118, 169; snakes as, 189, 19041; vestigial, 163; wine as, 197–202

Synod of Whitby, 210

Syracuse, 101

T

Talos, 122–123

Tao Te Ching, 38

Telemachus, 7, 80–81, 137, 144, 150, 161, 174

temple sexuality, 139

"Terrapins," 115

territory, 100

Thasos, 149

Thebes, 25, 66, 75, 97, 98, 99, 101, 102, 103–104, 104, 106, 135, 138, 171; connection with Crete, 104–105; establishment of male line and, 163; war and, 98, 165

Thera, 4, 11, 25, 32, 33, 51, 71–77, 72, 82, 83, 98, 101, 104, 107, 109, 112, 230; as center of influence, 22; trade and, 19; wall paintings from, 15, 16, 24, 108, 125, 152, 158, 226

Theran explosion, 71–77, 103–104, 108, 109, 111, 112, 122, 123, 226

Theseus, Prince, 17, 44, 100, 101, 135, 169, 175, 196

Thesmophoria, 175, 221, 229–230; fertility celebration of, 229

Thessaly, 66, 117; Jason and, 115, 122

thirteenth day, declaration of, as festival, 146

Thucydides, 10, 22, 74

Thunderer, 83, 109, 112

tidal wave, 72–73, 108, 109

time, 111; circular concept of, 33–43, 64, 151, 201, 228, 236; linear, 40, 65, 110, 111, 185

Tiryns, 75, 91, 96

Titans, 100, 103, 105–106, 130–131, 147, 165, 172

Tithonos, 131–132

Toynbee, Arnold, 203

Track II diplomacy, 5–6

trade, 11, 19, 82, 96; growth of, 79–81, 151; value of sons and, 226

trees, 64; in combination image, 16, 24–25, *25,* 27, *27;* fig, 96–97, 138, 139; olive, 16, 37, 71, 126, 141; sacred, 44

triangulation, 15

trident, 114

triparite worship of earth, water, and sky, 101

Triple Goddess, 14–15, *15,* 86, 111–112, 182

Trobrianders, 35–36

Trobriand Islanders, 33

Trojans, 44, 172

Trojan War, 1, 7, 47, 80–81, 82, 83–90, 91–92, 96, 99, 120, 128, 136, 143, 145, 157, 173, 176, 226

Troy, 82, 83–84, 125; allies of, 90; excavation of, 226; fall of, 175

Typhon, 103, 104, 105–106; Zeus and, 105

Typhoon, 104

U

Ugarit, 91, 96, 135

universe of daily life, 27

Uranus, 167, 185; castration of, 110, 111, 112, 165, 215

V

values: conflict of, 165–166; Greek, 124; of immortality, 132; Minoan cultural, 109, 196; at odds with patriarchy, 64–66; shaping of, by storytellers, 96–101, 113; suppression of Minoan, 67

vestigial symbols, 163

Vetruvius, 177

Vietnam War, 48, 239

Virgil, 74

virginity: patriarchal values of, 120–121; reciprocal value of marriage and, 176, 184–185, 186

Voltaire, 235

W

wage gap, 247–248

Walker, Barbara, 53, 201

war, 65; absence of, in Minoan war, 228–229; declining utility of, 238–240; heroics of, 1; peace and, 135; reasons for, 79; troubling question of, 44–51

war chariots, 69

war culture, emergence of, 68–70

Warlords, 113

warrior civilization: emergence of, 91–95; objections to, 195–196

water, diving into deep as metaphor for making love, 138

wealth, patriarchy and, 143

weddings, partying at, 119

West, M. I., 6, 7

Western civilization: foundations of, 5, 25, 75; influences on, 10–11; rewriting the story of, 1–8; template of values for, 96

wheat sheaves, 24, 25, 31, 37, 38, 71, *72,* 197, 201

wine: Eleusinian symbolism of, 197–202; transformation of, 199–200

witch burnings, 223, 224–225, 233

witchcraft, 220–221

women: arising out of the earth, *15,* 151–152; association with death, 31; attraction to Pelagius's teachings, 209; Augustine's attack on, 209–210; celebration of, 230; centrality of, 151, 227; in combination image, 16, 24–25, *25, 27, 27*; dancing, 13, *16,* 24, 33, 60, 62, 64, 183, 228; depreciation of, 151; domestic violence and, 236–237; elegantly dressed, *56,* 58; evil nature of, 150; exaltation of, 42, 43; with exposed breasts, 21, *22,* 29, *29,* 32, *41,* 56, *56,* 72; festivals of, 175; immortality and, 34; in Islam, 211–213; Jason's resistance of seductive, 113–123; marriageable, 141; in Minoan religion, 88; multitude of myths to tame, punish, and disparage, 161–168; rationale for controlling, 102–103; role of, 235–236; sexuality in, 52–59, 208; snakes and, 26, 97; stages of, 15; subordination of, on Parthenon frieze, 175–186, *180, 181, 182*; success and failure of wages and employment in America, 247–248; suppression of, 1, 79, 218–219; as symbol of recycling, 129; from tree trunks, 16, 24–25, *25,* 27, *27*; with uplifted arms, 62, *63*; vilification of, 92–93

women-centered religion, 158

women-centered societies, 8; end of, in Eastern Mediterranean, 82–90

World War II, 48, 239

X

Xerxes, 178

Z

Zakros: palace at, 17, 52, 53, 54, 55, 59, 72, 74, 98, 118; spiral frieze from, 28–29, *29,* 128, 129, 133, 152, 237

Zealots, 203–204, 207

Zeus, 3, 5, 8, 30, 42, 44, 73, 75, 84, 85, 100, 101, 104, 110, 111, 112, 119, 230; authority of, 119; birth of Athena from, 131, 137, 149, 182–183; brutalities of, 113; Calypso and, 128, 139; daughters of, 125; Demeter and, 153, 155; depiction of, on Parthenon, *181,* 182; as father figure, 175, 230; hegemony of, 227; marriage to Hera, 70, 76–77, 107, 124, 126–127, 172, 186; Persephone and, 156, 157; Rhea and, 145; sacrifices to, 117; Typhon and, 105

Zorastrians, 211

CRAIG BARNES began his career as a public interest lawyer dealing with women's rights and the environment, at one time trying a women's wage case before a federal judge who would not admit any evidence of historical discrimination. Spurred by this rejection, Barnes began the years-long research that eventually led to the remarkable revelations concerning the foundation of western culture, here spelled out in detail for the first time. Barnes has also been an essayist, editor, playwright, and negotiator in wars of ethnic cleansing in the Caucuses of the former Soviet Union as well as in water issues in Central Asia. He lives in Santa Fe, New Mexico.